Managing Democracy
Managing Dissent

First published 2013 by Corporate Watch
c/o Freedom Press
Angel Alley
84b Whitechapel High Street
London, E1 7QX

www.corporatewatch.org

British Library Cataloguing in Publication Data
A catalogue record for this book is available from the British Library

ISBN 978-1-907738-09-8

Edited by Rebecca Fisher

Cover design by Ally Arthur at TartanPixie.com and Rebecca Fisher

Layout and design by Ally Arthur at TartanPixie.com

Indexing by Michael Hamilton: mhindex[at]mail.com

Printed by Russell Press

Corporate Watch

Corporate Watch is an independent, not-for-profit research and publishing group that
investigates the social and environmental impacts of corporate power. Since 1996
Corporate Watch has been publishing corporate critical 'information for action' in the
form of books, reports, investigative articles, briefings and magazines.

Managing Democracy
Managing Dissent

Capitalism, Democracy and the Organisation of Consent

Edited by Rebecca Fisher

Corporate Watch
Corporate Critical Research Since 1996

www.corporatewatch.org

"The sharp increase in inequality, chronic high unemployment, and lack of response by nominal democracies to difficulties afflicting the majority, have made it clear to increasing numbers that so-called market-based democracy serves the market, not the demos. The growth of this understanding is a threat to dominant elites, so coping with it has become ever more urgent to those in command, who must engineer consent by hook or by crook. Managing Democracy, Managing Dissent has effective analyses of a wide range of these engineering techniques, from adapting language to make capitalism and democracy warm partners, to propaganda barrages in the press and on TV and movie screens, to philanthropic actions, to cooptation of progressive organizations and movements, and to the various forms of repression and violence. This book covers these techniques, and their mode of use at home and abroad. It is an eye-opener."

Edward S. Herman (among his other books, *Corporate Control, Corporate Power*, and *Manufacturing Consent* [with Noam Chomsky])

"In ancient times democracy was conceived as antagonistic to any class society. A remarkable change took place when the social technology required to combine the appearance of democracy and the reality of capitalist class rule was created in the late 18th century. This book, with daring clarity, opens the hood and investigates what machinery makes it possible to manage democracy and make it safe for capitalism. In chapter after chapter the reader is shown 'how it is done' without obscuration. It is a brave book and it should not be missed."

Silvia Federici, author of *Caliban and the Witch* and *Revolution at Point Zero.*

"The authors of this timely anthology, Managing Democracy, Managing Dissent deconstruct the democracy myth. They describe how outright repression has been legitimated-even by declaring rioters "brain damaged," and psychologists labeling anti-authoritarians as diseased. What makes this book essential reading is its description of the many ways in which influence is covert; how consent is obtained to inequality, corporate rule, imperialism, and war.

Journalists and academics, including some on the left, obey the silent rules of capitalist hegemony, regularly using language that disguises the deplorable inequality in political power and well-being that exists in the 'flagship' 'democracies'. Co-optation is subtle, and so far, it has been very effective. That is why we must become aware of its methods and thereby avoid those traps. Many positive-sounding civil society interventions have worked to stop liberation struggles in their tracks, while the liberal and reputedly impartial media generally echo corporate propaganda.

The book performs and important service by alerting those who wish to progress towards a truly democratic world."

Joan Roelofs, author of *Foundations and Public Policy: The Mask of Pluralism.*

"While capitalism has shown itself to be remarkably adaptable by turning the energies and ideas of its opponents into methods for its survival, radical movements have struggled to find ways to counter this recuperation. This book is an excellent step in countering that, moving from insightful analysis of co-optation not into defeatism, but a renewed spirit of revolt."

Stevphen Shukaitis, Autonomedia / University of Essex

"Understanding the continuing economic and political turmoil following the 'credit crunch' is a big project. This diverse collection of essays is an important contribution to unravelling the multiple threads and tensions obscured by the ongoing crisis of contemporary capitalism. Combining analysis of the internal dynamics and contradictions of neo-liberalism with rich accounts of events in Europe, America and the Middle East this collection begins to make sense of 'shock doctrine', the management of dissent and the massaging of the messages reaching the public sphere.

In an era that promotes experiments in participatory democracy with one hand, whilst simultaneously using anti-terrorist surveillance measures against citizens with the other, this is a book to read. The collection points the way towards meaningful democratic forms that can challenge institutional and corporate power. Don't expect to agree with everything in here but do expect to find clues and pointers towards a progressive politics for the contemporary milieu."

Ian Welsh, Reader in Sociology, Cardiff University

Because things are the way they are, things will not stay the way they are.

Bertolt Brecht

Contents

Foreword

Gerald Sussman

In 1971, Daniel Ellsberg, a former marine and military analyst for the Rand Corporation, after personally concluding that state secrecy and official propaganda about Vietnam were anathema to democracy, released thousands of pages of 'top secret' documents that exposed crucial details of the sordid history of U.S. policy toward that country going back to 1945 - *The Pentagon Papers*. A few years later, he was featured in the American documentary film *Hearts and Minds*, a hard-hitting indictment of America's militarized nationalist culture that undergirded the imperialist invasion of Vietnam. Commenting on the lies that each U.S. president since Truman had told about Vietnam, Ellsberg said: "It's a tribute to the American public that their leaders perceived that they had to be lied to. It's no tribute to us that it was so easy to fool the public."

Since Machiavelli, the most famous political consultant, it has been understood that successful authoritarian rulers exercise power not only through the imposition of fear but also by deception and the manipulation of public awareness, the manufacture of state legitimacy, and the active fostering of social and political consent amongst citizens - what Antonio Gramsci described as cultural 'hegemony'. It is no less a requirement in states with other forms of centralized power. The U.S. state's reliance on cultural hegemony has become all the more important during the past 40 years of declining real income for most Americans, the permanent loss of good paying jobs, and the now highest concentration of wealth since the eve of the Great Depression. The preservation of state power and political legitimacy under these circumstances requires a regime of expert political and commercial surveillance and heightened promotional activity (propaganda). With the panoptic vision of the Department of Homeland Security, FEMA, and other security agencies, thousands of Americans, involved in anti-war, environmental, social justice, animal protection, and other dissident organizations have come under an Orwellian purview of state security apparatuses. Even more pervasive is the corporate world's commercial surveillance of citizens that can track people via Internet, i-phone, credit card, GPS systems, CCTV, credit card purchases, and other electronic eavesdropping technologies.

In a capitalist economy based on information exchange, where more activity is focused on selling rather than making things, the role of surveillance and various forms of promotion (advertising, marketing, PR, sales management, branding, and the like) are central to wealth accumulation. The promotional industries have been rapidly expanding, while manufacturing employment is now below 10 percent (and only 11 percent of GDP). Moreover, the public is now more systematically integrated into the sphere of production, constantly giving out their identity information, voluntarily and involuntarily, in the creation of value. In the propaganda society, promotion is not just conventional persuasion; it is a central factor of production. Propaganda is *systemic*.

Industries also no longer rely on passive consumer behavior. Online crowdsourcing, appealing to people either desperately in search of minimally paid work or happily offering up their ideas for design, marketing, or engineering for nothing, has converted computer users into a labor force. In this form of labor, typically there are no benefits, no retirement savings, and no standard wage, just the status of having contributed to a corporate project or product. These patterns of exploitation represent the growing casualization, informalization, and precarity of labor. With little fixed capital, online businesses convert citizens into their 'prosumers' - exploited both at the producer end and as consumers doing the 'work' of consumption, such as by having themselves tracked online or in physical purchase centers by checking themselves out and thereby acting as unpaid cashiers and baggers at the point of sale. Online marketing has rapidly increased the velocity of circulation of goods from production to consumption, reducing investment costs and risks.

The maintenance of consumer ideology on which the propaganda society rests is still largely supported through mass media, whose role is to deliver audiences (the real merchandise) to advertisers. Mainstream media, including their news operations, do this by serving up platters of celebrity worship, spectacle, sensationalism, and other diversions that are designed to constantly reproduce the mood to consume. Vertically integrated corporate media, released from restraints by neoliberal economic mores, serve as agents of other corporate interests on whose ad revenues they depend. Among its many egregious practices, many TV news stations have permitted the airing of government- and commercial PR firm-produced video news releases, with actors posing as journalists, tricking unadvised audiences into watching fake news. Worse, advertisers and their television hosts shamelessly market consumer goods directly to children, bypassing parental filters, and prescription pharmaceutical products directly to adults, bypassing physicians. It is no wonder that network news is awash in pharmaceutical advertising.

Most workers in the entertainment industry have fared no better than other people. In local TV newsrooms across the country, advances in production technology have enabled stations to eliminate most behind-the-scenes personnel, allowing one 'operator' to put the news on the air by pre-programming a computer to advance, like an assembly line, the various segments of the newscast. This means piling demands that were once discrete tasks distributed to multiple employees on to an individual worker. One example of the workflow consolidation is seen in the deployment of a system called 'Ignite', produced by broadcast equipment-maker Grass Valley. Ignite has eliminated the jobs of camera operators, audio technicians, graphics generators, video rollers, and technical directors, replacing the human element of production with a computer and letting go many newsroom employees.

The same sort of consolidation is seen in the 'one-man-bands', TV journalists that are sent solo to cover stories, having to drive the station truck, hold the camera, set the lighting, interview the respondent, and send the story by microwave back to the studio, before rushing back to the station to put up a web version of the story online as well as deal with audience twitter and email feedback. This goes on day in and day out. The on-air product is often sloppy, and, worse, vacuous of any real news value. The days of investigative reporting are virtually over at most stations, replaced by quick and dirty stories, often nothing more than puff pieces serving the wishes of advertisers.

Media also play a central role in mythologizing electoral democracy. The political scientist Murray Edelman considered elections and other political events in America as *spectacles* that distract and disable people from political engagement and any meaningful form of citizenship. The cooptation of the electoral process by professionalization and corporate financing forecloses popular participation in politics. As a result, Americans have become mere spectators of government and the electoral process, which defies any serious notion of living in a real democracy. The cost of the federal electoral spectacle in the 2012 campaign was estimated to reach over $8 billion, two-thirds of which ended up as 30-second TV and radio political spots, for which political media consultants collect a cool 15 percent commission. As former Beltway political adviser, Bob Squier, once put it: "You'll find people in my business tend to use the word 'viewer' and 'voter' almost interchangeably." For broadcast stations, the national election season is a bonanza - paid political ad revenues rank third only behind automobiles and retail advertising.

Because it is so profitable, TV stations have a perverse incentive to radically reduce news coverage of campaigns in order to force candidates to invest more money in political advertising to get their messages across. The logic is flawless, with the result that news coverage of candidates has in fact radically declined since the 1980s, especially after the Supreme Court's Citizens United decision to unleash spending in the name of 'free speech' by unregistered special interest groups. Political consultants, whose regular employment is shilling for corporations, consider elections off-season work. In the corporate state, they're the nexus between the political parties and their candidates, the media, and the business tycoons. As long as media continue to turn elections into mass distractions, most people will have a hard time understanding who's really running the show and whose interests their 'representatives' (at least half of whom are millionaires or multimillionaires) actually serve. The 'horserace' is a popular but false image of election campaigns, as horserace winners are not determined by how much money is bet. American elections with all their hoopla and drama, would be better conceived as stockmarket investments, no different than pork belly futures transactions. In the ideal, systemic propaganda is designed to keep Humpty Dumpty on the wall and consumer-denizens in the mall.

Notes On Contributors

Matthew Alford

Matthew Alford is a Teaching Fellow at the University of Bath. He currently works on the relationship between entertainment, political power, and propaganda in the United States. His most recent book is *Reel Power: Hollywood Cinema and American Supremacy* (Pluto Press, 2010).

Tom Anderson

Tom Anderson is a researcher at Corporate Watch and an active campaigner against the occupation of Palestine, both in the UK and in Palestine as part of the International Solidarity Movement and other groups. He is also active in the Smash EDO campaign, against EDO MBM, an international arms company with a factory in Brighton. He is the co-author of Corporate Watch's *Targeting Israeli Apartheid: A Boycott, Divestment and Sanctions Handbook* and Corporate Watch's *2009 State Crackdown on Anti-Corporate Dissent* briefing, which looked at the repression of the animal rights movement in the UK. Tom's current research focuses on the companies profiting from Israeli apartheid, occupation and militarism and the arms trade.

Michael Barker

Michael Barker is an independent researcher and writer who has written extensively on the subject of corporate philanthropy, co-option and 'democracy promotion'.   He has been writing for alternative media outlets since 2006, and at present is a regular contributor to *Swans Commentary* and *Ceasefire Magazine*. His work and articles can be found at <http://michaeljamesbarker.wordpress.com>.

Edmund Berger

Edmund Berger is an independent writer/researcher and social activist based out of Louisville, Kentucky. He's written on the American political system, democracy promotion, activism, and arts and culture in *Swans Commentary, Dissident Voice*, and several other online outlets.

William K. Carroll

William K. Carroll is professor of Sociology at the University of Victoria in Canada, where he was founding Director of the Interdisciplinary Program in Social Justice Studies (2008-2012). His books include *The Making of a Transnational Capitalist Class, Remaking Media: The Struggle to Democratize Public Communication* (with Bob Hackett) and *Organizing Dissent: Contemporary Social Movements in Theory and Practice*. His current research project is a participatory study of transnational alternative policy groups and the production of knowledge for social change.

David Cromwell and David Edwards - Media Lens

David Cromwell and David Edwards are the co-editors of Media Lens, a UK-based online media watchdog at www.medialens.org. By highlighting the often glaring gaps between the views found in corporate media and in credible sources on vital issues - climate, war, the global economy and so on - Media Lens exposes how the corporate media consistently reports from the perspective of power. They encourage readers to follow the links and references they provide; to make up their own minds about the issues under discussion; and, if they wish, to challenge the journalists and editors responsible (and them!). They have co-authored two books, *Guardians of Power- The Myth of the Liberal Press* (London: Pluto Press, 2006) and *Newspeak in the 21st Century* (London: Pluto Press, 2009). David Cromwell's new book, *Why Are We The Good Guys?*, has just been published by Zero Books.

Matthew Greeno

Matthew Greeno completed his Master of Arts in Studies in Policy and Practice at the University of Victoria in 2012, with a focus on climate policy. Originally from Southern Alberta, Matthew now works, rides his bike, and tries to live up to his name's implications in Victoria, BC.

Rebecca Fisher

Rebecca Fisher is a researcher at Corporate Watch, where she has focused mainly on issues of democracy and consent, including in relation to the 2003 invasion and subsequent 'reconstruction' of Iraq. She has also been active in various grassroots movements, especially in alternative media and against border controls.

The Free Association

The Free Association is a writing collective loosely based in Leeds. Their virtual home can be found at www.freelyassociating.org; their book *Moments of Excess: Movements, Protest and Everyday Life* was published by PM Press in 2011.

Sibille Merz

Sibille holds a Master's degree in Postcolonial Studies from Goldsmiths, University of London, for which she carried out ethnographic research on NGOs in Palestine. She is currently studying for her PhD in Sociology at the same institution. Her main research interests include postcolonial studies and critiques of development, race and racism in Europe and labour in contemporary capitalism.

James Petras

James Petras has worked with the Brazilian Landless Workers Movement for the last eleven years in addition to his work with the unemployed workers movement in Argentina. He is also a Bartle Professor (Emeritus) of Sociology at Binghamton University, New York. His most recent book is *The Arab Revolt and the Imperialist Counterattack* (2011) and his articles in English can be found at <www.petras.lahaine.org>.

Katie Pollard and Maria Young

Katie Pollard and Maria Young both live in London and came together to write this one article.

William I. Robinson

William I. Robinson is a professor of sociology at the University of California, Santa Barbara. He is also affiliated with the Latin American and Iberian Studies Program, and with the Global and International Studies Program at UCSB. His scholarly research focuses on: macro and comparative sociology, globalization and transnationalism, political economy, political sociology, development and social change, Latin America and the Third World, and Latina/o studies. His most recent book is *Latin America and Global Capitalism: A Critical Globalization Perspective*, published by Johns Hopkins University Press in 2008. Many of his articles, speeches and interviews are available online at <http://www.soc.ucsb.edu/faculty/robinson/index.shtml>.

Gerald Sussman

Gerald Sussman is Professor of Urban Studies and Planning at Portland State University. His research interests include democracy studies, urban technological history and culture, labor conditions in the digital era, media and information systems, public policy, and theories of development. His most recent book publication (2011) is an edited volume titled *The Propaganda Society: Promotional Culture and Politics in Global Context*. He also authored the books *Branding Democracy: U.S. Regime Change in Post-Soviet Eastern Europe* (2010), *Global Electioneering: Campaign Consulting, Communications, and Corporate Financing* (2005), and *Communication, Technology and Politics in the Information Age* (1997).

Charles Thorpe

Charles Thorpe is Associate Professor of Sociology at the University of California, San Diego. His book on the atomic bomb and Cold War science, titled *Oppenheimer: The Tragic Intellect*, is published by the University of Chicago Press. He is currently writing about how contemporary technology and culture reflects and reinforces the condition of alienation under capitalism.

David Whyte

David Whyte is Reader in Sociology at the University of Liverpool where he conducts research on the relationship between the rule of law and state-corporate power. His books include *Crimes of the Powerful* (Open University Press, 2009) and *Regulatory Surrender* (Institute of Employment Rights, 2010, with Steve Tombs).

1. Introduction

Rebecca Fisher

Because they (citizens) press for more action to meet the problems they have to face, they require more social control. At the same time they resist any kind of social control that is associated with the hierarchical values they have learned to discard and reject. The problem may be worldwide.

The Crisis of Democracy 1975 Trilateral Commission Report[1]

This collection is centred on the fundamental problem of creating legitimacy for capitalism: how can an inherently and profoundly anti-democratic system contain and limit dissent and at the same time present itself as ostensibly 'democratic'? It will examine how ideological and material limits are placed on democratic practice, suppressing oppositional politics and restricting people's freedoms in order to protect the capitalist social order from challenges for greater social, economic and political equality and freedoms. It will argue that these limits are sustained using hollowed out, carefully managed versions of 'democracy', which exploit the popular appeal of democratic ideals while suppressing political dissent. Thus the grand promise of social and political equality is exploited to protect a system which requires gross social and political inequality.

Capitalism is dependent upon its relentless expansion and penetration into new spheres - such as land, resources and forms of labour - and consequently can permit only a very limited degree of popular participation. This is restricted to nominal political 'rights' which are separated from, and privileged over, socio-economic equality. Thus even while inequality deepens, our legal and social sanctioned political agency is largely limited to choosing between a selection of politically homogeneous parties once every four to five years. These elections have become empty, largely symbolic rituals, in which professionalised marketing campaigns elide any substantial political debate. Meanwhile, our legal avenues to hold our putative representatives to account, or to persuade them to take heed of our demands, are restricted to actions via pressure groups or tame and largely ineffectual protests about specific, isolated issues. This ensures that the capitalist system is able to reap catastrophic damage upon subject populations and the environment, even to the extent of threatening the habitability of the planet, while remaining, for the most part, insulated from public challenge.

Yet it is a widely held belief that, in an inseparable and providential union, democracy and capitalism have, in most countries of the world, defeated the forces of authoritarianism, and granted us universal political freedoms. Some also hold the less positive view that there is no other potential system which could meet our needs, wants and desires, and that 'democratic' capitalism is the least bad option. Such beliefs are crucial to the subtle and insidious processes of organising popular consent to the capitalist social order, and so to containing people's oppositional demands arising from the ever-worsening social polarity and economic oppression. The belief that we live in a democracy is also crucial to the legitimation of the use of repression, even military interventions to fight for 'democracy', when such demands are not successfully contained; demands which are so often cast as undemocratic and even pernicious.

As the contributions to this volume will show powerfully, a highly limited concept and practice of democracy, with its accompanying rhetoric, has been developed in parallel with the emergence of the capitalist system, to manage and contain dissent, shroud and legitimate the oppression that capitalism requires, and heavily confine our political responses to it. For capitalism requires firm limits on who has political power in order to function, and consequently, our political actions must be channelled into forms which do not fundamentally threaten its operations. Frequently this happens via subtle and obscure processes of co-option and neutralisation of public opinion and of what is termed civil society, i.e. social institutions that are, at least in theory, in a position to challenge the state or the market. Vital too is the reverse side of co-option - the marginalisation and repression of those elements which transgress the boundaries of safe, manageable dissent. Thus 'democracy' is *managed,* in order to contain dissent, and ensure it does not threaten transnational capitalism, corporate power and elite interests. *Managing Democracy, Managing Dissent* brings into sharp focus some of these mechanisms, and explores how limited and heavily circumscribed 'democratic' processes and ideology facilitates the organisation of consent, and legitimates the use of coercion when that consent is lacking, in order to constrain our political freedoms.[2]

Fundamentally, capitalism - the economic and political system by which goods and services are privately owned, commodified and distributed through the market - requires the majority to sell their labour in order to keep generating profits, while also relying upon both women's unpaid work in the private sphere to ensure the reproduction of labour power and the existence of a large pool of labour which remains unenfranchised and unintegrated into the formal wage economy. Such an exploitative system necessitates the majority relinquishing a great deal of their power over the political, social and economic forces that mould everyday life. In modern-day capitalism, political and economic decisions are made largely in the interests of corporations - the institutional managers of the capitalist system - their profit margins, and a transnational class of elites. Governments frequently serve as vital handmaids of the perpetual drive for the profits and resources. They create and maintain the conditions necessary for continual capitalist accumulation, and provides protection from the resistance capitalism inevitably provokes, via the legitimation of capitalism and repression of dissent. From political policing to generous corporate-friendly legislation, from massive bank bailouts to military interventions to secure corporate access to valuable resources and markets, governments protect the functioning of the market and the constant accumulation of capital above all other social or ecological considerations. Wide-ranging political and economic decisions which affect the lives of billions are made in largely unaccountable inter-governmental institutions such as the World Bank and the International Monetary Fund. Such anti-democratic forms of governance are necessary to ensure that the corporate engine continues to accumulate profit through new resources, new markets and ever cheaper sources of labour. The socio-political polarity thus intensifies as global capitalist penetration deepens, making the task of its legitimation increasingly difficult. For as social and economic oppression intensifies, so can the clamours for redress, clamours which must be contained. This is the contradiction at the heart of capitalism, and that which demonstrates the lie of democratic capitalism.

It is thus essential that the incompatibility of genuine democracy and capitalism is disguised, and for the majority to believe that democracy and capitalism are not only compatible but indivisible: that one engenders the other. And if this connection seems not to be quite watertight it is reinforced by the more negative notion that capitalism is the form of social organisation truest to basic human nature, and thus no more equitable, or sustainable system is possible. Together, they help to engender the widely held belief that challenging capitalism is not only misguided but unprogressive, even pernicious, and as a result, deserving of the marginalisation and repression it receives. This ideological perversion of 'democracy' is therefore used to create a hegemonic order in which a set of beliefs which broadly correspond to the 'democratic' nature or at least potential of capitalism becomes so accepted, even internalised, throughout the public mind, that it acquires the status of 'common-sense' or even of a self-evident 'truth', and thus opposing values or ideas are deemed 'illegitimate' or 'unacceptable' or even 'illogical'. Unlike more totalitarian systems, such ideological hegemony does not entail one particular dominant world-view, but allows for a variety of differing opinions as long as they do not transgress particular boundaries of 'legitimate' or 'reasonable' values, opinions and actions. In this way a semblance of plurality and open debate can be created, even though the overall limits can in effect be as in rigid as any totalitarian system, but without as much overt policing of thought and action. For if these notions are largely internalised, the need for them to be so visibly policed by overt propaganda or coercion, which would only expose the pretence of democracy, is obviated. The power of ideological hegemony results from its ability to limit or repress the imagination of the possible or even conceivable, thereby facilitating the implementation of policies and systems which might otherwise be deeply unpopular, and the incorporation, recuperation and neutralisation of forms of politics which might otherwise have remained fundamentally oppositional.

The belief in the inevitability, viability and democratic nature of capitalism within civil society leads to popular consent - that is, the majority participate in a social order even though it is inherently incapable of achieving social equality, or meeting our needs and interests, and is an order over which we have very little say. Today, most people have little choice but to sell their labour in return for the minimal freedoms granted by wages, although many others have not been granted even this, hard-fought, concession. Either way, labour provides the profit necessary for the continued accumulation of capital, and the majority are left with a meagre degree of wealth and freedom which suffices to contain antagonism and dissent. In addition, the jobs most of us are permitted are actively connected to the maintenance of capitalist systems of production, providing surplus profit for employers, providing the social welfare services that train and educate workers and providing services that seek to soften the worst effects of socio-economic inequalities. As the capitalist system is forced to become more coercive to protect the social and public order, so the security industry increases its share of the labour market - the army, police, prison officers, security guards, private mercenaries etc. In return we are 'rewarded' with grossly unequal wages, with which we are compelled to purchase or rent basic requirements for life, such as food and housing, which have all become ensnared by the market. Meanwhile, services such as education and healthcare are becoming even more overtly divorced from our control, increasingly placed in the hands of private companies over which we have even less authority than our governments. The idea of common ownership and entitlement of such provisions has been hacked away at to such an extent that to advocate more democratic control is to risk accusations of naivety or lunacy. Trapped in the capitalist system in which we must participate to gain the money necessary for survival, anti-capitalist, democratic notions contradict the prevalent 'common-sense' and are thus rarely heard, let alone heeded. Instead, we are force-fed the illogical 'truth' that capitalism is inevitable and progressive, and that, in spite of the inherent social limits to capital accumulation, and the obvious finiteness of the planet's resources, it will eventually provide for all; indeed, that it is the only system that ever will.

Of course, this is not to negate the reality of people's conflict with the system. People will continue to fight to improve their lives and the lives of others, in spite of the way economic dependence on work and economic insecurity limits the time and energy available for such efforts. But collective internalisation of the 'truth' of the 'democratic' nature of capitalism and its destiny to engender the best possible life for all, can limit such struggles, and heavily circumscribe their political intent, when they do emerge. For a collective belief in the illegitimacy of challenging the fundamentals of capitalism will engender only reformist political activity - that is, working to make certain changes which even if granted remain compatible with the functioning of the wider social order. Arguably, such actions which can be incorporated within the system actually strengthen the capitalist social order, insofar as they create the impression of a citizenry armed with democratic political freedoms to effect change. And so, great lengths are taken to co-opt resistance struggles, and to keep them within these boundaries, thereby protecting the capitalist system and reproducing the ideology of 'democracy'. And while activities which are not contained in this way, and which do fundamentally challenge that system, are deemed to be morally illegitimate, it becomes legitimate to use state (or privatised) repression against them, ironically in the name of protecting 'democracy'.

Today, the processes of managing dissent via the ideology of democratic capitalism are highly developed. Yet as a consequence of many processes, including the deepening globalising penetration of capitalism, the resulting financial crisis and the accompanying imposed austerity measures, the ecological crisis asserting the planetary limits on capitalist expansion, and the structural social limits to capital accumulation (the ability or willingness of workers to keep working and consumers to keep consuming), the hegemonic order is arguably becoming increasingly vulnerable. The myth of 'democracy' has to be carefully and constantly (re)created, not only in the media and other information-producing institutions, but also through the influencing, neutralising and outright repression of people's political agency. From the structures and nature of institutions through which people choose to take political action, to the sources of funding for political groups; from the the circumscription and control of information and culture to which people have access, to the manipulation of the very language we have to describe our realities, much of this channelling and influencing is subtle, insidious and, even covert, taking effect incrementally and cumulatively. But sometimes the process is forced to be more overt, risking exposure, particularly when people resist co-option and containment and so coercion must be applied. The struggles over the meanings and definitions of democracy form a fundamental battleground in the struggle for a just and equitable world. It is thus vital to try and understand this issue, from a theoretical, historical and contemporary perspective.

This volume thus aims to expose some of the overt and covert ways in which democracy is managed to protect unequal power structures of capitalism from the potential force of participatory democracy. It is made up of five sections, which together build a picture of how the hollow promise of capitalist 'democracy' is promoted, while our political thoughts and actions are heavily circumscribed through subtle and sometimes not so subtle methods, in order to protect capitalism and forestall genuine democracy. The articles vary in length, style and form, and do not correspond to a single, unified viewpoint, or way of addressing this problem, but we hope they will inspire debate. What they do share is a common critique of the current ideology of capitalist 'democracy', and a sense of the urgency with which it needs to be challenged.

The first section explores the relationship between capitalism and democracy, from both historical and contemporary angles. In the introductory chapter I trace the contradictions which underpin this symbiotic relationship, and continually shape both capitalism and democracy, demonstrating how liberal democracy has evolved into a means of achieving hegemonic control in tandem with the emergence and ongoing expansion of the capitalist system, even while the democratic claims of the capitalist order become ever more untenable. This is followed by David Whyte's exploration of how, as democratic rhetoric becomes increasingly unable to mask the anti-democratic practices and deepening inequalities that neoliberalism requires, naked economic coercion disguised as the public interest, which Whyte terms 'market patriotism', is promoted as an end in itself. William I. Robinson's examination builds on this analysis with an examination of the impact of the financial crisis on the organisation of consent and global hegemony, arguing that it has lead to the increased use of coercion, as consensual mechanisms of social control struggle to contain the massive structural inequalities of 21st century capitalism.

Section two provides a closer examination of how public opinion is manipulated to induce obedience to the prerogatives of corporate dominated capitalism. David Cromwell and David Edwards explore how the mainstream media slavishly protects corporate and state interests by ensuring that radical, challenging and systemically critical viewpoints are marginalised, excluded, and delegitimated, creating the sense that it is only 'common-sense' to endorse capitalism and state and corporate power, rather than to expose and challenge their patently destructive and catastrophic effects. This idea of 'common-sense' extends to the definition of democracy itself: the article illustrates how the media has become a crucial weapon in the ideological battle to confirm capitalism as democratic. This theme is broadened out in an interview with Matthew Alford in which he explains how the US entertainment industry has increasingly become effectively one large, multi-billion dollar profit making propaganda machine, in which state interference, corporate advertising and the supremacy of profits strictly, but covertly, police the messages emanating from mainstream film and television companies. In this way the likelihood that these cultural products will include viewpoints which challenge the status quo or capitalist logic is drastically curtailed, thereby providing vast amounts of ideological ammunition in defence of capitalism and US imperialism. Michael Barker then examines the close associations between several media celebrities and elite foundations and corporate and political interests in supposedly humanitarian interventions, exposing the neocolonial and neoliberal agendas this propaganda serves. Finally, James Petras demonstrates how the very language we have to describe our world is manipulated to hinder attempts to challenge fundamentally state and corporate agendas. He illuminates just how pervasively and perniciously propaganda can police our minds and our imaginations, and insists upon the rejection of euphemistic and deceptive terms and the development of new analytical frameworks which accurately describe the harsh conditions we face and enable radical struggle against them.

Sections three and four explore the subtle mechanisms through which public opinion and action are influenced and policed through the twin processes of co-option and repression, based on the understanding of civil society as a crucial battleground in the struggle to define democracy upon which rests the success or failure of the organisation of consent. This section begins with William K. Carroll and Matthew Greeno's examination of how consent is organised and social movements co-opted via cultural, economic and political processes that divide and rule while emptying democratic content from politics and instilling in us a possessive individualism and a faith in the global market. Sibille Merz's article focuses on the role of NGOs in co-opting, neutralising and disarming radical grassroots dissent, with a case study of the increasing presence of NGOs in Palestine, more precisely, the West Bank towns of Ramallah and al-Bireh. Using on her own fieldwork, she explores the effects of the neoliberal paradigm on the restructuring of social formations through the external funding and promotion of civil society groups, especially NGOs, arguing that neoliberal restructuring of international aid has aimed to transform societies and subjectivities around the notion of 'enterprise', via depoliticised concepts such as human rights, tolerance, and diversity. This has weakened the national resistance movement, diverting it away from collective resistance and towards individualised, depoliticised and professionalised forms of political agency.

Michael Barker continues this line of inquiry and delves into the murky world of corporate and elite philanthropy. His article highlights an often forgotten relationship of power, through which elites use funding to co-opt and de-fang political formations which threaten to disrupt capitalist social relations, with reference to historical examples of how this has been achieved. Edmund Berger pursues this topic further with an exploration into how political foundations seek to co-opt and neuter potentially revolutionary movements both domestically and internationally. The final article in this section is written by The Free Association and argues that stronger forms of political organisation can help mitigate the use of shock (i.e. panic, disorientation and exhaustion) which can discipline our thinking and induce us to fall back on reactionary tropes to try and understand our complicated and fast-changing world. They argue that stronger, flexible and resilient forms of political organisation are necessary to challenge more effectively neoliberalism's colonisation of the possible, and fight political and social transformation. Meanwhile, Katie Pollard and Maria Young contrast the state and media responses to the UK student protests and the August riots, concluding that the student demonstrations were recognised as a legitimate struggle and were thus more easily recuperated whereas the rioters, who did not make demands or appeal to the putative democratic nature of the state, were unco-optable and consequently received harsher condemnation and repression. Their analysis reveals the existence of fixed, often silent but always powerful, parameters of 'legitimate' and 'acceptable' dissent, which exist to safeguard the 'democratic' capitalist system.

Section four explores how comparable repression is legitimated when co-option does not work or is not possible. Charles Thorpe examines the imposition of an authoritarian, neoliberal model upon the University of California and the police repression of the student protests that these reforms prompted. He explores the university administration's attempts to legitimate its actions by using the language though not the substance of democracy, under which dialogue and political agency is tolerated only within strict parameters. His account provides a illuminating snapshot of the interrelations at one university between neoliberalism, education, co-option and repression. Meanwhile, Tom Anderson explores government attempts to repress dissent in the UK through legislation, extra-judicial measures, violence and the creation of a climate of fear. In doing so, he illustrates how such repression is ironically justified via the evocation of the 'rule of law', which is claimed will bring democracy and freedom. He then explores these issues further in an interview with Verity Smith about the use of undercover police officers to channel covertly and manipulate activists' political activities.

The final section examines the the practice of 'democracy promotion'; that is the deployment by US and European governments and their allies of 'assistance' to mould the political structures, civil society and media industries of countries of strategic interest. Here Edmund Berger examines the network of US organisations involved in democracy promotion, which he follows up with an investigation into how these organisations have used the opportunity provided by the uprisings in the Middle East and North Africa to attempt to try and ensure that the emerging political formations will facilitate corporate penetration into the region by acquiescing with US-led transnational elite and corporate interests. Finally, I examine the work of the UK-based Westminster Foundation for Democracy, a 'democracy promotion' organisation which has received remarkably little scrutiny, but which is integral to the UK government's efforts to shape the political landscapes of regions and countries in pursuance of its foreign policy strategy.

These mechanisms of manipulation, co-option, and coercion work in tandem to manage dissent, using an ideology of 'democracy' as justification. There are of course many other mechanisms and topics which this collection has not had the space to examine. For instance, the processes and impacts of the incorporation of labour movements, particularly trades unions, into structures of governance, have not been covered here. Nor have today's increasingly sophisticated propaganda, marketing and electioneering systems been given adequate attention,[3] nor the development of academic discourses which fuel the ideology of 'democracy'. In particular, there has been insufficient space here to detail how 'democracy' has been used to justify horrific levels of coercion, as exemplified in the invasion and so-called 'reconstruction' of Iraq. The ongoing subversion of 'democracy' in the wake of the uprisings in North Africa and the Middle East also requires deeper exploration. However, we hope this volume will have provided a snapshot of some of the mechanisms through which democracy is suppressed and consent organised, and will provoke readers' interest and encourage them to read further.

It is important to note that none of the submissions intend to pass judgement on social movements, organisations or individuals for the choices they have made whether or not to engage in powerful elite, state, or corporate institutions or processes; rather the aim is to point out the contradictions and risks of such choices. Nor has it been their intention to preach as if occupying some vantage point from which the obfuscation, propaganda and free-market ideologies are obvious. The book has been written in recognition of the power of propaganda and information control and in full awareness that difficult decisions are made often from compromised, marginalised and vulnerable positions, and also that elite agendas can be subtly subverted to progressive ends. Consent and co-option are far from a clear cut issues, but it is essential to remain constantly vigilant, and be keenly aware of the insidious forces and processes which impinge upon our freedom of choice, behaviour and thought. Such vigilance can help prevent diversion from one's original goals, while rigorous and continued exploration into these issues, and awareness of how others have addressed these thorny questions, can help provide the strength to repel co-option and fight back against repression. This volume attempts to aid this process.

What unites all the submission, and perhaps mitigates their

prevailing pessimism, is an understanding that the consent upon which this repressive social order depends is in fact unstable, built upon a precarious and impossible promise of democratic capitalism. This should inspire hope: the fact that ever greater lengths have to be undertaken each and every day to persuade us to believe in the patently contradictory notion of democratic capitalism in order to secure our participation, exposes the house of cards upon which capitalism is built. That it does so utilising such a grossly distorted version of 'democracy' indicates too the universal appeal and thus potential power of fully participatory democracy, in which equal access to political decision-making processes is protected.

We hope that this collection will help expose this fundamental weakness at the heart of the capitalist social order. The disconnection between the promise and the suppression of democracy will only intensify as capitalism becomes more and more coercive and as its claims to 'democracy' become increasingly spurious, opening up the possibility of radical challenge and change. This potential rests in our collective reclamation of democracy, from its grossly distorted capitalist form, into a genuinely participatory and egalitarian reality. Like a malevolent Tinkerbell from *Peter Pan*, capitalism only prevails when we collectively believe it can best deliver our wishes, and invest in it our hopes and desires, in spite of the catastrophic human and ecological costs of doing so. In fact, it rests with us, the governed, the consenters, to refuse to believe the fake promise, and instead to create instead genuine democracies - local and global - outside of capitalist relations, through which our voices can be heard and our needs, wants and desires met.

Acknowledgements

I would like to express firstly my thanks to all those who have participated in this project as authors, and to those who have engaged in discussions over its contents. In particular, I thank Edmund Berger, Nick Fisher, Chris Kitchen, Beth Lawrence, Kezia Rolfe and David Whyte for their insightful comments on earlier drafts. Members of the Corporate Watch co-operative also offered vital advice, and editorial and copy-editing assistance. I would also like to thank Peter Lang Publishers Inc. for allowing us to republish Michael Barker, 'Celebrity Philanthropy: In the Service of Corporate Propaganda' from Gerald Sussman (ed.) *The Propaganda Society: Promotional Culture and Politics in Global Context*, (New York: Peter Lang, 2011)

A Note on Referencing and Spellings

The referencing systems used in this book are not always consistent since they may reflect the system used on articles' first publication or authors' preferences. Similarly, the spellings use reflect authors' use of UK, US or Canadian English.

Notes

1   Michael Crozier, Samuel P. Huntington, and Joji Watanuki, *The Crisis of Democracy: Report on the Governability of Democracies to the Trilateral Commission* (New York: New York University Press, 1975), p. 21.

2   Of course, other ideologies can influence and police our consent and limit our political activity, such as nationalism and cultural superiority, or other systems of power relations such as patriarchy and racism, but these are beyond the scope of this volume.

3   However, I would recommend Gerald Sussman's *Branding Democracy: US Regime Change in Post-Soviet Eastern Europe,* which examines the uses of systemic propaganda in US foreign policy, as a very good starting point.

Part 1

The Contradictory Nature
of Democracy Under Capitalism

2. The Paradox of Democratic Capitalism: An Historical View

Rebecca Fisher

We can have democracy in this country, or we can have great wealth concentrated in the hands of a few, but we can't have both.

Supreme Court Justice Louis Brandeis[1]

Capitalism and democracy have been locked in a contradictory yet interdependent relationship throughout their history. Despite popular conceptions, liberal democracy has emerged as a mechanism which has in effect limited popular participation, and operated as a legitimating device to protect capitalism from more direct forms of democracy. This article will examine some of the ways in which ideals of democracy centred on wide public participation have been suppressed, and limited liberal democracy promoted, in order to mask the anti-democratic and oppressive nature of capitalism, and organise general consent. It will trace the historical evolution of this contradictory, yet mutually reinforcing relationship, suggesting that both capitalist and liberal democratic processes arose as defensive responses to subvert popular democracy and contain real and potential social rebellions. It will also show that this subversion is at times unstable, faced with inherent social and ecological limits to capital accumulation and continual opposition from advocates of a more genuine, popular democracy. The organisation of consent is necessarily a fraught, fluid and flexible process, and capitalist regimes are compelled to use increasingly overt anti-democratic practices, including exploitation, repression, and violence when consent is elusive. Thus the paradox is that liberal democracy must rely upon repressive means to contain social conflict, maintain the social order and pursue perpetual economic expansion, transgressing the rhetoric and language of democracy deployed to legitimate capitalism.

It is first worth noting some caveats. This article will only provide a brief and partial overview of some very complicated processes, over a long historical period. It is written from one particular angle and without intending to exclude others. It will bring out some of key the historical flashpoints in the use of democracy as an ideological cover to hide and mystify capitalism's oppression. The intention is to reveal some important aspects of how the capitalist social order has been legitimated via the language of democracy. Of course, liberal democracy is one of many disciplinary and ideological mechanisms by which general consent, or at least resignation, to capitalism are organised. Others - such as direct economic and political coercion - are not addressed here. This article does not purport to provide a comprehensive answer to the thorny question of how the capitalist order is sustained and (re)produced, but merely to suggest one perspective from which it can be tackled. In doing so, it will employ Antonio Gramsci's ideas concerning hegemony, which was described by Gramsci as "consensus protected by the amour of coercion".[2] This seems to offer a useful method of understanding the mutually dependent and dynamic relationship between consent and coercion, in particular in relation to the limited practice of democracy, and brings to light the dynamic and sometimes tenuous attempts to contain resistance and legitimate the capitalist system.[3]

Defining Democracy

> *When we say that the voters 'choose' their representative, we are using a language that is very inexact. The truth is that the representative* has himself elected by the voters. *[Emphasis in original]*
>
> Gaetano Mosca[4]

While liberal, representative democracy has clearly taken varying forms over time and place, for the purposes of this article it is worth emphasising the basic constants, which Goran Therborn defines as:

> a form of state with all the following characteristics. It has 1. a representative government elected by 2. an electorate consisting of the entire adult population, 3. whose votes carry equal weight, and 4. who are allowed to vote for any opinion without intimidation by the state apparatus.[5]

In addition, there should be a constitutionally protected separation of the executive and the judiciary, some level of accountability of the leaders and some civil and political rights, including freedom of speech, association, organisation and the press. However, overstating these apparent constants elides important elements which limit democratic participation, without necessarily diminishing the claims to constitute a democracy. For instance, legal rights to protest are subjected to continually changing restrictions in response to changing political agendas and priorities. (See also Anderson, Chapter 16.) But further restrictions on popular political participation lie deeper within the 'democratic' system.

The emphasis purely on the procedural aspects - primarily elections typically held every few years - to define democracy is a fundamental mechanism by which the popular participation in decision-making is suppressed, and social antagonism caused by capitalism's structural inequalities contained. As William I. Robinson writes, the term 'polyarchy' is more accurate to describe this system in which "a small group actually rules and participation in decision-making by the majority is confined to choosing among competing elites in tightly controlled electoral processes."[6] Labelling such a system 'democracy', simply by virtue of holding elections, and without reference to who is in a position to muster the political and cultural resources to become a candidate, or what other forces wield power over those candidates or exert power over and above the sphere of representative politics, is a powerful ideological weapon with which to manipulate public opinion and engineer consent, especially given the power of naming - or mis-naming - to shape how we understand our world. Conversely, a more participatory form of democracy would prescribe a far deeper engagement in political decision-making by the entire populace, and ensure equality of access to political power. It would thus be likely to constitute a means to fundamentally alter the unjust and unequal power relations, divisions and hierarchies imposed through economic, social and political structures and traditions.[7] In order to understand how these unequal structures of power operate, it is thus essential to examine how democracy's radical, egalitarian meanings have been subverted in order to protect an elitist form of government which serves to prevent the development of more participatory system.

The Emergence of Capitalism and Democracy

> *The ground of the late war between the King and you [Parliament] was a contest whether he or you should exercise the supreme power over us.*

> *Is not all the controversy, whose slaves the poor shall be?*

> Levellers' pamphlets, 1648 and 1649[8]

Both representative democracy and capitalism emerged as defensive strategies against social struggles for a more equitable and less exploitative system. The inauguration of early capitalist relations, roughly from 1450-1650, should be understood in the context of the crisis of the feudal order in Europe: as an attempt to restore class power of the privileged elites who struggled to maintain their power amid a more powerful labour force and high wages resulting in part from the labour shortage following the Black Death; and to quell the "vast communalistic social movements and rebellions against feudalism" which "offered the promise of a new egalitarian society built on social equality and cooperation."[9] Space constraints here necessitate a severely truncated and simplified account of what was a long, complex and extremely bloody historical process, which only gains a linear appearance of a transition from feudalism to capitalism when viewed with hindsight. The reality was that the emergence of capitalism was far from certain, and other forms of social organisation were possible. Yet, by means of instigating new and brutal hierarchies of race, gender and geography the foundations of capitalism were laid down "in the relentless attempt to appropriate new sources of wealth, expand its economic base, and bring new workers under its command."[10] This was achieved through vast enclosures of common land; through the suppression of working class, and in particular women's, social and economic status; through territorial conquest in the 'New World' and the ensuing genocides and enslavements of its populations; and through the transatlantic slave-trade. The new social differences, hierarchies and inequalities, in particular in relation to gender, class and race, that emerged as a result weakened the ties of communal solidarity and resistance, and have since become paradigmatic of capitalist development. For instance, the commodification of common land, and therefore access to food, dramatically altered gender relations through making survival conditional upon having a wage, or access to one. This consequently feminised, devalued and hid the work of the reproduction of labour - producing and looking after children, the household and healthcare - since it did not receive a wage.[11] It also increased the rates of capital accumulation possible since wages now only had to cover a portion of the costs of production. The colonial conquest and enslavement of the 'New World' also inaugurated new methods of increased capitalist production and exploitation that still exist today, including the model of an internationally divided yet economically integrated labour force and an export-oriented system of production. Thus, to counter ongoing and bloody struggles for greater social equality, capitalist relations, and the patriarchal and colonial practices they depend upon, gradually developed mechanisms to control and exploit both waged and unwaged labour, and appropriate new sources of surplus wealth and accumulate capital. Such mechanisms are very much in existence today, ensuring that capitalism is still "necessarily committed to racism and sexism."[12]

The new capitalist system that slowly and bloodily emerged out of the decaying feudal order required new conceptions of political, economic and individual rights. In opposition to older notions of the 'divine right' of the feudal aristocracy, the notion of a 'social contract' emerged which served to justify the new economic freedoms for the merchants, traders and industrialists that capitalist expansion required. Under this 'social contract' everyone would supposedly be equal before the law, rather than before God, as self-contained individuals with innate rights and liberties. This became known as liberalism and assisted the growth of the institutions of the nation state in order to supposedly protect citizens' new-found juridical equality and political freedoms and to protect private property rights.

The logic of free and equal individuals and the relaxation of the feudal bonds also contained within it the threat of rebellion from those supposedly free and equal individuals who remained oppressed and exploited: precisely the threat which had precipitated the emergence of capitalism and which it was required to suppress. As capitalist relations emerged, the unsustainability and instability of ruling "exclusively by means of hunger and terror"[13] was well understood, leading to the augmentation of the repressive power of the state as "the only agency capable of confronting a working class that was regionally unified, armed, and no longer confined in its demands to the political economy of the manor". This development has continued ever since.[14] This increase in state repression helped to restrict the new economic power and freedoms to the privileged classes, thereby enabling the appropriation of wealth among the newly created social elites necessary for capital accumulation. The state had accrued a new and contradictory role which it still inhabits today, as both the impartial judge protecting the supposedly innate and universal rights of the individual, and the authority entrusted with protecting private property rights, and thus the unequal social order, from challenges from the dispossessed majority.

The contradiction in the state's function arises from the formal separation of the political and economic spheres that the new system of capitalist relations ushered. Under the previous feudal system political power - the state - was intrinsically linked to economic power (note its linguistic derivation from the word 'estate', that is the site of both political and economic power) and the landed aristocrat was at once both economic and political authority.[15] However, under capitalism these two sites of authority formally separated and the political elites were no longer necessarily the primary wielders of economic power. In this new capitalistic order economic power became in theory private and non-political, comprising of private relations of market exchange between individual agents of production. Meanwhile, political power became the preserve of the state, that is of public, political relations, comprising of the government, its executive, administration and coercive apparatus, i.e. the site of 'democracy' as it developed. Occupying supposedly separate spheres, the idea that political universal freedoms could exist alongside social and economic inequality could then gain legitimating power. As Perry Anderson writes,

> The fact is that this cultural domination is embodied in certain irrefutable concrete institutions: regular elections, civic freedoms, rights of assembly - all of which exist in the West and none of which directly threaten the class power of capital. The day-to-day system of bourgeois rule is thus based on the consent of the masses, in the form of the ideological belief that they exercise self-government in the representative State.[16]

The Limitations of Liberal Democracy and the Growth of the Corporation

> *How has is come about that, in the major and most advanced capitalist countries, a tiny minority class - the bourgeoisie - rules by means of democratic forms?*
>
> Goran Therborn[17]

In reality however, political and economic power are never possible to separate, and this reveals the root of the contradictory and complicated relationship between capitalism and popular democracy. It has therefore required a long, contested and far from inevitable set of processes to apply the ideology of liberal democracy in legitimating capitalism, as the social, economic and political polarity produced by capitalism can never be wholly reconciled with the ideology of democracy. As Ralph Miliband writes,

> Political equality, save in formal terms, is impossible in the conditions of advanced capitalism... Unequal economic power on the scale and of the kind encountered in advanced capitalist societies, inherently *produces* political inequality, on a more or less commensurate scale, whatever the constitution may say... the state in these class societies is primarily and inevitably the guardian and protector of the economic interests which are dominant in them. Its 'real' purpose and mission is to ensure their continued predominance, not to prevent it.[18]

Thus, despite the formal separation, the political sphere - the state - frequently finds itself the target of the social conflict deriving from capitalism's systemic socio-economic inequalities, a dynamic which has convinced many political elites that democracy would be unable to maintain the social order. For instance, James Madison, one of the 'Founding Fathers' of the United States, wrote that "democracies have ever been spectacles of turbulence and contention; have ever been found incompatible with personal security, or the rights of property."[19] Indeed, many liberal elites of the 18th and 19th centuries opposed the extension of democratic rights to the masses out of a fear that "the levelling instincts of democracy were a great threat to the liberties which had only just been wrestled from monarchs and autocrats".[20] Universal suffrage, also referred to as the franchise, was eventually won after long and often bloody political struggles. Frequently, extensions of the franchise were introduced as defensive measures against the risk of social unrest in the context of preparing for or recuperating from wars, when securing popular participation in nationalist projects was of paramount importance to the social order. In Italy and Canada franchisement was extended in advance of mobilisations, in order to engineer consent, while in Great Britain, Denmark, Holland, and the United States, the franchise was extended following the effects of the popular integration in the national war-effort, as rewards, and to counter the threat of discontent in the wake of the terrible impacts of war.[21] For instance, in Great Britain all men over the age of twenty-one, and women over thirty were allowed to vote only in 1918, at a time when the political establishment was especially eager to placate the masses. Such a relationship with war and voting continued well into the 20th century: Therborn writes that the right to vote for African-Americans in the South were "first enforced during the Vietnam War, quite possibly as a result of the Government's concern with a crumbling home front marked by black rebellion, student movements and opposition to the war."[22] Hobson observes that the problem for elite liberal thinkers who opposed political, and thus potentially economic and social, equality, was the universalist language in which liberalism was couched, "which made it difficult to limit indefinitely calls for extension of basic rights and the franchise"; he argues that "the subsequent appearance of liberal democracy was not so much due to most liberals wishing for it" but "in part from a miscalculation in the strategy used to entrench liberal rights, combined with a gradual recognition that the best way to manage democracy's seemingly unavoidable rise was to limit and control it as best they could."[23]

Indeed, restricting the franchise to those sufficiently economically integrated into the capitalist system in order to render them unlikely to pressure for systemic change ensured that, eventually, even near universal franchise could prove a highly effective mechanism to contain social discontent, and insulate the economic sphere from political challenge. As Claus Offe states, enfranchisement served to placate the public and stave off clamours for systemic change:

> [t]he mechanism through which democratic equality would lead to the peaceful and stable (rather than revolutionary and disruptive) processing of conflict, its accommodation, and change was thought... to reside in the voting and bargaining powers with which those inferior in socioeconomic power were to be compensated for their

relative powerlessness through the constitutional provision of political resources... If every interest was given a 'voice', nobody had any reason to 'exit' to a radical anti-systemic opposition. By virtue of its procedures, democracy is able to reconcile conflict to the extent which is necessary for the maintenance of stability and do so more effectively than any other regime form.[24]

Economic integration of non-elite groupings was partly achieved through granting real or perceived social advancements in terms of wealth, social mobility or access to relative luxuries, provided by imperial expansion. Thus, in Western Europe, mirroring the development of early capitalist relations, the social conflict engendered by the industrial revolution was partly offset by intensified efforts to colonise new places, exploit their populations' labour and resources and extract more surplus capital. This process enriched the burgeoning 'middle-class', and enabled an increase in their political power by various means, including the extension of the franchise to wider groups of property-owners, and eventually, to the whole adult population (barring such groups as prisoners and foreign-nationals). Thus, the development of liberal democracy and the extension of the franchise can be understood to have emerged as a means of providing political stability as a defensive response to real or threatened social and political unrest.[25] This demonstrates how capitalism and liberal democracy evolved symbiotically, and explains why the limited 'democratic' systems are most stable in the "centers of the world system, where wealth is concentrated and the process of capital accumulation most dynamic".[26] It also demonstrates that, just as when capitalist relations first emerged, state repression (through facilitating and legitimating capitalist and imperial expansion) constitutes a determinant feature of capitalism, and further illustrates its structural incompatibility with, and thus inherently hollow claims to co-exist with, popular participation in democracy.

The process of perpetual expansion into new places, resources and services continues today in the pursuit of capital accumulation, class power and legitimation of the capitalist social order. For instance, recent years have seen new patterns of enclosure encompassing entirely new spheres of the commons, such as the financialisation of nature and commercialisation of social media. This has brought a raft of new commodities, with everything from pollution rights and genetic traits to ecosystem services becoming incorporated within the market.[27] The global economic crisis has also resulted in entrenchment and expansion of privatisation around the world accelerating the transfer of resources from public to private. Such 'new enclosures' are continually met with resistance, chiming with the first struggles against land enclosure, and embodying the social contradictions that have always been inherent to the capitalist system.[28]

The maintenance of the formal separation between the economic and political spheres, insulating the former from the latter, was also aided by the creation of the corporation. Having been illegally transformed from charitable, not-for-profit organisations to commercial entities without legal challenge, exemplified by the East India Company in the late 17th century, corporations rapidly proliferated. A major advantage was that since these new corporations were legal entities separate from the persons running it, those persons could not be held responsible for 'the corporation's' actions, thereby enabling economic activity to be separated from the political sphere of the courts and the state. A corporation's various social, political or moral responsibilities were instead replaced with a singular responsibility to shareholders to maximise profit, making it the ideal agent of capitalist expansion.[29] The proliferation of corporations accelerated the process of capital accumulation and commodification of goods and services, as their novel ability to "combine the capital, and thus the economic power of unlimited numbers of people", opened up opportunities for the growing middle-classes to buy shares.[30] Corporations thus unlocked far more capital investment than had been previously available from elite individuals, which was crucial to the financing of both colonialism and industrialisation and in particular the expensive canal and railway building programmes upon which the development of industrial capitalism in Europe and North America depended.[31] The purchasing of company shares was facilitated by the introduction of limited liability, meaning that investors were liable only to the value of their investment, reducing the risks involved (in Britain this occurred in 1855). This reduced still further the responsibilities of the shareholders for their business activities and intensified many people's integration into the globalising economy, helping to stabilise the capitalist social order by deepening people's dependence upon its operations. As an article in the Edinburgh Journal in 1853 stated, "The workman does not understand the position of the capitalist. The remedy is, to put him in the way by practical experience... Working-men, once enabled to act together as the owners of a joint capital, will soon find their whole view of the relations between capital and labour undergo a radical alteration."[32]

Information Control for Social Control

> *The twentieth century has been characterised by three developments of great political importance: the growth of democracy, the growth of corporate power, and the growth of corporate propaganda as a means of protecting corporate power against democracy.*

> Alex Carey[33]

The eventual extension of the franchise to all adult citizens, and both sexes strengthened the imperative for those in power to find effective means to discipline people's choices and behaviours via social control and to influence public opinion and understandings via ideological means. Space does not permit a detailed discussion here into the means of social control utilised by 'democracies', which include the laying on of putatively beneficent state services such as pensions, hospitals, schools, and so on, to encourage popular support for the status quo by giving the impression that the state exists to serve the public interest, and help to maintain the day-to-day running of the capitalist system, e.g. by providing education, and indoctrination where required for its workers, health services to ensure enough survive to provide and reproduce their labour, and arguably to discipline people into assenting to the capitalist order.[34] However, more explicit forms of public manipulation of opinion are more directly connected to the development of liberal democracy as a mechanism to contain the social discontent and rebellion that capitalism produces, and so deserve a brief examination here.

While propaganda is of course an ancient art, modern propaganda techniques - in particular the public relations industry - can be traced to the United States in the early 20th century, and in particular as a defensive strategy to contain social unrest and to promote perpetual consumerist behaviour amongst the population.[35] (See also Sussman, Foreword.) The massive appropriation of wealth among a political and economic elite had been met by the rise of organised labour and immigrant movements which demanded greater economic and political rights. Corporations in the United States responded by developing ways to control their reputations among the public, as a "response to the threat of democracy and the need to create some kind of ideological link between the interests of big business and the interests of ordinary Americans."[36] This dynamic has continued ever since: in 1938 the National Association of Manufacturers warned of "the hazard facing industrialists" in "the newly realized political power of the masses," and noted that "unless their thinking is directed we are definitely headed for adversity".[37] Meanwhile, S.C. Allyn of National Cash Register explicitly named the goal as to "indoctrinate citizens with the capitalist story" until "they are able to play back the story with remarkable fidelity".[38] The PR industry has now grown into a massive enterprise, manipulating public opinion by frequently injecting stories, marketing and disinformation into the news and popular culture, often without direct attribution to the corporate and elites interests from which they originate. In addition, the mainstream media, entertainment and culture industries are largely dominated by huge corporations, and other state and elite interests. (See also Cromwell and Edwards, Chapter 5 and Alford and Fisher, Chapter 6.) The cumulative effect is to glorify the benefits provided by capitalism, and its corporate servants, and to mystify and disguise the violent and exploitative reality of its operations.

Unsurprisingly, propaganda techniques were also used to subvert even the limited democracy permitted in the US and manipulate public opinion for political ends, in ways which have become systemic in modern global capitalism.[39] The Committee for Public Information, also known as the Creel Commission, was created to generate public approval for US intervention in World War One. To do so, it claimed that sending troops to fight in the war was necessary in order to 'make the world safe for democracy'. This use of democratic rhetoric to legitimate foreign, and often military interventions has since been an essential weapon of US global and imperial power. Public Relations pioneer Edward Bernays was part of the Creel Commission, and when the war ended put his expertise to use in developing peacetime PR methods for companies including Proctor and Gamble, CBS, General Electric and Dodge Motors.[40] Using his uncle Sigmund Freud's theories about social psychology, and in particular those concerning unconscious desires, he pioneered a now ubiquitous form of advertising which equated the product with symbolic qualities - such as status, dominance or freedom - often qualities which people felt were missing from their lives.[41] He was well aware of the political impact of his methods, both in terms of helping to deflect energies away from political struggles via consumerism and in the more general influence on people's perceptions of themselves and their society. [42] Bernays believed that such direct manipulation was necessary in order to limit liberal democracy, in order to protect it from the 'ignorant masses', whose empowerment he believed would lead inevitably to Fascism:

> The conscious and intelligent manipulation of the organized habits and opinions of the masses is an important element in democratic society... We are governed, our minds are moulded, our tastes formed, our ideas suggested, largely by men we have never heard of... who understand the mental processes and social patterns of the masses. It is they who pull the wires which control the public mind.[43]

The developments in propaganda, public relations and consumerist ideology had important political implications, promulgating the notion that the route to freedom and happiness lay not in winning political freedoms but in material possessions, which were advertised as quick-fix solutions to social and personal malaise, and tickets to a liberated, meaningful and connected life. This both served to militate against over-production by persuading people to purchase goods for which they had no need and to dampen social discontent with the capitalist system responsible for many of the alienations. Those with enough disposable income were to be liberated by the market, and in this way their very tangible lack of freedom over their everyday lives - their choices in regards to work, education, housing, leisure etc. - was hidden behind their new wealth of consumer choices. Consumerist ideology serves to depoliticise social behaviour, including of those who are unable to afford to purchase the goods on offer, through encouraging the psychological fixation upon material possessions, individually owned or craved, rather than political causes, inducing debilitating alienation, atomisation and marginalisation.[44] (See also Carroll and Greeno, Chapter 9.) As Kaela Jubas writes, "the ideology of consumerism functions to conflate the concepts of consumption and citizenship and capitalism and democracy, as if consumption offered a resolution to social and political struggles".[45]

Another crucial mechanism is the supposedly philanthropic funding of education programmes, public policy research, cultural and knowledge production and civil society organisations. Particularly in the United States, where welfare and philanthropic activity was less monopolised by the state or the church than in European capitalist societies,[46] wealthy elite foundations operate significant ideological influence to limit the radical potential of knowledge and culture, by co-opting and neutralising the political activities of NGOs, civil society and grassroots organisations, and social movements. As Arnove, whose seminal work has helped to expose this hidden nexus of unaccountable and unregulated power, puts it, philanthropic "foundations like

Carnegie, Rockefeller, and Ford have a corrosive influence on a democratic society... they buy talent, promote causes, and, in effect, establish an agenda of what merits society's attention" and "serve as 'cooling out' agencies, delaying and preventing more radical, structural change".[47] (For a far more extensive examination of this process see Barker, Chapter 11.)

Such ideological methods of social control are at their most insidious, pervasive and sophisticated where capitalism is most developed and where its political legitimacy is most reliant upon the myth of popular empowerment and political freedoms.[48] Such a social order can therefore be described as hegemonic as consensual methods of social control - especially the promotion of an ideology of democracy - mitigate the necessity for overt coercion, ensuring that domination or large-scale overt policing of thought and behaviour, more redolent of totalitarian societies, is not required. Rather, hegemony operates when dominant groups can define "the limits of what is possible" and "inhibits the growth of alternative horizons and expectations."[49] Thus, techniques to manipulate and influence the cultural production of knowledge - via such mechanisms as education, intellectual research, propaganda and the media - serve to establish a set of multiple ideas, morals and values as determinative of commonly accepted, or legitimate opinion. The power and complexity of hegemony lies in its ability to tolerate and accommodate a shifting range of values, meanings, and opinions, and in the process often recuperating and neutralising erstwhile radical positions, always within certain parameters of 'legitimacy'. In the context of this discussion, these silent rules of permissible opinion induce tacit or active endorsement of capitalism and market democracy, to the extent that, within mainstream discourses these opinions are held as 'common-sense', or even self-evident. This can delegitimise as irrational, illogical or even dangerous views which break the implicit rules.

The process of building ideological hegemony is not automatic, certain or uncontested however. As Thompson writes, "[s]uch hegemony can be sustained by the rulers only by the constant exercise of skill, of theatre and of concession".[50] It is far from overt or even necessarily consciously planned, for it lacks the required centralised organisation. Instead, hegemony is the aggregate results of shared values by those monopolising both political and economic power to shape the dominant discourses. Thus ideological hegemony can have much more powerful effects than a mere ideology. As Raymond Williams observes, "if what we learn... were only the isolable meanings and practices of the ruling class, or of a section of the ruling class, which gets imposed on others, occupying merely the top of our minds, it would be - and one would be glad - a very much easier thing to overthrow", but instead it is "continually active and adjusting... more substantial and more flexible than any abstract ideology".[51] Thus,

> hegemony is not to be understood at the level of mere opinion or mere manipulation. It is a whole body of practices and expectations; our assignments of energy, our ordinary understanding of the nature of man [sic] and of his world. It is a set of meanings and values which as they are experienced as practices appear as reciprocally confirming. It thus constitutes a sense of reality for most people in the society, a sense of absolute because experienced reality beyond which it is very difficult for most members of the society to move, in most areas of their lives.[52]

Consequently, the implicit rules that define 'common-sense' are as invisible as "the air we breathe".[53]

Capitalism's Inherent Instability

> *We have 50 percent of the world's wealth, but only 6.3 percent of its population... In this situation we cannot fail to be the object of envy and resentment. Our real task in the coming period is to devise a pattern of relationships which will permit us to maintain this position of disparity.*
>
> George F. Kennan[54]

However, capitalism is continually, and inevitably, beset by crises arising from its inherent social contradictions and its dependence upon inequality, exploitation and violence which is likely to breed social rebellion. When the patterns of capital accumulation are severely disrupted then the political system of 'democracy' too is precarious. In such circumstances, consensual mechanisms may be discarded and replaced by more coercive means of control, as occurred during the 1930s in Japan, Germany and Italy. Frequently, however, new, apparently more benign, forms of state intervention are developed, in response to a crisis of legitimacy and capital accumulation. The New Deal and other state interventionist policies in welfare provision and job creation were direct responses to the very real threat of social rebellion against the capitalist social order during the Great Depression. Similarly, the post-War adoption of Keynesian, corporatist economic and political policies were designed to ameliorate the worst effects of capitalism in the regions where capitalism was most developed and stave off social unrest. They produced a fragile compromise between capital and labour which included state intervention and political concessions such as a degree of accommodation of trade union power, controls over the free movement of capital and extended public expenditure, particularly in the development of the welfare state, all with the promise of full employment, welfare provision and continued economic growth. Such provisions - such as the welfare state and the National Health Service in the UK- were often the result of hard-fought struggles which forced the politically powerful to concede to many of their demands. This compromise, or settlement as it became known, was accompanied with promises of fairer redistribution of the capitalist rewards, in order to ensure sufficient public purchasing power to maintain levels of consumerism to keep the economy growing. It introduced a complex web of state imposed constraints on entrepreneurial and corporate activities and market processes, and so represents yet another instance of state intervention in the functioning of market exchange relations, prioritising the organisation of popular consent over the independence and separation of the market, the economic sphere, from the state, the political sphere, and demonstrating the mutually reinforcing relationship between capitalism and the supposedly 'democratic' state.

The rewards redistributed as part of this settlement arose from surplus capital accumulated via repressive means, in particular via the importation of cheap migrant labour in the centre, and abroad through colonial, and following successive decolonisation struggles, neo-colonial interventions. The globalising post-war economy was also managed by new intra-governmental institutions, in particular the Bretton Woods Institutions, the World Bank and the International Monetary Fund, created in an attempt to ensure that global economic growth would never again stall so dramatically as it had done during the Great Depression. They have come to deploy coercive economic disciplinary mechanisms, often involving debt, to police countries' macro-economic policies, often contrary to democratically mandated political and economic decisions. This process has created an increasingly integrated world economy and intensified capitalism's structural contradictions, provoking social and political instability. It also demonstrates the inherent violence and repression upon which the maintenance of the capitalist system, particularly in times of crisis, depends. Thus in the post-war period liberal democracy was increasingly used as a rhetorical device to mask the repression required to police and enforce countries' compliance with and integration into the globalising capitalist world-system.

The Contradiction of Imperialist Democracy

> *A genuinely populist democracy has never before attained international supremacy. The pursuit of power and especially the economic costs and human sacrifice that the exercise of such power requires are not generally congenial to democratic instincts. Democratization is inimical to imperial mobilization.*

> Zbigniew Brzezinski[55]

Following in the path set by the Creel Commission, the United States government and corporate elites used a rhetoric of democracy to advance highly undemocratic, imperial practices in the pursuit of greater global capital accumulation. Unlike the European empires, US imperial power was based less on direct colonialism, but on equally coercive indirect mechanisms, providing military and financial support to frequently authoritarian client regimes.[56] Consequently, the US form of imperialism did not claim that its subject populations were unable to eventually govern themselves, and instead claimed the role of benevolent tutor to as yet untrained pupils: as Woodrow Wilson wrote, "We must govern those who learn; and they must obey as those who are in tutelage. They are children and we are men in the deep matters of government and justice."[57] This important difference helped American imperialism to hide its economic motivations to expand and deepen capitalism behind the mask of spreading democracy, while in fact frequently subverting and obstructing popular democracy. As we shall see, this has become a crucial narrative for engineering popular consent for capitalist brutality, and suppress popular movements demanding systemic economic and political change.

US political intervention to manipulate, influence and control the political behaviours and choices of subject populations has been particularly deployed on movements which chose to support left-wing or communist causes. Then US National Security Advisor, Henry Kissinger, stated in 1970, "I don't see why we need to stand by and watch a country go communist because of the irresponsibility of its own people".[58] At this stage the US government largely restricted itself to manipulating, even selecting or removing, the political elites in the target countries through economic and military aid, coups d'état and assassinations, and military invasions, rather than attempting to manipulate the political choices made by the countries' general populations. Several democratically elected governments which looked unlikely to create sufficiently hospitable environments for foreign capital were summarily removed by successive US governments, both Republican and Democrat. In 1953 the CIA and British MI6 engineered a coup d'etat which replaced the democratically elected, left-wing Iranian prime minister, Mohammed Mossadegh with the Shah of Iran, who repaid the favour by awarding the recently-nationalised oil contracts to American companies. In Guatemala, Jacobo Árbenz's elected government instituted land reforms which directly threatened the agricultural monopoly of US United Fruit Company (now known as Chiquita). The CIA - at the behest of the United Fruit Company - removed the Arbenz government in a coup d'état, in order to counter a democracy that was likely to be more responsive to popular demands, than to corporate or US state interests, and to prevent such radical and democratic ideas from taking root in the area. As a State Department official explained: "Guatemala has become an increasing threat to the stability of Honduras and El Salvador. Its agrarian reform is a powerful propaganda weapon; its broad social program, of aiding the workers and peasants in a victorious struggle against the upper classes and large foreign enterprises, has a strong appeal to the populations of Central American neighbors, where similar conditions prevail."[59]

In places such as Nicaragua, Indonesia and the Philippines political interference took the form of propping up authoritarian client regimes which served US and corporate interests. Nicaragua from the 1920s onwards was a paradigm example. Following a protracted guerilla insurgency led by Sandino against the country's US military occupation successive US governments provided the Somoza family dictatorship with economic and military aid and close diplomatic ties which helped ensure the defeat of Sandino's movement, despite the US government's growing reliance upon democratic rhetoric. In return the Somoza regime kept the country open to foreign capital, and ensured that Nicaragua could become "the bastion of US domination throughout the Caribbean Basin" providing "a launching pad for the 1954 CIA-organized coup d'état in Guatemala and for the aborted 1961 Bay of Pigs invasion of Cuba".[60] (However, in 1979 Somoza was overthrown by the Sandinista movement.) Such political interference was not limited to peripheral regions: after the Second World War the CIA bankrolled both French and Italian centre-right and conservative parties to prevent communist success in the post-war elections, while also working to destroy the political left in Greece.[61]

However, the support of dictatorial regimes severely undermined the image of the US as leader of the free world, upon which the Cold War propaganda efforts were based, and ironically, made it harder to contain communism or other opposition movements. In Iran for instance, the CIA-installed Shah was, after twenty-years on the throne, struggling to remain in power against a rising Islamic fundamentalist movement and popular opposition to his slavishly pro-American and free-market policies. Without a strategy that could establish client regimes which would remain stable and resistant to popular pressures, by the mid-1970s the CIA's unsubtle methods were widely discredited: as Robinson writes, "the capable hands of a political surgeon were needed, not the heavy hand of a paramilitary assassin."[62] In the early 1970s information about its covert operations became public via Congressional hearings, the defection of top-level CIA operatives who then defected and sold their stories and investigative journalists who exposed unsavoury details. The CIA found it next to impossible to find support domestically or in countries and communities subject to their interference, where "association with CIA programmes meant instant repudiation".[63] Direct military invasions to quell socially responsive or left-wing governments, such as occurred in Korea and Vietnam, were even more difficult to legitimate.

In conjunction, by the end of the 1960s the post-War settlement was clearly breaking down in the wake of the stagnating global economy and rising social and political instability. Rates of capital accumulation decreased dramatically as unemployment and inflation surged; wealthy elites found their investment returns suffering, while others suffered from severely diminished buying power of their wages. Social disorder, from riots and strikes in the more advanced capitalist countries to revolts and uprisings against their imperial rule and authoritarian puppets in the periphery, further threatened the accumulation of capital. US imperial might was fundamentally shaken, in particular by its defeat in Vietnam, the collapse of the Shah's client regime in Iran in early 1979 and the Nicaraguan revolution in the same year. In short, the capitalist system faced a crisis of legitimacy. While corporatist solutions were still proffered, and often adopted, (particularly in Scandinavian countries with a strong tradition of a social-democratic welfare state), by the 1970s an alternative solution was devised; this sought increased corporate power and greater market freedoms in order to restore the class power of the most wealthy and capitalist expansion was gaining sway. This strategy became known as neoliberalism, and along with it emerged its political counterpart, created in order to restore global legitimacy, which, ironically, commonly goes by the name of 'democracy promotion'.

Neoliberalism and Democracy Promotion

> *A US stance in favor of democracy helps get the Congress, the bureaucracy, the media, the public, and elite opinion to back US policy. It helps ameliorate the domestic debate, disarms critics (who could be against democracy?)... It helps bridge the gap between our fundamental geopolitical and strategic interest and our need to clothe those security concerns in moralist language... The democracy agenda, in short, is a kind of legitimacy cover for our more basic strategic objectives.*

Howard Wiarda[64]

The ascendency of neoliberalism was a gradual process.[65] Its adherents had been circling the political and academic establishment since the late 1930s, gathered around Friedrich von Hayek and Milton Friedman, and in think-tanks such as the Mont Pelerin Society (created in 1947) and offshoots such as the Institute of Economic Affairs (created in 1955), one of the most influential free-market think tanks in the UK. Until the 1970s the neoliberal movement remained on the fringes of both the academic and policy-making stage, but as a result of the crisis of capital accumulation and legitimacy in the 1970s it garnered more interest, funding and influence, including two Nobel Prizes in economics for Hayek and Friedman (in 1974 and 1976 respectively). Certain neoliberal policies began to creep into political decision making, for instance President Carter's deregulation of the US economy to combat the chronic 'stagflation' (the existence of high inflation, low rates of economic growth and high employment) of the 1970s. However, neoliberalism's first testing ground was predictably enough in a country peripheral to the world system, Chile. Here, Augusto Pinochet had been established as dictator via a military coup planned and orchestrated by the CIA and US corporations which resulted in the death of the socialist leader, Salvador Allende, whose election was described by Kissinger as a "fluke of the Chilean political system".[66] Pinochet enlisted the so-called 'Chicago Boys' to restructure the economy. These were Chilean students who the US government and 'philanthropic' foundations had paid to study under free-market champion, Milton Friedman and his colleagues at the University of Chicago, as part of an exchange programme launched in 1956, in the hope that they would spread neoliberal economic ideas across Latin America. As Juan Gabriel Valdés, Chilean foreign minister in the 1990s, noted, this was "a striking example of an organized transfer of ideology from the United States to a country within its direct sphere of influence."[67] Reliant on Pinochet's brutal regime, Chile was envisaged as a blank canvas onto which the Chicago Boys could paint their imagined neoliberal future.[68]

The programme issued by Pinochet and the Chicago Boys, who were quickly installed in the government, was fundamentally faithful to the neoliberal theory, including privatisation, deregulation and cuts to social spending. These were all measures for which the Chicago Boys had tried and failed to generate any popular support during Allende's time in government. When visiting the new Chilean regime, Friedman used the term 'shock treatment' for the first time in prescribing the economic policies he thought "the only medicine", and this became the prescription for many other countries following the Chilean experiment.[69] As Klein writes, "Chile under Chicago School rule was offering a glimpse of the future of the global economy, a pattern that would repeat again and again, from Russia to South Africa to Argentina: an urban bubble of frenetic speculation and dubious accounting fueling superprofits and frantic consumerism, ringed by the ghostly factories and rotting infrastructure of a development past; roughly half the population excluded from the economy altogether; out-of-control corruption and cronyism; decimation of nationally owned small and medium-sized businesses; a huge transfer of wealth from public to private hands."[70] This first appearance of neoliberalism theory in practice occurred without the cover of any form of democracy, but through brute force. As Allende's former defence minister, Orlando Letelier explained, this "economic plan has had to be enforced, and in the Chilean context that could be done only by the killing of thousands, the establishment of concentration camps all over the country, the jailing of more than 100,000 persons in three years... Regression for the majorities and 'economic freedom' for the small privileged groups are in Chile two sides of the same coin."[71] Letelier himself paid the price for this outspokenness when he was assassinated by a car-bomb in Washington D.C. planted by Pinochet's agents in 1976.

Although in other countries similar neoliberal policies have been carried out with less ideological purity and more pragmatism, the Chilean experience showed the germ of a brutal economic doctrine which was to be expanded throughout the world following its experiment in the periphery. A crucial lesson learnt during this experiment was that such unpopular economic measures with such destructive socio-economic impacts could not be reliably imposed solely through the use of force. Although Pinochet remained in power for 16 years his repressive regime became an international pariah, accepted only by such neoliberal devotees as Margaret Thatcher. As Hayek had correctly predicted, the battle of ideas had to be won to combat both Marxism, state-planning and Keynesian interventionism.[72] Neoliberal ideas had to become an intrinsic part of the dominant discourses, and an unquestioned part of the ideological landscape. It therefore became clear to corporate and government elites that capitalism's insatiable demand for new markets and resources would require even more sophisticated mechanisms of social control and ideological hegemony to achieve the legitimacy necessary to engineer consent. As in the regions central to the capitalist world system, these would need to address more than the governing elites, but instead engineer consent at the level of the general populace. In short, as capitalist relations expanded and deepened under neoliberalism, hegemonical forms of political control which aimed to infiltrate the consciousness of the masses were required in the periphery as well as the centre, and once again the ideology of democracy proved integral to these efforts.

The Trilateral Commission reached the same conclusion when in 1975, they authored an influential report called "the Crisis of Democracy". They believed the industrialised world was experiencing "an excess of democracy" in which "[t]he pursuit of democratic virtues of equality and individualism has led to the delegitimation of authority" and so prescribed "a greater degree of moderation in democracy" by which they meant less popular participation: "the effective operation of a democratic political system usually requires some measure of apathy and nonviolence on the part of some individuals and groups".[73] This crisis was caused by the mobilisation and empowerment within the formal democratic institutions of popular demands from oppressed groups, which risked pulling apart the fragile and paradoxical union of the ideology of democracy with the inherently oppressive social order. The report reflected that "in recent years, the operations of the democratic process do indeed appear to have generated a breakdown of traditional means of social control" and "a delegitimation of political and other forms of authority" producing what it called "dysfunctions of democracy" as "the vitality of democracy in the 1960s raised questions about the governability of democracy in the 1970s".[74] The circularity of the report's logic - that too much democracy was threatening democracy - reflects its reliance on contradictory definitions of the word 'democracy' as both popular participation and a stable, although oppressive, social order which seeks to limit popular participation. For the Commission, restricted democracy was required to contain and limit mass participation, rather than to enable it. With the Chilean experience in mind, the report recommended "experiment[ing] with more flexible models that could produce more social control with less coercive pressure."[75]

For the Commission, the kind of democracy that was required was one in which the civil society would be better controlled and manipulated in order to neuter public opinion and resistance, and militate against the risks of social rebellion against the capitalist, undemocratic and unequal social order. This, it was hoped, would correct the "flukes" and "dysfunctions" of democracy, without the risks to legitimacy posed by direct coercive force. Ideological hegemony has long been attempted in the central regions, in order to try and embed acceptance, participation and consent to the capitalist order. As two consultants on Project Democracy (see below) noted, "In international affairs, organization is now as important as issues, just as has always been the case in domestic politics."[76] Thus, concerted efforts to fund and cultivate civil society organisations in US state foreign policy interventions constituted a major shift to a focus on so-called 'soft-power' consensual means to try and manipulate and influence social and political behaviour from within. As Robinson writes, this was "a shift from social control 'from above' to social control 'from below' (and within) for the purpose of managing change and reform so as to preempt any elemental challenge to the social order. This explains why the new political intervention does not target governments *per se*, but groups in civil society itself - trade unions, political parties, the mass media, peasant associations, women's, youth and other mass organizations."[77] In this way it would be hoped that populations in peripheral regions into which transnational capital was expanding, would consent to accommodate US and neoliberal interests, and 'choose' their leaders accordingly.

Democracy promotion thus became the primary rhetorical device in order to legitimate imperial and inherently anti-democratic ventures. In 1982, President Reagan launched a new policy to help "foster the infrastructure of democracy around the world", which became known as Project Democracy. Raymond D. Gastil, a consultant on the project, described the goals as: "The preservation of democracies from internal subversion by either the Right or the Left" and noted that they would require the US to "struggle militarily, economically, politically and ideologically."[78] There were also three component parts to how these goals were to be achieved: propaganda, to win both domestic and international support for U.S. foreign policy; an expansion of covert operations, some of which were later exposed during the Iran-Contra scandal of the late 1980; and the creation of a 'quasi-governmental institute' in order to engage in 'political action strategies' abroad. This last measure led to the creation of the National Endowment for Democracy in 1983, which was intended, as Gastil noted, to "become an increasingly important and highly cost-effective component of... the defense effort of the United States and its allies".[79] Although it did not replace the CIA, it's similarity to the CIA in both means and goals was noted by former CIA director, William Colby: "Many of the programs which... were conducted as covert operations [can now be] conduced quite openly, and consequentially, without controversy."[80] While organisations providing similar 'support' in the name of democracy had existed before this point, none had been so directly connected to state foreign policy agendas, nor as intensively intervened to manipulate civil society organisations. As Robinson notes, in 1980 the NED served "as the midwife of the new political intervention, bringing together centrifugal forces in a cohesive new policy orientation."

The NED has spawned a large, growing and networked industry of similar organisations which use democracy promotion as a discursive strategy to gain access to foreign countries, and influence, mould and control their political landscapes, thereby helping to insulate transnational elites and corporate interests from popular opposition and provide stable conditions for capital accumulation and resource extraction. Democracy promotion has been an integral part of "the genius of neoliberal theory to provide a benevolent mask full of wonderful-sounding words like freedom, liberty, choice and rights to hide the grim realities of the restoration or reconstitution of naked class power."[81] (See also, Berger, Chapter 18 and Chapter 19, and Fisher, Chapter 20.)

Concluding Thoughts

> ... *democracy is an historical process which began under capitalism but can only be consummated with the supersession of capitalism.*

> William I. Robinson[82]

As this article has demonstrated, the efforts to spread the ideology and practice of profoundly limited democracy are a direct result of the fraught and contradictory relationship between capitalism and democracy, and their ultimate incompatibility. As capitalist expansion deepens, enclosing more and more of the world's commons and commodifying more goods and services, particular democratic practices - primarily voting in elections - emerged to contain the resistance that these enclosures generate. However, these democratic practices have had to be continually restricted and limited in order to insulate the processes of capitalist capture from political pressure from subjugated classes and groups. As we have seen, this has resulted in an unstable and sometime precarious hegemonic order in which, by virtue of its multiple and contradictory meanings, democracy is both a mask to legitimate capitalist coercion, and a direct threat to those coercive forces. Thus the existing supposedly democratic systems have to become ever more anti-democratic in line with capitalist expansion, thereby jeopardising the claims made that capitalism is, or can be, democratic, which remains a crucial means of securing public consent.

In the present neoliberal era we are therefore experiencing increasing corporate domination of many allegedly 'democratic' decision-making processes - from the revolving doors between companies and government, to the large-scale corporate bankrolling of election campaigns to encourage candidates' loyalty to corporate, rather than public, interests; from the insulation of monetary policy making from any form of even nominally democratic control, to the deployment of corporations to rebuild the political structures of Iraq's 'democratic' government, and even its basic economic and monetary systems following the invasion.[83] Other interventions in the market permitted by neoliberalism are insulated from popular participation: the IMF and the World Bank, whose membership is made up of 'democratic' states, serve the needs of transnational capitalism by imposing brutal economic regimens bypassing any sovereign democracies they encounter and remaining themselves impenetrable to public pressures. Meanwhile, ever more brutal disciplinary measures are deployed against those who rebel: note the growing rates of incarceration and social exclusion from state provisions. This is perhaps most starkly revealed in the story of migration under neoliberalism, in which while capital is increasingly free to move people's movement is 'managed', in order to discipline people into working for low wages in the periphery or in inhumane conditions as 'illegal' migrants in the centre.[84]

Corporations too are entrusted with the task of mystifying and disguising this shocking reality via the manipulation of public opinion using the powerful public relations and promotional industries, and their dominance within the mainstream media, entertainment and cultural industries. Dominant political and cultural discourses are now routinely constructed to promote capitalist narratives of democracy, freedom and individual choice. This has been the case even in the wake of public outcry and social unrest following the financial crisis and ongoing recession, which has seen the readiness of the state to prioritise the maintenance of the capitalist system, with massive injections of state money to bail out the financial system, brutal cuts to public spending, and drives to privatise even more of the public sector and enclose more and more of the commons. This has resulted in another crisis of legitimacy and an increase in the use of coercive strategies to control restive populations, such as increased militarisation. (See also Whyte, Chapter 3 and Robinson, Chapter 4.) Thus we see that the ideological hegemony based on the false belief in the notion of the inevitable and inviolable union between democracy and capitalism is increasingly difficult to manufacture, as social and ecological limits to capital accumulation are reached. Ultimately, the need to achieve hegemony - which includes both coercive and consensual mechanisms - is a sign of weakness, as it entails a reliance upon legitimating, masking and enforcing an increasingly violent system. That capitalist propagandists must make appeals to democracy, which stands in contradiction to capitalism, shows their fundamental vulnerability. Only time will tell whether the ideological hegemony that protects capitalism will rehabilitate itself sufficiently in order to hide its contradictory relationship with democracy and (re)organise sufficient levels of popular consent to protect elite wealth and power from demands for greater social equality. Alternatively, this time, clamours for systemic change may assert themselves more effectively against the dominance of capital, and force open new directions that will overcome the hegemonic forces and the structural socio-economic and political structures of capitalism, both of which currently promote democracy while simultaneously, and forcefully, denying it.

Notes

1   Quoted in Gerald Sussman, *Branding Democracy; U.S. Regime Change in Post-Soviet Eastern Europe* (New York: Peter Lang, 2010), p. 30.

2   Antonio Gramsci, *Selections from the Prison Notebooks*, edited and translated by Quintin Hoare and Geoffrey Nowell Smith (New York: Lawrence and Wishart, 1971), p. 263.

3   Perry Anderson helpfully used the analogy of gold and paper to illustrate the relationship: while paper is itself worthless, when people believe that it substitutes for gold it acquires great power as money. Similarly, coercion does not have to be directly applied to wield power, if enough people are persuaded via ideological mechanisms to believe in and consent to the capitalist system. However, it must exist in the background, as a reserve measure: just as gold, or higher value currencies are automatically reached for during credit crises, so too do ruling elites resort to coercion when consent is unreliable. Anderson writes, "The normal conditions of ideological subordination of the masses – the day-to-day routines of a parliamentary democracy – are themselves constituted by a silent, absent force which gives them their currency: the monopoly of legitimate violence by the State. Derived of this, the system of cultural control would be instantly fragile, since the limits of possible actions against it would disappear. With it, it is immensely powerful – so powerful that it can, paradoxically, do 'without' it: in effect, violence may normally scarcely appear within the bounds of the system at all… in the most tranquil democracies today, the army may remain invisible in the barracks, the police appear uncontentious on its beat." See Perry Anderson, 'The Antinomies of Antonio Gramsci', in *New Left Review*, vol. 100, Nov 1976-Jan 1977, p.43.

4   Gaetano Mosca, *The Ruling Class*, (New York: McGraw-Hill, 1965), p. 51. Quoted in William I. Robinson, *Promoting Polyarchy: Globalization, US Intervention, and Hegemony* (Cambridge: Cambridge University Press, 1996), p. 63.

5   Goran Therborn, 'The Rule of Capital and the Rise of Democracy', *New Left Review*, 1/103, (May/June 1977), pp. 3-41, p. 4.

6   William I. Robinson, *A Theory of Global Capitalism. Production, Class, and State in a Transnational World* (Baltimore: The John Hopkins University Press, 2004), p. 82.

7   See Robinson, *Promoting Polyarchy*, p. 57.

8   Quoted in Paul Z. Simons, 'A True Account of the New Model Army', *Anarchy: A Journal of Desire, Armed*, #42 Fall (1995) Vol. 14, No. 4. <http://theanarchistlibrary.org/library/paul-z-simons-a-true-account-of-the-new-model-army>

9   Silvia Federici, *Caliban and the Witch* (New York: Autonomedia, 2004), p. 61.

10 Ibid., p. 62.

11   Ibid., p. 75.
12   Ibid., p. 17.
13   Ibid., p. 84.
14   Ibid.
15   See Robinson, *Promoting Polyarchy*, p. 353.
16   Perry Anderson, 'The Antinomies of Antonia Gramsci', p. 42.
17   Therborn, 'The Rule of Capital', p. 3.
18   Ralph Miliband, *The State in Capitalist Society* (Pontypool: Merlin Press, 2009),
     p. 193
19   James Madison, 'Federalist No. 10', 23 November, 1787.
     <http://www.foundingfathers.info/federalistpapers/fed10.htm>
20   Christopher Hobson, 'Beyond the End of History: The Need for a 'Radical
     Historicisation' of Democracy in International Relations', in *Millennium –
     Journal of International Studies*, vol. 37 (2009), pp. 361-657, p. 341.
21   See Therborn, 'The Rule of Capital', pp. 19-23.
22   Ibid., p. 23.
23   Hobson, 'Beyond the End of History', p. 643.
24   Claus Offe, 'Crisis and innovation of liberal democracy: Can deliberation be
     institutionalized?', in *Czech Sociological Review*, vol. 47, no. 3 (2011), pp. 447-
     473, p. 449.
25   Other alternatives were opted for to try and resolve these contradictions,
     including different forms of the state (such as republic, constitutional
     monarchy) or other political forms (such as authoritarianism and
     'Bonapartism'). See Robinson, *Promoting Polyarchy*, p. 361.
26   Ibid, p. 348.
27   For more on neoliberal commodification and enclosure see Larry Lohman,
     'Performative Equations and Neoliberal Commodification: The Case of
     Climate', 15 September, 2012.
     <http://www.thecornerhouse.org.uk/resource/performative-equations-and-
     neoliberal-commodification>
28   In 'Feminism and the Politics of the Commons', Silvia Federici examines
     contemporary struggles against 'new enclosures', and notes how women are,
     and have been, very often the commons' staunchest defenders, since as
     primary subjects of reproductive work they are more dependent upon access
     to communal natural resources. See: Silvia Federici, 'Feminism and the
     Politics of the Commons', in *The Commoner*, 24 January 2011.
     <http://www.commoner.org.uk/?p=113>
29   For more on the development of corporate structures see Corporate Watch,
     'Corporate Law and Structures: Exposing the roots of the problem', 2004.
     <http://www.corporatewatch.org.uk/?lid=2592>
30   Joel Bakan, *The Corporation. The Pathological Pursuit of Profit and Power*,
     (London: Constable, 2004), p. 9-11.
31   Ibid.
32   Quoted in ibid., p. 12.

33 Alex Carey, *Taking the Risk Out of Democracy: Corporate Propaganda versus Freedom and Liberty,* ed. Andrew Lohrey (Urbana and Chicago: University of Illinois Press, 1997), p. 18.

34 See especially Michel Foucault, *Discipline and Punish. The Birth of the Prison,* trans. *Alan Sheridan* and, *Madness and Civilisation. A History of Insanity in the Age of Reason* (New York: Random House, 1998). Also relevant are the writings of R.D. Laing, in particular, *The Politics of Experience* (Harmondsworth: Penguin, 1967).

35 For more information on the PR industry, especially in Britain see Corporate Watch, 'All the Rest is Advertising: the Public Relations Industry and the Decline of Trust', 2010 <http://www.corporatewatch.org.uk/?lid=3685>; David Miller and William Dinan, *A Century of Spin: How Public Relations Became the Cutting Edge of Corporate Power* (London: Pluto Press, 2007); David Miller and William Dinan (eds.), *Thinker, Faker, Spinner, Spy: Corporate PR and the Assault on Democracy* (London: Pluto Press, 2007).

36 Quoted in Corporate Watch, *All the Rest is Advertising,* p. 4.

37 Quoted in Noam Chomsky, *Year 501, The Conquest Continues* (Boston: South End Press, 1993). <http://books.zcommunications.org/chomsky/year/year-c11-s04.html>

38 Quoted in Elizabeth A. Fones-Wolf, *Selling Free Enterprise: The Business Assault on Labor and Liberalism* (Urbana and Chicago: University of Illinois Press, 1994), p. 177.

39 For more on systemic propaganda see the work of Gerald Sussman, including his foreword to this volume as well as: *Branding Democracy,* and Sussman (ed.), *The Propaganda Society. Promotional culture and Politics in Global Context* (New York: Peter Lang Publishers, 2011).

40 Corporate Watch, 'All the Rest is Advertising', p. 4.

41 See Adam Curtis, *The Century of the Self* (BBC Four, 2002). <http://www.youtube.com/watch?v=OmUzwRCyTSo>

42 A prime example was his work for American Tobacco for whom in 1929 he staged publicity events promoting cigarettes as symbols of female liberation, calling them 'Torches of Freedom', having been advised by a Freudian psychiatrist to connect smoking with challenging male power. See ibid.

43 Quoted in Corporate Watch, 'All the Rest is Advertising', p. 4.

44 See Robinson, *Promoting Polyarchy,* p. 378.

45 Kaela Jubas, 'Conceptual Con/fusion in Democratic Societies: Understandings and Limitations of Consumer-Citizenship', *Journal of Consumer Culture,* vol. 7, no. 2 (2007), pp 231-254, p. 251.

46 Robert F. Anove, 'Introduction ' in Arnove ed., *Philanthropy and Cultural Imperialism: The Foundations at Home and Abroad* (Bloomington: Indiana University Press, 1982), p. 4.

47 Ibid. The work of Joan Roelofs exposing the influence of foundations is also vital. See especially her *Foundations and Public Policy: The Mask of Pluralism* (New York: State University of New York Press, 2002).

48 Chomsky and Mermet, 'Democracy's Invisible Line', *Le Monde Diplomatique*, August 2007. <http://mondediplo.com/2007/08/02democracy>

49 E. P. Thompson, "Eighteenth-Century English Society: Class Struggle without Class?", *Social History*, vol. 3 (May 1978), pp. 133-165, p. 164.

50 Ibid., p. 158.

51 Raymond Williams, 'Base and Superstructure in Marxist Cultural Theory' in *New Left Review*, No. 83, Nov-Dec, 1973, p. 9-10.

52 Ibid. p. 9.

53 Chomsky and Mermet, "Democracy's Invisible Line".

54 George F. Kennen, Policy Planning Study (PPS) 23 (PPS23), *Foreign Relations of the United States (FRUS)*, 1948. Quoted in Gilles D'Aymery, 'Context and Accuracy. George F. Kennan's Famous "Quotation"', *Swans Commentary*, 28 March, 2005. <http://www.swans.com/library/art11/ga192.html>

55 *Zbigniew Brzezinski, The Grand Chessboard* (New York: Basic Books, 1998), p. 36. Quoted in Roelofs, *Foundations and Public Policy*, p. 5.

56 See David Harvey, *A Brief History of Neoliberalism* (New York: Oxford University Press, 2005), p. 27.

57 Woodrow Wilson, 'The Ideals of America', *The Atlantic Monthly*, December 1902. <http://www.theatlantic.com/past/docs/issues/02dec/wilson.htm>

58 Quoted in Robinson, *Promoting Polyarchy*, p. 146.

59 See Noam Chomsky, *Deterring Democracy*, (Boston: South End Press 1991, 1992). <http://books.zcommunications.org/chomsky/dd/dd-after-s06.html>

60 See Harvey, *A Brief History of Neoliberalism*, p. 27; Robinson, *Promoting Polyarchy*, p. 208-211.

61 Gerald Sussman, *Branding Democracy*, p. 39; Robinson, *Promoting Polyarchy*, p. 109.

62 Robinson, *Promoting Polyarchy*, p. 86.

63 Ibid.

64 Howard Wiarda, *The Democratic Revolution in Latin America*, (New York: Holmes and Meier, 1990), p. 270. Quoted in Robinson, *Promoting Polyarchy*, p. 73.

65 See Harvey, *A Brief History of Neoliberalism*, esp. pp.19-22.

66 Quoted in Robinson, *Promoting Polyarchy*, p. 68.

67 Quoted in Naomi Klein, *The Shock Doctrine. The Rise of Disaster Capitalism*, (London: Allen Lane, 2007), p. 62.

68 This story is depressingly similar to Indonesia following the 1965 CIA-backed coup which installed General Suharto. Here the CIA provided Indonesian forces with arms, field radios and even "shooting lists" of four to five thousand leftists to assassinate. According to Klein, "the CIA crossed names off their lists until they were satisfied that the Indonesian left had been annihilated". In addition to aiding such brutality, the US also provided economic training at the University of Berkeley to a group of Indonesian economists, known as the Berkeley Mafia, who, while not as faithful to neoliberal economic theory as the Chicago Boys, nonetheless managed to

embed themselves in Suharto's new government and helped to transform Indonesia "into one of the most welcoming environments for foreign multinationals in the world". (Klein, *The Shock Doctrine,* p. 70). The parallels were noted at the time as graffiti in Santiago before the coup which ousted Allende warned: "Jakarta is coming" (Klein, *The Shock Doctrine,* p. 70). For more information, see Klein, *The Shock Doctrine,* pp. 67-70.

69   Quoted in Klein, *The Shock Doctrine,* p. 81.

70   Ibid., p. 87.

71   Quoted in ibid., p. 99.

72   See Harvey, *A Brief History of Neoliberalism,* p. 21.

73   Michael Crozier, Samuel P. Huntington, and Joji Watanuki, The Crisis of *Democracy: Report on the Governability of Democracies to the Trilateral Commission* (New York: New York University Press, 1975), pp. 113, 161, 113, 114.<http://www.trilateral.org/download/doc/crisis_of_democracy.pdf>

74   Ibid., pp. 8, 161, 64.

75   Ibid., p. 55.

76   Michael A. Samuels and William A. Douglas, 'Promoting Democracy', *Washington* Quarterly, Vol. 4, no 3 (1981), pp. 52-66, pp. 52-3. Quoted in Robinson, *Promoting Polyarchy,* p. 83.

77   Robinson, *Promoting Polyarchy,* p. 69.

78   Quoted in ibid., p. 92.

79   Quoted in ibid.

80   Quoted in ibid., p. 88.

81   See Harvey, *A Brief History of Neoliberalism,* pp. 21, 119.

82   Robinson, *Promoting Polyarchy,* p. 355.

83   See for instance the employment by the UK's Department for International Development of consultancy company and private sector devotees Adam Smith International to provide "Economic Support to Coalition Provisional Authority" and "Support to the Centre of Government", see Corporate Watch, 'Corporate Carve-Up: UK Companies in Iraq. Second Edition', (2006) <http://www.corporatewatch.org.uk/?lid=2646>; and the $79.5m USAID contract awarded to BearingPoint, a US consultancy giant, to bypass any 'democratic' processes and draw up what is essentially the blueprint for the new post-invasion Iraqi economy, see <http://www.sourcewatch.org/index.php?title=BearingPoint,_Inc.>; David Whyte, 'Market Patriotism and the War on Terror', in *Social Justice,* vol. 34, issue 3-4 (2007-8), pp. 111-131, p. 123.

84   See Dimitris Papadopoulos, Niamh Stephenson, and Vassilis Tsianos, *Escape Routes: Control and Subversion in the Twenty-first Century* (London: Pluto Press, 2008). <http://www.elimeyerhoff.com/books/Escape_routes.pdf>

3. Market Patriotism:
Liberal Democracy Unmasked

David Whyte

We are living in confusing times. This is an age in which liberal democracy is being extended across the globe by ever more awesome and terrifying forms of policing and military violence. It is an age in which liberal democracy is being imposed without choice upon the most vulnerable economies by faceless and unaccountable financial institutions. And it is an age in which the most extreme forms of violence and economic force are produced by liberal democracies. Yet a close look at world history shows us that there is no contradiction between the model of liberal democracy and the violence that is necessary to ensure its prevalence. The history of both British and American Imperialisms, although their paths of development have been wholly different, show this umbilical connection between extreme violence and the spread of the model of liberal democracy most openly. In the British Empire, the open acknowledgment of this close connection is written into the blueprint for colonisation. Simply read John Locke's theory of property; which is nothing less than a rationale for a very Christian form of pillage and theft (Meiksins Wood, 2003). At the height of the American Empire, in the late 20th century, the doctrine of liberal democracy was rhetorically trawled out in US foreign policy as the same government sponsored and ensured the survival of regimes that routinely practised torture and organised death squads (Herman, 1982).

The starting point for the argument I will develop here is not a particularly new one. Yet it is one that is - perhaps as a result of its obviousness - commonly missed in debates about the nature of power in contemporary capitalist societies. This point is that we need to distinguish between what liberal democracy *does* and what it *says* it does. This may seems obvious, but this basic conflation remains the source of so much obfuscation and mystification that it continues to obscure our view of how the world really works. Most contemporary social theory that has become prominent in academic disciplines and political debates suffers from a basic misunderstanding of liberal democracy: that liberal democracy is democratic. Yet the political and economic systems that we know as 'democracies' are far from what they claim to be. Consider the Chambers dictionary definition of the term:

Democracy (Noun)
1 *A form of government in which the supreme power is vested in the people collectively, and is administered by them or by officers appointed by them*
2 *The common people*
3 *The state of society characterised by the recognition of equality of rights and privileges of all people*
4 *Political social or legal equality*

The argument that will be briefly developed in what follows is that liberal democracy remains the same as it ever was: a set of political principles that claims to guarantee equality of access and collective decision making to all, but delivers the opposite. Further, the argument will be that in current times of 'turbo-capitalism' or 'neo-liberalism', those myths of equality and universal access are quickly evaporating.[1]

The Universalising Myths of Liberal Democracy

In every system of social organisation, those that rule must provide a narrative which on one hand justifies the ruling elite's right to rule and on the other hand justifies the pre-eminence of *systems* of social and political organisation which enable them to rule. (See in the specific context of a university Thorpe, Chapter 15.) The various forms of liberal democracy that have evolved over the past 400 years are no different. They have evolved as the political system that best supports capitalist social orders. And in liberal democratic capitalist states, those that rule have required a legitimate narrative that justifies *capitalist* rule. The ways in which bids for capitalist legitimacy change across history and across different national and local contexts are infinitely complex. Yet, if we look at how the system of liberal democratic rule in capitalist social orders has been historically legitimised, there are some remarkably consistent themes. The argument here is that two of those themes are of particular significance, and, as we shall see, are now becoming more vulnerable to challenge than before.

First, liberal democracy makes claim to a principle of *universal political representation*. From this perspective, parliamentary democracy, although rarely presented to us as a form of 'perfect' representation, is nonetheless depicted in its liberal incarnation as a more or less efficient means of ensuring that governments can faithfully reflect the will of the people. Political apparatuses and public institutions are conceptualised as relatively open systems of power, whereby citizens have equal rights to representation, and the government's right to impose obligations on citizens is in turn limited by ensuring that the democratic rights of citizens are upheld. (See also Fisher, Chapter 2.)

Second, justifications for capitalist social orders have historically been rooted in a rationale of *universal prosperity* which sets out a technical case for capitalism. Central to this rationale is the claim that the general social wealth is improved by encouraging particular forms of economic activity. The benefits from economic growth, measured in terms of gross national product (GNP) will be universally experienced as economic prosperity in absolute terms, no matter how unequal this prosperity is. Claims of universal economic benefit are always posited using the language of economic freedoms, whereby the 'freedom' to act in commoditised systems - to engage in contracts with employers, to buy and sell in markets, to make investments and so on - is guaranteed by liberal democratic rules and institutions. Thus, for example, employment rights and working conditions are guaranteed by labour law, by arbitration systems and by the various tribunal systems and commissions that ensure such freedoms are upheld.

Most forms of liberal democracy also claim to guarantee some form of universal access to social support, to public amenities and services or social welfare. Typically, social supports - just like access to political representation and participation in the economy - are conceptualised in highly individualised terms and are always qualified in relation to political and economic freedoms. Thus, in liberal democracies with high levels of access to social welfare and health care, the 'right' to such provision is always defined as an element of political citizenship. In liberal democracies with relatively low levels of social provision, social provision is always conceptualised as being reducible to economic and political freedoms, and is often posed in opposition to undue government intervention in the lives of citizens.

In liberal democratic thought and practice, political and economic freedoms are generally seen to be complementary; there is always a *positive* mutually re-enforcing relationship between the way that individual freedoms are realised in markets and in the sphere of production, and the way that such freedoms are realised politically, in terms of civil liberties, political rights to representation and so on. The realization of individual freedoms are partly guaranteed by the formal separation of powers within government. This model divides the state into branches with separate and independent powers; divisions are normally drawn across separate branches of legislature, executive, and judiciary. Liberal democracies are also guaranteed by a formal segregation of the public and private spheres. It is assumed that in liberal democratic systems, public policy-making is insulated from the corrupting influence of private interest; the political order is based upon the formal constitutional segregation between public and private spheres. It is this barrier that ostensibly ensures governments protect the public interest. (See also Fisher, Chapter 2.)

Liberal democracy is therefore a system of political organisation that does not recognize any conflict between the realization of political and economic freedoms; or between the realization of public and private interests. Yet it is when those conflicts rise to the surface that liberal democratic narratives of equality and universality, and of formal organization are rendered fragile and vulnerable to exposure for the legitimating *myths* that they are. It is the argument here that those narratives are facing renewed challenges to their credibility. (See also Robinson, Chapter 2.)

The Mask Slips

The process of *neo-liberal* capitalist social ordering, which intensified in the latter part of the 20th and early part of the 21st centuries, has brought with it growing levels of highly visible *inequality* in political representation and material wealth. Increased access to mass media and to the internet has increased our capacity to know about inequality and patterns in relative wealth, just as it has improved access to *some* information about political institutions. This is not to argue, like Bill Gates does, that access to the internet itself is a new form of liberal universalism; merely that internet access has expanded our capacity to see power in different ways. The volume of information and analyses about the post-2008 financial crash means that we can quickly access detailed information about executive wage inflation, and about the devastating impacts of public spending cuts on communities. Our knowledge about power has found a far from perfect, but nonetheless far reaching means of dissemination. Raw data about social inequality has become more accessible and visible. It is no longer possible to hide the fact that whilst Phil Knight in his last year as CEO of Nike earned a total of $3.7 million, many of Nike's workers in Indonesia were kept on the poverty line, earning as little as 50c an hour (Karmini and Wright, 2011). As such evidence becomes more easily disseminated, it becomes much more difficult for anyone to seriously claim that capitalism offers a way to universal prosperity.

In any case, the idea that, as the rich accumulate more wealth, a portion of this wealth will stimulate the economic growth necessary to raise the living standards of even the lowest socio-economic groups (often called 'trickle down' economics), is now doubted even by neo-liberalism's most enthusiastic champions. Indeed, in economic research, there has never existed a body of empirical evidence which supports a 'trickle down' thesis. The idea is sometimes articulated in rhetorical political discourse (and surfaces intermittently in right-wing political arguments for high end tax cuts) but rarely in a carefully supported economic strategy. But increasingly the 'trickle down' perspective is presented in much more naked terms as something that should be defended on its own terms: to increase prosperity for the rich, rather than to spread the benefits of wealth creation. Take this recent statement from the World Bank in answer to the question, why should we care about inequality?

> Some studies show that high inequality [encourages] poor people to choose very high tax rates on the rich, which reduces investments and growth rates. That's one [reason we should care].
>
> (World Bank, 2012).

Thus we are experiencing a period in which when low taxes for the rich can be pursued by international financial institutions (IFIs) as ends in themselves, regardless of their consequences, and combating inequality can only be justified as a safeguard against the poor demanding tax increases for the rich! Evidence produced by both the World Bank and the IMF shows that we have faced unprecedented rises in global inequality in the past 2 decades (Milanovic, 2011; Wade, 2001). This general trend is being experienced across most liberal democracies. In the UK, as the OECD has noted recently, annual average income of the top 10% is about 12 times higher than that of the bottom 10%, a multiplier that has risen from 8:1 in 1985 (OECD, 2011).

The promise of universal prosperity is rarely based upon trickle down theory alone, but is increasingly expressed in conditional terms. Prosperity is thus guaranteed to the poor if they adapt to the demands of the new economy. For individuals in the labour market, this means learning 'flexible' skills and being prepared to follow the demands of the market. For developing countries in the global economy, this means accepting unequal trading relationships in exchange for incorporation into those markets. In contemporary forms of capitalism, the conditions which enable entry into a system of (claimed) universal prosperity are shaped more than ever before by the realities of gross socio-economic inequalities. Relatively weak economies are often forced to accept the neo-liberal restructuring as a condition for membership of the international trade system, or as pre-conditions for IFI loans and debt relief.

Similarly, neo-liberalism implies both material losses and economic insecurity for the most vulnerable sections of domestic populations even in the strongest nation states. Neo-liberalism has deepened economic inequalities in the US and the UK. The coercive and anti-democratic way that those policies are implemented poses a problem for the organisation of the legitimacy of both the ruling elite and the capitalist system in core and periphery countries. The perennial problem of capitalist social orders is that the real experienced conditions of capitalism render its legitimising myths impossible to sustain.

The Public/Private Veil Slips

Rising inequality has a negative impact on the functioning of electoral systems, especially upon the participation of lower socio-economic groups in elections and their inclusion in the democratic processes. As one recent study of the declining participation of the poor in elections in liberal democracies notes:

> Economic inequality shapes the quality of democratic life. Greater inequality concentrates power among a smaller group of people and increases politicians' responsiveness to a smaller group of advantaged citizens.
> (Anderson and Beramendi, 2012: 732)

Growing disparities between rich and poor - the legacy of the neo-liberal period - has undermined the institutional basis of democracy. This has meant, as Rita Abrahamsen has shown in her analysis of the relationship between structural adjustment and democracy in the majority world, that:

> the influence of citizens has been severely curtailed by the power of international financial institutions and Africa's dependence on continued development assistance. In fact it could be asked whether multi-party democracy has any meaning at all.
>
> (Abrahamsen, 2000: 134)

Whilst the declining representativeness of the democratic process and of representation in political institutions undermines the legitimacy of liberal democracy, many of the most far-reaching political decisions are made without reference to those political institutions in the first place.

When the UK Chancellor of the Exchequer Alistair Darling completed his £500 billion bank bail-out deal in October 2008, he did so before it could be debated in Parliament. This decision, perhaps the most high-impact political decision in recent memory, that has ensured that Britain will remain in a fiscal and public sector funding crisis for a long time to come, was thrashed out behind close doors between leading bankers, politicians and senior civil servants.

The bank bailout was one of those moments of exposure that revealed the 'market autonomy' dogma so often relied upon by governments as nonsense. For here was a moment in which national governments intervened to save 'private' banks from the ravage of market forces, something that is so often disavowed as a strategy when jobs are threatened by offshoring production, or when meaningful curbs on executive pay are suggested. In the bank bail-out, the 'invisible' hand of the market began to look like the very clearly visible hand of the state. It was a moment at which the illusion of the formal separation of bureaucratic power between the public and the private sector/civil society was shattered as governments around the globe scrambled to save *their* banks.

Perhaps the formally separate relationship between public and private spheres has never been able to mask entirely the embeddedness of states in markets (Polanyi, 1962). But the interconnectedness of public and private has certainly become more *visible* under contemporary capitalism. This is, of course, partly as a result of the very real transfer of public social and economic functions to private corporations and the rash of privatisations that all liberal democracies have experienced in recent years. It is also a result of the tendency in neo-liberal capitalism to encourage closer collaboration between government and capital at an institutional and individual level. An increasingly visible manifestation of this process is the 'revolving door' that often facilitates the movement of personnel between public and private sectors and provides the social networks that are ultimately used to concentrate power in social elites. In some industrial sectors, revolving door appointments make it difficult to draw a formal distinction between 'public' and 'private' interest. Amy Goodman's book *Exception to the Rulers* (2004) is one example amongst a huge body of literature attesting to this process in the global arms industry. At the time of writing this article, a British newspaper investigation revealed that over the previous 16 years, senior military officers and officials from the Ministry of Defence took up more than 3,500 jobs in arms corporations (*The Guardian*, 15th October, 2012).

A further indicator of the way that the veil between public and private interest is visibly slipping is that even under the most criminal of circumstances, corporations and their senior officers still enjoy relative impunity. This is the issue at stake in the consistent interventions of the British government to prevent the prosecution of BAE Systems for alleged corruption in arms deals with a number of governments.[2] As Charles Ferguson's book and documentary *Inside Job* showed with great skill and clarity, there are a large number of individuals in the US finance industry that could be held accountable and prosecuted for a range of serious frauds that were causal in the 2008 financial crash (Ferguson, 2012). Almost all have been granted immunity from prosecution.

The general acceptance, and in many industries, the normalization of revolving door appointments between government and industry, and generalised immunity granted to the most serious fraudsters suggests that we are witnessing a more open corruption of the political system in the neo-liberal period. This is empirically most obvious in relation to the effects of political strategies that place corporate executives at the heart of political decision-making, and the growing influence of the corporate lobby in most liberal democracies. In other words, the idea that liberal democracies preserve the neutrality of government and 'state' - and ensure their insulation from corporate interests - has become barely credible.

The same crisis in legitimacy that has its roots in the deepening of inequalities and the intensification of economic insecurity for the majority also stems from the visibility of the common interest that corporate officials share with government officials. The legitimacy of liberal democracy is melting before our eyes.

Market Patriotism

Unlikely though it may seem in a world that we are continually being told is a global village, or is more interconnected and unified than ever before, a key response by governments to the melting legitimacy of liberal democracy is a very traditional form of nationalism, or what I describe here as 'market patriotism'. This resort to market patriotism is becoming more prevalent as a replacement form of legitimation for the fading myths of liberal universalism.

In place of those universalising premises of liberal democracy, the rationale for neo-liberalism is very often reduced to the economic 'success' of a given nation state. In some contexts a particular supra-nation state grouping (such as the European Union) or urban area can be promoted as a 'patriotic' territory for the purposes of reshaping economic policy (Coleman, 2009). Ideological supports for capitalist social orders defend 'market' and 'nation' in equal measure. The term 'market patriotism' is used here to describe the hegemonic attempt to crudely couple the public interest to the economic interest of the ruling elite. It is in market patriotism that we find the most open ideological defence of the naked brutality and economic egoism of neo-liberalism.

Elsewhere, I have shown how, under conditions of a 'war on terror' (no matter how contrived this 'war' might be), market patriotism has been mobilised to facilitate the un-interrupted accumulation of profits, to provide a basis for heightened collaboration between corporations and government institutions, and to provide a more general 'common' sense basis for the mobilisation of public and private apparatuses to 'secure the imperium' at home and abroad (Whyte, 2008). Thus, following the September 2001 attacks on the World Trade Centre and the Pentagon, ideologies of market supremacy became prominent in relation to the defence of 'our' markets and 'our' market system against the 'terrorists'. Typically, such national security crises are coupled with appeals to 'consumer patriotism'. Thus former President of the US Bill Clinton took to the streets in a public shopping spree for ties in order to remind citizens of their "patriotic duty to spend money" (Whyte, 2002). When the New York Stock Exchange re-opened on 17th September 2001 it organised a ceremony that included a recital of God Bless America led by a US Marine. The traders themselves were lauded as "heroes" after they managed to buy and sell a record value in shares that day (*The Financial Times*, 22nd/23rd September, 2001).

When Tony Blair recently argued at a conference of the Iraq British Business Council, that British companies are obliged to take advantage of Iraq's economic opportunities because British troops fought there with "heroism and sacrifice", he was merely articulating what many already suspected about the motivations for war (*The Telegraph*, 5th November 2012). It was the unashamed way that he directly described the war as a business opportunity that surprised many. And in this respect it was a moment reminiscent of US Deputy Secretary of State Paul Wolfowicz's admission, 3 months after the invasion, that the motivation for war was that Iraq "swims in a sea of oil" (*The Guardian*, 4th June, 2003). We now know that major figures in the US and UK oil companies had been involved in the planning of the invasion and even in the capture of the oil fields (Whyte, 2008). And we know that UK ministers intervened directly on behalf of the British oil company BP in the negotiations of the carve-up of Iraq's oil fields (Muttitt, 2011). But what is significant about both Wolfowicz and Blair's statements was that they were made in public, not in private, and yet, they were not scandalised in the mass media. Such statements - which link war to national economic, or even business interests - are becoming part and parcel of normal political discourse.

As the preceding section indicates, a key problem for ruling elites seeking to maintain their grip on power at this juncture, is the apparent paradox of how to maintain legitimacy in an economic system that continually undermines the stated basis of this legitimacy; this problem is essentially one of how to maintain enough popular support to guarantee stable hegemonic rule. As the liberal mask begins to slip, glib claims about universal prosperity, representation or 'freedoms' are less likely to have popular appeal. Consent or social incorporation is now less likely to be secured consensually with reference to universality, and is increasingly sought through a more naked brand of economic force. Thus ruling elites must find ways of securing consent for neo-liberal policies and strategies that are increasingly pared down to a purely economic rationale. There is no sophisticated way to do this. Neo-liberalism in the present era is reliant upon ever more vulgar means of seeking consent for ever more vulgar forms of social organisation.

Now, the argument here is not that the universalising claims that underpin capitalist social orders can or will be abandoned in political discourse entirely. Politics, as the Italian Marxist, Antonio Gramsci argued, is always underpinned by hybrid philosophies and ideas (Gramsci, 1996). No government rules with reference to one intellectual tradition and discourse is never formed around a fully coherent conceptual architecture (also, Foucault, 1991). Claims to universal prosperity, representation and freedom have been central ideological supports for the ruling elite in capitalist societies for three centuries and are not likely to be erased overnight. Indeed, conditional versions of those universalising myths remain central to the rhetoric that the G8 and G20 governments use to defend neo-liberalism. Those governments continue to make claims that are located in, for example, the idea that universal prosperity can be achieved *if* poor nations liberalise their economies and 'trade' their way out of poverty; or that excluded groups will be included and prosper *if* they adapt themselves to the flexibility required by the new economy. Rather than obliterating the universalising premises that have been historically important in legitimising capitalist social orders, the preceding argument proposes that the claims on which those premises are based are increasingly conditional. They are also accompanied by a growing small print of exceptions to the rule of universality.

Typically, market patriotism is opportunistic. In times of war or acute economic crisis, nation states have traditionally relied upon some kind of market patriotism as a technique of popular mobilisation. In the Second World War, appeals for people to adapt their patterns of consumption in line with the war effort were commonplace (Calder, 1969). In this respect it is also worth recalling 'Buy British' and 'Buy American' campaigns that surface intermittently during economic crises. In the context of the 'war on terror', market patriotism has been used as a means of abstracting crises in uneven-development or the uneven distribution of profits by conflating a common security threat to the general population (terrorism) with a threat to uninterrupted profit accumulation. The new market patriotism therefore couples the common public interest to the unobstructed accumulation of profits by capital in a way that does not rely on - and explicitly eschews - principles of universal prosperity and representation. Market patriotism ensures that states as well as market actors are brought into line with the exigencies of neo-liberal markets.

Five days after the bank bail-out was announced, British Prime Minister Gordon Brown invoked the "spirit of the blitz" as the way out of the deepening financial crisis and argued that Britain's economy - the government alongside the banks alongside the people - could lead the global recovery (*Sunday Mirror*, 12th October, 2008). No political party challenged this appeal. Indeed, there was a remarkable solidarity amongst political elites that the way out of the crisis was to donate enormous sums to the banks and get everyone else to pay for it. This manufactured national unity - that we are "all in this together" - is a seductive reflex for governments caught in a fiscal crisis.[3] It enables governments to appeal to a unity that is not based upon unsustainable myths of universalism, but merely based upon an appeal for economic success, as measured in neo-liberal terms. A more openly economically egotistic premise is revealed at the core of those appeals, whereby economic success is justified not as a means to achieve socially useful or politically fair ends, but is simply sought as an end in itself (Tombs, 2001). Contemporary capitalism has created the necessity for a more nakedly *economic/egotistic* rationale in its legitimating narratives. It is this gradual rejection of any other reasoning for the spread of neo-liberal capitalism other than for economic growth and the accumulation of profit as ends in themselves that marks out the contemporary brand of liberal democracy as particularly brutal.

Brown's successor, David Cameron has taken the same approach in his appeal for unity. In his 2012 Conservative Party Conference, he argued:

> We are in a global race today. And that means an hour of reckoning for countries like ours. Sink or swim. Do or decline... Today I'm going to set out a serious argument to this country about how... we compete and thrive in this world... how we can make sure in this century, like the ones before, Britain is on the rise. Nothing matters more. Every battle we fight, every plan we make, every decision we take is to achieve that end... Britain on the rise.[4]

It is an approach that sidesteps the political reasons behind the deepening economic inequalities that characterise the governments' response to *crisis*, and at the same time recasts both the cause of the fiscal crisis and the political response as collective responsibilities. There is, in the logic of market patriotism, no alternative to embedding the interests of capital in public mechanisms of political representation:

> To get Britain on the rise we need a whole new economy... more enterprising, more aspirational... Britain leading; Britain on the rise... When I became Prime Minister I said to the Foreign Office: those embassies you've got... turn them into showrooms for our cars, department stores for our fashion, technology hubs for British start-ups. Yes, you're diplomats but you need to be our country's salesforce too. ... And to those who question whether it's

right to load up a plane with businesspeople - whether we're flying to Africa, Indonesia, to the Gulf or China... whether we're taking people from energy, finance, technology or yes - defence... I say - there is a global battle out there to win jobs, orders, contracts... and in that battle I believe in leading from the front.[5]

Market patriotism mobilises general support for a project of 'national unity' in which the interests of state-corporate elites are aligned with the general public interest. At the same time, it seeks to reconcile conflict between different sections of the ruling elite. The key effects of market patriotism are the development of intellectual legitimacy for, and the provision of momentum towards, particular formations of government-capital symbiosis. It is concerned on the one hand with organising the support of subordinate groups for projects of national unity and on the other with organising unity across ruling elites. Market patriotism directs us away from asking about the politics and economics that is taking some of the worlds most developed countries to the brink of collapse.

The post-2008 fiscal crisis and the post-2001 'war on terror' - have both been legitimised by a form of market patriotism which asserts that we are "all in this together" and, therefore, that we share a common interest in refusing to deviate from a broadly neo-liberal social and economic strategy.

Conclusion

The mechanisms that deepen inequalities and intensify insecurity for most of the world's population are precisely the same ones that create a crisis in legitimacy in global capitalism. Neo-liberal governments are set to fall back upon market patriotism more frequently as a means of legitimising a literally bankrupt economic system, as a means of justifying the intensification of state attacks upon individual liberties and as a means of excusing the extreme violence used against subordinate populations to secure the 'national interest' at home and abroad. (See also, Robinson, Chapter 4.) Yet it is not market patriotism that is behind the brutal turn in neo-liberalism; market patriotism is merely a surface reflection of the need for ruling elites to find new ways to justify policies that are increasingly being seen as unjust.

Market patriotism seeks to provide the same universalising function that the myths of classical liberal theory provide. But in so far as it seeks a promotion of purely sectional interests, its potential for *universal* appeal is, by definition, limited. Indeed, it is probably a measure of the brutality of contemporary capitalism that the legitimating narratives which claim to be *inclusive* rather than *exclusive* are in decline. As Christian Parenti (2004) perceptively observed in the wake of the 2003 invasion of Iraq, the bluntness of official arguments justifying American domination of the globe has left little room for critique. In one sense, market patriotism is the last refuge for systems of government caught in a remarkably intricate, and now public, web of personal connections that inter-link senior politicians with monopoly capital. Their personal and class interests are impossible to mask, so the legitimating narrative cannot now seek to hide those interests. It must find a narrative that openly acknowledges the corruption and violence that is part of the not-so-hidden structure of liberal democracy.

Yet, corporate and political elites still cannot risk being too open about their ambitions. State-market symbiosis, the source of the material strength of ruling elites is at the same time a source of its vulnerability. As the real consequences of state-capital symbioses - the corruption of political authority and the untrammelled violence of Imperialist wars - are laid bare, too much is revealed about the capitalist social order. Market patriotism, then, has limits in terms of its ability to forge a consensus across social classes. And it is at the openly violent frontiers of the neo-liberal market that consensus is less likely, and yet all the more necessary for the future of liberal democracy. Market patriotism is therefore unlikely to provide a stable basis for securing the social order.

Our times have been characterised by the routine resort to military invasions and occupations initiated by liberal democratic governments, particularly by the US and its allies. It is in this context that we can see the universalising liberal myths slowly begin to evaporate. Because of the volatility of economic cycles and the embeddedness of structural disadvantage to the poor that neo-liberalism demands the deepening of long term economic exclusion (whether we are talking in terms of individual incorporation into labour markets or in terms of the subordination of national economies within the global system) is a real prospect for a growing proportion of the world's population. It is for this reason that the basis for social incorporation under neo-liberal forms of capitalism is now sought with less reference to universality and consensus, but is sought by force, under conditions whereby refusal to be incorporated by harsh economic regimes has serious consequences.

Crucially, the lack of popular support and the volatility and insecurity that this implies for the lives of the citizens subject to neo-liberal policies means that they are implemented using techniques of economic coercion. The coruscating inequalities created by neo-liberal policies that leave large numbers of people dispossessed and impoverished provides stark evidence for everyone to see that the 'benefits' of neo-liberal economic policy are not universalised.

Alan Badiou has argued: "The only way to make truth out of the world we're living in is to dispel the aura of the word democracy and assume the burden of not being a democrat and so being heartily disapproved of by 'everyone'" (2010: 7). Yet, we should be wary of being forced into a false choice of being either 'with democracy or against democracy'. The fact is that economic force now more easily brushes aside the civil and political protections that come, selectively, with citizenship in more brutal and chaotic ways than we have recently known. We might, under those circumstances, begin to feel quite nostalgic about good old fashioned forms of democratic inequality. Yet what we are experiencing is merely a more open and visible administration of the gross inequalities that have *always* been inscribed into systems of liberal democracy. If the replacement discourse is no less mythical, its consequences are every bit as violent.

To make truth out of the world we are living in requires us to face up to the new barbarism. And one way to do this is to recognise 'democracy' for the mystified structure it is. In the world we find ourselves in, it has at least become easier to distinguish between what liberal democracy says it does and what it actually does.

Notes

1   Neo-liberalism is used here to describe the term that we use for the system of socio-economic organization that emerged to dominate global politics in the late 20th/early 21st century - often referred to as the Washington consensus - in which social relations are increasingly commoditised, and economic relations are structured around the intensification of regimes of capital accumulation.

2   See The Corner House, 'Legal challenge to blanket immunity given to BAE Systems', first published 7 January, 2011.
<http://www.thecornerhouse.org.uk/resource/legal-challenge-blanket-immunity-given-bae-systems>

3 I refer to the current economic crisis here as a fiscal crisis in order to emphasise the point that the current 'crisis' can be understood less as an abstract 'financial' crisis, but as a result of decisions made to change government expenditures and revenues. The burden of the current 'crisis' is being transferred to the majority of taxpayer, ultimately through cuts in public sector jobs and services at the same time as corporate taxation levels are being reduced. In the 2012/2013 tax year, the main rate of corporation tax in the UK will be reduced from 26% to 25%.

4 The full text of this speech is available at: http://www.newstatesman.com/blogs/politics/2012/10/david-camerons-speech-conservative-conference-full-text.

5 See footnote 3 above.

References

Abrahamsen, R (2000) *Disciplining Democracy: development discourse and good governance in Africa*, London: Zed.

Calder, A (1969) *The People's War. Britain, 1939-1945*, London: Pimlico.

Coleman, R (2009) Policing the Working Class in the City of Renewal in Coleman, R, Sim, J, Tombs, S and Whyte, D (eds.) *State, Power, Crime*, London: Sage.

Badiou, A (2010) 'The Democratic Emblem', in Agamben, G, Badiou, A, Bensaid, D, Brown, W, Nancy, J-L and Rancière, J *Democracy in What State*, New York: Colombia University Press.

Ferguson, C (2012), *Inside Job*, Oxford: Oneworld Publications Limited.

Foucault, M (1991) 'Politics and the Sudy of Discourse', in Gordon, Colin (ed) *The Foucault Effect: studies in governmentality*, London: Harvester Wheatsheaf.

Goodman, A (2004) *Exception to the Rulers: exposing oily politicians, war profiteers and the media that love them*, London: Arrow.

Gramsci, A (1996) *Selections from the Prison Notebooks, vol. 1*, London: Lawrence and Wishart.

Herman, E (1982) *The Real Terror Network*, Boston: South End Press.

Karmini, N and Wright, S (2001) Nike faces new worker abuse claims, *Associated Press*, Sukabumi, Indonesia, July 13th.

Klein, N (2001) 'McWorld and Jihad', *The Guardian*, 5th October.

Meiksins Wood, E (2003) *Empire of Capital,* London: Verso.

Milanovic, B (2011) *The Haves and the Have-Nots: A Brief and Idiosyncratic History of Global Inequality*, New York: Basic Books.

Muttitt, G (2011) *Fuel on the Fire: Oil and Politics in Occupied Iraq*, London: The Bodley Head.

OECD (2011) *Divided We Stand*, Paris: OECD.

Parenti, C (2004) *The Freedom: Shadows and Hallucinations in Occupied Iraq*, New York: The New Press.

Polanyi, Karl (1962) *The Great Transformation: the political and economic origins of our time*, Boston: Beacon.

Smith, A (1776) *Inquiry into the Nature and Causes of the Wealth Of Nations, book V, Part III. Of the Expence of Public Works and Public Institutions.*

Tombs, S (2001) 'Thinking About White-Collar Crime', in Lindgren, S., ed. (2001) *White Collar Crime Research. Old Views and Future Potentials, BRA-report*, Stockholm: The National Council for Crime Prevention.

Wade, R (2001) The Rising Inequality of World Income Distribution, *Finance and Development*, vol. 38, no. 4.

World Bank (2012) *Why We Should Care About Inequality*, Washington: World Bank.
<http://web.worldbank.org/WBSITE/EXTERNAL/TOPICS/EXTPOVERTY/0,,cont entMDK:23157030~pagePK:210058~piPK:210062~theSitePK:336992,00.html>

Whyte, D (2008) 'Market Patriotism and the 'War on Terror', *Social Justice*, vol. 35, nos 2-3, pp 111-131.

Whyte, D (2002) 'Business as Usual? Corporate Crime Regulation and the War on Terrorism', in Scraton, P (ed.) *Beyond September 11th*, London: Pluto.

4. Global Rebellion: The Coming Chaos?*

William I. Robinson

As the crisis of global capitalism spirals out of control, the powers that be in the global system appear to be adrift and unable to propose viable solutions. From the slaughter of dozens of young protesters by the army in Egypt to the brutal repression of the Occupy movement in the United States, and the water cannons brandished by the militarised police in Chile against students and workers, states and ruling classes are unable to hold back the tide of worldwide popular rebellion and must resort to ever more generalised repression.

Simply put, the immense structural inequalities of the global political economy can no longer be contained through consensual mechanisms of social control. The ruling classes have lost legitimacy; we are witnessing a breakdown of ruling-class hegemony on a world scale.

To understand what is happening in this second decade of the new century we need to see the big picture in historic and structural context. Global elites had hoped and expected that the 'Great Depression' that began with the mortgage crisis and the collapse of the global financial system in 2008 would be a cyclical downturn that could be resolved through state-sponsored bailouts and stimulus packages. But it has become clear that this is a structural crisis. Cyclical crises are on-going episodes in the capitalist system, occurring and about once a decade and usually last 18 months to two years. There were world recessions in the early 1980s, the early 1990s, and the early 21st century.

Structural crises are deeper; their resolution requires a fundamental

---

* This article was first published in *Al Jazeera*, 4 December 2011. <http://www.aljazeera.com/indepth/opinion/2011/11/20111130121556567265.html>

restructuring of the system. Earlier world structural crises of the 1890s, the 1930s and the 1970s were resolved through a reorganisation of the system that produced new models of capitalism. 'Resolved' does not mean that the problems faced by a majority of humanity under capitalism were resolved but that the reorganisation of the capitalist system in each case overcame the constraints to a resumption of capital accumulation on a world scale. The crisis of the 1890s was resolved in the cores of world capitalism through the export of capital and a new round of imperialist expansion. The Great Depression of the 1930s was resolved through the turn to variants of social democracy in both the North and the South - welfare, populist, or developmentalist capitalism that involved redistribution, the creation of public sectors, and state regulation of the market.

Globalisation and the Current Structural Crisis

To understand the current conjuncture we need to go back to the 1970s. The globalisation stage of world capitalism we are now in itself evolved out the response of distinct agents to these previous episodes of crisis, in particular, to the 1970s crisis of social democracy, or more technically stated, of Fordism-Keynesianism, or of redistributive capitalism. In the wake of that crisis capital went global as a strategy of the emergent Transnational Capitalist Class and its political representatives to reconstitute its class power by breaking free of nation-state constraints to accumulation. These constraints - the so-called 'class compromise' - had been imposed on capital through decades of mass struggles around the world by nationally-contained popular and working classes. During the 1980s and 1990s, however, globally-oriented elites captured state power in most countries around the world and utilised that power to push capitalist globalisation through the neo-liberal model.

Globalisation and neo-liberal policies opened up vast new opportunities for transnational accumulation in the 1980s and 1990s. The revolution in computer and information technology and other technological advances helped emergent transnational capital to achieve major gains in productivity and to restructure, 'flexibilise,' and shed labour worldwide. This, in turn, undercut wages and the social wage and facilitated a transfer of income to capital and to high consumption sectors around the world that provided new market segments fuelling growth. In sum, globalisation made possible a major extensive and intensive expansion of the system and unleashed a frenzied new round of accumulation worldwide that offset the 1970s crisis of declining profits and investment opportunities.

However, the neo-liberal model has also resulted in an unprecedented worldwide social polarisation. Fierce social and class struggles worldwide were able in the 20th century to impose a measure of social control over capital. Popular classes, to varying degrees, were able to force the system to link what we call social reproduction to capital accumulation. What has taken place through globalisation is the severing of the logic of accumulation from that of social reproduction, resulting in an unprecedented growth of social inequality and intensified crises of survival for billions of people around the world.

The pauperising effects unleashed by globalisation have generated social conflicts and political crises that the system is now finding it more and more difficult to contain. The slogan 'we are the 99 per cent' grows out of the reality that global inequalities and pauperisation have intensified enormously since capitalist globalisation took off in the 1980s. Broad swaths of humanity have experienced absolute downward mobility in recent decades. Even the IMF was forced to admit in a 2000 report that "in recent decades, nearly one-fifth of the world's population has regressed. This is arguably one of the greatest economic failures of the 20th century".

Global social polarisation intensifies the chronic problem of over-accumulation. This refers to the concentration of wealth in fewer and fewer hands, so that the global market is unable to absorb world output and the system stagnates. Transnational capitalists find it more and more difficult to unload their bloated and expanding mass of surplus - they can't find outlets to invest their money in order to generate new profits; hence the system enters into recession or worse. In recent years, the Transnational Capitalist Class has turned to militarised accumulation, to wild financial speculation, and to the raiding of sacking of public finance to sustain profit-making in the face of over-accumulation.

While transnational capital's offensive against the global working and popular classes dates back to the crisis of the 1970s and has grown in intensity ever since, the Great Recession of 2008 was in several respects a major turning point. In particular, as the crisis spread it generated the conditions for new rounds of brutal austerity worldwide, greater flexibilisation of labour, steeply rising under and unemployment, and so on. Transnational finance capital and its political agents utilised the global crisis to impose brutal austerity and attempting to dismantle what is left of welfare systems and social states in Europe, North America, and elsewhere, to squeeze more value out of labour, directly through more intensified exploitation and indirectly through state finances. Social and political conflict has escalated around the world in the wake of 2008.

Nonetheless, the system has been unable to recover; it is sinking deeper into chaos. Global elites cannot manage the explosive contradictions. Is the neo-liberal model of capitalism entering a terminal stage? It is crucial to understand that neo-liberalism is but one model of global capitalism; to say that neo-liberalism may be in terminal crisis is not to say that global capitalism is in terminal crisis. Is it possible that the system will respond to crisis and mass rebellion through a new restructuring that leads to some different model of world capitalism - perhaps a global Keynesianism involving transnational redistribution and transnational regulation of finance capital? Will rebellious forces from below be co-opted into some new reformed capitalist order?

Or are we headed towards a *systemic* crisis? A systemic crisis is one in which the solution involves the end of the system itself, either through its supersession and the creation of an entirely new system, or more ominously the collapse of the system. Whether or not a structural crisis becomes systemic depends on how distinct social and class forces respond - to the political projects they put forward and as well as to factors of contingency that cannot be predicted in advance, and to objective conditions. It is impossible at this time to predict the outcome of the crisis. However, a few things are clear in the current world conjuncture.

The Current Moment

First, this crisis shares a number of aspects with earlier structural crises of the 1930s and the 1970s, but there are also several features unique to the present:

▪   The system is fast reaching the ecological limits of its reproduction. We face the real spectre of resource depletion and environmental catastrophes that threaten a system collapse.

▪   The magnitude of the means of violence and social control is unprecedented. Computerised wars, drones, bunker-buster bombs, star wars, and so forth, have changed the face of warfare. Warfare has become normalised and sanitised for those not directly at the receiving end of armed aggression. Also unprecedented is the concentration of control over the mass media, the production of symbols, images and messages in the hands of transnational capital. We have arrived at the society of panoptical surveillance and Orwellian thought control.

▪ We are reaching the limits to the extensive expansion of capitalism, in the sense that there are no longer any new territories of significance that can be integrated into world capitalism. De-ruralisation is now well-advanced, and the commodification of the countryside and of pre- and non-capitalist spaces has intensified, that is, converted in hot-house fashion into spaces of capital, so that intensive expansion is reaching depths never before seen. Like riding a bicycle, the capitalist system needs to continuously expand or else it collapses. Where can the system now expand?

▪ There is the rise of a vast surplus population inhabiting a planet of slums, alienated from the productive economy, thrown into the margins, and subject to sophisticated systems of social control and to crises of survival - to a mortal cycle of dispossession-exploitation-exclusion. This raises in new ways the dangers of a 21st-century fascism and new episodes of genocide to contain the mass of surplus humanity and their real or potential rebellion.

▪ There is a disjuncture between a globalising economy and a nation-state based system of political authority. Transnational state apparatuses are incipient and have not been able to play the role of what social scientists refer to as a 'hegemon', or a leading nation-state that has enough power and authority to organise and stabilise the system. Nation-states cannot control the howling gales of a runaway global economy; states face expanding crises of political legitimacy.

Second, global elites are unable to come up with solutions. They appear to be politically bankrupt and impotent to steer the course of events unfolding before them. They have exhibited bickering and division at the G-8, G-20 and other forums, seemingly paralysed, and certainly unwilling to challenge the power and prerogative of transnational finance capital, the hegemonic fraction of capital on a world scale, and the most rapacious and destabilising fraction. While national and transnational state apparatuses fail to intervene to impose regulations on global finance capital, they *have* intervened to impose the costs of the crisis on labour. The budgetary and fiscal crises that supposedly justify spending cuts and austerity are contrived. They are a consequence of the unwillingness or inability of states to challenge capital and their disposition to transfer the burden of the crisis to working and popular classes.

Third, there will be no quick outcome of the mounting global chaos. We are in for a period of major conflicts and great upheavals. As I mentioned above, one danger is a neo-fascist response to contain the crisis. We are facing a war of capital against all. Three sectors of transnational capital in particular stand out as the most aggressive and prone to seek neo-fascist political arrangements to force forward accumulation as this crisis continues: speculative financial capital, the military-industrial-security complex, and the extractive and energy sector. Capital accumulation in the military-industrial-security complex depends on endless conflicts and war, including the so-called wars on terrorism and on drugs, as well as on the militarisation of social control. Transnational finance capital depends on taking control of state finances and imposing debt and austerity on the masses, which in turn can only be achieved through escalating repression. And extractive industries depend on new rounds of violent dispossession and environmental degradation around the world.

Fourth, popular forces worldwide have moved quicker than anyone could imagine from the defensive to the offensive. The initiative clearly passed this year, 2011, from the transnational elite to popular forces from below. The juggernaut of capitalist globalisation in the 1980s and 1990s had reverted the correlation of social and class forces worldwide in favour of transnational capital. Although resistance continued around the world, popular forces from below found themselves disoriented and fragmented in those decades, pushed on to the defensive in the heyday of neo-liberalism. Then the events of September 11, 2001, allowed the transnational elite, under the leadership of the US state, to sustain its offensive by militarising world politics and extending systems of repressive social control in the name of 'combating terrorism'.

Now all this has changed. The global revolt underway has shifted the whole political landscape and the terms of the discourse. Global elites are confused, reactive, and sinking into the quagmire of their own making. It is noteworthy that those struggling around the world have been shown a strong sense of solidarity and are in communications across whole continents. Just as the Egyptian uprising inspired the US Occupy movement, the latter has been an inspiration for a new round of mass struggle in Egypt. What remains is to extend transnational coordination and move towards transnationally-coordinated programmes. On the other hand, the 'empire of global capital' is definitely *not* a 'paper tiger'. As global elites regroup and assess the new conjuncture and the threat of mass global revolution, they will - and have already begun to - organise coordinated mass repression, new wars and interventions, and mechanisms and projects of co-optation in their efforts to restore hegemony.

In my view, the only viable solution to the crisis of global capitalism is a massive redistribution of wealth and power downward towards the poor majority of humanity along the lines of a 21st-century democratic socialism in which humanity is no longer at war with itself and with nature.

Part 2

Masking the Contradiction

5. The Liberal Gatekeepers:
State-Corporate Power's Little Helpers

David Cromwell and David Edwards, Media Lens

On the BBC Six O'Clock News on March 20, 2006, diplomatic correspondent Bridget Kendall declared solemnly: "There's still bitter disagreement over invading Iraq. Was it justified or a disastrous miscalculation?" It was a wonderful illustration of how the world's most respected broadcaster limits the range of acceptable debate; even thought. Kendall could have asked: "There's still bitter disagreement over invading Iraq. Was it justified or an example of the supreme war crime, the waging of a war of aggression?"

But this is what the media does relentlessly: exclude possible viewpoints - in fact, accurate depictions of events - that would lead the public to fundamentally question the motives and legitimacy of power. Silence is to Western democracy what the iron fist is to Big Brother-style totalitarianism.

But how can silence about Western crimes reign in ostensible democracies? First, consider that most of what the public hears about politics, including foreign policy and environmental issues, comes from the corporate media. The industry is mostly made up of large profit-seeking corporations whose main task is to sell audiences to wealthy advertisers - also corporations, of course - on whom the media depend for a huge slice of their revenues. This advertising revenue is as much as 75% of a newspaper's total income, even for the so-called quality press like the *Guardian* and the *Independent*.

Remember, too, that media corporations are typically owned by wealthy individuals or giant conglomerates, and are answerable to shareholders which means they are legally obliged to subordinate human and environmental health to maximise revenues in minimum time at minimum cost to themselves.[1]

The consequences for democracy of such media ownership are normally brushed aside, but sometimes the truth pops up comically. Thus, after giving evidence to the Leveson inquiry in April 2012, the owner of the *Independent*, Evgeny Lebedev, tweeted:

> Forgot to tell #Leveson that it's unreasonable to expect individuals to spend £millions on newspapers and not have access to politicians.

Even a *Guardian* report had to note:

> It was a funny and refreshingly honest message after all the recent humbug and hypocrisy from media magnates about not wanting to influence the political class.[2]

The Leveson inquiry also delivered a nugget from David Yelland, the former Sun editor, who said that all Rupert Murdoch's editors "go on a journey where they end up agreeing with everything Murdoch says... 'What would Rupert think about this?' is like a mantra inside your head".[3]

But corporate news agendas are not only shaped by the commercial and profit interests of owners and shareholders. The corporate media is heavily dependent on governments, the military and big business sources for an endless supply of cheap news. News media are also subject to intense pressures from big business and establishment interests that control the economy and politics. An oil giant is far more able to intimidate a newspaper than, say, Greenpeace.

What kind of a view of the world would we expect to emerge out of this system? Obviously, it would be one that represents elite interests, the business sector, the government and other institutions and people with power. And, indeed, that's how it turns out.

Let's be clear: the system is not one giant conspiracy. To understand why, imagine making a shallow square wooden frame and pouring a bucket-load of marbles over it. You'll find the marbles arrange themselves into a regular pyramid structure. The marbles aren't conspiring; they're responding to framing conditions that inevitably build a pyramid. A few marbles bounce out because they don't find a place in the structure. And that's basically how the corporate news system works too.

The media's framing conditions were explained by Edward Herman and Noam Chomsky's propaganda model in their landmark book, *Manufacturing Consent*.[4] They began their analysis by pointing to the highly concentrated nature of media ownership in private hands. This acts as an effective 'filter' that helps to shape the news that's 'fit to print', to quote the *New York Times* masthead logo. Then add the other four news filters of the propaganda model: advertising as the primary income source of the mass media; the reliance of the media on information provided by government, business, and 'experts' funded and approved by these primary sources and agents of power; 'flak' as a means of disciplining the media if they deviate too far from state-corporate ideology; and 'anticommunism' - or, more recently, 'anti-terrorism' - as a patriotic pressure and control mechanism; and Beeb's your Big Brother! The model provides a powerful means of understanding how news agendas are routinely shaped in the interests of elite sectors of society. (For its application in relation to the entertainment industry, see Alford and Fisher, Chapter 6.)

This Far and No Further

The most highly respected 'liberal' media in this country - notably the BBC, Channel 4 News, the *Guardian* and the *Independent* - play a special role in this propaganda system. How? By delimiting the 'progressive' end of the acceptable spectrum for 'mainstream' news and debate. In effect: this far, and no further.

Consider first the role of the corporate media as a whole in supporting the aims of power. So, for example, if the US and UK governments decide that Iraq or Libya or Iran should be the focus of attention and concern, then news reports heavily reinforce that focus. In a world full of suffering and violence, the government is able to highlight just *this* suffering or *that* alleged threat by a 'rogue' country, which then becomes 'the story'. Regardless of whether the threat is real - a 'nuclear-armed' Iran? - government and media propaganda have the power to make it seem of overwhelming importance requiring urgent attention; perhaps even 'humanitarian' intervention by Western forces.

Media editors perceive their job as being one of supporting 'democracy' by reporting the opinions of political leaders and government spokespeople at face value. To seriously challenge government claims and motivations, to highlight state hypocrisy and point to past and current crimes, is seen as sabotaging this democracy-supportive role; perhaps even undermining Western democracy itself.

This is denounced as 'biased', 'partial' or 'crusading' journalism.

This does not mean that there is no dissent in the corporate media. On the contrary, the system strongly requires the appearance of openness. In an ostensibly democratic society, a propaganda system must incorporate occasional instances of dissent. Like vaccines, these small doses of truth inoculate the public against awareness of the rigid limits of media freedom. The honest dissident pieces which occasionally surface in the 'mainstream' are almost as important to the successful functioning of the propaganda system as the vast mass of power-friendly journalism. Dissidents - whatever tiny number of them are permitted - also have their place in the pyramid. The end result, however, is an overall performance that tends strongly to mould public opinion to support the goals of state-corporate power.

Is the appearance of honest dissent in the corporate media really so damaging? Why does it matter so much? How can it possibly do any harm? It does when you realise that a crucial limiting feature of liberal dissent is that it takes as a given the key propaganda claim that the state is basically benevolent and well-intentioned. So, as we saw above, the BBC's Bridget Kendall reported that the 2003 invasion of Iraq might be considered 'justified' or a 'mistake', but not what it very obviously was: a major war crime. Reporting the West's war of aggression on Iraq as 'the supreme international crime', the legal term adopted by the post-WW2 Nuremberg judges, would threaten to undermine the legitimacy of the 'democracy' which the BBC is supposed to support.

Why should there be such scepticism about the BBC? It is paid for by the British public and it is obliged to uphold high standards of fair and accurate journalism. So what is our problem with it? Well, just ask yourself: how can the BBC possibly be relied upon for 'balanced' news when its senior managers, invariably high establishment figures, are appointed by the state? When 'impartiality' is upheld by the BBC Trust whose members are Establishment grandees with fingers in numerous state and corporate pies? And when the BBC's 'public service' remit is under the thumb of governments whose policies are distorted by the dictates of power and elite financial-economic interests?

Likewise the *Guardian*, famously owned by the non-profit Scott Trust - as the paper's editors and journalists are fond of reminding their readers - is managed and operated by influential people with extensive ties to the establishment, political parties, banks and big business.[5]

The *Guardian* is just as grubbily commercial as other corporate media organisations. A media insider revealed to us recently that the *Guardian* has a business plan to address its current massive loss-making (a common affliction in today's newspaper industry with the increasing leakage of advertising from papers to the internet). Apparently, when a media website is ranked in the top 10 in the US, the floodgates of online advertising open and its coffers fill up. The online *Guardian* has therefore been marketing itself to US audiences as heavily as it can; its Comment is Free website being one of the key components of that strategy. The *Guardian* is at the threshold of accessing that advertising revenue.

Even debating any of the above issues is forbidden in the corporate media; and the liberal component of the system is no exception. Indeed, as Media Lens has found, to criticise journalists for their silence and hypocrisy is to become an instant hate figure; someone intolerable, and to be ignored.

The Golden Rule of State Violence

One of the cardinal principles of Western elites is that 'we' are, by definition, 'the good guys' and anyone 'we' attack are 'the bad guys'. You could say that the golden rule of Western state violence is: terrorism is what they do; counterterrorism is what we do.

In 2007, we wrote a joint media alert with Nikolai Lanine, a journalist and former Soviet soldier who had taken part in Moscow's occupation of Afghanistan which lasted from 1979-1989. The aim of the alert was to highlight the extraordinary similarities between the Soviet media's earlier coverage of the Soviet occupation, and British media coverage of the current occupation of Afghanistan. The parallels are uncanny. For example, in 1980, the Soviet newspaper *Izvestiya* wrote that the invasion was an act of self-defence to prevent a "neighbouring country with a shared Soviet-Afghan border... [from turning] into a bridgehead for... [Western] aggression against the Soviet state".[6]

The leading Soviet newspaper, *Pravda*, insisted that the Soviet-backed Afghan army had conducted military operations "at the demand of the local population" and because of "the danger to lives and property of citizens" posed by the Afghan resistance. The Soviet government insisted that its aim was "to prevent the establishment of... a terrorist regime and to protect the Afghan people from genocide", and to provide "aid in stabilising the situation and the repulsion of possible external aggression". The rhetoric will be familiar to consumers of Western propaganda about 'our peace mission' and the 'battle for hearts and minds' in Afghanistan today.

Reporters in the West are happy to pour scorn on the obvious rhetoric of enemy states, but have done very little, if anything, to expose the shame of Western propaganda. Not even the *Guardian*'s Seumas Milne or the *Independent*'s Robert Fisk would ever offer an institutional analysis of the corporate media, especially the liberal newspapers that employ them, as a system of propaganda. For example, they could look into the history and theory of elite control of society, as Noam Chomsky often does. The facts are easily accessible to them and not at all too complex to understand and explain. But they never write about them.[7]

It's easy to understand why Milne, Fisk, George Monbiot, Jon Snow and the tiny handful of other 'crusading' journalists don't expose the propaganda system, especially their own employer's role. To do so is to risk alienating influential elements on the paper - the costs of even minor dissent could be high and ultimately career-terminating. Anyone who has worked in a corporation knows that everything revolves around profit-maximisation - woe betide anyone who criticises the senior management, the product, or the advertisers, in front of customers. If that criticism seriously cost the company, it would certainly not be tolerated. And remember - these are some of the most progressive and prominent journalists working in the corporate media. They are about as radical as it is possible to be and still appear regularly in the media. So this is why the *Guardian*, *Independent*, Channel 4 News and the BBC are crucial to upholding the façade of liberal democracy in this country.

Consider the glaring lack of historical context provided by corporate journalism when reporting on issues of UK foreign policy, even in the best liberal media. Often journalists simply don't know much of it. We have found in over 11 years of running Media Lens that journalists are surprisingly ignorant about the history and wider political context of what they're reporting. The real problem is that explaining the historical context tends to complicate the media's Manichean - 'us' good, 'them' bad - view of the world.

If you accept the evidence that the corporate media is a system designed to serve corporate profits and the state power that supports business, then it's clear that the media is not in the business of making sense of the world. Quite the reverse: 'Ignorance is Strength.'

Game Over for the Climate

It's not just foreign policy. Take the very real risk of climate catastrophe. Leading climate scientist James Hansen, who was the first to alert the US Congress of the dangers of global warming in 1988, warns that:

Presdident Obama speaks of a "planet in peril," but he does not provide the leadership needed to change the world's course.

He adds:

> The science of the situation is clear - it's time for the politics to follow. ... Every major national science academy in the world has reported that global warming is real, caused mostly by humans, and requires urgent action. The cost of acting goes far higher the longer we wait - we can't wait any longer to avoid the worst and be judged immoral by coming generations.[8]

If proper action doesn't happen soon, Hansen says it's "game over for the climate".

And yet even liberal media outlets repeatedly present as fact that there has been government 'failure' to respond to climate change. They do very little to report that big business, acting through and outside government, and the media itself, have been fighting tooth and nail to prevent the required action.

We have seen for ourselves that media debate on how best to respond to environmental crisis has barely moved in a generation. For years, the public has been assailed by the same anodyne editorials urging 'the need for all of us to act now'. But how serious can the corporate media be about challenging the lethal activities of their big business allies when, for example, the *Guardian* and the *Independent* rely so heavily on advertising revenue?

The media are silent about the inherently biocidal logic of corporate capitalism. They are silent about the reality that politics in the US and UK is "a two-party dictatorship in thraldom to giant corporations," as Ralph Nader has observed.[9] They are silent about the role of the media, and media advertising, in normalising what should be an obviously untenable notion, given the planetary limits, of unrestrained consumption. The corporate media are key elements of a system that, as mentioned above, puts profits above all other concerns.

As for media employees themselves - especially those well-rewarded as editors, senior journalists and influential columnists - they are an integral part of a corporate system that, unsurprisingly, selects for servility to the needs and goals of corporate power. Just like senior officials in any corporation, they are expected to toe the company line. And all the more effective if they are untroubled by doing so, or even blind to the limits of permissible reporting and commentary. 'Nobody ever told me what I can or can't say' is the familiar refrain from corporate journalists. It's not a sensible argument. Typically, media professionals are recruited precisely because they believe the right things and hold the right values.

Of course there are exceptions, but these individuals soon learn to compromise or they end up being filtered out of the system. This isn't merely our view; it's the view of honest voices from within the system. So, for example, the former *Guardian* journalist Jonathan Cook once told us:

> Every time we *Guardian* journalists walked into the office, we subtly realigned our personal views to accord with those of our employer. For most *Guardian* journalists, this was rarely a dramatic realignment. The paper seems leftish to most; the few there who struggled ideologically, eventually myself included, drifted away or were forced out.[10]

A Sustained Act of Mass Deception

Corporate media reporting of the global financial and economic crisis of recent years fits the pattern we've presented so far. From the perspective of power, it is important that a steadying hand is applied to the tiller of news and commentary on the crisis, as well as the global economy itself. The liberal media has its role to play in shoring up public confidence in a discredited, unjust system.

In the *Guardian*'s comment pages, star columnist Jonathan Freedland was permitted to express a glimmer of dissent in 2008, near the start of the current crisis. "Turbo-capitalism is not just unfair," he wrote, "it is dishonest and dangerous." He pleaded: "surely this is the moment when Labour and the centre-left can dare to question the neoliberal dogma that has prevailed since the days of Thatcher." Any hope that the then Labour government would step in to challenge neoliberalism was seriously misguided, given its egregious record in expanding Thatcherism after the party came to power in 1997. But since this timid expression of dissent, somehow Freedland's blind faith in Labour had been restored.[11]

And so his dissection of the crisis was limited at best, timidly suggesting that "you could argue" that "capitalism is always... parasitical on the state." What Freedland called for was a kinder, gentler form of capitalism instead of the "turbo-capitalism" which is happy to rely "on

us, the public, and our instrument, the state, when it gets in trouble."
Thin on details, he concluded weakly: "Now we should demand a say the
rest of the time, too." It was grim fare indeed.

Economist Harry Shutt, author of several books including *The
Trouble with Capitalism,* notes astutely that one of the most striking
features of the ongoing crisis is:

> the uniformly superficial nature of the analysis of its causes
> presented by mainstream observers, whether government
> officials, academics or business representatives.' This
> applies very much to journalists too, not least in the liberal
> media.

Shutt continues:

> Thus it is commonly stated that the crisis was caused by a
> combination of imprudent investment by bankers and
> others... and unduly lax official regulation and supervision
> of markets. Yet the obvious question begged by such
> explanations - of how or why such a dysfunctional climate
> came to be created - is never addressed in any serious
> fashion.

He sums up:

> The inescapable conclusion... is that the crisis was the
> product of a conscious process of facilitating ever greater
> risk of massive systemic failure.[12]

Shutt observes that an alarming symptom of what is wrong with
current economics is the increasingly desperate and cynical measures
taken by powerful states, corporations and investors to maintain
faltering public confidence in global capitalism. Just as Enron,
WorldCom and a host of other large corporations committed accounting
fraud, so governments have falsified figures on inflation, output and
unemployment to present a false picture of a healthy economy up to,
and even including, the current global recession.

For example, the US government deliberately exaggerated GDP
growth rates in order to disguise the economy's poor performance since
the mid-1970s; in the developed world, growth rates actually declined
over succeeding decades. As David Harvey notes in *A Brief History of
Neoliberalism,*[13] aggregate global growth rates stood at around 3.5 per cent

in the 1960s. Even during the difficult 1970s, marked by energy shortages and industrial 'unrest', it only fell to 2.4 per cent. But later growth rates languished at 1.4 per cent and 1.1 per cent in the 1980s and 1990s, respectively, and struggled to reach even 1 per cent after 2000.

In terms of managing public perception, however, Western governments and financial institutions have largely succeeded. They have maintained the fiction that they can manage the economy effectively and that global capitalism is the only game in town. How has this been possible? Shutt points to a "media campaign of uncritical propaganda and pro-market hype". This "sustained act of mass deception (in which the establishment has seemingly come to believe in its own propaganda) has had disastrous consequences."[14]

Those consequences encompass wars motivated by the desire for geostrategic power, including access to, and control of, hydrocarbon resources and economic markets; crushing levels of poverty and inequality; global climate instability; and the most rapid loss of species in the planet's history.

Beyond the Propaganda Wall

The best way to break down the wall of silence surrounding the corporate media's role in global crimes and abuses - with the liberal media a vital accessory - is to work hard collectively to expose and challenge it. First, one has to show that the corporate media is less a window on the world than a barrier to understanding. Then one has to highlight the hidden assumptions and expose them with rational arguments and credible facts and sources.

At a larger scale throughout society, what needs to be done is the same as it's always been: to build and strengthen grassroots efforts to raise public awareness of the issues confronting humanity, and to challenge the powerful elite interests that are crushing so much of the planet's people and ecosystems. Tackling the serious risk of climate instability with the required radical action represents a very real threat to elite interests in the corporate, financial, media, government and military sectors. We could begin by challenging corporate media to reject advertising for climate-wrecking products and services; just as tobacco advertising is now regarded as unacceptable.

We need to challenge the mantra of endless economic growth and rampant mass consumption. We need to expose the myth that 'our' leaders have essentially benevolent aims and humane priorities; as opposed to so-called 'national interests', a phrase which is all too often newspeak for corporate greed, imperialism and military violence. We need to confront political and media elites, and show that what passes for 'democracy' is largely a sham so long as people are immersed in a propaganda system of relentless brainwashing to promote state-corporate goals.

But people can and do resist this brainwashing. The power of propaganda is only as effective as we allow it to be.

Notes

1   See Joel Bakan, *The Corporation: The Pathological Pursuit of Profit and Power* (London: Constable, 2004).

2   Simon Hatterstone, 'Evgeny Lebedev: Don't call me an oligarch', *guardian.co.uk*, 5 May, 2012.
    <http://www.guardian.co.uk/media/2012/may/05/evgeny-lebedev-evening-standard-oligarch>

3   Michael White, 'Rupert Murdoch killed softly with Leveson lawyer's words', *guardian.co.uk*, 26 April, 2012.
    <http://www.guardian.co.uk/media/2012/apr/26/rupert-murdoch-leveson-lawyers-words>

4   Edward S. Herman and Noam Chomsky, *Manufacturing Consent: The Political Economy of the Mass Media* (New York: Pantheon, 1988).

5   As we discussed at greater length in our book, *Newspeak in the 21st Century* (London: Pluto Press, 2009).

6   Media Lens media alert, 'Invasion – A Comparison Of Soviet And Western Media Performance', 20 November, 2007.
    <http://www.medialens.org/index.php?option=com_content&view=article&id=526:invasion-a-comparison-of-soviet-and-western-media-performance&catid=21:alerts-2007&Itemid=38>

7   See Media Lens media alert, 'Silence of the Lambs: Seumas Milne, George Monbiot & "Media Analysis" In The Guardian Wonderland', 25 January, 2012.
    <http://www.medialens.org/index.php?option=com_content&view=article&id=662:silence-of-the-lambs-&catid=25:alerts-2012&Itemid=9>

8   James Hansen, 'Game over for the climate', *New York Times*, 9 May, 2012.
    <http://www.nytimes.com/2012/05/10/opinion/game-over-for-the-climate.html>

9   Interview with Paul Jay, The Real News Network, 4 November, 2008.

10 Jonathan Cook, email to editor@medialens.org, 4 March, 2011.
    <http://www.medialens.org/forum/viewtopic.php?t=3173>

11 Jonathan Freedland, 'The free-marketeers abhor the crutch of the state - until they start limping', *The Guardian*, 23 January, 2008. <http://www.guardian.co.uk/commentisfree/story/0,,2245256,00.html>

12 Harry Shutt, *Beyond the Profits System* (London: Zed Books, 2010), p. 6.

13 David Harvey, *A Brief History of Neoliberalism* (New York: Oxford University Press, 2005).

14 Harry Shutt, *The Decline of Capitalism* (London: Zed Books, 2005), pp. 36-7.

6. Screening Our Screens:
Propaganda and the Entertainment Industry

An Interview with Matthew Alford.
By Rebecca Fisher

Rebecca Fisher: You wrote your first book, Reel Power: Hollywood Cinema and American Supremacy, *in 2010. What have you been working on lately?*

Matthew Alford: I have been watching recent movies that received on-set production support from the US Defense Department, such as *Battleship, Act of Valor,* and *Battle: Los Angeles.* They're terrific recruitment tools - even I now want to join the Army in Afghanistan, though only so I never have to go to the cinema again.

RF: Could you discuss the rules which ensure that the content of Hollywood films fall largely within state-friendly ideological parameters?

MA: Jack Valenti, the Motion Picture Association of America President used to explain it most succinctly: Washington and Hollywood are "sprung from the same DNA". Accordingly, Hollywood follows the script, especially on foreign policy issues.

More specifically, there are four factors that determine and degrade the politics of Hollywood: only half a dozen huge companies own all the movies; advertisers play a central part in most films; the CIA and Pentagon have major roles in affecting the politics of scripts (they work on at least a third of modern films depicting US foreign policy); and powerful organisations will punish professionals who challenge the system.

The resultant underlying rules for movie content have remained consistent, implicit, and well-observed: do not question the benevolence of the US system (extra marks for gormless nationalism), do not question or call attention to the egregious power wielded by private interests (such as the oil and arms industries, the Israeli lobby), and feel free to vilify and patronise people that don't come from countries allied to the US - especially Middle Eastern Muslims.

RF: Are these ideas formalised within the industry or are they just accepted implicitly?

MA: Both. From 1934 to 1968, there was an explicit document - the Production Code - that formalised many important elements of conformist cinema, notably 'Section X', which dealt specifically with the protection of 'National Feeling'. The Code was used by its anti-Semitic head, Joseph Breen (dubbed 'The Hitler of Hollywood'), to justify blocking scripts that opposed Nazi Germany right up to January 1940. Gotta love that National Feeling.

RF: Did the demise of the Production Code signal the end for formal controls over the industry?

MA: Far from it. Nowadays, the potential political messages emanating from the mainstream media and entertainment industry are constrained by effective informal controls, including concentrated corporate ownership; the centrality of advertising; the pervasiveness of the government as a source of information; the ability of the powerful to issue flak, and the self-serving notion that we in the West are superior and benevolent and that those who do not accept our economic and political models are backward or even hostile.

Not to mention direct interference in production. When 'advising' on-set, for example, the Pentagon ties the producers into a contract and ensures script alterations in exchange for providing air craft carriers, tanks, etc. If anything, this practice has escalated in recent years, and has been applied to higher budget productions than ever before, such as the *Transformers* series.

The role of the White House itself is often overlooked too. In the 1990s, the Clinton administration was secretly spending tens of millions of dollars paying the major networks to inject War on Drugs plots into the scripts of prime-time series such as *ER, The Practice, Sabrina the Teenage Witch, Smart Guy,* and *Beverley Hills 90210.* To cite just one example, an inferior script for *Chicago Hope* was produced solely because it had anti-drug theme. In the episode, ravers endured drug-induced death, rape, psychosis, a nasty two-car wreck, a broken nose and a doctor's threat to skip life-saving surgery unless the patient agreed to an incriminating urine test. You know what, kids - 'Just say no... to government propaganda'.

RF: Do the rules include 'do not question the basic free market system' or 'do not provide positive examples of any alternatives to capitalism' in addition to 'do not question American imperial power'?

MA: The Pentagon, CIA, and White House almost never worry about the portrayal of capitalism in entertainment products. The advertisers and corporate owners do that for them, largely because if you leave the cinema thinking 'That film really made me question the profit motive', you're not likely to buy into the franchise. There's a reason Ken Loach doesn't sell many lunchboxes.

It's also important that the major studios are almost all based in New York and LA, dominated by lawyers and bankers, with a few outspoken 'free market' ideologues from General Electric CEO, Jack Welch to Arnold Schwarzenegger thrown in for good measure. So of course the idea of questioning the American-led economic system is just inconceivable.

Ed Herman and Noam Chomsky emphasise that the real product is not the news programme, or film, or whatever, but rather us, the audience. It all sounds a bit *Matrix*-y but of course it stands to reason that we are being sold to advertisers by media producers. The result is that they can charge advertisers more money if they guarantee that the film will reach a sufficiently large, affluent audience, and that it will strive to ensure that this audience is receptive to that advertising. This explains that feeling maybe you have when you watch a Bond film - it's quite enjoyable but also feels a bit like a cheesy commercial for razors. *Die Another Day* had twenty companies place products on set, for which the producers received $120m.

RF: But not all Hollywood films that depict foreign policy themes are blatant paeans to American power, are they? Does the fact that some films flirt with more radical ideas indicate that Hollywood is not always so controlled?

MA: Yes, although many productions give the impression of being radical but on closer inspection are timid, misleading, or even deceptively pro-establishment narratives.

In *Munich*, Spielberg's "evenhanded cry for peace", for example, the most celebrated "anti-war" scene in the film is a two-and-a-half minute exchange between an Arab and an Israeli, which at best points out that Palestinians are motivated by a desire for 'home' but, more saliently, suggests that their struggle is both futile and immoral. *Hotel Rwanda* (2004) condemns America's unwillingness to stop the 1994 Rwandan genocide. In fact, the film whitewashes the Rwandan Patriotic Front's invasion of Rwanda and apparent Presidential assassinations that triggered the crisis, its facilitation of the Tutsi and Hutu genocides, its support from the US, and its current activities in the Congo that the UN calls 'near genocidal', all of which have been explained by diligent on-the-ground reporters like Keith Harmon Snow.

TV series such as *24* and *Alias* received government cooperation but also raise the spectre of nefarious strains within government. Nevertheless, these products still fit comfortably into the myth of American Exceptionalism and promote the virtues of a national security state. *24* was created by Joel Surnow - buddy to Rush Limbaugh and open advocate of Dick Cheney's political perspective - and promoted the use of torture and hyperbole on terrorism and official state enemies (a thinly veiled portrayal of an aggressive, nuclear Iran, for instance, throughout series eight). In other words, even conspiracy plotlines are often utilised to show the essential righteousness of the American system and its ability to weed out its own 'bad apples'.

The same principle is advanced in some of the most celebrated 'critical' programmes. So Aaron Sorkin's *The West Wing* (1999-2006) was indeed liberal but the White House team itself is well-meaning, competent, and idealistic, thereby preserving the idea of America as the 'exceptional nation'. According to actor Rob Lowe, who spoke to Bill Clinton in 2000, the White House staff was "obsessed with the show" and the President himself thought it was "renewing people's faith in public service". *The West Wing* bromide worked for the Bush administration too - just after 9/11 Sorkin rushed through production a special episode about a massive terrorist threat to America entitled 'Isaac and Ishmael'. "I'm going to blow them [the Jihadists] off the face of the earth with the fury of God's thunder," says Martin Sheen's President Bartlet, in rhetoric even more Biblical than that of the real-world incumbent. In series two, the anti-globalisation movement is cut down in a stylish and impassioned speech by a White House official that concludes: "... Free trade stops wars! And we figure out a way to fix the rest. One world, one peace."

Sorkin has a new series now, *The Newsroom*, which he calls "a love letter to journalism". He says, "I love the idea that there is this small group of people, way up high in a skyscraper, in the middle of Manhattan, beaming this signal out into the night." Really? I don't.

Sounds like Sorkin enjoys celebrating fantasy-world groups of wealthy professionals who are insulated from the lives of ordinary people and have an unhealthy amount of power. Bit weird.

So there is some political variety if you look around. It's just that you're very unlikely to find a mainstream film, video game, or TV show that challenges the righteousness of the American system, and plenty that laud it to the Heavens.

RF: What are the similarities and/or differences between how this works within different entertainment industries?

MA: Let's first be clear first that all these commercial and political pressures, or "filters" as Herman and Chomsky call them, do come into play in more populist media. This is not usually acknowledged, but at the Leveson enquiry News Corp's CEO Rupert Murdoch kindly made the point for me when he rebutted suggestions that he unduly influenced *The Times* [a respectable broadsheet newspaper] by saying "*The Times*? No. ... If you want to judge my thinking, look at *The Sun* [his downmarket tabloid]."

Certainly, the TV industry is subject to the same pressures. Quite apart from the apolitical (*Big Brother*) and some real throwback products (ever see *Flavor of Love*?) that characterise American network television, even many of the most political, intelligent TV series are paeans to the national security state, such as *E-Ring, Profiles From the Front Line, NCIS, JAG* (all of which had DOD cooperation)*, and The Agency, The Company, Covert Affairs* (all made with CIA cooperation), as well as other sympathetic products that didn't receive the government's stamp of approval, such as *Last Resort, Tour of Duty* and *Homeland*.

Political interference can actually go right down to seemingly apolitical cultural industries such as sporting events. The military schedules aircraft flyovers or the unfurling of giant stars and stripes to coincide with the precise moment that fans cheer to mark the start of the game, meaning that the audience suddenly find themselves supporting an overt display of American military prowess.

When athletes decide for religious or pacifist reasons not to salute the flag or sing the national anthem they quickly become the subject of audience vitriol, abandoned or punished by the authorities, and their right to express their viewpoint stymied.

The Pentagon will also spin sports stories. Pat Tillman played football for the Arizona Cardinals before giving up a three-year $3.6m contract to join the U.S. Army in 2002. Sadly, Tillman died in Afghanistan in 2004. The military granted him a posthumous Silver Star and publicly grieved that hostile forces had ended his life, all the while knowing that Tillman had been killed by friendly fire. They lied to Tillman's family and the American public.

Of course, there are inconsistencies in the way each cultural industry is constrained ideologically. So, when you pick up a copy of *Hello!* magazine or read your horoscopes, though these won't be politically enriching experiences and may even play into something worse (irrationality, celebrity worship, materialism), there is rarely a calculated, nefarious political agenda behind the product. Don't rule it out though - even poor Spiderman and his buddies in kids' comic strips have been paid off by the government at various times - especially to push the clunky old 'drugs are bad' message.

RF: What about series like The Wire, which present a more sophisticated view of drugs?

MA: Yes, *The Wire* provides an unsentimental view of law-enforcement self-interest, which acts as a metaphor for the War on Terror. This series would surely not have emerged on any channel except HBO.

RF: How is it that more critical outputs are able to emerge from HBO?

MA: Firstly, because it is funded by subscription rather than by adverts, so it can afford to appeal directly to viewers rather than its corporate sponsors. Secondly, the board of directors at its parent company, Time Warner, has close ties to the powerful liberal organization, the Council on Foreign Relations (President Jeffrey L. Bewkes is a directors-board member of the Council on Foreign Relations, for example), so the studio itself is much less likely to receive flak internally if it pursues a liberal agenda.

This doesn't mean that HBO is completely free, though. Exeter University researcher Matt Barber looked into a major TV movie starring Glenn Close, *Strip Search*, which juxtaposed China's treatment of a detained American with the FBI's detention of a Muslim - where both are terrorist suspects who are forcibly strip searched. In other words, the film directly criticised Bush's Patriot Act by comparing it to a dictatorship's legal system. Barber found that: the film was aired on a Tuesday rather than the usual Saturday or Sunday night; screener tapes were not sent out to television critics; there was minimal marketing, and the original 88 minute running length was trimmed to 55 minutes. Furthermore, HBO airbrushed *Strip Search* from its back catalogue and have not released it on DVD, though a version is available from Amazon if you have a spare $99.

RF: How well are the parameters enforced - what, if anything, slips through the net, and how?

MA: A handful of genuinely dissenting films are made that break down these barriers but they usually emerge in unusual circumstances and are poorly distributed. I was amazed when I saw that Warren Beatty's explicitly pro-Socialist *Bulworth* had been distributed by Rupert Murdoch's Fox. I soon discovered, though, that Beatty made the 1998 film "in complete stealth", without revealing any political content to the studio, and skilfully negotiated complete creative control owing to Fox having backed out of making *Dick Tracy*. In response, Fox released *Bulworth* to compete with the blockbusting *Godzilla*.

The rules can be bent, of course, if the film maker is extraordinarily rich and powerful - hence James Cameron's *Avatar*, which presented Americans invading a peaceful planet to plunder resources. Some of my colleagues feel differently but the film left me rather underwhelmed, though, since the lead hero was a Marine, Cameron sold it in pro-military language, and the Pandoran people were dull. Undeniably, though, *Avatar* was a mile away from Pentagon-supported tripe like *Stargate*, which had a similar political narrative but with utterly moronic indigenous people who learn that they must rise up against their ~~Muslim~~ Alien masters after the Americans introduce them to guns, cigarettes, and democracy. So it's a case of 'small mercies', Becca.

RF: And why do you think that Cameron fell short of making the film more radical?

MA: Because it was sponsored by MacDonalds ("The Big Mac is all about the thrill of your senses" so it's a "perfect match" for the movie, apparently). And because Cameron sees himself as an entertainer, not a political activist. In fact, back on planet Earth, one charity, Survival International appealed directly to Cameron through a full page advert in Variety magazine, asking him to help the "real-life Na'vi" Dongria Khond tribe in India, whose people and environment are being ruthlessly uprooted by British mining corporation Vedanta. I don't think anyone is obliged to support a charity just because they're asked, but if one stumped up a few grand just to nudge me into making a single public utterance about an issue I'd just made a movie about, I think I'd probably accommodate them. Survival International told me that Cameron's disinterest was "unfortunate" and added that "It is a classic example of where a simple quote could have had a massive impact on a campaign."

RF: What happens if industry professionals break the rules?

MA: On the rare occasions that entertainment figures become politically active, then they can get burnt quite badly. Historically, the FBI mounted vicious campaigns against people like Charlie Chaplin, Orson Welles, Jean Seberg, and Jane Fonda - in Seberg's case, J. Edgar Hoover leaked the lie that she was carrying another man's baby, which triggered her miscarriage and suicide. Maybe Cameron is right to keep his head down.

Others just lose their jobs. One of the most radical contemporary political films to emerge from a major studio is *Fight Club* (1999), the explosive Brad Pitt/ Ed Norton feature which attacked ideas like consumerism and credit-culture. In this case, Rupert Murdoch, rather than the politicos at the Pentagon or Langley, declared "You have to be sick to make a movie like that". Murdoch's personal dislike of the "dark tone" of films like *Fight Club* and *The Beach* led to the unexpected resignation of 20th Century Fox's head, Bill Mechanic, and a renewed trend towards conservative pictures coming from the studio.

RF: To what extent do film-makers consciously censor themselves in order to secure their film's funding or distribution, or to what extent is it so internalised that these issues aren't even raised or questioned?

MA: I haven't come across much evidence of film-makers saying, 'We really didn't want to make an imperialist piece of junk but the studio made us'. I'd guess that few film-makers in the Hollywood system have any interest in pushing political boundaries because they are almost all political conformists - and more worryingly, several of them are real advocates of the American empire. For instance, Peter Berg, director of *Battleship*, recently went on Israeli TV making the case for Israel bombing Iran - this from the man who created *The Kingdom*, a supposedly 'balanced' film set against the background of the US-Saudi relationship.

But the main issue is that political responsibility just isn't on the agenda. To illustrate, in response to the allegation that Americans are "widely perceived to be selfish and self-indulgent", Geoff Zucker, director of NBC Entertainment said "Listen, we are not culpable for the images we portray on television". That's right, they have no responsibility. He actually goes on to say that "News informs the American public and keeps our politicians honest" - well, maybe, if you take your view of the news from Aaron Sorkin.

RF: The counter argument of course is that that customers vote with their wallets, and so get what they ask for. Is this fair?

MA: Partly, but government and commercial organisations routinely make changes to scripts that have nothing to do with public demand and everything to do with their desire to spin a story for PR ends. Would audiences have baulked at *Counter Measures*, a film starring Geena Davis about government corruption? We will never know, since the Pentagon refused the necessary cooperation to get the film into production on the grounds that they have "no reason to denigrate the White House" or to "remind the public of the Iran-Contra scandal". Was that what audiences wanted?

Sometimes studios assume that audiences want reactionary drivel. In 1981, MGM released *Inchon*, a $46m nationalist movie about the Korean War that starred Laurence Olivier and was endorsed by Ronald Reagan. *Inchon* took just five million dollars, was never released on video or DVD, and is widely cited as being the worst film of all time. Sometimes studios just assume wrong.

Actually, some of the mythologizing movies are 'successful' largely because they are pushed so hard by the studios. For example, Disney doubled the usual release dates for *Pearl Harbor*, which meant it just about turned a profit. On the flip side, it is true that the *Transformers* films, which were also designed extensively for Pentagon recruitment, were highly successful, but here profits were almost guaranteed since they were a mega-budget extension of the long-standing Hasboro franchise.

RF: What are the impacts in terms of capitalism, consent and dissent of these rigid controls over our culture and entertainment?

MA: Hollywood studios are uniquely important in selling political messages, according to a very wide range of sources, including the FBI, CIA, Pentagon, and a war-time Senate Investigation that called them "gigantic engines of propaganda".

It's hard to measure effects, but obviously if entertainment systems work hard to promote consent, then they're going to have a significant degree of success. I'd say that Hollywood provides very infrequent inspiration for dissent, with occasional exceptions, such as the V masks from the excellent *V for Vendetta* that have been increasingly popular with Anonymous and Occupy protesters.

I don't actually think that Hollywood does endorse capitalism in clear terms, certainly not as vociferously as it endorses the national security perspective on foreign policy. Many films make villains of corporate leaders.

RF: But wouldn't you say that even if not able to glorify corporate values of greed and corruption - something which surely wouldn't chime with the general mood today - doesn't Hollywood nonetheless consistently endorse state-capitalism?

MA: Some films do indeed take active steps towards endorsing the miracle of the American market system (even *Ghostbusters*, to some degree, if you watch it as an adult). It's just not an over-riding trend.

I think a recent study for the journal Managerial and Decision Economics gets it about right when is says "it is not business that film-makers dislike but rather the control of firms by profit-maximizing capitalists" and that "film-makers display little concern with workers' problems and only rarely blame firms' social irresponsibility on the fact that capital rather than labour is in control."

Certainly there is almost no sense of worker solidarity on screen, which I think is a vital omission for the sake of America's rulers. It calls to mind an episode of the [British comedy series] *Comic Strip Presents...* in which Hollywood money men turn a gritty script about the British miner's strike into a schlock action piece with the ball-busting hero [union leader] Arthur Scargill, renamed "Scarface". Hollywood loves a lone hero and displays of solidarity as in *V For Vendetta*, *Salt of the Earth*, and *Spartacus*, are as rare as they are inspirational.

RF: What, if anything, exists to challenge this status quo? What useful things could be done to move things forward?

MA: We should kick the CIA, Pentagon and White House out of the industry. It's do-able - the Pentagon's Hollywood liaison was almost axed in budget cuts during the 1990s, and a single Congresswoman forced the closure of Homeland Security's Hollywood PR unit just on the grounds that it was a waste of $130k. In 2012, the press rounded on the Obama White House, Pentagon, and CIA for allegedly providing classified information to Kathryn Bigelow and Mark Boal for their feature about the assassination of Osama Bin Laden, and also raised concerns about the movie being as party political propaganda in Obama's re-election campaign.

For us as audiences, we should not capitulate to the idea that we are just products to be sold to advertisers and recruiters. If Hollywood presents bullshit on screen we should subject it to ridicule, protest, critique, and/or abandon it at the box office in the name of creative and political freedom. I look forward to the day when the only people in the cinema enduring films like *Battleship* are me and Peter Berg.

7. Celebrity Philanthropy:
In the Service of Corporate Propaganda[*]

Michael Barker

In the era of mass society, the mainstream media have long demonstrated a fixation on celebrities. The public are regaled daily with spectacular stories of their dramatic personal lives and are invited to engage as voyeurs of their glamour-to have a peek in on their soirées with the rich and powerful. In his seminal book, *The Power Elite* (1956), C. Wright Mills dedicated an entire chapter to celebrities, observing how, with the rise of national means of mass communication, "the institutional elite must now compete with and borrow prestige from these professionals in the world of the celebrity" (p. 71). He outlined the integral social function their lives fulfill in the management of democracy, noting that "the liberal rhetoric-as a cloak for actual power-and the professional celebrity-as a status distraction-do permit the power elite conveniently to keep out of the limelight" (p. 91). Writing so many years ago, Mills was unsure as to whether the power elite would be content to remain uncelebrated. Now, however, under the liberating permissiveness of the neoliberal regime of media indoctrination and social management, the differences between the jet-set crowd and the power elite are melting (per Marx's observation: "All that is solid melts into air, all that is holy is profaned..."). Actors become political leaders, while politicians become world class "actors." The real power behind these figureheads, however, remains in the hands of what has become an

---

[*]   This article was first published in Gerald Sussman (ed.), *The Propaganda Society: Promotional Culture and Politics in Global Context* (New York: Peter Lang Publishing, 2011), pp. 145-158. Republished with the kind permission of Peter Lang Publishing Inc.

increasingly concentrated economic elite. The basis of elite legitimacy rests largely with the mainstream media, which sanction their behavior as part of the emerging military-industry-infotainment complex.

With global media conglomerates now acting as powerful political actors, the profitable returns of the *culture industry*-be they musicians, film and TV stars, or all three-are now integral to the hegemony of neoliberalism. Capital "takes the risk out of democracy" (Carey, 1997) by replacing thoughtful public discourse with corporate propaganda and promotion. However, while celebrity promotional culture is often intimately related to propaganda (Alford, 2010; Peck, 2008), perhaps its most enduring utility lies in its ability to legitimize and promote "humanitarian" interventions, giving a human face to the depredations of transnational capital. Drawing upon the liberal proclivities of a handful of the talented entertainers, such as Oprah Winfrey, Wyclef Jean, Bono, Angelina Jolie, Demi Moore, Madonna, George Clooney, and others who have worked their way to the top of the culture industry, power elites meld their celebrity status to their own agendas. Then there are celebrity capitalists such as Bill Gates and Warren Buffett, who enjoy the favorable epithet of philanthropist. The benevolent rhetoric of humanitarianism puts a sparkle on charitable aid givers, while aggressive corporate behavior in poor countries largely goes unheeded (Bricmont, 2007), shielded by a lack of media scrutiny.

The larger discourse of human rights and democracy assistance has always provided stellar rhetorical cover for all manner of unjust state and corporate policies, even more so in the post-Soviet era. Organisations such as the National Endowment for Democracy (established in the United States in 1983) were created to overtly carry out the anti-democratic actions (e.g., destabilisation) that were formerly undertaken covertly by the Central Intelligence Agency (CIA). In the U.K. its equivalent organization is the Westminster Foundation for Democracy. With Orwellian instrumentalism, "democracy" is rendered as a low-intensity *market*-based notion of democracy that prevails against the best interests of a global public-and without a hint of criticism from the mainstream media (Sussman, 2005).

In many ways, the work undertaken by such government-funded "non-governmental" organisations (NGOs) was modeled upon the longstanding philanthropic work of not-for-profit corporations, otherwise known as foundations. And while right-wing foundations played an integral role in financing the neoliberal revolution, liberal foundations, such as Ford, Rockefeller, and Carnegie, also worked to promote neoliberalism, and did so through a subtle process of co-opting what would otherwise have been its progressive dissenters (see Barker,

2008; Berman, 1983). This chapter critiques celebrity-driven liberal philanthropy by providing a critical interrogation of humanitarian responses to the poverty and health crisis in parts of the African continent and by problematising celebrity activism in this context.

Feeding the Humanitarian Industry

The use of humanitarian aid by Western donor organisations in the pursuit of geostrategic interests is well documented. Western governments do not donate food out of generosity; rather their food distribution networks are considered to be an *integral* weapon through which they promote their foreign policies and secure economic access to the targeted region. John F. Kennedy explicitly made the manipulation of foreign aid a strategic aspect of foreign policy (see Sussman & Lent, 1991, p. 4). George (1976, p. 193) points out how Herbert Hoover, working through allied "relief" agencies, was the "first modern politician to look upon food as a frequently more effective means of getting one's own way than gunboat diplomacy or military intervention." Hoover's use of food aid as a weapon was initially developed during and after World War I, and his notable success in this project led to his coordinating American relief in Europe after World War II. In the latter instance, Hoover institutionalized his "humanitarian" operations by bringing various civic, religious, charitable, and farm groups together in 1945 under an umbrella body known as the Cooperative for American Remittances to Europe-now simply known as CARE (Carnoy & Levison, 1974, p. 122). This selective provision of food aid through ostensibly independent bodies like CARE provided a valuable means of promoting hegemonic relations in the world and has been utilized in that way ever since (Schwartz, 2008).

Ethiopia during the famine of the early 1980s was a take-off point for celebrity activism and philanthropy in Africa. Bearing in mind the malevolent history of food imperialism, the record-breaking humanitarian activities of the celebrities who came together in 1984 as Band Aid under the guidance of Bob Geldof should be viewed in a critical light. For those who missed the media frenzy surrounding this venture, Band Aid's humanitarian anthem "Do They Know It's Christmas?" was released in December 1984 and became the fastest-selling U.K. single of all time. Considering the massive support this campaign received from the mainstream media, it is all the more important to scrutinize Band Aid's history. Band Aid did not, and could not, simply give food to the starving in Ethiopia without involving itself in regional politics; to claim otherwise, as Geldof has, is simply disingenuous.[1]

To begin with, Ethiopia was "reaping of the whirlwind of the fall-out of the then raging Cold War between the West and the former Soviet bloc" (Shaw, 2007, p. 393) and was in the grip of a protracted Civil War fighting against rebels of the Tigrayan People's Liberation Front (TPLF). Under these circumstances, the Ethiopian government was deliberately withholding food aid from the "huge areas of Tigray where TPLF guerrillas held sway" because, as their acting foreign minister Tibebu Bekele made clear at the time: "Food is a major element in our strategy against the secessionists" (Shaw, 2007, p. 393). Additionally, more recent reports reveal that some of the relief monies entering Ethiopia were used to buy arms for the rebels, which were distributed through the TPLF's aid front-group, the Relief Society of Tigray. The U.S. government was well aware of this situation, as a now-declassified CIA report written in 1985 made clear. The report observes that: "Some funds that insurgent organizations are raising for relief operations, as a result of increased world publicity, are almost certainly being diverted for military purposes" (Prashad, 2010).

Ironically, if one returns to the initial 7-minute BBC report (broadcast on October 24, 1984) that fueled Bob Geldof's initial humanitarian efforts in the region, it turns out that the two reporters who filed the BBC report (Mo Amin and Michael Buerk) were working under the auspices of World Vision-a well publicized, right-wing, evangelical Christian organisation. Little wonder that the report described Ethiopia as the scene of a "biblical famine" that was the "closest thing to hell on earth." It is also significant that journalists in the United States (for example, David Kline) had been attempting to air this famine story for some time with no interest from the mainstream media. As Bosso (1990, p. 157) observed: "It was not 'new' news, for the roots of the 1984 disaster lay in conditions known for years before the disaster hit the headlines." During the seemingly endless deluge of one-dimensional coverage of Ethiopia's human disaster, at no stage did the mainstream media make any significant effort to explain the root causes of the famine. This of course would require the mainstream media to challenge the dominant developmentalist narrative upon which NGOs in the aid industry then relied-and continue to rely (Miller, 2006; Petras, 1999).

Media elites and the international aid community were not interested in the historical background that led to anti-colonial and political conflicts in the region and to the catastrophe and instead simply latched upon well-worn neo-Malthusian environmental degradation narratives to justify ongoing aid in the post-famine period (1985-1990). This badly conceived developmentalist narrative was supremely useful to imperialist donors, as it promoted an intervention in a geostrategically important region that "was narrowly technical, largely bypassed the Ethiopian government, was targeted directly on the rural poor and would be welcomed by the growing environmental lobby in Washington" (Hoben, 1995, pp. 1013-1014).

Engineering Comic Relief

Building upon the momentum gathered by the aid industry in Ethiopia, in 1985 a host of celebrities came together to rally around a new humanitarian project called Comic Relief (a name that, like Band Aid, can be construed as a cynical way of branding philanthropic efforts in post-colonial Africa). The key person behind this venture was the influential comedy scriptwriter Richard Curtis, who during the Ethiopian famine had visited refugee camps as a guest of Oxfam. To this day Comic Relief remains a regular and important fundraising fixture in Britain, a spectacular event occurring every two years. Broadcast live on television, courtesy of the BBC, Comic Relief presents a veritable celebrity feast, which is regularly criticized in the alternative media "for their distinct lack of politics and inaccurate portrayal of Africa as a continent-come-country [sic] ravaged by natural disasters and warring tribes," and for the way in which they totally ignore root causes of poverty (i.e., colonialism, neocolonialism, and devastating IMF and World Bank structural adjustment programs) (Hodkinson, 2005).

In recent years, Richard Curtis has also proved to be a key mover behind another well-publicized humanitarian endeavor, the Make Poverty History coalition. With Curtis's assistance, reams of celebrities were enlisted to the campaign, and Curtis was even able to "convinc[e] Scottish multi-millionaire business tycoon, Sir Tom Hunter, to donate a [sic] £1m to the campaign, and [to encourage] advertising executives to donate more than £4m of free airtime" (Hodkinson, 2005). Following in the footsteps of the founding father of public relations, Edward Bernays-who is famous for authoring the 1948 essay "The Engineering of Consent"-Richard Curtis epitomizes the neoliberal celebrity icon of the new world order. Yet, while Bernays gained fame for using independent authorities (i.e., doctors) to engineer public consent, Curtis has proved willing and able to harness non-experts (read: celebrity comedians) to work the "humanitarian" propaganda mill.

In keeping with the power structure research of scholars like William Domhoff, tracing the personal relationships and networks maintained among corporate elites remains as important for critical research as it is for celebrity magazines. Thus keeping the public mind adjusted to celebrity status seems to have been something of a tradition in Curtis's family, as his wife and well-known current affairs reporter, Emma Freud, is the great-granddaughter of the famed psychoanalyst (Bernays was Freud's nephew). One might also add that Emma's younger brother, Matthew Freud, is also integrated into the mainstream propaganda apparatus-as in addition to being a trustee of Comic Relief and one of the most powerful PR men in London, he is married to Rupert Murdoch's daughter, Elisabeth Murdoch, who in turn has her own connections to Bob Geldof's celebrity entourage.

In 2001, Elisabeth Murdoch, with the assistance of Lord Waheed Alli, founded Shine Entertainment, a TV production company whose "key brands" include Gladiators, The Biggest Loser, and Banged Up. Some years earlier, in 1992, Lord Alli, who is the former boss of Carlton TV's production business, teamed up with Geldof (along with Charlie Parsons) to form the TV production company Planet 24 Productions. Planet 24's most enduring contribution to TV is its long-running and immensely profitable reality show Survivor, a television program that makes a fetish of competition and encapsulates the neoliberal (and Social Darwinist) view of human nature (Smith & Wood, 2003)-demonstrating the stark disconnect between Geldof's business sense and his humanitarian media persona. When Planet 24 was purchased by Carlton TV in 1999, Lord Alli, Geldof, and Parsons retained the rights to produce this program by transferring them to a new company, Castaway Television Productions (BBC, 2002).

Musical Campaigns

To take another example, artist-manager Simon Fuller, best known for being the creator of the *Idol* franchise (*Pop Idol, American Idol,* and some hundred other versions around the world), literally creates celebrities. The media phenomenon that was the Spice Girls was Fuller's doing, and former Spice Girl Geri Halliwell, singer-songwriter and now "philanthropist," is just one of Fuller's success stories. Another solo artist nurtured under Fuller's wing (since the early 1990s) is Annie Lennox, a singer who has created an activist reputation for herself working to promote humanitarian causes with Amnesty International,

Oxfam, and Comic Relief. Liberal activism of this sort secures the endorsement of many of the world's most powerful capitalists, and Lennox is one of only a handful of celebrities to be invited to serve alongside Richard Curtis on the advisory council of the prestigious Global Philanthropy Forum. Two other notable members of this Forum include Vartan Gregorian (president of the Carnegie Corporation of New York and former board member of the Bill and Melinda Gates Foundation), and William H. Gates, Sr., the father of the world's richest philanthropist (Bill Gates). Liberal activists appear to keep well-endowed company.

As a result of a pitch from Curtis in 2007, Fuller and *American Idol* supported a two-night celebrity extravaganza called "Idol Gives Back," the expressed intention of which was to provide aid for young people in need in the United States and Africa. Three years later, Bill Gates and his wife Melinda were invited as *Idol Gives Back*'s special guests to discuss the work of the world's largest foundation, the Bill and Melinda Gates Foundation, which distributed $3 billion in grants the previous year. (For a critique of the Gates Foundation's work, see Barker, 2008.)

This brings us to the king of contemporary rock, Bono, who in 2005, together with Bill and Melinda Gates, was voted *Time* magazine's "person of the year." Bono has a long interest in working within the aid industry. Not only did he sing on the initial Band Aid track (and played at the Live Aid gig in 1985), but he subsequently went on to volunteer for 6 weeks at an orphanage in Ethiopia. Bono's open commitment to Christian missionary work was then put on hold until 1997 when he became a spokesperson for a church-based coalition known as Jubilee 2000, which campaigned to cancel Third World debt. This political reawakening was catalysed by Jamie Drummond, global strategist for Jubilee 2000, an individual who had previously worked for Christian Aid in Ethiopia (Tyrangiel, 2005). The long-standing president of Jubilee 2000, Michael Taylor, formerly served as the head of Christian Aid for twelve years (1985 to 1997), and from 2001 to 2004 he acted as the director of the World Faiths Development Dialogue-a group that had been set up in 1998 by the then-Archbishop of Canterbury, Lord Carey of Clifton, and the head of the World Bank, James Wolfensohn, a powerful clerico-capitalist combo.[2]

Following the U2 frontman's spiritual revival, inspired by Drummond in 1997, Bono began spending weekends at the World Bank with his friend Bobby Shriver, whose brother-in-law is the film-star-turned-California-Governor Arnold Schwarzenegger (Tyrangiel, 2005). Bobby had been close to the World Bank's then-president James Wolfensohn (1995-2005) through his earlier employment within the venture capital division of the Wolfensohn firm.

Having gained such an apprenticeship under world financial leaders like Wolfensohn, it is appropriate that "Eventually, Bono's education was taken over by economist Jeffrey Sachs." Bono was pioneering new ground within the realm of celebrity activism, moving from the former archetypal celebrity-as-fundraiser to the realm of celebrity-as-lobbyist (for corporate wealth, not people power) (Tyrangiel, 2005). To this day Bono maintains close ties to Sachs, and with George Soros and BP's latest chairman, Carl-Henric Svanberg, he sits on the advisory board of Sachs's free-market environmental research group, the Earth Institute.

With the zeal of a born-again missionary, Bono endeavoured to work the circuits of power of the nonprofit sector, and Bob Geldof (his "close friend") devised the name DATA (Debt, AIDS, Trade, Africa) to christen his and Bobby Shriver's new group in 2002. As one might have expected, DATA was born to great power, with $1 million start-up grants flowing in from the likes of George Soros and the Bill and Melinda Gates Foundation. Moreover, once set up, DATA recruited like-minded, high-profile corporate lobbyists-the two main ones being the Democrat AIDS activist Tom Sheridan and defence contractor lobbyist Scott Hatch, who formerly ran the National Republican Campaign Committee (Tyrangiel, 2005).

In 2004, Bono extended his activist commitments, and with the backing of Bread for the World, the Better Safer World coalition, and the Bill and Melinda Gates Foundation, he created "ONE: The Campaign to Make Poverty History"-which subsequently merged with DATA in 2007 and is now known as ONE Campaign. Almost all the members of the board of directors of ONE are leading members of the U.S. power elite, but of particular interest are the two media big hitters, board chair Tom Freston (who is the former CEO of Viacom and MTV Networks), and Joe Cerrell (who presently works for the Gates Foundation, but formerly served as assistant press secretary to former U.S. Vice President Al Gore). Another notable ONE board member is Helene Gayle, who since 2006 has served as the president of CARE, and prior to this had worked for the Bill and Melinda Gates Foundation.

On top of all this, one might observe that in 2006 Bono and Bobby Shriver launched Product (RED) at Davos-a business venture to raise money from corporations to buy AIDS drugs for poor Africans. Here it is useful to turn to Naomi Klein (2007), who with regard to Bono's longstanding economic guru (Sachs) and the validity of RED's neoliberal approach to social change, noted how, unlike Jeffrey Sachs, I actually don't believe that what is lacking is political will at the highest levels, cooperation between world leaders. I don't think that if we could just present our elites with the right graphs and PowerPoint presentations-no offense-that we would finally convince them to make poverty history. I don't believe that. I don't believe we could do it, even if that PowerPoint presentation was being delivered [by] Angelina Jolie [who is also a member of the elite think-tank, the Council on Foreign Relations] wearing a (Product) Red TM Gap tank top and carrying a (Product) Red cell phone. Even if she had a (Product) Red iPhone, I still don't think they would listen. That's because elites don't make justice because we ask them to nicely and appealingly. They do it when the alternative to justice is worse.

Solutions to poverty, catastrophic diseases such as AIDS, high infant mortality, and other crises that stem from poverty will come from organized people power, not from more intensive lobbying efforts for more humane corporations. Bono's refusal to acknowledge this point helps explain why he puts so much faith in the power of high finance. Indeed, in 2004 Bono became an early founding partner of a "private equity firm that makes large-scale investments in market-leading media, entertainment, and consumer-related businesses" known as Elevation Partners (http://www.elevation.com/), a group whose current portfolio companies include Forbes and Facebook. This partnership saw Bono join forces with the former chief financial officer of Apple Computers and, among others, two former senior executives of the private investment banking firm The Blackstone Group (Reeves, 2006). Once again revealing his commitment to corporate solutions, in 2005 Bono and his wife, Ali Hewson, co-founded EDUN, a fashion label for organic clothing. Basic EDUN T-shirts cost $57 and so should be seen as luxury commodities; thus it is fitting that EDUN's creative director has previously designed products for Louis Vuitton. Furthermore, in 2009 the French luxury brand house LVMH decided to take a minority stake in the company (Oxberry, 2010).

Sir Bob Geldof's Aid Redux

While the musicians involved in the first Band Aid project might argue that they were unaware of the means by which food aid is tied to imperialism, the same could be not true of the actions of some of the same singers who participated in the corporate "aid" bonanza, Live 8. It was here that Geldof introduced Bill Gates to the millions watching Live 8 as "the world's greatest philanthropist." The political world had been turned upside down, and as George Monbiot (2005) commented, "Geldof and Bono's campaign for philanthropy portrays the enemies of the poor as their saviours."

In the past, Geldof had preferred to refer to his humanitarian work as apolitical, but now the ante has been raised and his actions, like Bono's, are firmly aimed at achieving tightly defined political objectives. Their calling is not one of humanitarianism as much as to deliver Africa to transnational corporate partners by trading on their celebrity capital. That their objectives work hand in hand with neoliberal elites, not in solidarity with the poor, is to be expected of two individuals who are highly successful businessmen in their own right.

For example, Geldof was on hand in 2004 when the British Prime Minister Tony Blair set up the Commission on Africa (with Gordon Brown as another of its members) to "take a fresh look at Africa's past and present and the international community's role in its development path" (LIVE 8, 2010). Yet, given Britain's ongoing commitment to exploiting the natural wealth and the poor in Africa (Curtis, 2004), especially in its former colonies, it is impossible to see this commission as anything other than a whitewash of British foreign policy, and so it is fitting that Geldof was invited to participate. While the Commission clearly served a useful PR function for world leaders, it also provided a vital strategizing function for neoliberal politicians (including those of African origins), as it was tasked with producing clear recommendations for the G8 summit that was to be held in Gleneagles, Scotland, in 2005. This was ground on which Geldof was comfortable, and he joined the former head of the IMF, Michel Camdessus (1987-2000), and many of Africa's most powerful elites in planning the historical, continuing, and expanded exploitation of the African continent (oil and other strategic resources, commercial ventures, arms sales, etc.).

Under Blair's watchful leadership, Geldof worked with and defended fellow neoliberal dealmaker and now prime minister of Ethiopia, Meles Zenawi, who in 2010 was accused of diverting aid funds to purchase weapons. Another key person in the Commission on Africa was former World Bank chief economist Lord Stern, who acted as the Commission's director of policy and research. A notable individual who worked closely with Lord Stern on the Commission was Paul Vallely, the person who ghost-wrote Geldof's autobiography, *Is That It?* (1985) and had "travelled with Geldof across Africa to decide how to spend the £100m raised by Live Aid" (*About Paul Vallely*, 2010). Vallely himself is a leading theorist of Christian-inspired humanitarianism and is the author of numerous books, although perhaps his most influential contribution was *Bad Samaritans: First World Ethics and Third World Debt* (1990), which is widely credited as inspiring the Jubilee 2000 campaign. He was also involved with the organization of Live 8, and in 2005 he coauthored (with Geldof) a book modestly titled *Geldof in Africa*.

The final and perhaps most significant person other than Geldof, who worked with Stern and Vallely in organizing the Commission on Africa, was the Head of the Secretariat to the Commission, "food aid" impresario Myles Wickstead, who just prior to joining the Commission had been based in Addis Ababa as the British Ambassador to Ethiopia and Djibouti. Wickstead's resume reveals that after completing his work at the Commission, he went on to serve on Comic Relief's international grants committee, become vice chair of the Westminster Foundation for Democracy, and chair of One World Media. In 2008, One World Media teamed up with the Television Trust for the Environment to support five journalists to go to developing countries to provide supportive journalism for the Millennium Development Goals (MDGs). With regard to the feel-good PR of celebrity philanthropists such as Geldof and friends, Ian Taylor (2006, p. 378) brings us back to earth in pointing out that "to set in place structures to allow Africa to reach the MDGs would require a fundamental political and societal change, not some mere technocratic policy tinkering, nor a development policy merely predicated on increased aid giving." Such changes are certainly not on the cards. Taylor's scathing criticisms of both the Commission on Africa and the MDGs were received with hostility by Wickstead (2006) and the developmentalist establishment.

Given this history, it is unsurprising that at Live 8, prior to the British general election, Geldof publicly supported Tony Blair's neoliberal political agenda for the 2005 G8 meeting. However, it was not just Geldof who succeeded (against much popular resistance) in coupling the Make Poverty History coalition, noted above, to the neoliberal agenda of the G8 leaders. As previously noted, Richard Curtis also acted as a driving force behind the coalition (Monbiot, 2005). Curtis's Scottish business friend, Sir Tom Hunter, who regards himself as a modern-day Andrew Carnegie, assisted by putting his philanthropic might behind the task of co-opting the Make Poverty History coalition (Hodkinson, 2005). Carnegie, of course, was a famous Scottish plutocrat who founded an array of philanthropic bodies that, while casting themselves as apolitical charitable institutions, went on to help consolidate the power of capital worldwide (Berman, 1983).

Repealing Philanthropic Propaganda

Celebrity activists of the "humanitarian" brand identified in this chapter actually represent, contrary to their cultivated image, a threat to democracy worldwide. Through their widely publicized good work with the world's leading financial elites-who in turn are tied in with powerful media corporations and philanthropic (non-profit) corporations-celebrity philanthropists help foster social exploitation throughout the African continent, even while undertaken in the rhetoric of "peace" and "justice." This manipulation of the body politic by the *culture industry* is not a new phenomenon. What's different is that the agents of neoliberalism are now able to employ more sophisticated forms of propaganda in their cynical abuse of public sentiment.

What to do? To begin with, we need to decertify the misleading representations of catastrophes, such as they are regularly reported in the mainstream media, and actively work to publicize and address the root causes, not the symptoms, of such disasters, which are embedded in the neocolonial system of Western aggression (and support for domestic aggression) on the continent. To help more people to understand how human crises can be averted in the future requires a commitment to exposing the falsehoods and negative consequences that the celebrity-foundation-media complex and neoliberal order exerts over society. In equal measure we can also encourage and support alternative media in the form of locally produced films, video, and other informational and cultural networks as well as celebrate the ingenuity of small budget productions and help nurture local talent (producers, directors, writers, actors, set designers, web site creators, and the like). In this way we can ensure that in the future we will have an entertainment structure that fosters participation and diversity (and that benefits the majority of citizens) instead of apathetic spectatorship and celebrity worship. The former strengthens democracy; the latter can only weaken it.

Notes

1   Geldof was also involved in the U.S. version of Band Aid, which under the organization of Harry Belafonte released the song "We Are the World" in March 1985. The song became the fastest-selling American pop single in history.
2   The current executive director of the World Faiths Development Dialogue, Katherine Marshall, previously served for many years in a senior capacity at the World Bank and presently sits on CARE's program and policy committee.

References

About Paul Vallely. (2010). Retrieved from http://www.paulvallely.com/?page_id=2

Alford, M. (2010). *Reel power: Hollywood cinema and American supremacy.* London: Pluto Press.

Barker, M. (2008, July 6-9). Bill Gates as social engineer: Introducing the world's largest liberal philanthropist. Refereed paper presented to Australasian Political Science Association Conference, University of Queensland, Australia.

BBC (2002, September 27). Geldof takes action against "Celebrity," *BBC News.* Retrieved from http://news.bbc.co.uk/1/hi/entertainment/2284706.stm

Berman, E. (1983). *The influence of the Carnegie, Ford, and Rockefeller foundations on American foreign policy: The ideology of philanthropy.* Albany: State University of New York Press.

Bosso, C. (1990). Setting the agenda: Mass media and the discovery of famine in Ethiopia. In M. Margolis & G. Mauser (Eds.), *Manipulating public opinion: Essays on public opinion as a dependent variable* (pp. 153-174). Pacific Grove, CA: Brooks/Cole.

Bricmont, J. (2007). *Humanitarian imperialism: Using human rights to sell war.* New York: Monthly Review Press.

Carey, A. (1997). *Taking the risk out of democracy: Corporate propaganda versus freedom and liberty.* Champaign: University of Illinois Press.

Carnoy, J., & Levison, L. (1974). The humanitarians. In Weissman, S. (Ed.), *The Trojan horse: A radical look at foreign aid.* Palo Alto: Ramparts Press.

Curtis, M. (2004). *Unpeople: Britain's secret human rights abuses.* London: Vintage.

George, S. (1976). *How the other half dies: The real reasons for world hunger.* New York: Penguin.

Hoben, A. (1995). Paradigms and politics: the cultural construction of environment policy in Ethiopia. *World Development, 23*(6), 1007-1021.

Hodkinson, S. (2005, June 28). Inside the murky world of the UK's Make Poverty History campaign. *Znet.* Retrieved from http://www.zcommunications.org/inside-the-murky-world-of-the-uks-make-poverty-history-campaign-by-stuart-hodkinson

Klein, N. (2007, August 16). From think tanks to battle tanks. *Znet.* Retrieved from http://www.zcommunications.org/from-think-tanks-to-battle-tanks-by-naomi-klein

LIVE 8 (2010). *Africa Commission.* Retrieved from http://www.live8live.com/whatsitabout/

Miller, E. (2006). *Viewing the South: How globalization and western television distort representations of the developing world.* Cresskill, NJ: Hampton Press.

Mills, C.W. (2000). *The power elite.* New York: Oxford University Press. (Original work published 1953)

Monbiot, G. (2005, June 21). Bards of the powerful. *Guardian* (UK). Online edition.

Oxberry, E. (2010, January 20). Edun names Sharon Wauchob creative director. *DrapersOnline.* Retrieved from http://www.drapersonline.com/news/womenswear/news/edun-names-sharon-wauchob-creative-director/5009705.article

Peck, J. (2008). *The age of Oprah: Cultural icon for the neoliberal era.* Boulder: Paradigm.

Petras, J. (1999). NGOs: In the service of imperialism. *Journal of Contemporary Asia, 29*(4), 429-40.

Prashad, V. (2010, March 29). Bad aid: Throw your arms around the world. *Counterpunch.* Retrieved from: http://www.counterpunch.org/prashad03292010.html

Reeves, S. (2006, August 7). Private Equity Group Buys into Forbes. *Forbes.* Retrieved from http://www.forbes.com/2006/08/07/forbes-invest-elevation-cx_sr_0807forbes.html

Schwartz, T. (2008). *Travesty in Haiti: A true account of Christian missions, orphanages, fraud, food aid and drug trafficking.* Charlestown, SC: BookSurge Publishing.

Shaw, I.S. (2007). Historical frames and the politics of humanitarian intervention: from Ethiopia, Somalia to Rwanda. *Globalisation, Societies and Education, 5*(3), 351-371.

Smith, M.J., & Wood, A.F. (Eds.). (2003). *Survivor lessons: Essays on communication and reality television.* Jefferson, NC: McFarland & Company.

Sussman, G. (2005). *Global electioneering: Campaign consulting, communications, and corporate financing.* Lanham, MD: Rowman & Littlefield.

Sussman, G., & Lent. J.A. (1991). Introduction: Critical perspectives on communication and Third World development. In G. Sussman, & J.A. Lent (Eds.), *Transnational communications: Wiring the Third World* (pp. 1-26). Newbury Park, CA: Sage.

Taylor, I. (2006). The millennium development goals and Africa: Challenges facing the Commonwealth. *The Round Table: The Commonwealth Journal of International Affairs, 95*(385), 365-382.

Tyrangiel, Josh (2005, December 19). The constant charmer. *Time.* Retrieved from http://www.time.com/time/magazine/article/0,9171,1142270,00.html

Wickstead, M.A. (2006). The millennium development goals and Africa: A response to Ian Taylor. *The Round Table: The Commonwealth Journal of International Affairs, 95*(385), 383-386.

8. The Politics of Language and the Language of Political Regression[*]

James Petras

Capitalism and its defenders maintain dominance through the 'material resources' at their command, especially the state apparatus, and their productive, financial and commercial enterprises, as well as through the manipulation of popular consciousness via ideologues, journalists, academics and publicists who fabricate the arguments and the language to frame the issues of the day.

Today material conditions for the vast majority of working people have sharply deteriorated as the capitalist class shifts the entire burden of the crisis and the recovery of their profits onto the backs of wage and salaried classes. One of the striking aspects of this sustained and on-going roll-back of living standards is the absence of a major social upheaval so far. Greece and Spain, with over 50% unemployment among its 16-24 year olds and nearly 25% general unemployment, have experienced a dozen general strikes and numerous multi-million person national protests; but these have failed to produce any real change in regime or policies. The mass firings and painful salary, wage, pension and social services cuts continue. In other countries, like Italy, France and England, protests and discontent find expression in the electoral arena, with incumbents voted out and replaced by the traditional opposition. Yet throughout the social turmoil and profound socio-economic erosion of living and working conditions, the dominant ideology informing the movements, trade unions and political opposition is reformist: Issuing calls to defend existing social benefits,

---

[*] This article was first published on James Petras' website, 18 May 2012.
<http://petras.lahaine.org/?p=1898>

increase public spending and investments and expand the role of the state where private sector activity has failed to invest or employ. In other words, the left proposes to conserve a past when capitalism was harnessed to the welfare state.

The problem is that this 'capitalism of the past' is gone and a new more virulent and intransigent capitalism has emerged forging a new worldwide framework and a powerful entrenched state apparatus immune to all calls for 'reform' and reorientation. The confusion, frustration and misdirection of mass popular opposition is, in part, due to the adoption by leftist writers, journalists and academics of the concepts and language espoused by its capitalist adversaries: language designed to obfuscate the true social relations of brutal exploitation, the central role of the ruling classes in reversing social gains and the profound links between the capitalist class and the state. Capitalist publicists, academics and journalists have elaborated a whole litany of concepts and terms which perpetuate capitalist rule and distract its critics and victims from the perpetrators of their steep slide toward mass impoverishment.

Even as they formulate their critiques and denunciations, the critics of capitalism use the language and concepts of its apologists. Insofar as the language of capitalism has entered the general parlance of the left, the capitalist class has established hegemony or dominance over its erstwhile adversaries. Worse, the left, by combining some of the basic concepts of capitalism with sharp criticism, creates illusions about the possibility of reforming 'the market' to serve popular ends.

This fails to identify the principal social forces that must be ousted from the commanding heights of the economy and the imperative to dismantle the class-dominated state. While the left denounces the capitalist crisis and state bailouts, its own poverty of thought undermines the development of mass political action. In this context the 'language' of obfuscation becomes a 'material force' - a vehicle of capitalist power, whose primary use is to disorient and disarm its anti-capitalist and working class adversaries. It does so by co-opting its intellectual critics through the use of terms, conceptual framework and language which dominate the discussion of the capitalist crisis.

Key Euphemisms at the Service of the Capitalist Offensive

Euphemisms have a double meaning: what terms connote and what they really mean. Euphemistic conceptions under capitalism connote a favorable reality or acceptable behavior and activity totally dissociated from the aggrandizement of elite wealth and concentration of power and privilege. Euphemisms disguise the drive of power elites to impose class-specific measures and to repress without being properly identified, held responsible and opposed by mass popular action.

The most common euphemism is the term 'market', which is endowed with human characteristics and powers. As such, we are told 'the market demands wage cuts' disassociated from the capitalist class. Markets, the exchange of commodities or the buying and selling of goods, have existed for thousands of years in different social systems in highly differentiated contexts. These have been global, national, regional and local. They involve different socio-economic actors, and comprise very different economic units, which range from giant state-promoted trading-houses to semi-subsistence peasant villages and town squares. 'Markets' existed in all complex societies: slave, feudal, mercantile and early and late competitive, monopoly industrial and finance capitalist societies.

When discussing and analyzing 'markets' and to make sense of the transactions (who benefits and who loses), one must clearly identify the principal social classes dominating economic transactions. To write in general about 'markets' is deceptive because markets do not exist independent of the social relations defining what is produced and sold, how it is produced and what class configurations shape the behavior of producers, sellers and labor. Today's market reality is defined by giant multi-national banks and corporations, which dominate the labor and commodity markets. To write of 'markets' as if they operated in a sphere above and beyond brutal class inequalities is to hide the essence of contemporary class relations.

Fundamental to any understanding, but left out of contemporary discussion, is the unchallenged power of the capitalist owners of the means of production and distribution, the capitalist ownership of advertising, the capitalist bankers who provide or deny credit and the capitalist-appointed state officials who 'regulate' or deregulate exchange relations. The outcomes of their policies are attributed to euphemistic 'market' demands which seem to be divorced from the brutal reality. Therefore, as the propagandists imply, to go against 'the market' is to oppose the exchange of goods: This is clearly nonsense. In contrast, to identify capitalist demands on labor, including reductions in wages, welfare and safety, is to confront a specific exploitative form of market behavior where capitalists seek to earn higher profits against the interests and welfare majority of wage and salaried workers.

By conflating exploitative market relations under capitalism with markets in general, the ideologues achieve several results: They disguise the principal role of capitalists while evoking an institution with positive connotations, that is, a 'market' where people purchase consumer goods and 'socialize' with friends and acquaintances. In other words, when 'the market', which is portrayed as a friend and benefactor of society, imposes painful policies presumably it is for the welfare of the community. At least that is what the business propagandists want the public to believe by marketing their virtuous image of the 'market'; they mask private capital's predatory behavior as it chases greater profits.

One of the most common euphemisms thrown about in the midst of this economic crisis is 'austerity', a term used to cover-up the harsh realities of draconian cutbacks in wages, salaries, pensions and public welfare and the sharp increase in regressive taxes (VAT). 'Austerity' measures mean policies to protect and even increase state subsidies to businesses, and create higher profits for capital and greater inequalities between the top 10% and the bottom 90%. 'Austerity' implies self-discipline, simplicity, thrift, saving, responsibility, limits on luxuries and spending, avoidance of immediate gratification for future security - a kind of collective Calvinism. It connotes shared sacrifice today for the future welfare of all.

However, in practice 'austerity' describes policies that are designed by the financial elite to implement class-specific reductions in the standard of living and social services (such as health and education) available for workers and salaried employees. It means public funds can be diverted to an even greater extent to pay high interest rates to wealthy bondholders while subjecting public policy to the dictates of the overlords of finance capital.

Rather than talking of 'austerity', with its connotation of stern self-discipline, leftist critics should clearly describe ruling class policies against the working and salaried classes, which increase inequalities and concentrate even more wealth and power at the top. 'Austerity' policies are therefore an expression of how the ruling classes use the state to shift the burden of the cost of their economic crisis onto labor.

The ideologues of the ruling classes co-opted concepts and terms, which the left originally used to advance improvements in living standards and turned them on their heads. Two of these euphemisms, co-opted from the left, are 'reform' and 'structural adjustment'. 'Reform', for many centuries, referred to changes, which lessened inequalities and increased popular representation. 'Reforms' were positive changes enhancing public welfare and constraining the abuse of power by oligarchic or plutocratic regimes. Over the past three decades, however, leading academic economists, journalists and international banking officials have subverted the meaning of 'reform' into its opposite: it now refers to the elimination of labor rights, the end of public regulation of capital and the curtailment of public subsidies making food and fuel affordable to the poor. In today's capitalist vocabulary 'reform' means reversing progressive changes and restoring the privileges of private monopolies.

'Reform' means ending job security and facilitating massive layoffs of workers by lowering or eliminating mandatory severance pay. 'Reform' no longer means positive social changes; it now means reversing those hard fought changes and restoring the unrestrained power of capital. It means a return to capital's earlier and most brutal phase, before labor organizations existed and when class struggle was suppressed. Hence 'reform' now means restoring privileges, power and profit for the rich.

In a similar fashion, the linguistic courtesans of the economic profession have co-opted the term 'structural' as in 'structural adjustment' to service the unbridled power of capital. As late as the 1970's 'structural' change referred to the redistribution of land from the big landlords to the landless; a shift in power from plutocrats to popular classes. 'Structures' referred to the organization of concentrated private power in the state and economy. Today, however, 'structure' refers to the public institutions and public policies, which grew out of labor and citizen struggles to provide social security, for protecting the welfare, health and retirement of workers. 'Structural changes' now are the euphemism for smashing those public institutions, ending the constraints on capital's predatory behavior and destroying labor's capacity to negotiate, struggle or preserve its social advances.

The term 'adjustment', as in 'structural adjustment' (SA), is itself a bland euphemism implying fine-tuning, the careful modulation of public institutions and policies back to health and balance. But, in reality, 'structural adjustment' represents a frontal attack on the public sector and a wholesale dismantling of protective legislation and public agencies organized to protect labor, the environment and consumers. 'Structural adjustment' masks a systematic assault on the people's living standards for the benefit of the capitalist class.

The capitalist class has cultivated a crop of economists and journalists who peddle brutal policies in bland, evasive and deceptive language in order to neutralize popular opposition. Unfortunately, many of their 'leftist' critics tend to rely on the same terminology.

Given the widespread corruption of language so pervasive in contemporary discussions about the crisis of capitalism the left should stop relying on this deceptive set of euphemisms co-opted by the ruling class. It is frustrating to see how easily the following terms enter our discourse:

- 'Market discipline' - The euphemism 'discipline' connotes serious, conscientious strength of character in the face of challenges as opposed to irresponsible, escapist behavior. In reality, when paired with 'market', it refers to capitalists taking advantage of unemployed workers and using their political influence and power lay-off masses workers and intimidate those remaining employees into greater exploitation and overwork, thereby producing more profit for less pay. It also covers the capacity of capitalist overlords to raise their rate of profit by slashing the social costs of production, such as worker and environmental protection, health coverage and pensions.

- 'Market shock' - This refers to capitalists engaging in brutal massive, abrupt firings, cuts in wages and slashing of health plans and pensions in order to improve stock quotations, augment profits and secure bigger bonuses for the bosses. By linking the bland, neutral term, 'market' to 'shock', the apologists of capital disguise the identity of those responsible for these measures, their brutal consequences and the immense benefits enjoyed by the elite.

- 'Market Demands' - This euphemistic phrase is designed to anthropomorphize an economic category, to diffuse criticism away from real flesh and blood power-holders, their class interests and their despotic strangle-hold over labor. Instead of 'market demands', the phrase should read: 'the capitalist class commands the workers to sacrifice their own wages and health to secure more profit for the multi-national corporations' - a clear concept more likely to arouse the ire of those adversely affected.

- 'Free Enterprise' - An euphemism spliced together from two real concepts: private enterprise for private profit and free competition. By eliminating the underlying image of private gain for the few against the interests of the many, the apologists of capital have invented a concept that emphasizes individual virtues of 'enterprise' and 'freedom' as opposed to the real economic vices of greed and exploitation.

- 'Free Market' - A euphemism implying free, fair and equal competition in unregulated markets glossing over the reality of market domination by monopolies and oligopolies dependent on massive state bailouts in times of capitalist crisis. 'Free' refers specifically to the absence of public regulations and state intervention to defend workers safety as well as consumer and environmental protection. In other words, 'freedom' masks the wanton destruction of the civic order by private capitalists through their unbridled exercise of economic and political power. 'Free market' is the euphemism for the absolute rule of capitalists over the rights and livelihood of millions of citizens, in essence, a true denial of freedom.

- 'Economic Recovery' - This euphemistic phrase means the recovery of profits by the major corporations. It disguises the total absence of recovery of living standards for the working and middle classes, the reversal of social benefits and the economic losses of mortgage holders, debtors, the long-term unemployed and bankrupted small business owners. What is glossed over in the term 'economic recovery' is how mass immiseration became a key condition for the recovery of corporate profits.

- 'Privatization' - This describes the transfer of public enterprises, usually the profitable ones, to well-connected, large scale private capitalists at prices well below their real value, leading to the loss of public services, stable public employment and higher costs to consumers as the new private owners jack up prices and lay-off workers - all in the name of another euphemism, 'efficiency'.

- 'Efficiency' - Efficiency here refers only to the balance sheets of an enterprise; it does not reflect the heavy costs of 'privatization' borne by related sectors of the economy. For example, 'privatization' of transport adds costs to upstream and downstream businesses by making them less competitive compared with competitors in other countries; 'privatization' eliminates services in regions that are less profitable, leading to local economic collapse and isolation from national markets. Frequently, public officials, who are aligned with private capitalists, will deliberately disinvest in public enterprises and appoint incompetent political cronies as part of patronage politics, in order to degrade services and foment public discontent. This creates a public opinion favorable to 'privatizing' the enterprise. In other words 'privatization' is not a result of the inherent inefficiencies of public enterprises, as the capitalist ideologues like to argue, but a deliberate political act designed to enhance private capital gain at the cost of public welfare.

Conclusion

Language, concepts and euphemisms are important weapons in the class struggle 'from above' designed by capitalist journalists and economists to maximize the wealth and power of capital. To the degree that progressive and leftist critics adopt these euphemisms and their frame of reference, their own critiques and the alternatives they propose are limited by the rhetoric of capital. Putting 'quotation marks' around the euphemisms may be a mark of disapproval but this does nothing to advance a different analytical framework necessary for successful class struggle 'from below'. Equally important, it side-steps the need for a fundamental break with the capitalist system including its corrupted language and deceptive concepts. Capitalists have overturned the most fundamental gains of the working class and we are falling back toward the absolute rule of capital. This must raise anew the issue of a socialist transformation of the state, economy and class structure. An integral part of that process must be the complete rejection of the euphemisms used by capitalist ideologues and their systematic replacement by terms and concepts that truly reflect the harsh reality, that clearly identify the perpetrators of this decline and that define the social agencies for political transformation.

Part 3

Co-opting Dissent

9. Neoliberal Hegemony and the Organization of Consent *

William K. Carroll and Matthew Greeno

In December of 1972, three astronauts were locked in a capsule barreling toward the moon. The crew captured a picture of Earth in its full illumination, which came to be known as "The Blue Marble." It was not the first picture of our planet, but it is the most significant, showing Earth in full view contrasted against the vast darkness of space. Released during a period of widespread environmental protests, the image provided significant meaning to a social movement that, at its boldest, called for radical departures from the status quo of the era. By the 1980s, the discourse had shifted substantially to 'sustainable development' as the mainstream environmental movement embraced the free market. Today's carbon taxes and carbon trading schemes are the legacy of the notion of sustainable development and an explicitly capitalist environmentalism.

Environmentalism has been co-opted; indeed, mainstream corporate environmentalism helps disable more radical ideas. But it is by no means the only movement that has suffered this fate; another is the labour movement. A major force for social transformation in the 19th and early 20th centuries, labour (specifically in the global North) traded its radicalism for membership in the consumer-capitalist 'affluent society' of the second half of the 20th century, and has been hobbled in recent decades by the internationalization of labour markets, among other factors. Each of these movements have largely accepted capitalist

---

*   This article is based on a previous article by William K. Carroll: W. K. Carroll, 'Hegemony, counter-hegemony, anti-hegemony', *Socialist Studies*, Vol. 2 No. 2, (2006), pp. 9-42.

growth as an imperative and presumed that progressive politics could be added 'on top' of the basic structure. These movements underestimated, or have been relatively powerless to oppose, the totalizing dynamic of capitalism: its capacity to mute dissent by incorporating into its circuitry the immediate concerns of oppositional movements - as in the 'green economy' or, earlier, high-wage Fordism.

Today the ongoing global economic crisis, coupled with deteriorating ecological conditions across the globe, demands a coherent and organised radical alternative. Yet despite signs of impending ecological catastrophe and the deepening inequalities that consign billions to lives of permanent privation, the solution offered from on high is fiscal austerity, more free trade and an increase in economic globalization while environmental protections are scaled back. Governments and corporations increasingly act to create short-term economic growth, to the benefit of a tiny minority - the investors and executives who comprise the ruling class.

To struggle effectively for a better world, we need to seek to understand how co-optation occurs, and how consent is managed. This article offers an analysis of how, despite its deepening crisis, contemporary capitalism co-opts its potential opposition and organizes consent to an unjust, unsustainable way of life. We will use the concept of hegemony, which Antonio Gramsci described as a state in which "spontaneous consent [is] given by [civil society]... to the general direction imposed on social life,"[1] as a method to understand co-optation. Consent is established historically through the continued prestige of intellectual concepts, the free market being the case in point. It is actively reinforced through institutions that support and expand these concepts as the 'common sense' of an era. But hegemony is more than ideology; it is also closely linked to capital accumulation, the profit-seeking process at the heart of the world economy.

Capital accumulation is commonly called 'economic growth' but regardless of the terminology, it is capitalism's driving force. Without growth, capitalism spirals downward, in crisis. Companies reduce their workforces, and this in turn shrinks the overall demand for goods and services and the tax revenues that governments collect. If prospects for growth flag, capitalists hold back from investment, further amplifying the crisis. In 2008, it was this meltdown scenario of under-investment/under-consumption that led many of the world's governments to provide banks and corporations with billions in public money to erase bad debt and encourage further investment. Having bailed out corporate capital in its moment of global crisis, the same governments now insist on austerity for the masses as a means of paying the bail-out bill.

The various programs that institutions create to support the continued capital accumulation embody neoliberal capitalist hegemony, which is based around the norm of an unfettered free market. In this deeper, structural sense, hegemony has to do with "the cohesion of the social system. It secures the reproduction of the mode of production and other basic structural processes."[2] In short, capitalist hegemony creates a material basis for its own reproduction while securing a manner of cohesion around the market. (See also Whyte, Chapter 3.)

Amid an ongoing global economic and ecological crisis, the question of hegemony looms larger than perhaps at any time since the Great Depression of the 1930s, yet the challenges of constructing a political alternative to the rule of capital seem more daunting than ever. We will focus on the three 'mechanisms' that underlie neoliberal hegemony: cultural fragmentation; market insulation and dispossession; and globalization from above. In combination, these mechanisms disorganize, disable and defang movements. However, if we are to move beyond our deeply flawed contemporary world order we must build stronger forms of organisation that can repel co-optation. (See also, The Free Association, Chapter 13.) To do this we must examine the processes of co-optation.

Cultural Fragmentation:

Hegemony is often conceptualized as a condition of cultural and political consensus, yet today one of its most important bases is the *cultural fragmentation* that issues from advanced consumer capitalism as a way of life, particularly in the global North. The full flowering of consumer capitalism has brought the commodification of everyday life, including culture. Beginning in the 1970s, aided by information technologies, corporations in the global North began to produce not only for mass consumer markets but for niche markets. This meant more than a shift in business strategy. Over time, it fragmented culture into many pieces, each of which can be cultivated and exploited for its commercial value. Each subculture and identity group offers a niche market to corporate capital. As market principles invade culture they absorb and commodify the voices of subjugated groups within the chain of production and consumption. As David Teztlaff explains, "The genius of capitalism is its simplicity of motive. As long as profit can be accumulated and maximized, other considerations are secondary. This gives capital great flexibility, allowing it to form alliances of convenience with other centers of power."[3] To manage consent, any combination of ideologies that instills compliance in the workforce while discouraging challenges to the system is acceptable. Forces of capitalism organize society explicitly with that motive, in a governance strategy of "divide and conquer."[4]

Take for example the actions of Dove Cosmetics starting in 2004 when it established its "Self-esteem Fund" and its "Campaign for Real Beauty."[5] Dove's campaign claimed to work towards a diversification of beauty and spawned commercials with the slogan "let's make peace with beauty." Dove reported constructing this campaign because a study they commissioned showed that the vast majority of women were feeling alienated by the media and its idealization of women's bodies. Their rationale suggests that this campaign was about a company's growing awareness of a social problem. However, grassroots activists and academics have been analyzing the negative social effects of the media's idealization of women's bodies at least since the early 1990s. Dove picked up on this social movement and saw an opportunity to capitalize; Dove was attempting, through this marketing campaign, to sell a version of women's diversity and then fuse the Dove brand to the idea. The intended effect was for Dove to appear socially responsible, but the end goal was always capital accumulation. To that end, the marketing campaign succeeded: according to one account, "the campaign returned $3 for every $1 spent."[6]

The result of corporations seeking to appear socially responsible and agreeable to the progressive goals of various social movements is the commodification of those movements and division within these movements. In the example above, Dove commodified the alienation of women by the media and made the purchase of their products seem politically motivated. This organizes people around a product as opposed to a collectively transformative project. Dove's campaign is sharply contrasted by groups like Pretty, Porky, and Pissed Off from Toronto, who are critical of consumer culture and involved in grassroots activism about women's body image.[7] The radical viewpoints of such a group, which are less compliant with the chain of production and consumption, are alienated from mainstream culture.

The Dove example serves to show how marketing creates culture, but a divided culture. Dove made great efforts to differentiate itself within a broad category of beauty products by marketing a social mission. This marketing effort blurred the line between the actual products Dove sells and consumers' sense of identity. This is generally true about marketing. Marketing attempts to define experience by associating a brand with symbols that people recognize about that experience, but through this process, as corporations continue to jostle for competitive position, marketing helps produce a culture that is fragmented. Products are created for increasingly esoteric markets and take increasingly divergent forms. Today our culture produces markets for cable channels designed for classic movie fans, smart phones designed for being dropped in the mud, and board games designed for miniature train collectors. Niche markets are created first by marketers as they try to differentiate their product and then are adopted by the masses. As Apple Computer former CEO, Steve Jobs, advocated, "people don't know what they want until you show it to them."[8]

From this perspective, the hegemonic significance of cultural fragmentation lies in a *consent without consensus* that is sustained by two mechanisms:

• *ideological diversification*: the proliferation of many distinct style cultures and subcultures - divided by age, gender, ethnic and other differences - that prevent subjugated groups from understanding one another and undertaking the difficult work of constructing solidarities; for example, there is a conflict between younger generations, who blame baby-boomers for economic and environmental woes, and the baby-boomers who perceive youth as entitled and lazy.

• *implosion of meaning*: the cultural fixation on superficial symbols and televisual spectacle - the Olympics, endlessly replayed footage of the latest militarized conflict or natural disaster, etc. - all of which distracts people from imagining a collectively transformative project.[9]

Within "the cultural logic of late capitalism,"[10] consent is organized around the market and fostered by the lack of other forms of social cohesion. The divisions between social groups pose a challenge to oppositional movements intent on moving beyond the fragments of single-issue politics and liberal multiculturalism that reinforce the pattern of ideological diversification.

Insulation and Dispossession:

In the 1970s and 1980s, neoliberal politics, best exemplified by Thatcherism and Reaganomics, reorganized hegemony, and government efforts enabling this project were explicit. The main tenets of neoliberalism are the priority of 'sound money' and low inflation, attacks on unions, flexible labour markets, policies of fiscal retrenchment, deregulation, and free trade - all of which are meant to strengthen the role of markets in human affairs. These policies have indeed amplified the impact of global market forces on working people and communities, thereby shifting the balance of class power toward those who command capital.[11] Neoliberalism strives to restore the optimal conditions for capital accumulation at the expense of social protections inscribed within welfare state institutions: social housing provisions, public pensions etc.

At the heart of neoliberal economic policies is the *insulation* of both capital and the state from democratic control. A key hegemonic claim is that the market provides a natural mechanism for rational economic allocation. Thus, attempts to regulate capital via political decisions produce suboptimal outcomes. This hegemonic claim is based on the fiction of a free market comprised of many small firms. In fact, giant corporations and financial institutions, commanded by members of a transnational capitalist class, dominate contemporary capitalism.[12] Deregulating these centres of class power insulates them from democratic control. The promise of increased freedom is belied by the reality of ever-more concentrated economic power.

By the same token, neoliberalism insists that key state agencies be insulated from popular will. Central banks and institutions like the International Monetary Fund must be insulated from "myopic" elected governments, so that they can foster "sustainable real economic growth."[13] Allowing politics to influence monetary policy would result in unstable financial markets, reduced growth, or a recession. This perspective assumes that managing the economy independently from politics results in increases in private investment. However, the opposite has been shown. Since the 1970s, investment has decreased in relation to GDP.[14] Profits for many businesses have increased as a result of market liberalization, but that capital is accumulating as private wealth. This is referred to as the phenomenon of over-accumulation. As Jim Stanford observed, "while neoliberalism has been successful in restoring business profitability and, more generally, business power, it has not lead to stronger world growth."[15]

We can see neoliberal insulation at work in the paradigm shift from the welfare state to the "competition state."[16] In a competition state, the state's role is to promote its territory as a site for investment. To accomplish this, the state must be insulated from popular will, and free to enact business-friendly policies. Promoting individual economic freedom as the highest virtue is at the core of this aspect of hegemony.

Citizens are asked to trade away any modicum of democratic control over economic decisions for the promise of enhanced personal opportunities in markets buoyed by pro-business policies.

Alongside what we have called insulation, a second hegemonic element in neoliberal economic policies arises from what David Harvey calls *accumulation by dispossession*.[17] The insulation of capital and the state from democratic constraint is directed at promoting depoliticized economic activity within liberalized markets. In contrast, accumulation by dispossession refers to the process of *privatizing commonly-held assets* (or rights to assets). These include public utilities, educational institutions, and transportation networks among others. By selling these assets, governments free up new venues into which over-accumulated capital can flow. Harvey has connected the dots between a wide range of examples - biopiracy and the wholesale commodification of nature, commercialization of culture and intellectual creativity, corporatization and privatization of public institutions and utilities - in short, the enclosure of the commons. What gives these initiatives persuasive power in managing dissent is the disempowering implications of successful enclosure. As the elements of life are privatized, people lose collective capacity to resist. They become increasingly 'free agents' acting individually in various markets, rather than members of communities knit together through social stewardship.

However, as a stable material basis for social cohesion, neoliberal capitalism remains problematic. Both aspects of neoliberal hegemony - insulation and dispossession - create unstable material conditions. Corporate profits have increased since the economic crises of the 1970s and early 1980s, but so have the economic shocks that accompany accumulation by dispossession. Such shocks can be observed as a result of the cumulative privatization campaigns in Argentina and elsewhere, which initially brought massive inflows of over-accumulated capital and a boom in asset values, followed by collapse into general impoverishment and social chaos as capital fled the scene.[18] Similarly, market liberalization may boost profitability in the short term, but it "will not produce a harmonious state in which everyone is better off."[19] Market liberalization and the global integration of deregulated national economies resulted in the most recent, and ongoing, global financial crisis. As of early 2012, large multinational corporations were sitting on trillions of dollars, and even the US[20] and UK[21] governments, which have been the sites of much deregulation, struggle to get those companies to spend the capital on hiring or investment. Moreover, the result of insulation through market liberalization nationally and internationally has been economic polarization - the growing gap between the 99% and the 1% - even during boom times. Neoliberalism's brutalizing ramifications render claims to hegemony tenuous. (See also Fisher, Chapter 2 and Whyte, Chapter 3.)

Against these weaknesses, however, consider neoliberalism's strategic advantages:

▪ To the extent that 'the economy' is imagined to be an autonomous rational machine, capitalism becomes an inaccessible topic to opponents of neo-liberal ideology.

▪ To the extent that the state becomes seen simply as the protector of economic growth, policies that counter-balance the power of capital by addressing the needs of workers, communities and ecology become marginalized. They are viewed as incompatible with the state's main mission.[22]

▪ To the extent that markets become society's guiding principles, the actions of individuals and social movements conform to market guidelines and must fit institutionally within market confines. Notions of competition and individual or organizational self-interest may come to dominate the social missions of many non-governmental organizations (NGOs). This can render activists and movements disciplined by the market and can instill a kind of fatalism in the general population, setting limits to dissent. However, the full hegemony of market discourse is constantly subverted by the economic and social polarization that stem from neoliberal policy, giving activists fresh opportunities to contest neoliberal hegemony.

The current Conservative federal government of Canada has attempted to mobilize these advantages to suppress environmental concern in the country. The Conservatives are ideologically opposed to accepting climate change and conservation forms of environmentalism alike. This government places emphasis on extraction of natural resources, like bitumen from the Tar Sands in Alberta, above all else and recently put its considerable weight behind the efforts of a multinational corporation called Enbridge. Enbridge has proposed to run a pipeline from the Tar Sands over hundreds of kilometres of remote terrain between the provinces of Alberta and British Columbia (BC) to an inlet in a small community called Kitimat, where the bitumen would be loaded into supertankers, which will attempt to navigate through waters better fit for canoes, eventually bound for China. Despite mass opposition to the pipeline by the citizens of BC and the nation, the

Conservative Minister of Natural Resources stated: "unfortunately, there are environmental and other radical groups that would seek to block this opportunity to diversify our trade."[23] The reactionary accusations of the government framed the dissent as 'radical' and as attempting to undermine the economic good of the nation. In other words, dissent that ignores the economic benefits in favor of an environmental risk assessment cannot be valid. This government has continued this rhetoric stating, "science, not politics, will decide the fate of the pipeline"[24] while also "streamlining" the country's environmental review process for resource extraction projects. This example shows a government attempting to discipline social movements by critiquing their actions against the insulated economy while attempting to isolate the project from the popular will of the citizenry.[25]

Globalization from Above:

Globalization from above is the final mechanism to consider in the recent hegemonic transition.

Globalization is the complex and emergent product of various practices and processes operating on many scales,[26] but our focus here is on the hegemonic implications of international capital accumulation. This form of globalization occurs 'from above', as the quest for profit pushes capitalists into a "chase across the globe"[27] and reshapes the world in the image of capital, as more and more people are drawn into commodity relations.

Although capital has been globalizing for half a millennium, a turning point occurred in 1971, when then US President Richard Nixon announced that America was abandoning the fixed exchange rates that made the US dollar the standard for other currencies.[28] Previously, fixed currency exchange rates inhibited the international movement of capital to help prevent the massive financial shocks that were associated with the Great Depression. With Nixon's decision the globalization of capitalism's financial circuitry began in earnest.

It is not surprising that globalization in this sense has gone hand-in-hand with neoliberal political transformations.[29] Globalization from above expands the volume and extent of international trade and investment, enabling capital to play some communities and workforces off against others in the competition for jobs and revenue. As capital becomes more internationalized, its structural power, exercised through financial institutions and markets, is amplified, along with the risks of cascading global crisis.

As a hegemonic idea, 'globalization' conveys a metanarrative that trumps Fordist-era narratives of national development. The story suggests that international trade and investment provide *the* formula for development. The implications of globalization from above for the organization of consent are important. Where the Fordist-era narrative presented a collective whose unity was based on national identity,

> The global narrative displaces human subjectivity, dramatizing instead the integration of markets... 'Globalization' offers a story in which the new world order will culminate, not in an undifferentiated whole, but in an endlessly differentiated circuit of exchangeability. It tells a story, not about our sameness, but about our fungeabilty.[30]

To be fungible is to be universally exchangeable, and interchangeable. This applies not only to objects, but to human beings and their capacities. Each location for investment, each job, is interchangeable as far as international capital is concerned and organizations have been created to extend this sensibility. The World Trade Organization, for example, "provides a forum for negotiating agreements aimed at reducing obstacles to international trade and ensuring a level playing field for all, thus contributing to economic growth and development."[31] The aim is to eliminate the so-called myopic public control of investment and trade. Global governance recognizes the need to solve 'world problems' such as economic instability, poverty, and ecological destruction, cooperatively and in dialogue by bringing together not only state actors, but also NGOs and private enterprises from civil society. As the state withdraws from interventionist public policy, NGOs often step in to fill the void, but the playing field is hardly level and they do this from a position of vulnerability and often marginality. The key global actors appear as hierarchical and corporatized organizations, for instance, the powerful corporate alliances that have repeatedly scuttled any real progress toward an international agreement on preventing catastrophic climate change. As one author observed, "international relations have become 'privatized'... Non-state actors are increasingly integrated in the operations of the liberal world market which has affected even the NGO sector where the corporate model of organization has grown in popularity."[32] (See also Merz, Chapter 10.)

The phenomenon of 'NGO-ization' vividly illustrates how globalization-from-above co-opts its own potential opposition. This refers to the creation of non-government organizations (NGOs) as a way of organizing around an issue like environmental degradation or the oppression of women. These organizations become the institutional representatives of social movements, often to the detriment of grassroots democracy. The dependence of NGOs on foundation funds can cause them to act as brakes upon radical ideas from the global South. To secure and maintain funds from liberal-humanitarian foundations, many NGOs must moderate and 'mainstream' the radical demands and visions that often come from the grassroots. Such NGOs act as social control agents, policing social movements through the management of dissent. Only movement groups whose projects fit within the overall agenda of the foundations get promoted and supported.[33] (See also Barker, Chapter 11.) In this and other ways, global organizations of many different stripes have embraced the formation and indeed the goals of neoliberal capitalism. Within this framework, the economy is the place of legitimate competition; politics is the place where cooperation smooths out the rough edges of the primary competitive process.[34]

Conclusion

The prioritization of the market links the practices and projects discussed here to the deeper structures of transnational neoliberal capitalism. Throughout cultures of the Global North, it naturalizes market relations and infuses them into an organization of consent that operates both locally and globally. This hegemonic system tends to co-opt dissenting groups through commodification of subcultures and the active expansion of neoliberal projects that limit politics to 'what works' within an increasingly international and privatized economic framework. Yet this is an unstable, crisis-ridden way of life. The paradigm shift has accomplished only a *thin* hegemony and weak basis for social cohesion.

Neoliberal hegemony's key elements - cultural fragmentation, dispossession and market insulation, and globalization-from-above - do not comprise a singular project created from a conspiracy to construct a new world order. Instead, these elements have come together as an *assemblage*. What unites them is the support they provide for a certain form of capitalism. Commodification, deregulation, and the expanding transnational reach of accumulation together enable a lifestyle of affluence for the elect, and the semblance of that lifestyle for affluent segments of the working class in the global North. However, the social and ecological base for this assemblage is shrinking. Capital makes allegiances of convenience and may abandon them during times of crisis; this has been the fate of organized labour in the North. Less favoured groups are actively repressed in the interest of capital accumulation and demonized in the corporate media as welfare cheats, illegal migrants, treacherous environmentalists, overpaid unionized labour and violent radicals. Ecosystems at varying scales also are harmed through capital's endless expansion, whose effects include resource depletion, pollution, species loss and most significantly, climate change. In short, the system tends to undermine its own human and natural infrastructure while sharpening social inequities.

None of the hegemonic mechanisms we have reviewed here hold a lock upon popular consciousness. Indeed, particularly since the rise of alter-globalization politics in the 1990s, social movements and communities across the globe have resisted neoliberalism while attempting to construct new paths to an alternative future. Although the question of how to transform the global structure remains to be answered, our analysis suggests several important points worth considering to avoid the trail of co-optation:

▪ Each of the mechanisms we have discussed tends to disorganize the opposition and to recruit support for the current regime of transnational neoliberal capitalism. Democratic movements need to counter them, with an alternative social vision that inspires people to struggle for a better world. But constructing such a counter-hegemony does not mean simply reversing or inverting the dominant perspective.

▪ In the case of cultural fragmentation, democratic movements need to foster political organisation, discussion and networking across and within the different stands of activism, North and South, without repressing cultural difference. Diversity and solidarity must be core values of any post-capitalist world.

▪ In the case of neoliberal insulation of economics from politics, democratic movements need both to demand the democratization of economic life and to put such demands into practice by creating participatory-democratic alternatives, as in co-operatives, participatory budgeting and the like. Likewise, effective responses to dispossession and privatization need both to insist on the value of public goods as a basis for democracy itself and to create new commons, as in cyberactivist open-source initiatives and the land invasions of Brazil's landless workers' movement (MST).

- Finally, in response to globalization-from-above, democratic movements need to build upon the globalization-from-below exemplified by movements like La Via Campesina, but they also need to ensure that any engagement with the existing organizations of global governance, such as the UN institutions, is conducted with critical awareness of their power. The UN institutions, particularly those involved in development, aid or so-called 'democracy promotion' are themselves mechanisms of co-optation, and have swallowed up and diverted the paths of many well-meaning NGOs and social movements. Any engagement with these institutions is perilous, and must proceed from an insistence on their democratization and extrication from the global nexus of elite and corporate power. Enacting this risky form of engagement requires that movements retain at their core a commitment to democratic practice (again, La Via Campesina offers an example) while building alliances with other democratic actors at the international level. At the same time, local bases for activism need to be cultivated: globalization-from-below can only develop from democratic initiatives at the grassroots.

In our view, the most compelling counter-hegemonic vision that can respond to the deepening economic and ecological crisis of our time is what Foster and Magdoff have called "sustainable human development": a transformation in community, culture and economy that reduces humanity's ecological footprint while producing "*enough* for everyone, and no more."[35] Valuing human thriving and ecological health rather than unsustainable capital accumulation, this vision provides a basis for both North-South solidarity and solidarity across the domains of social and environmental justice. The challenge for activists is to find, or create, pathways in the present toward this alternative future.

Notes

1   A. Gramsci, *Selections from the Prison Notebooks of Antonio Gramsci* (New York: International Publishers, 1971), p. 12.
2   J. Joseph, *Hegemony: A Realist Analysis* (London: Routledge, 2002), p. 211.
3   D. Tetzlaff, 'Divide and Conquer: Popular Culture and Social Control in Late Capitalism.', *Media, Culture and Society*, Vol. 13, (1991), pp. 9-33, p. 22.
4   Ibid.
5   Tinted Lens: Musings on Culture and Beyond, 'The Beauty Myth: Dove Cosmetics rides the wave', 28 February, 2008.

<http://interculturaljournal.wordpress.com/2011/02/28/women-and-advertising-the-power-myth/>

6   O. Falcione, and L. Henderson, 'The Dove Campaign for Beauty', 1 March, 2009. <http://psucomm473.blogspot.ca/2009/03/dove-campaign-for-real-beauty.html>

7   J. Johnston, and J. Taylor, 'Feminist Consumerism and Fat Activists: A Comparative Study of Grassroots Activism and the Dove Real Beauty Campaign', *Signs*, Vol. 33 (2008), pp. 941-966.

8   C. Mui, 'Five Dangerous Lessons to Learn From Steve Jobs'", 17 October, 2011. <http://www.forbes.com/sites/chunkamui/2011/10/17/five-dangerous-lessons-to-learn-from-steve-jobs/>

9   W. K. Carroll, 'Hegemony, counter-hegemony, anti-hegemony', pp. 29-30.

10 P. Anderson, *The Origins of Postmodernism* (London: Verso, 1998), p. 131.

11 G. Teeple, *Globalization and the Decline of Social Reform* (Second Edition, Aurora, Ontario: Garamond Press, 2000).

12 W. Carroll, *The Making of a Transnational Capitalist Class* (London: Zed Books, 2006).

13 T. Lybek, 'Central Bank Autonomy, Accountability, and Governance: Conceptual Framework', (2004), p. 2. <www.imf.org/external/np/leg/sem/2004/cdmfl/eng/lybek.pdf>

14 J. Stanford, *Economics for Everyone: A short guide to the economics of capitalism* (Halifax, NS: Fernwood Publishing, 2008).

15 Ibid, p. 149.

16 J. Hirsch, 'Globalisation of Capital, Nation-States and Democracy', *Studies in Political Economy*, Vol. 54 (1997), pp. 39-58.

17 D. Harvey, *A Brief History of Neoliberalism* (New York: Oxford University Press, 2005).

18 L. Evans, 'The Crisis In Argentina', *UCLA International Institute*, 4 April, 2003. <http://www.international.ucla.edu/article.asp?parentid=3566>

19 Harvey, D., *The New Imperialism*, (New York: Oxford University Press, 2005), p. 114.

20 M. Aneiro, 'U.S. Companies Sitting on $1.24 Trillion Cash Hoard', *Barron.com's Income Investing blog*, 14 March, 2012. <http://blogs.barrons.com/incomeinvesting/2012/03/14/u-s-companies-sitting-on-1-24-trillion-cash-hoard/>

21 P. Aldrick, 'Budget 2012: UK companies are sitting on billions of pounds, so why aren't they spending it?', *The Telegraph*, 17 March, 2012. <http://www.telegraph.co.uk/finance/budget/9150406/Budget-2012-UK-companies-are-sitting-on-billions-of-pounds-so-why-arent-they-spending-it.html>

22 This strategic advantage is particularly tenuous as it hinges on popular acceptance of the claim that the state should be handmaiden to corporate business. Critics of neoliberalism and advocates of radical democratization can contest this claim, not only when markets fail to meet needs (e.g. for

housing) but in general. In fact, the neoliberal state subverts democracy. It enables the market and the powerful players within the market, at the expense of all those positioned disadvantageously, and often at the expense of ecological well being.

23 L. Payton, 'Radicals Working Against Oilsands, Ottawa Says', *CBC News*, 9 January, 2012. <http://www.cbc.ca/news/politics/story/2012/01/09/pol-joe-oliver-radical-groups.html>

24 P. O'Neal, 'B.C.-Alberta pipeline dispute: Stephen Harper says science, not politics, will determine route', *The Vancouver Sun*, 8 August 8 2012. <http://www.vancouversun.com/business/energy-resources/Alberta+pipeline+dispute+Stephen+Harper+says/7053256/story.html>

25 The fate of the project is still to be determined. The major provincial parties in BC have expressed opposition to the pipeline, and in August 2012, 59% of citizens in BC were reported to be opposed to the pipeline.

26 B. Jessop, *The Future of the Capitalist State* (Cambridge: Polity, 2002), p. 113.

27 D. Bryan, *The Chase across the Globe: International Accumulation and the Contradictions for Nation States* (Boulder, Colorado: Westview Press, 1995).

28 N. Beams, 'When the Bretton Wood System Collapsed', *World Socialist Web Site,* 2001. <http://www.wsws.org/articles/2001/aug2001/bw-a16.shtml>

29 G. Teeple, *Globalization and the Decline of Social Reform.*

30 L. Medovoi, 'Nation, Globe, Hegemony: Post-Fordist Preconditions of the Transnational Turn in American Studies', *Interventions*, Vol 7, No. 2, (2005), pp. 162-79, p. 169.

31 World Trade Organization, 2012. <http://www.wto.org/index.htm>

32 R. Väyrynen, 'Political Power, Accountability, and Global Governance', (2003). <www.tampereclub.org/e-publications/11Vayrynen.pdf>

33 A. Choudry, D. and Kapoor (eds), *Learning from the Ground Up: Global Perspectives on Social Movements and Knowledge Production,* (London: Palgrave Macmillan, 2010). This critique of NGOs is not intended to be universal. Some NGOs are able to maintain their autonomy and political integrity by accessing resources outside of corporate philanthropy and state funding agencies. Others inhabit the grey zone between autonomy and co-optation.

34 U. Brand, 'Order and Regulation: Global Governance as a Hegemonic Discourse of International Politics?', *Review of International Political Economy*, Vol. 12, No. 1, (2005) pp. 155-76, p. 166.

35 J.B. Foster, and F. Magdoff, *What Every Environmentalist needs to know about Capitalism* (New York: Monthly Review Press, 2011).

10. Reforming Resistance:
Neoliberalism and the Co-option of Civil Society Organisations in Palestine*

Sibille Merz

This article explores the effects of the neoliberal development paradigm on the restructuring of social formations through the external funding and promotion of civil society groups, especially non-governmental organisations (NGOs). It uses the case study of the increasing presence of NGOs in Palestine,[1] more precisely in the West Bank towns of Ramallah and al-Bireh. Based on fieldwork, it argues that neoliberal rationality aims at transforming societies and subjectivities around the notion of 'enterprise' and weakens the collective national resistance movement.

The subject of the international aid regime as well as the role of non-governmental organisations and especially their often depoliticising and de-democratising effects has been researched and criticised by various scholars in the past. Nonetheless, little has been said about the role of NGOs in an explicitly neoliberal development project that aims at the transformation of social relations, general conduct and subjectivities. In a neoliberal rationality, civil society is not - or not only - a philosophical concept and by no means a neutral space between the state and the

---

*   This article is based upon a longer article by Sibille Merz: '"Missionaries of the new era": neoliberalism and NGOs in Palestine', *Race & Class*, vol. 54, no. 1, pp. 50-66.

market but rather the correlate of governmental techniques where many, even though by no means all, international and local NGOs function as handmaiden for or even pioneers of neoliberalism's reformulation of society. The resulting emphasis on individualism as well as the organisation of the social around the notion of 'enterprise' often leads to a further depoliticisation and fragmentation of a society's social relations. In the example of Palestine which serves as a case study here, it has led to the further weakening of the collective resistance movement against the Israeli occupation.

Since the concept of civil society has been rediscovered in the wake of the revolutions against the Stalinist states in Central and Eastern Europe in the 1980s it has become very much a buzzword on the political agenda. While previously it represented a sphere where people, organised in groups and initiatives, could pursue democratic projects in freedom from authoritarian state power in these regions, it has since been massively flattened out and is now commonly perceived by donors as a guarantee for democracy. Together with a few other key terms such as democracy, human rights, participation, self-help and empowerment, it is on the very top of a neoliberal development agenda which, powered by the twin motors of neoliberal economics and liberal democratic theory, sees private agencies and NGOs as main agents for democratisation.

Following the utter failure of the World Bank driven approach of development via Structural Adjustment Programmes (SAPs) in the 1980s and early 1990s, the 1990s and 2000s have brought a shift of the development agenda from mere economic adjustment to a focus on participation, civil society, good governance and poverty reduction. With the expansion of the market into areas that it had previously not encroached upon, this new focus also implied a shift from a 'negative' or conservative neoliberalism which merely aimed to keep the state out of the market, to a more 'positive' or inclusive neoliberalism of empowerment, market enablement, participation and community and NGO partnerships. In development policy, the idea of civil society, mostly reduced to NGOs and aimed at the exclusion of other forms of collective action for the benefit of society as a whole, is closely tied up with the notion of good governance and often equated with political as well as economic liberalisation.

The NGO approach to development is thereby exemplary of this (neo)liberal logic. On the one hand, the needs of marginalised groups are addressed in terms of encouraging self-help or empowerment which reflects the neoliberal dogma of individualising risk and responsibility and fosters the privatisation of social services and institutions. On the other hand, neoliberal thought and policies perfectly exemplify forms of biopolitical[2] governmentality since they aim at governing subjects and the population as a whole through the transformation of general conduct, rationalities, and self-conceptions. As Nicolas Rose and Peter Miller argue, political power in terms of "'political rationalities' and 'technologies of government'... draws attention to the diversity of regulatory mechanisms which seek to give effect to government, and to the particular importance of indirect mechanisms that link the conduct of individuals and organizations to political objectives".[3] Neoliberalism is a paradigm of indirect social control. The neoliberal "self as enterprise highlights... [the] dynamics of control in neoliberal regimes which operate through the organized proliferation of individual difference in an economized matrix."[4] Essentially, neoliberal development discourses and practices attempt to govern "from a distance", from an almost invisible position through localised institutions and practices and the transformation of individual subjectivities into "enterprise men and women".[5]

Nonetheless, it is important to stress that the neoliberal project has been contested since its very emergence. NGOs, citizens' movements, transnational corporations, academia and mass media were turned into accomplices in these new forms of governance, but never completely nor without resistance, slippages or subversion. Many Palestinian NGOs, for example, refused to sign an agreement drafted by an important international donor guaranteeing that the undersigned denounce all forms of terrorism, given that all forms of opposition to the Oslo Process are labelled terrorist, and thus sacrificed potentially vital sources of income.[6]

The emergence of new forms of governance was further intensified and obfuscated by the increasing securitisation of international relations since the Cold War and the so-called war on terror expressed by the idea of development *as* security in the name of opportunity and empowerment. It was down to global security concerns, involving the security of people and the environment besides the security of nation states, that the concept of good governance was introduced into development programmes and governance redefined to involve non-state actors and organisations. As David Craig and Doug Porter explain:

> ... the IMF, all MDBs [Multilateral Development Banks] and multi-/bi-laterals were through 'good governance' able to accomplish the full convergence of risk, crisis and security management, all joined to the adoption of slightly more 'inclusive' neoliberal market reforms by what was seen as the

unassailable 'moral duty to reach the poor and needy'.[7]

This focus on security further exemplifies how development has become a biopolitical security mechanism to contain the marginalised in their peripheral spaces.

In order to produce broad-based consent to these measures the new approach of security through development plus good governance must involve civil society and the private sector. In the case of Palestine, security has always played a key role for international donors' funding conditionalities, and the focus on NGOs represents the attempt to 'pacify' the Arab-Israeli conflict through stimulating civic modes of action. Of course, the containment of Palestinians is additionally massively reinforced by the Israeli occupation and mechanisms of control, especially the separation barrier with all its economic and political restraints.

Hence whilst the support of NGOs represents the inclusive neoliberal approach of framing poverty not in politico-economic terms but as local vulnerability, NGOs can also function as the filters for international political and economic interests trying to produce widespread consent, and the correlate of governmental techniques through disciplining and normatively regulating bodies and societies. Sari Hanafi and Linda Tabar thus observe for the Palestinian case a "displacement of a political mode of action, in the form of mobilization, by a civic mode of action, promoting new subjectivities and a new reflexivity on social norms"[8] in the trajectory of Palestinian civil society organisations.

Palestinian NGOs and the National Resistance Movement

Palestinian non-governmental organisations have historically secured legitimacy and popular support in the absence of a national government and have therefore acted as local political leaders since the military occupation of the West Bank, East Jerusalem and the Gaza Strip in 1967. While secular and religious charitable societies and organisations committed to providing basic social services as well as voluntary work committees have always been relevant in Palestinian society, the development of explicitly political civil society organisations has been triggered by the ongoing occupation and the lack of an officially acknowledged government, which allowed them also to respond to the political needs of the communities.[9] During the 1980s, factionalisation and growing competition between the different initiatives and groups resulted in the institutionalisation of the grassroots movement against the occupation, the formalisation and professionalisation of its executive structures and staff, and to the increasing demand for external funding which led to the establishment of first links to donor NGOs in the global North.

Palestinian NGOs were crucial in organising the population to resist the Israeli occupation. The first *Intifada* (1987-1993) consolidated their roles as local political leaders and reasserted their embeddedness in the local communities. The popular committee structures that had served as the frontline in the first two years of the uprising were made possible by the mobilising and organising skills of the various grassroots organisations. They provided not only the framework and the avant-garde of the uprising, but also formed its source of direction, cohesion and continuity.

However, this heyday of NGOs as pure activists was short-lived and soon to be overshadowed by their increasing 'professionalisation' and the international recognition of their contributions to service delivery accompanied by financial support. The transformation of many of the mass-based national movements into elitist, professional and politically independent NGOs intensified during the Oslo negotiations and the establishment of the Palestinian Authority (PA) in 1994. As the newly founded PA attempted to ensure its legitimacy and control over the political field, it was expected that Palestinian NGOs would engage in the building of a civil society independent of the new interim government. This task was further underlined by the pivotal role played by international support, leading to the dependence of roughly 30 percent of the indigenous NGOs on financial aid in the mid-1990s.[10] This dependence has led to a greater influence of international policy trends on local agendas, which in the 1980s had shifted from 'relief' to 'development' and since the 1990s has focused on the role of private and non-governmental institutions.

This new focus on civil society and NGOs was aimed at ensuring that the Palestinians saw concrete improvements in their daily lives in order to minimise resistance to the peace process. This has left deep marks on the Palestinian civil society sector. One of the most noticeable changes has been a gradual neutralisation of a formerly highly active and political civil society as donor funds to various organisations secured the retrenchment of NGOs from popular support, diminished their mobilising potential and consequently hindered mass mobilisation during the second *Intifada*. This is exemplified by a new focus of many foreign funded Palestinian NGOs on civic education programmes, human rights trainings, awareness raising activities and advocacy work as a result of their entry into complex relations with various international donors.

The outbreak of the *al-Aqsa Intifada* in 2000 clearly exposed a disconnection between the largely professionalised, elitist NGOs and popular, anti-colonial movements in Palestine. The lack of synergy between civil society actors and political forces or the local population dramatically weakened the collective act of resistance against the Israeli occupation, which had metamorphosed into an apartheid regime of checkpoints and permit systems.[11] The NGOs' absence from popular demonstrations, their reluctance to be associated with the popular National and Islamic High Committee (NIHC) as well as their refusal to take a position in the widespread calls for the resignation of Israeli Prime Minister Ariel Sharon exemplified the NGOs' attempts to occupy an apolitical, 'neutral' position in the midst of a national and anti-colonial struggle.[12] Their failure to advance alternative modes of resistance while critiquing the armed struggle left them open to de-legitimisation.

This transformation however was not the product of an internal process but a largely external one, the result of an international aid industry that envisions society as neatly divided into either political or 'civil' spheres. Various Palestinian NGOs have increasingly internalised the (imagined) global aid community's mantra of professionalisation and political neutrality and, as a result, disengaged from the explicitly political, nationalist project. Many other organisations, secular and Islamist, however, opposed such a neutralisation, while others used the opportunity to gain decent and relatively well-paid jobs without giving up their political stand towards the occupation. Most of the Palestinian NGO critics cited in this article are actually affiliated with NGOs as researchers, consultants or project coordinators.

The *al-Aqsa Intifada* nonetheless provides a good example of the absurdity of a vision of society as partitioned into a civil and a political sphere, with no regard to the social reality in Palestine, since it positions the Palestinian NGOs in an antagonistic relationship to the mass-based national struggle. Western donors' conceptualisations of civil society have therefore undermined the stated aim of strengthening Palestinian society and instead contributed to its fragmentation. The international aid regime and the globally popular ideas of individual responsibility, self-empowerment, professionalisation and political neutrality thus increasingly (re-)shape local agendas and power relations.

Neoliberalism, Development and NGOs in Palestine Today

Since 2011, Prime Minister Salam Fayyad's statehood-programme and especially the 2008 Palestinian Reform and Development Plan (PRDP) it incorporates, to promote Palestinian statehood, development and independence, further redefines and diverts the Palestinian liberation struggle. Even though they represent a 'home-grown' approach to development and state-building, they are inspired by a "model of neoliberal governance increasingly widespread in the region, indeed in neocolonial states around the world, but which socially, culturally, and politically remains an alien creation of the Washington-based international financial institutions".[13] Built on the premise that Palestinians have to prove their ability to build a state despite the occupation in order to be well prepared at the time of final status agreements between Israel and the PLO originally scheduled for mid-2011, its architects mainly invest in neoliberal institution building. This will, in effect, increase Palestinian dependence on Israel, further reinforcing the latter's quest for security as it formalises a truncated network of industrial zones entirely dependent on the Israeli infrastructure of control, providing a pool of cheap Palestinian labour to be exploited by Israeli and other capitalist interests in the region. The transformations that Palestinian society is witnessing must be understood in the context of the significant shifts in the Palestinian labour force over the last fifteen years, which have been mainly caused by Israel's refusal to employ Palestinians from Gaza and the West Bank after the second intifada. This has meant that employment by the PA (or NGOs) has become a major means of survival. The likely outcome of the PRDP is even greater economic and political dependence on Israel - and thus, the normalisation of the occupation - and the strengthening of informal economic activities, which has itself become a new target of development, bolstered by micro-credits, technical equipment or managerial training.

Deeply pervaded with this neoliberal rationality, the Plan does not only redefine economic and political but also social structures and relations. Indeed, its success, as well as the long-term goal of the construction of a single neoliberal economic zone across the Middle East which the US envisions, is dependent on a fracturing of the resistance movement, of the national unity and the reshaping of people's self-conceptions as atomised, private individuals working for their own economic success rather than for the collective goal of a wider political liberation. Through the simultaneous maintenance of a semblance of stability and the incentive of personal economic gains, the motivation to resolve the conflict declines. As a Palestinian taxi driver rightfully noted to an Al-Jazeera correspondent: "They want to distract us with roads until our country is gone".[14]

This attempt to manufacture a consensus on national and individual goals, i.e. freedom, individualism, consumption, choice, responsibility and competition, is, needless to say, conducted via an increased focus on civil society organisations, especially NGOs. Further consolidating the international financial institutions' role in this regard, the Palestinian NGO Development Centre, for example, has received a ten million US-Dollar grant from the World Bank to implement a third phase of the Palestinian NGO Project which is directed towards improving the effectiveness, self-reliance and sustainability of the Palestinian NGO sector.

According to the parameters of the neoliberal development agenda, the buzzwords of democratisation, community participation and grassroots mobilisation have thereby made it into most of the Palestinian NGOs' funding applications and project descriptions. The community's role in the decision-making process and a deep connection to the 'grassroots' has to be ensured in order to secure international funding. Yet, in contrast to the international donors' democratising aspirations, the various studies on the de-democratising effects of the "NGOisation of Palestinian social movements"[15] have shown that international donors largely ignore popular committees, trade unions or political councils and prefer working with NGOs that are trained in writing applications, managing large grants and setting up glittery websites. Standardising, bureaucratising and normalising goals and forms of action contribute to the displacement of explicitly *political* in favour of *civic* modes of action.

Changing NGO Agendas: A Case Study

As my ethnographic fieldwork[16] in the West Bank has shown, in hardly any of the project proposals by the Palestinian NGO (PNGO) was any community representative involved nor was there any assessment of the respective community's needs. Rather, the responsible employees of the PNGO thought about what would sound most attractive in a proposal for international donors. 'Youth' and 'women' therefore seemed to be the most lucrative target groups, and their 'participation' and 'empowerment', in the form of drawing contests, was included as a remunerative project aim. The two Western European interns' experiences in proposal writing were thereby seen as authoritative and most auspicious for attracting donor funding, despite their lack of deep knowledge of the Palestinian context. A one-size-fits-all approach according to globally standardised models, discursively homogenising 'underdeveloped' regions, is apparently more beneficial than knowledge about the 'facts on the ground'. As a result there has never been an attempt to assess the gender relations that were apparently in need of intervention, nor the local youth's actual concerns. Thus the generation of ideas or the development of proposals for new activities seldom occurred through meetings with the local population, and if it did it was only with its - mostly male - leaders, rather than via a representative survey evaluating the current requirements of the community.

For example, in a meeting with a German donor, the director of the PNGO was told that the donor attaches great importance to the promotion of women's rights and the enforcement of gender equality. While this reflects Kanishka Goonewardena and Katharine N. Rankin's statement that the significance of gender equality is even more insisted on "when the Empire embarks on the Middle East",[17] it also demonstrates the scale Palestinian NGOs are supposed to fulfil the donor's expectations: while the organisation had not had a special focus on women's rights and sees much larger gender inequalities in the urban middle-classes than in the more traditional countryside which the German donors wished to target, the director affirmed their request and emphasised the PNGO's explicit commitment to women's equality. This illustrates how the donor's agenda and not the actual needs of the respective community shapes local organisations' projects, leading to a further alienation of people from many established NGOs. In an informal talk, a young Palestinian activist explained that:

> the NGOs especially in Ramallah appropriate the normative power to define our struggles. They mainly work for global capitalism and the ruling classes, sometimes for the PA, and legitimise the Israeli occupation but pretend they contribute to our national liberation. I wish there were no NGOs here. Then there would be truly political resistance (an architect and activist living in Ramallah).

Asked for her opinion on the large presence of international and foreign funded NGOs in Ramallah, a Palestinian-American student active in the Boycott, Divestment and Sanctions Movement (BDS) in the US similarly stated that "they all mainly engage in normalisation work and try to spread consent on giving up resistance, just as Israel and the US want them to" (a student and researcher from Washington).

Furthermore, despite their emphasis on 'promoting democracy', Western donors sharply limited their aid expenditures after Hamas had been democratically elected and secured a majority within the Palestinian Legislative Council (PLC) in 2006. This refusal of any contact with Islamist organisations such as Hizbollah or Hamas while at the same time calling for democracy and free elections has been characteristic especially of the US-American stand towards democracy in the Middle East in recent years and is also reflected in the donors' funding conditions. The PNGO has, consciously or subconsciously, internalised this mantra of secularisation and the de-radicalisation of religio-political movements and is increasingly committed to promoting religious tolerance and secularism. Their projects are shaped through an explicitly anti-Islamist lens in which forms of organisation, collectivity or political action not defined by secular norms are at best ignored, and at worst made the target of an education or de-radicalisation project. For example, the tolerance and human rights programme, conforming to its self-definition, focuses on trying to reform religious ideology by emphasising connections between religious thought and human rights. As Nasser, one of their employees, explained, every criticism of Israel in a project proposal lessened the chance to receive funding, despite the fact that religious and political factionalisation and radicalisation are fuelled by the Israeli occupation, the ongoing forced eviction of people from their lands and the daily discrimination of Palestinians by Israeli soldiers.

Not only does this exclude large segments of society as potential target groups or partner organisations but also it reflects the international agenda to refuse support to Islamic or Islamist groups and parties, or indeed to anything related to Islam, no matter its deep roots in society. Leone gives the example of a Palestinian NGO she worked with which had developed a project with the women of the community about the rule of law aiming at supporting women in learning what elements of Islamic law are supportive of their own rights. However, the international donor they had approached made it clear that one could only propose topics in civil law, no matter which law is actually locally prevalent. "Anything related to Islamic law, she [the USAID officer] said, would not be considered".[18]

Hence far from implementing projects with a strong connection to the grassroots, strengthening participatory development and democratisation, the daily work of many NGOs is dominated by donor-driven agendas and the implementation of an international neoliberal agenda that supports institutions and rules which provide the framework for the conduct of public and private businesses. Despite donors' explicit aim of democratisation, democracy is only desirable if certain groups that would threaten the neoliberal, imperial project in the region, such as Islamist movements, remain excluded. Formerly popular civil society and community organisations are often re-organised hierarchically and played off against each other in the competition for funding, driving a wedge between Palestinian institutions and dismantling social cohesion. NGOs are co-opted, turned into consensual governing partners and serve or even actively promote the neoliberal agenda of privatisation and deregulation. Disseminating values and concepts like good governance and democracy skills has thereby become a means of redirecting the focus of the NGOs toward implementing universalised standards of behaviour and away from active political resistance.

Secondly, the main focus of the PNGO on human rights, tolerance and diversity, all catchphrases on the current development agenda, also exemplifies the organisations', and their donors', depoliticised approach to development, since these concepts cover up current power asymmetries and sources of social injustice such as political and economic restrictions caused by the Israeli occupation. The idea of human rights, for example, seen in narrowly humanitarian terms of merely preventing suffering, has been shown to implicitly or explicitly prevent the formation of a collective political project and of real socio-political transformations.[19] The PNGO implements this depoliticised concept of human rights, deemed universal, which has become one of the main pillars of international development aid that often postpones a politico-economic transformation by treating only the symptoms, not the causes of 'poverty' and 'underdevelopment'. This is in spite of the fact that many of its employees believe that "universal human rights declarations cannot contribute to any solution of our struggle and only serve the powerful to reinforce their power" (a PNGO employee). Human rights advocates and NGOs often treat political, economic or colonial conflicts as if they were mere humanitarian crises that can be solved by preventing immediate suffering through the provision of food, shelter or (human) rights. Such humanitarianism "presents itself as something of an anti-politics, a pure defence of the innocent and the powerless against power, a pure defence of the individual against immense and potentially cruel or despotic machineries of culture, state, war, ethnic conflict, tribalism, patriarchy, and other mobilizations or instantiations of collective power against individuals."[20] The concept of human rights thus relies on a violent de-politicisation and victimisation of the subject, a private individual that is, more often than not, a Third World rather than a First World subject as the 'authentic' victim subject. Such a conception of human rights does not only rely on an individualised, atomised notion of the subject but also depoliticises conflicts and 'underdevelopment'.

The PNGO's focus on tolerance and diversity similarly exemplifies a depoliticised approach to development and social justice. Whilst the concept of tolerance is based on the passive acceptance of the (subaltern) 'Other', defined in terms of 'I suffer your presence because I cannot get rid of you', it does not challenge the processes of othering *per se* and thus only targets, like human rights concepts, the symptoms but not the root causes of social injustice. It rather affirms the tolerating subject's powerful position from which it can represent itself as philanthropic and altruistic and hence reproduce itself as the norm. Thus the NGO elite presents itself as part of the international aid regime that sets out to promote plurality and inclusion, plays off different sections of society against each other, and consolidates the construction of a new bourgeois elite. The 'tolerated' Other thereby remains trapped in its 'being-Other'. The PNGO's self-conception clearly expresses this narrow approach as it defines tolerance as the willingness to recognise and respect the beliefs of others and *to allow* others to be different.

A third example of the effects of the aid industry on local NGOs' agendas and hence on social formations and subjectivities in the West Bank is the increasing number of projects on entrepreneurship, business skills, artistic trainings and other projects such as writing proposals or managing funds, thereby contributing to the production of new subjectivities according to a globally standardised model. In this way the idea of training relies on the assumption that the body politic, as well as the individual, can and has to be shaped by various governmental techniques and interventions.

Most of those under the age of thirty in Ramallah who were interviewed for this article had previously participated in at least one workshop or training sponsored by an international, mostly European or US-American organisation. The underlying idea of the subject as both a producer of goods and as a producer of her- or himself clearly originates in the international neoliberal paradigm. Accordingly, one of the most popular forms of training is in entrepreneurship bolstered by the notion, increasingly favoured within development circles, that entrepreneurs make model citizens. This approach reflects the current neoliberal development agenda to attempt to transform subjects into little enterprises and divert their attention away from politics. On the one hand, they aim at transforming subjectivities around the notions of enterprise, consumerism, individualism and freedom; on the other hand they often result in increased economic dependency on international aid, declining voluntarism, and political apathy. A weakening of the collective project of national resistance, 'violent' or 'non-violent', is a likely result of the dissemination of individualistic, profit-oriented and competitive ideas and values.

Similarly, local and international NGOs in Ramallah offer numerous artistic trainings and workshops for aspiring artists, film-makers and musicians in the region. Nearly all of the trainings were short-term, often conducted by a 'generous' foreign artist or trainer flown in for just a few days, and did not result in the establishment of any durable structures such as art or music schools, let alone in regular employment for the participants.

Rather, they are based on the idea of producing human capital and subjectivities which conform to the idea of 'enterprise men and women'. The marketisation and commodification of social relations eventually also encompasses individuals and subjectivities and engenders the biopolitical production of new entrepreneurs in all areas of life. In the case of the arts and music scene in the West Bank, this implies that the young artists are being trained to become or lay bare their human capital, their potential and talent to be commodified, capitalised and sold.

Many of the young artists seem highly critical of these singular events, even though they admitted that they are a good opportunity for them to forge links with the international arts community. One of them, an actor and trainer for theatre and performance also complained about his decreasing income opportunities. Earlier, he explained, he was a freelance instructor working for different theatres and film productions all over the West Bank. Today, theatres and theatre schools do not hire Palestinians any longer but prefer working with foreign funded NGOs which can offer trainings for free. Consequentially, he himself relies on tedious application procedures with NGOs, all requiring English language skills. This is only one of many examples of the NGO sector constantly reproducing itself and penetrating every possible space, physical or imagined, in the West Bank today in order to neutralise and depoliticise behaviour, aspirations and self-conceptions.

Hence with this focus on the production of subjectivities as self-entrepreneurs, the aspired penetration of virtually all space and the consequential dependency of many areas of life on the aid industry, the neoliberal development regime constantly reproduces the conditions for its own intervention and thus secures its own survival. Social formations increasingly disperse through the promotion of neoliberal conceptions of work, life and the subject. The fragmentation of political resistance to the occupation is one among many potential results of these processes: "People are tired, you know. They have been doing politics for all their lives, but now, with the economic boom and all the NGOs offering jobs, they can actually make a living and do not need to care about politics anymore" (a PNGO employee). Also, another PNGO worker, states: "I am not doing this job because I believe in it. It is a good way to make money to survive, but in the long run, all these NGOs destroy the base for a political struggle which is what we actually need". These and other statements provide strong indications that the processes of the NGOisation of Palestinian social movements beginning in the 1990s might even have increased due to the intensification of neoliberal policies and the consequent atomisation, individualisation and depoliticisation of society. In a meeting with political activists who organised demonstrations in the wake of the 63rd anniversary of the *Nakba*, the founding of the State of Israel or the *catastrophe*, for the Palestinians, the participants similarly bemoaned the decreasing willingness of Palestinians inside the West Bank to engage in political demonstrations and direct actions. One of them explained that:

> people have always been afraid, but while they did not have anything to lose before, they are now promised personal economic gains if there is political stability. They are being bought by the government and the United Nations! How can there be stability and peace without justice and our right to return [one of the main claims of the resistance movement that the PA has abandoned]?

Repression, fear, exhaustion but also the governmental techniques of the development regime and the perspective of economic rewards in exchange for political rights seem to have further fragmented the resistance movement in the urban centres of Ramallah and al-Bireh.

New Forms of Resistance?

While the traditional Palestinian resistance movement has been weakened through the increased influence of international interests and donor money in the West Bank, new forms of opposing the occupation, the deprivation of political rights and the many forms of everyday discrimination have nonetheless emerged. As the large demonstrations at Israel's borders on *Nakba* Day, the 15 May 2011, have shown, Palestinian refugees in Lebanon, Syria and Jordan, indeed across the globe, demand their right to return with all possible insistence. Embedded within a broader anti-imperialist struggle within and outside Palestine and inspired by the revolutions almost everywhere in the Arab world, these newly emerging networks might mark a new era of collective movements. Characterised by their independence from one specific centre, network or individual leadership figure, they cannot easily be closed, manipulated, controlled or co-opted by the regime as could more traditional forms of protest such as leftist movements, Islamic initiatives or labour protests prevalent in the region (which, of course, simultaneously still exist). Together with the popular non-violent initiatives such as the BDS or the Stop the Wall Campaign, they may give rise to a new national collective identity which transcends political cleavages and, surely, will continue to play a significant role in the political processes of the region.

Hence while traditional forms of protests have been repressed by the increasingly authoritarian regime of the PA, redefined due to the lack of international support of armed resistance and transformed through the attempted construction of a neoliberal consent in civil society, these and other new forms of resistance have emerged. Alongside decentralised actions, newly emerging *ad hoc* popular committees, such as the Popular Committee for Ending the Division which contributed to the reconciliation of the political rivals Fatah and Hamas in May 2011, show that the Palestinian struggle is far from co-opted, neutered or depoliticised.

Notes

1   I favour the term 'Palestine' over 'Occupied Palestinian Territories' to highlight Palestine as an entity that is the reference point for its inhabitants and refugees, not just disconnected 'territories' whose inhabitants could live in 'any other Arab country as well', as the Zionist narrative would have it. Nonetheless, my hypothesis cannot be generalised to the situation in the Gaza Strip, but is specific to that in the central West Bank, recently bolstered with massive development and reconstruction aid. Throughout this article, unattributed quotes are taken from the author's research and interview data.

2   The Foucaldian concept of biopolitics or biopower refers to a specific governmental technique which, according to him, emerged at the beginning

of the eighteenth century. In contrast to earlier forms of sovereign government, biopolitical techniques are utilised by emphasis on the protection of life rather than the threat of death. They target the individual body as well as the population, representing "an explosion of numerous and diverse techniques for achieving the subjugations of bodies and the control of populations"; (Foucault 1998: 140) . Today, biopolitics comprises various forms of regulating, managing and normalising the individual body and the body politic as a whole. Ref.: M. Foucault, *The History of Sexuality Vol.1: The Will to Knowledge* (London: Penguin, 1998). See also: M. Foucault, *Security, Territory, Population. Lectures at the College de France 1977-1978* (New York: Palgrave Macmillan, 2009) and M. Foucault, *The Birth of Biopolitcs. Lectures at the College de France 1978-1979* (New York: Palgrave Macmillan, 2008).

3   N. Rose and P. Miller, 'Governing Economic Life', *Economy and Society,* Vol. 19, No. 1 (1990) p. 1.

4   L. McNay, 'Self as enterprise: dilemmas of control and resistance in Foucault's *The Birth of* Biopolitics', *Theory, Culture & Society,* Vol. 2, No. 6 (2009) pp. 55-77, p. 55.

5   T. Mitchell, *Colonising Egypt* (Berkeley and Los Angeles: University of California Press, 1988), p. 28.

6   N. Abdo, 'Imperialism, the State, and NGOs: Middle Eastern Contexts and Contestations', *Comparative Studies of South Asia, Africa and the Middle East,* Vol. 30, No 2 (2010), p. 245.

7   D. Craig and D. Porter, *Development beyond Neoliberalism? Governance, Poverty Reduction and Political Economy* (London and New York: Routledge, 2006), p. 77.

8   Hanafi, Sari and Linda Tabar, *The Emergence of a Palestinian Globalized Elite: Donors, Organizations and Local NGOs* (Jerusalem: Institute for Jerusalem Studies/Muwatin, 2005), p. 30.

9   R. Hammami, 'NGOs: "The Professionalisation of Politics"', *Race and Class* Vol. 37, No. 2 (1995), 51-63, p. 53; and S. A. Shawa, 'NGOs and Civil Society in Palestine: A Comparative Analysis of Four Organization', in *NGOs and Governance in the Arab World,* ed. by Sarah Ben Néfissa, Nabil Abd al-Fattah, Sari Hanafi, and Carlos Milani, (Cairo: The American University in Cairo Press, 2005) p. 210.

10   Shawa, 'NGOs and Civil Society', p. 212.

11   Many Palestinian NGOs used their funds and international recognition gained during the last decade for advocacy, the provision of up-to-date information on Palestinian fatalities and the frequent human rights violations by the Israeli military operations and organised an international protection and solidarity movement. Nonetheless, they did not take any active leadership role, failed in developing non-violent forms of resistance and entirely ignored popular calls for the boycott of Israeli goods. Likewise, they did not use their experience and resources to organise popular committees that would have sustained the socio-economic steadfastness

(*sumoud*) of the population as they did during the first *Intifada*.

12 S. Hanafi and L. Tabar, 'The Intifada and the Aid Industry: the impact of the New Liberal Agenda on the Palestinian NGOs', *Comparative Studies of South Asian and the Middle East,* Vol. 23 Nos 1/2 (2003), pp. 205-214, p. 206.

13 R. Khalidi and S. Sobhi, 'Neoliberalism as Liberation: The Statehood Program and the Remaking of the Palestinian National Movement', *Journal of Palestine Studies* Vol. 40, No. 2 (2011), pp. 6-25, p. 8.

14 N. Odeh, 'Money can't buy you Love', *Al-Jazeera English*, 26 March 2010. <http://blogs.aljazeera.com/blog/middle-east/money-cant-buy-you-love>

15 I. Jad, 'NGOs between buzzwords and social movements', *Development in Practice,* Vol. 17, No.4 (2007), pp. 622-9, p. 622.

16 I spent six weeks in Ramallah and conducted twelve semi-structured interviews, as well as recording numerous impromptu conversations with those I met during my daily work as an intern with a Palestinian NGO and in meetings with foreign donors.

17 K. Goonewardena and K. N. Rankin, 'The desire called civil society: a contribution to the critique of a bourgeois category', *Planning Theory,* Vol. 3, No. 2 (2004), pp. 117-49, p. 132.

18 A. Leone, 'International development assistance and the effects on Palestinian community mobilization', unpublished MA thesis (Centre for Arab Studies, Georgetown University, Washington, 2010), p. 34.

19 Žižek, Slavoj, 'Against Human Rights', New Left Review, Vol. 34 (2005), 115-131; Douzinas, Costas, *Human Rights and Empire: The Political Philosophy of Cosmopolitanism* (London: Routledge-Cavendish, 2007).

20 Brown, '"The Most We Can Hope For...": Human Rights and the Politics of Fatalism', *The South Atlantic Quarterly,* Vol. 103, Nos 2/3 (2004), pp. 451-463, p. 453.

11. Do Capitalists Fund Revolutions?[*]

Michael Barker

To date capitalists have financially supported two types of revolution: they have funded the neoliberal revolution to "take the risk out of democracy",[1] and they have supported/hijacked popular revolutions (or in some cases manufactured 'revolutions') in countries of geostrategic importance (i.e. in counties where regime change is beneficial to transnational capitalism).[2] The former neoliberal revolution has, of course, been funded by a hoard of right wing philanthropists intent on neutralising progressive forces within society, while the latter 'democratic revolutions' are funded by an assortment of 'bipartisan' quasi-nongovernmental organizations, like the National Endowment for Democracy (NED), and private institutions like George Soros' Open Society Institute.

The underlying mechanisms by which capitalists hijack popular revolutions have been outlined in William I. Robinson's seminal book, *Promoting Polyarchy: Globalization, US Intervention, and Hegemony* (1996), which examines elite interventions in four countries - Chile, Nicaragua, the Philippines, and Haiti.[3] Robinson hypothesized that as a result of the public backlash (in the 1970s) against the US government's repressive and covert foreign policies, foreign policy making elites elected to put a greater emphasis on overt means of overthrowing 'problematic' governments through the strategic manipulation of civil society. In 1984,

---

[*] This article was first published in two parts on *Znet*, 4 and 9 September 2007.
Part One <http://www.zcommunications.org/do-capitalists-fund-revolutions-part-1-of-2-by-michael-barker>
Part Two <http://www.zcommunications.org/do-capitalists-fund-revolutions-by-michael-barker>

this 'democratic' thinking was institutionalised with the creation of the National Endowment for Democracy, an organisation that acts as the coordinating body for better funded 'democracy promoting' organisations like US Agency for International Development and the Central Intelligence Agency. (See also Fisher, Chapters 2 and 20, and Berger, Chapter 18.) Robinson observes that:

> ... the understanding on the part of US policymakers that power ultimately rests in civil society, and that state power is intimately linked to a given correlation of forces in civil society, has helped shape the contours of the new political intervention. Unlike earlier interventionism, the new intervention focuses much more intensely on civil society itself, in contrast to formal government structures, in intervened countries. The purpose of 'democracy promotion' is not to suppress but to penetrate and conquer civil society in intervened countries, that is, the complex of 'private' organizations such as political parties, trade unions, the media, and so forth, and *from therein*, integrate subordinate classes and national groups into a hegemonic transnational social order... This function of civil society as an arena for exercising domination runs counter to conventional (particularly pluralist) thinking on the matter, which holds that civil society is a buffer between state domination and groups in society, and that class and group domination is diluted as civil society develops.[4]

Thus it is not too surprising that Robinson should conclude that the primary goal of 'democracy promoting' groups, like the NED, is the promotion of polyarchy or low-intensity democracy over more substantive forms of democratic governance.[5] Here it is useful to turn to Barry Gills, Joen Rocamora, and Richard Wilson's work which provides a useful description of low-intensity democracy, they observe that:

> Low Intensity Democracy is designed to promote stability. However, it is usually accompanied by neoliberal economic policies to restore economic growth. This usually accentuates economic hardship for the less privileged and deepens the short-term structural effects of economic crisis as the economy opens further to the competitive winds of the world market and global capital. The pains of economic adjustment are supposed to be temporary, preparing the

society to proceed to a higher stage of development. The temporary economic suffering of the majority is further supposed to be balanced by the benefits of a freer democratic political culture. But unfortunately for them, the poor and dispossessed cannot eat votes! In such circumstances, Low Intensity Democracy may 'work' in the short term, primarily as a strategy to reduce political tension, but is fragile in the long term, due to its inability to redress fundamental political and economic problems.[6]

So while capitalists appear happy to fund the neoliberal 'revolution', or geostrategic revolutions that promote low-intensity democracy, the one revolution that capitalists will not bankroll will be the revolution at home, that is, here in our Western (low-intensity) democracies: a point that is forcefully argued in INCITE! Women of Color Against Violence's book *The Revolution Will Not Be Funded*. Of course, liberal-minded capitalists do support efforts to 'depose' radical neoconservatives, as demonstrated by liberal attempts to oust Bush's regime by the Soros-backed Americans Coming Together coalition.[7] But as in NED-backed strategic 'revolutions,' the results of such campaigns are only ever likely to promote low-intensity democracy, thereby ensuring the replacement of one (business-led) elite with another one (in the US's case with the Democrats).

So the question remains: can progressive activists work towards creating a more equitable (and participatory) world using funding derived from those very groups within society that stand to lose most from such revolutionary changes? The obvious answer to this question is no. Yet, if this is the case, why are so many progressive (sometimes even radical) groups accepting funding from major liberal foundations (which, after all, were created by some of most successful capitalists)?

Several reasons may help explain this contradictory situation. Firstly, it is well known that progressive groups are often underfunded, and their staff overworked, thus there is every likelihood that many groups and activists that receive support from liberal foundations have never even considered the problems associated with such funding.[8] If this is the case then hopefully their exposure to the arguments presented in this article will help more activists begin to rethink their unhealthy relations with their funders.

On the other hand, it seems likely that many progressive groups understand that the broader goals and aspirations of liberal foundations are incompatible with their own more radical visions for the future; yet, despite recognizing this dissonance between their ambitions, it would seem that many progressive organizations believe that they can beat the foundations at their own game and trick them into funding projects that will promote a truly progressive social change. Here it is interesting to note that paradoxically some radical groups do in fact receive funding from liberal foundations. And like those progressive groups that attempt to trick the foundations, many of these groups argue that will take money from anyone willing to give it so long as it comes with no strings attached. These final two positions are held by numerous activist organizations, and are also highly problematic. This is case because if we can agree that it is unlikely that liberal foundations will fund the much needed societal changes that will bring about their own demise, why do they continue funding such progressive activists?

Despite the monumental importance of this question to progressive activists worldwide, judging by the number of articles dealing with it in the alternative media very little importance appears to have been attached to discussing this question and investigating means of cultivating funding sources that are geared towards the promotion of radical social change. Fortunately though, in addition to INCITE!'s aforementioned book, which has helped break the unstated taboo surrounding the discussion of activist funding, another critical exception was provided in the June 2007 edition of the academic journal *Critical Sociology*. The editors of this path breaking issue of *Critical Sociology* don't beat around that bush and point out that:

> The critical study of foundations is not a subfield in any academic discipline; it is not even an organized interdisciplinary grouping. This, along with concerns about personal defunding, limits its output, especially as compared to that of the many well-endowed centers for the uncritical study of foundations.[9]

Despite the dearth of critical inquiry into the historical influence of liberal foundations on the evolution of democracy, in the past few years a handful of books have endeavoured to provide a critical overview of the insidious anti-radicalising activities of liberal philanthropists. Thus the rest of this article will provide a brief review of some of this important work, however, before doing this I will briefly outline what I mean by progressive social change (that is, the type of social change that liberal foundations are loath to fund).

Why Progressive Social Change?

With the growth of popular progressive social movements during the 1960s in the US (and elsewhere), the global populace became increasingly aware of the criminal nature of many of their government's activities (both at home and abroad) which fuelled increasing popular resistance to imperialism. This in turn led influential scholars, working under the remit of the Trilateral Commission (a group founded by liberal philanthropists, see note 53), to controversially conclude (in 1975) that the increasing radicalism of the world's citizens stemmed from an "excess of democracy" which could only be quelled "by a greater degree of moderation in democracy".[10] This elitist diagnosis makes sense when one considers Carole Pateman's observation that the dominant political and economic elites in the US posited that true democracy rested "not on the participation of the people, but on their nonparticipation."[11] However, contrary to the Trilateral Commission's desire to promote low-intensity democracy on a global scale, Gills, Rocamora, and Wilson suggest that:

> Democracy requires more than mere maintenance of formal 'liberties'. [In fact, they argue that t]he only way to advance democracy in the Third World , or anywhere else, is to increase the democratic content of formal democratic institutions through profound social reform. Without substantial social reform and redistribution of economic assets, representative institutions - no matter how 'democratic' in form - will simply mirror the undemocratic power relations of society. Democracy requires a change in the balance of forces in society. Concentration of economic power in the hands of a small elite is a structural obstacle to democracy. It must be displaced if democracy is to emerge.[12]

In essence, one of the most important steps activists can take to help bring about truly progressive social change is to encourage the development of a politically active citizenry - that is, a public that participates in democratic processes, but not necessarily those promoted by the government. Furthermore, it is also vitally important that groups promoting more participatory forms of democracy do so in a manner consistent with the participatory principles they believe in.[13]

Michael Albert is an influential theorist of progressive politics, and he has written at (inspiring) length about transitionary strategies for promoting participatory democracy in both his classic book *Parecon: Life After Capitalism*, and more recently in *Realizing Hope: Life Beyond Capitalism*. Simply put, Albert observes that: "A truly democratic community insures that the general public has the opportunity for meaningful and constructive participation in the formation of social policy." However, there is no single answer to determining the best way of creating a participatory society, and so he rightly notes that Parecon (which is short for participatory economics) "doesn't itself answer visionary questions bearing on race, gender, polity, and other social concerns, [but] it is at least compatible with and even, in some cases, perhaps necessary for, doing so."[14]

Finally, I would argue that in order to move towards a new participatory world order it is vitally important that progressive activists engage in radical critiques of society. Undertaking such radical actions may be problematic for some activists, because unfortunately the word radical is often used by the corporate media as a derogatory term for all manner of activists (whether they are radical or not). Yet this hijacking of the term perhaps makes it an even more crucial take that progressives work to reclaim this word as their own, so they can inject it back into their own work and analyses. Indeed, Robert Jensen's excellent book *Writing Dissent: Taking Radical Ideas from the Margins to the Mainstream* reminds us that:

> ... the origins of the word - radical, [comes] from the Latin *radicalis*, meaning 'root.' Radical analysis goes to the root of an issue or problem. Typically that means that while challenging the specific manifestations of a problem, radicals also analyse the ideological and institutional components as well as challenge the unstated assumptions and conventional wisdom that obscure the deeper roots. Often it means realizing that what is taken as an aberration or deviation from a system is actually the predictable and/or intended result of a system.[15]

The Liberal Foundations of Social Change

Now that I have briefly outlined why progressive social change is so important, it is useful to examine why liberal philanthropy - which has been institutionalised within liberal foundations - arose in the first place. Here it is useful to quote Nicolas Guilhot who neatly outlines the ideological reasons lying behind liberal philanthropy. He observes that in the face of the violent labor wars of the late 19th century that "directly threatened the economic interests of the philanthropists", liberal philanthropists realized:

> ... that social reform was unavoidable, [and instead] chose to invest in the definition and scientific treatment of the 'social questions' of their time: urbanization, education, housing, public hygiene, the 'Negro problem,' etc. Far from being resistant to social change, the philanthropists promoted reformist solutions that did not threaten the capitalistic nature of the social order but constituted a 'private alternative to socialism'.[16]

Andrea Smith notes that:

> From their inception, [liberal] foundations focused on research and dissemination of information designed ostensibly to ameliorate social issues-in a manner, however, that did not challenge capitalism. For instance, in 1913, miners went on strike against Colorado Fuel and Iron, an enterprise of which 40 percent was owned by Rockefeller. Eventually, this strike erupted into open warfare, with the militia murdering several strikers during the Ludlow Massacre of April 20, 1914. During that same time, Jerome Greene, the Rockefeller Foundation secretary, identified research and information to quiet social and political unrest as a foundation priority. The rationale behind this strategy was that while individual workers deserved social relief, organized workers in the form of unions were a threat to society. So the Rockefeller Foundation heavily advertised its relief work for individual workers while at the same time promoting a pro-Rockefeller spin to the massacre.[17]

Writing in 1966, Carroll Quigley - who happened to be one of Bill Clinton's mentors[18] - elaborates on the motivations driving the philanthropic colonisation of progressive social change:

> More than fifty years ago [circa 1914] the Morgan firm decided to infiltrate the Left-wing political movements in the United States. This was relatively easy to do, since these groups were starved for funds and eager for a voice to reach

the people. Wall Street supplied both. The purpose was not to destroy, dominate, or take over but was really threefold: (1) to keep informed about the thinking of Left-wing or liberal groups; (2) to provide them with a mouthpiece so that they could 'blow off steam,' and (3) to have a final veto on their publicity and possibly on their actions, if they ever went 'radical.' There was nothing really new about this decision, since other financiers had talked about it and even attempted it earlier. What made it decisively important this time was the combination of its adoption by the dominant Wall Street financier, at a time when tax policy was driving all financiers to seek tax-exempt refuges for their fortunes, and at a time when the ultimate in Left-wing radicalism was about to appear under the banner of the Third International.[19]

One of the most important books exploring the detrimental influence of liberal foundations on social change was Robert Arnove's *Philanthropy and Cultural Imperialism*. In the introduction to this edited collection Arnove notes that:

A central thesis [of this book] is that foundations like Carnegie, Rockefeller, and Ford have a corrosive influence on a democratic society; they represent relatively unregulated and unaccountable concentrations of power and wealth which buy talent, promote causes, and, in effect, establish an agenda of what merits society's attention. They serve as 'cooling-out' agencies, delaying and preventing more radical, structural change. They help maintain an economic and political order, international in scope, which benefits the ruling-class interests of philanthropists and philanthropoids - a system which, as the various chapters document, has worked against the interests of minorities, the working class, and peoples.[20]

With the aid of Nadine Pinede, Arnove recently updated this critique noting that, while the Carnegie, Rockefeller, and Ford foundations' "are considered to be among the most progressive in the sense of being forward looking and reform-minded", they are also "among the most controversial and influential of all the foundations".[21] Indeed, as Edward H. Berman demonstrated in his book, *The Influence of the Carnegie, Ford, and Rockefeller Foundations on American Foreign Policy: The Ideology of*

Philanthropy,[22] the activities of all three of these foundations are closely entwined with those of US foreign policy elites. This subject has also been covered in some depth in Frances Stonor Saunders book *Who Paid the Piper?: CIA and the Cultural Cold War.* She notes that:

> During the height of the Cold War, the government committed vast resources to a secret programme of cultural propaganda in western Europe. A central feature of this programme was to advance the claim that it did not exist. It was managed, in great secrecy, by America's espionage arm, the Central Intelligence Agency. The centrepiece of this covert campaign was the Congress for Cultural Freedom [which received massive support from the Ford Foundation and was] run by CIA agent Michael Josselson from 1950 till 1967. Its achievements - not least its duration - were considerable. At its peak, the Congress for Cultural Freedom had offices in thirty-five countries, employed dozens of personnel, published over twenty prestige magazines, held art exhibitions, owned a news and features service, organized high-profile international conferences, and rewarded musicians and artists with prizes and public performances. Its mission was to nudge the intelligentsia of western Europe away from its lingering fascination with Marxism and Communism towards a view more accommodating of 'the American way.'[23]

So given the elitist history of liberal foundations it is not surprising that Arnove and Pinede note that although the Carnegie, Rockefeller, and Ford foundations' "claim to attack the root causes of the ills of humanity, they essentially engage in ameliorative practices to maintain social and economic systems that generate the very inequalities and injustices they wish to correct."[24] Indeed they conclude that although the past few decades these foundations have adopted a "more progressive, if not radical, rhetoric and approaches to community building" that gives a "voice to those who have been disadvantaged by the workings of an increasingly global capitalist economy, they remain ultimately elitist and technocratic institutions."[25]

Based on the knowledge of these critiques, it is then supremely ironic that progressive activists tend to underestimate the influence of liberal philanthropists, while simultaneously acknowledging the fundamental role played by conservative philanthropists in promoting neoliberal policies. Indeed, contrary to popular beliefs amongst progressives, much evidence supports the contention that liberal philanthropists and their foundations have been very influential in shaping the contours of American (and global) civil society, actively influencing social change through a process alternatively referred to as either channelling[26] or co-option.[27]

> Co-optation [being] a process through which the policy orientations of leaders are influenced and their organizational activities channeled. It blends the leader's interests with those of an external organization. In the process, ethnic leaders and their organizations become active in the state-run interorganizational system; they become participants in the decision-making process as advisors or committee members. By becoming somewhat of an insider the co-opted leader is likely to identify with the organization and its objectives. The leader's point of view is shaped through the personal ties formed with authorities and functionaries of the external organization.[28]

The critical issue of the cooption of progressive groups by liberal foundations has also been examined in Joan Roelofs seminal book *Foundations and Public Policy: The Mask of Pluralism*.[29] In summary, Roelofs argues that:

> ... the pluralist model of civil society obscures the extensive collaboration among the resource-providing elites and the dependent state of most grassroots organizations. While the latter may negotiate with foundations over details, and even win some concessions, capitalist hegemony (including its imperial prerequisites) cannot be questioned without severe organizational penalties. By and large, it is the funders who are calling the tune. This would be more obvious if there were sufficient publicized investigations of this vast and important domain. That the subject is 'off-limits' for both academics and journalists is compelling evidence of enormous power.[30]

Defanging the Threat of Civil Rights

The 1960s civil rights movement was the first documented social movement that received substantial financial backing from philanthropic foundations.[31] As might be expected, liberal foundation support went almost entirely to moderate professional movement organizations like, the National Association for the Advancement of Colored People and their Legal Defense and Education Fund, the Urban League, and foundations also helped launch President Kennedy's Voter Education Project.[32] In the last case, foundation support for the Voter Education Project was arranged by the Kennedy administration, who wanted to dissipate black support of sit-in protests while simultaneously obtaining the votes of more African-Americans, a constituency that helped Kennedy win the 1960 election.[33]

One example of the type of indirect pressure facing social movements reliant on foundation support can be seen by examining Martin Luther King, Jr.'s activities as his campaigning became more controversial in the years just prior to his assassination. On 18 February 1967, King held a strategy meeting where he said he wanted to take a more active stance in opposing the Vietnam War: noting that he was willing to break with the Johnson administration even if the Southern Christian Leadership Conference lost some financial support (despite it already being in a weak financial position, with contributions some 40 percent less than the previous year). In this case, it seems, King was referring to the potential loss of foundation support as, after his first speech against the war a week later (on 25 February), he again voiced his concerns that his new position would jeopardize an important Ford Foundation grant.[34]

Thus, by providing selective support of activist groups during the 1960s, liberal foundations promoted such groups' independence from their unpaid constituents working in the grassroots, facilitating movement professionalization and institutionalization. This allowed foundations "to direct dissent into legitimate channels and limit goals to ameliorative rather than radical change",[35] in the process promoting a "narrowing and taming of the potential for broad dissent".[36] Herbert Haines supports this point and argues that the increasing militancy of the Student Non-Violent Coordinating Committee and the Congress for Racial Equality meant most foundation funding was directed to groups who expressed themselves through more moderate actions.[37] He referred to this as the "radical flank effect" - a process which described the way in which funding increased for nonmilitant or moderate groups (reliant on institutional tactics) as confrontational direct action protests increased.[38] As Jack Walker concludes, in his study of the influence of foundations on interest groups, the reasoning behind such an interventionist strategy is simple. He argues that:

[f]oundation officials believed that the long run stability of the representative policy making system could be assured only if legitimate organizational channels could be provided for the frustration and anger being expressed in protests and outbreaks of political violence.[39]

From Apartheid to 'Democracy' and Onwards

Moving to South Africa's transition to 'democracy', Roelofs observes that:

> In the case of South Africa , the challenge for Western elites was to disconnect the socialist and anti-apartheid goals of the African National Congress. Foundations aided in this process, by framing the debate in the United States and by creating civil-rights type NGOs in South Africa . In 1978 the Rockefeller Foundation convened an 11-person Study Commission on US Policy Toward Southern Africa, chaired by Franklin Thomas, President of the Ford Foundation; it also included Alan Pifer, President of the Carnegie Corporation of New York . In Eastern Europe, the 1975 East-West European Security agreement, known as the "Helsinki Accords" prompted the foundations to create Helsinki Watch (now Human Rights Watch), an international NGO for monitoring the agreements; Rockefeller, Ford, and Soros Foundations are prominent supporters.[40]

Roelofs also points out that in addition to coopting social movements, foundations have played an important role in promoting 'identity politics' which has served to promote fragmentation between similarly minded radical social movements.[41] Madonna Thunder Hawk also critiques the narrow scope of most activists work:

> Previously, organizers would lay down their issue when necessary and support another issue. Now, most organizers are very specialized, and cannot do anything unless they have a budget first. More, foundations will often expect organizations to be very specialized and won't fund work that is outside their funding priorities. This reality can limit an organization's ability to be creative and flexible as things change in our society.[42]

Stephanie Guilloud and William Cordery support such ideas, and suggest that activist:

> ... work becomes compartmentalized products, desired or undesired by the foundation market, rated by trends or political relationships rather than depth of work. How often do we hear that 'youth work is hot right now'? Funders determine funding trends, and non-profits develop programs to bend to these requests rather than assess real needs and realistic goals. If we change our 'product' to meet foundation mandates, our organizations might receive additional funding and fiscal security. But more often than not, we have also compromised our vision and betrayed the communities that built us to address specific needs, concerns, and perspectives.[43]

Likewise, Ana Clarissa Rojas Durazo launches a similar broadside against multiculturalism, arguing that:

> The existence of 'special' and 'non-white' programs emerges from the logic of the liberalist project of multiculturalism. While there are clear racial hierarchies structured into organizations, these programs are developed under a multiculturalist model that renders race marginal by heralding the primacy of culture... While culturally specific services and programs might appear to address the injuries of racism, this organizational strategy actually displaces race from the broader analysis effectively ignoring the power structure of white supremacy and the structured subjugation of people of color, which affects countless forms of violence against women. By adding a program ostensibly designed to serve the needs of a given community of color, the larger organization avoids direct accountability to that community. In other words, the organization's own white supremacy remains intact and fundamentally unchallenged, as are the countless forms of violence against women perpetuated by racism.[44]

> ... Thus, 'culturally competent' and/or multicultural organizational structures collude with white supremacy and violence against women of color, namely because this logic enables organizations to dismiss the centrality of

racism in all institutions and organizations in the United States.[45]

World Social Forum: Funders' Call the Tune

As a result of the lack of critical inquiry into the influence of liberal philanthropy on progressive organizations, liberal foundations have quietly insinuated their way into the heart of the global social justice movement, having played a key role in founding the World Social Forum (WSF). Furthermore, it is not surprising that, when critiques of the WSF are made, they tend to be met with a resounding silence by progressive activists and their media (most of which have been founded and funded by liberal foundations, see later).[46]

As the Research Unit for Political Economy astutely observes, the WSF "constitutes an important intervention by foundations in social movements internationally" because (1) many of the NGO's attending the WSF obtain state and/or foundation funding, and (2) "the WSF's material base - the funding for its activity - is heavily dependent on foundations."[47] It is perhaps stating the obvious to note that more attention should be paid to such important critiques; however, if further critical investigations then determined that such claims were unsubstantiated then the WSF could only be strengthened. On the other hand, if activists collectively decided that the receipt of liberal foundation funding is problematic - as happened at the 2004 WSF in Mumbai - then further steps must be immediately taken to address the issue. Yet, as the Research Unit for Political Economy point out, although:

> ... the WSF India committee's decision to disavow funds from certain institutions marked a victory for the critics of the WSF, it did not really resolve the issue. If the organizers disavowed funds from these sources on principle (rather than merely because uncomfortable questions were raised), it is difficult to understand why the prohibition did not extend as well to organizations *funded* by them. This left scope for the WSF to accept funds from organizations funded in turn by Ford. Moreover... the bulk of the WSF's expenses are borne by participating organizations, many of which are in turn funded by Ford and other such 'barred' sources.[48]

Clearly important (and concerning) questions have been raised about the democratic legitimacy of the WSF, but most activists still remain unaware of the existence of such well founded critiques. This is problematic and, as Stephanie Guilloud and William Cordery argue, although fundraising is "an important component of most organizing efforts in the United States", it:

> ... is usually perceived by activists as our nasty compromise within an evil capitalist structure. As long as we relegate fundraising to a dirty chore better handled by grant writers and development directors than organizers, we miss an opportunity to create stepping stones toward community-based economies.[49]

However, as Dylan Rodriguez observes:

> ... when one attempts to engage [in] a critical discussion regarding the political problems of working with these and other foundations, and especially when one is interested in naming them as the gently repressive 'evil' cousins of the more prototypically evil right-wing foundations, the establishment Left becomes profoundly defensive of its financial patrons. I would argue that this is a liberal-progressive vision that marginalizes the radical, revolutionary, and proto-revolutionary forms of activism, insurrection, and resistance that refuse to participate in the [George] Soros charade of 'shared values,' and are uninterested in trying to 'improve the imperfect.' The social truth of the existing society is that it is *based on* the production of massive, unequal, and hierarchically organized disenfranchisement, suffering, and death of those populations who are targeted for containment and political/social liquidation-a violent social order produced under the dictates of 'democracy,' 'peace,' 'security,' and 'justice' that form the *historical and political foundations* of the very same white civil society on which the NPIC [Non-Profit Industrial Complex] Left is based.[50]

Guilloud and Cordery "believe it is better to be dissolved by the community than floated by foundations." Indeed, they go on to correctly state the obvious, by noting that community supported organizations will, by necessity, have to serve the needs of democracy because "[m]embers who contribute to an organization will stop contributing when the work is no longer valuable."[51]

Moving Beyond the Non-Profit Industrial Complex

> People in non-profits are not necessarily consciously thinking that they are 'selling out'. But just by trying to keep funding and pay everyone's salaries, they start to unconsciously limit their imagination of what they *could* do. In addition, the non-profit structure supports a paternalistic relationship in which non-profits from outside our Communities fund their own hand-picked organizers, rather than funding us to do the work ourselves.[52]

Given the historical overview of liberal foundations presented in this article it is uncontroversial to suggest that liberal philanthropists - who also support elite planning groups - will not facilitate the massive radical social changes that will encourage the global adoption of participatory democracy.[53] Taking a global view, James Petras and Henry Veltmeyer argue that most funding "for poverty alleviation through NGOs also has had little positive effect" and:

> On the contrary, foreign aid directed toward NGOs has undermined national decision-making, given that most projects and priorities are set out by the European or US-based NGOs. In addition, NGO projects tend to co-opt local leaders and turn them into functionaries administering local projects that fail to deal with the structural problems and crises of the recipient countries. Worse yet, NGO funding has led to a proliferation of competing groups, which set communities and groups against each other, undermining existing social movements. Rather than compensating for the social damage inflicted by free market policies and conditions of debt bondage, the NGO channelled foreign aid complements the IFIs' [international financial institutions'] neo-liberal agenda.[54]

Referring to the detrimental influence of the liberal philanthropy in the US, Andrea Smith also observes that:

[T]he NPIC [Non-Profit Industrial Complex] contributes to a mode of organizing that is ultimately unsustainable. To radically change society, we must build mass movements that can topple systems of domination, such as capitalism. However, the NPIC encourages us to think of social justice organizing as a career; that is, you do the work if you can get paid for it. However, a mass movement requires the involvement of millions of people, most of whom cannot get paid. By trying to do grassroots organizing through this careerist model, we are essentially asking a few people to work more than full-time to make up for the work that needs to be done by millions.

In addition, the NPIC promotes a social movement culture that is non-collaborative, narrowly focused, and competitive. To retain the support of benefactors, groups must compete with each other for funding by promoting only their own work, whether or not their organizing strategies are successful. This culture prevents activists from having collaborative dialogues where we can honestly share our failures as well as our successes. In addition, after being forced to frame everything we do as a 'success', we become stuck in having to repeat the same strategies because we insisted to funders they were successful, even if they were not. Consequently, we become inflexible rather than fluid and ever changing in our strategies, which is what a movement for social transformation really requires. And as we become more concerned with attracting funders than with organizing mass-based movements, we start niche marketing the work of our organizations.[55]

Amara H. Perez and Sisters in Action for Power also add that:

In addition to the power and influence of foundation funding, the non-profit model itself has contributed to the co-optation of our work and institutionalized a structure that has normalized a corporate culture for the way our work is ultimately carried out.[56]

Fortunately, the answers to the funding problems raised in this article are rather simple. However, given the lack of critical inquiry into the anti-democratic influence of liberal foundations on progressive social change, first and foremost progressive activists need to publicly acknowledge that a problem exists before appropriate solutions can be devised and implemented. Therefore, the first step that I propose needs to be taken by progressive activists is to launch a vibrant public discussion of the broader role of liberal foundations in funding social change - an action that will rely for the most part upon the interest and support of grassroots activists all over the world.

Given the insidious activities of liberal foundations, the "very existence of many social justice organizations has often come to rest more on the effectiveness of professional (and amateur) grant writers than on skilled-much less 'radical' - political educators and organizers".[57] So now more than ever, it is vital that progressive citizens committed to a participatory democracy work to develop alternate funding mechanisms for sustaining grassroots activism so they can break the "insidious cycle of competition and co-optation" set up by liberal foundations and their cohorts.[58] Indeed as Guilloud and Cordery point out, "[d]eveloping a real community-based economic system that redistributes wealth and allows all people to gain access to what they need is essential to complete our vision of a liberated world. Grassroots fundraising strategies are a step in that direction."[59]

Unfortunately, raising awareness of the vexing issues raised in this article may be harder than one might first expect. This is because in some instances the progressive media themselves may be preventing an open discussion of the influence of liberal philanthropy on social change - due to their reliance (or at least good relations) with liberal foundations. So sadly, as Bob Feldman observes, "[w]hen the rare report calls attention to the possibility of foundation influence over the left-wing media or think tanks, a typical attitude is unqualified denial."[60] Feldman concludes:

> ... that organizations and media generally considered left-wing have in recent years received substantial funding from liberal foundations. This information alone is significant, as left activists and scholars are either unaware of or uninterested in examining the nature and consequences of such financing. Furthermore, although a definitive evaluation would require a massive content analysis project, there is much evidence that the funded left has moved towards the mainstream as it has increased its dependence on foundations. This is shown by the 'progressive,' reformist tone of formerly radical organizations; the gradual disappearance of challenges to the economic and political power of corporations or United States militarism and

imperialism; and silence on the relationship of liberal foundations to either politics and culture in general, or to their own organizations. Critiquing right wing foundations, media, and think tanks may be fair game, but to explain our current situation, or to discover what has happened to the left, a more inclusive investigation is needed.[61]

It is clear that the barriers to spreading the word about liberal philanthropy's overt colonization of progressive social change are large but they are certainly not insurmountable to dedicated activists. There are still plenty of alternative media outlets that should be willing to distribute trenchant critiques of liberal philanthropy given persistent pressure from the activist community, while internet blogs can also supplement individual communicative efforts to widen the debate. If activists fail to address the crucial issue of liberal philanthropy now this will no doubt have dire consequences for the future of progressive activism - and democracy more generally - and it is important to recognise that liberal foundations are not all powerful and that the future, as always, lies in our hands and not theirs.

Notes

1   Damien C. Cahill, *The Radical Neo-liberal Movement as a Hegemonic Force in Australia, 1976-1996* (Unpublished PhD Thesis: University of Wollongong, 2004); Alex Carey, *Taking the Risk out of Democracy: Propaganda in the US and Australia* (Sydney, N.S.W.: University of New South Wales Press, 1995); Sally Covington, *Moving a Public Policy Agenda: The Strategic Philanthropy of Conservative Foundations* (Washington, DC: National Committee for Responsive Philanthropy, 1997).
2   Michael Barker, 'Taking the Risk Out of Civil Society: Harnessing Social Movements and Regulating Revolutions', Refereed paper presented to the Australasian Political Studies Association Conference, 25-27 September 2006.
    http://www.newcastle.edu.au/school/ept/politics/apsa/PapersFV/IntRel_IPE/Barker,%20Michael.pdf>.
3   Here it is important to note that in all four countries that Robinson examined, the 'democratic transitions' "were touted by policymakers, and praised by journalists, supportive scholars, and public commentators, as 'success stories' in which the United States broke sharply with earlier support for authoritarianism and dictatorship and contributed in a positive

way to 'democracy,' and therefore as 'models' for future US interventions of this type." William I. Robinson, *Promoting Polyarchy: Globalization, US Intervention, and Hegemony* (Cambridge: Cambridge University Press, 1996), p. 114.

4   Robinson, *Promoting Polyarchy*, pp. 28-9. For related online resources see, William I. Robinson, *A Faustian Bargain: Intervention in the Nicaraguan Elections and American Foreign Policy in the Post-Cold War Era* (Westview Press, 1992), <http://www.soc.ucsb.edu/faculty/robinson/Assets/pdf/faustista.pdf>.

5   However, he does specify that it is important to note that the US "is not acting on behalf of a 'US' elite, but [instead is] playing a leadership role on behalf of an emergent transnational elite"; and that the "impulse to 'promote democracy' " essentially arises from the need "to secure the underlying objective of maintaining essentially undemocratic societies inserted into an unjust international system."Robinson, *Promoting Polyarchy*, pp. 20, 6. Robinson also adds that: "A caveat must be stressed. US preference for polyarchy is a general guideline of post-Cold War foreign policy and not a universal prescription. Policymakers often assess that authoritarian arrangements are best left in place in instances where the establishment of polyarchic systems is an unrealistic, high-risk, or unnecessary undertaking." Robinson, *Promoting Polyarchy*, p. 112.

6   Barry Gills, Joen Rocamora, and Richard Wilson, *Low Intensity Democracy: Political Power in the Order* (London: Pluto Press, 1993), pp. 26-7.

7   Leslie Wayne, 'And for His Next Feat, a Billionaire Sets Sights on Bush', *New York Times*, May 31, 2004.

8   Indeed as INCITE! note in their book *The Revolution Will Not Be Funded*: "We took a stand against state funding since we perceived that antiviolence organizations who had state funding had been co-opted. It never occurred to us to look at foundation funding in the same way. However, in a trip to (funded, ironically, by the Ford Foundation), we met with many non-funded organizations that criticized us for receiving foundation grants. When we saw that groups with much less access to resources were able to do amazing work without funding, we began to question our reliance on foundation grants." Andrea Smith, 'Introduction: The Revolution Will Not Be Funded', In: INCITE! Women of Color Against Violence (eds.) *The Revolution Will Not Be Funded: Beyond The Non-Profit Industrial Complex* (Boston: South End Press, 2007), p. 1.

9   Annon, 'Note on this Special Issue of Critical Sociology', *Critical Sociology*, 33 (2007), p. 387.

10 Crozier, M., S. P. Huntington and J. Watanuki, *The Crisis of Democracy: Report on the Governability of Democracies to the Trilateral Commission* (New York: New York University Press, 1975), p. 134.

11 Carole Pateman, 'The Civic Culture: A Philosophical Critique', In: G. A. Almond and (eds.) *The Civic Culture: A Philosophical Critique* (Newbury Park, Calif.: Sage Publications, 1989), p. 79.

12 Gills, Rocamora, and Wilson, *Low Intensity Democracy*, p. 29.

13 For a major critique of 'progressive' activism in the US see Dana Fisher's
    *Activism, Inc.: How the Outsourcing of Grassroots Campaigns Is Strangling
    Progressive Politics in America*, (Stanford: Stanford University Press, 2006).
    Similarly, also see my article 'Hijacking Human Rights: A Critical
    Examination of Human Rights Watch's Branch and their Links to the
    'Democracy' Establishment', *Znet*, 3 August 2007.
    <http://www.zmag.org/content/showarticle.cfm?ItemID=13436 >

14 Michael Albert, *Realizing Hope: Life Beyond Capitalism* (London: Zed Books,
    2006), pp. 24, 185.

15 Robert Jensen, *Writing Dissent: Taking Radical Ideas from the Margins to the
    Mainstream* (New York: Peter Lang, 2004), p. 7.

16 Nicolas Guilhot, 'Reforming the World: George Soros, Global Capitalism and
    the Philanthropic Management of the Social Sciences', *Critical Sociology*,
    Volume 33, Number 3, 2007, pp. 451-2.

17 Andrea Smith, 'Introduction: The Revolution Will Not Be Funded', p. 4.

18 Daniel Brandt, 'Clinton, Quigley, and Conspiracy: What's going on here?'
    NameBase NewsLine, No. 1 (April-June 1993).
    <http://www.namebase.org/news01.html>

19 Carroll Quigley, *Tragedy and Hope: A History of the World in Our Time* (New
    York: Macmillan, 1966), p. 938.

20 Robert F. Arnove, 'Introduction', In: Robert F. Arnove, (ed.), *Philanthropy and
    Cultural Imperialism: The Foundations at Home and Abroad* (Boston, Mass.: G.K.
    Hall, 1980), p. 1.

21 Robert Arnove and Nadine Pinede, 'Revisiting the "Big Three" Foundations',
    Critical Sociology, Volume 33, Number 3, 2007, p. 391.

22 Edward H. Berman, *The Influence of the Carnegie, Ford, and Rockefeller
    Foundations on American Foreign Policy: The Ideology of Philanthropy* (Albany:
    State University of New York Press, 1983). For excerpts:
    <http://www.icdc.com/%7Epaulwolf/oss/ideologyofphilanthropy.htm>

23 Frances Stonor Saunders, *Who Paid the Piper?: CIA and the Cultural Cold War*
    (London: Granta Books, 1999), p. 1.
    For a useful review of Saunders' book see, James Petras, 'The CIA and the
    Cultural Cold War Revisited', *Monthly Review*, November 1999.
    <http://monthlyreview.org/1999/11/01/the-cia-and-the-cultural-cold-war-
    revisited>
    Also see Hugh Wilford, *The CIA, the British Left, and the Cold War: Calling the
    Tune?* (London: Frank Cass, 2003); and Paul Wolf, 'OSS and the Development
    of Psychological Warfare'.
    <http://www.icdc.com/~paulwolf/oss/foundations.htm>

24 Robert Arnove and Nadine Pinede, 'Revisiting the "Big Three" Foundations',
    p. 393.

25 Robert Arnove and Nadine Pinede, 'Revisiting the "Big Three" Foundations',
    p. 422.

26 Craig J. Jenkins, 'Channeling Social Protest: Foundation Patronage of
     Contemporary Social Movements', In: W. W. Powell and E. S. Clemens, (eds.),
     Private Action and the Public Good (New Haven, CT: Yale University Press,
     1998), pp. 206-216.
27 Robert F. Arnove (ed.), *Philanthropy and Cultural Imperialism*; Donald Fisher,
     'The Role of Philanthropic Foundations in the Reproduction and Production
     of Hegemony: Rockefeller Foundations and the Social Sciences', *Sociology*,
     vol. 17, no. 2 (1983), pp. 206-233; Joan Roelofs, *Foundations and Public Policy:
     The Mask of Pluralism* (Albany: State University of New York Press, 2003).;
     John Wilson, 'Corporatism and the Professionalization of Reform', *Journal of
     Political and Military Sociology*, vol. 11 (1983), pp. 52-68.
     Few researchers would argue that all foundations actively attempt to
     deliberately co-opt all social movements, although the larger ones like the
     Ford and Rockefeller Foundations have certainly successfully done this in
     the past. Craig Jenkins (1998, p. 212) proposes his channeling thesis is more
     appropriate than the cooption model because it: (1) considers "that
     foundation goals are complex, ranging from genuine support of movement
     goals to social control" (a point the co-option thesis also acknowledges), (2)
     identifies the trend towards professionalization (a process also identified by
     the co-option thesis) and (3) this professionalization has led to greater
     mobilizations and successes than would have occurred otherwise. This last
     point is certainly debatable, as the history of social change seems to suggest
     that mass grassroots campaigns have far more progressive influence on
     political institutions than professional advocacy groups.
     Deborah McCarthy (2004, p. 254) suggests that the "social relations"
     approach to grantee/funder relations "presents a dialectical model in which
     both grantees and funders influence each other" as opposed to "the
     channeling and co-optation theories [which she argues] present a one-way
     model in which foundations influence grantees but not the other way
     around." In response, I would argue that it is clear that foundation funding
     is dialectical, and it is important not to write off the work of those she
     presents as "one-way models" because clearly each funding relationship will
     vary from another, and the latter models benefit by incorporating the
     unequal power evident between funders' and grantees. McCarthy (2004, p.
     258) notes that activist/funders often have to trick their foundations to
     support environmental justice projects by using "terminology with issues
     that their foundation's boards and donors already fund." McCarthy
     discusses some ways in which activists and funders' may begin to work
     around three major problems associated with foundation funding of the
     environmental justice movement which are: "programmatic emphases on
     project-specific grants, outcome-specific evaluation criteria, and short-term
     grants" (2004, p. 263). See Deborah McCarthy, 'Environmental Justice
     Grantmaking: Elites and Activists Collaborate to Transform Philanthropy',
     Sociological Inquiry, Vol. 74, No. 2 (2004) pp. 250-270.

28 Raymond Breton, *The Governance of Ethnic Communities: Political Structures and Processes in Canada* (Westport, CT: Greenwood, 1990).

29 Joan Roelofs, *Foundations and Public Policy: The Mask of Pluralism* (Albany: State University of New York Press, 2003). Extracts from this book can be found online <http://www.icdc.com/~paulwolf/oss/maskofpluralism.htm>

30 Joan Roelofs, 'Foundations and Collaboration', *Critical Sociology*, Vol. 33,No. 3 (2007) p. 502. Roelofs' talk, 'The Invisible Hand of Corporate Capitalism' summarises the arguments presented in her book and is available here: <http://www.grassrootspeace.org/edrussell/JoanRoelofs18April07AImedia.mp 3>

31 Foundation funding for social movements was for the most part nonexistent before the 1960s, with foundation grants tending to focus on more general issues like education. By 1970 this had changed and 65 foundations distributed 311 grants to social activists worth around $11 million.

32 Craig J. Jenkins and Craig M. Eckert, 'Channeling Black Insurgency: Elite Patronage and Professional Social Movement Organizations in the Development of the Black Movement', *American Sociological Review*, vol. 51(1986).

33 Craig J. Jenkins, 'Channeling Social Protest: Foundation Patronage of Contemporary Social Movements', p.. 212.

34 David J. Garrow, *Bearing the Cross: Martin Luther King, Jr., and the Southern Christian Leadership Conference* (Random House, 1988), pp. 545-6.

35 Frances B. McCrea and Gerald E. Markle, *Minutes to Midnight: Nuclear Weapons Protest in America* (Newbury Park, Calif.: SAGE, 1989), p. 37.

36 John D. McCarthy, David W. Britt, and Mark Wolfson, 'The Institutional Channeling of Social Movements by the State in the United States', In: L. Kriesberg and M. Spencer (eds.) *Research in Social Movements, Conflicts and Change* (Greenwich, CT.: JAI Press, 1991), pp. 69-70.

37 Herbert H. Haines, *Black Radicals and the Civil Rights Mainstream, 1954-1970* (Knoxville: University of Tennessee Press, 1988), pp. 82-99.

38 Herbert Haines, 'Black Radicalization and the Funding of Civil Rights', *Social Problems*, vol. 32 (1984), pp. 31-43.

39 Jack L. Walker, 'The Origins and Maintenance of Interest Groups in', *American Political Science Review*, vol. 77 (1983) p. 401.

40 Joan Roelofs, 'Foundations and Collaboration', *Critical Sociology*, Vol. 33, No. 3, 2007, p. 497.

41 Joan Roelofs, *Foundations and Public Policy*, p. 44. For more on this subject see David Rieff, 'Multiculturalism's Silent Partner', *Harper's*, August 1993, pp. 62-72.
Alisa Bierria (2007) points out that: "All too often, inclusivity has come to mean that we start with an organizing model developed with white, middle-class people in mind, and then simply add a multicultural component to it. We should *include* as many voices as possible, without asking what exactly are we being included in? However, as Kimberle Crenshaw has noted, 'it is

not enough to be sensitive to difference, we must ask what difference the difference makes. That is, instead of saying, how can we *include* women of color, women with disabilities, etc., we must ask, what would our analysis and organizing practice look like if we centered them in it? By following a politics of re-centering rather than inclusion, we often find that we see the issue differently, not just for the group in question, but everyone.'" Alisa Bierria, 'Communities against rape and abuse (CARA)', In: INCITE! Women of Color Against Violence (eds.) *The Revolution Will Not Be Funded: Beyond The Non-Profit Industrial Complex* (Boston: South End Press, 2007), pp. 153-4.

42 Madonna Thunder Hawk, 'Native Organizing Before the Non-Profit Industrial Complex', In: INCITE! Women of Color Against Violence (eds.) *The Revolution Will Not Be Funded: Beyond The Non-Profit Industrial Complex* (Boston: South End Press, 2007), p. 106.

43 Stephanie Guilloud and William Cordery, 'Fundraising is Not a Dirty Word', In: INCITE! Women of Color Against Violence (eds.) *The Revolution Will Not Be Funded: Beyond The Non-Profit Industrial Complex* (Boston: South End Press, 2007), p. 108.

44 Ana Clarissa Rojas Durazo, '"we were never meant to survive" Fighting Violence Against Women and the Forth World War', In: INCITE! Women of Color Against Violence (eds.) *The Revolution Will Not Be Funded: Beyond The Non-Profit Industrial Complex* (Boston: South End Press, 2007), pp. 115-6.

45 Ibid., p. 116.

46 Michael Barker, 'The Liberal Foundations of Media Reform? Creating Sustainable Funding Opportunities for Radical Media Reform', Global Media (Submitted); Bob Feldman, 'Report from the Field: Left Media and Left Think Tanks - Foundation-Managed Protest?', *Critical Sociology,* 33 (2007).

47 Research Unit for Political Economy, 'Foundations and Mass Movements: The Case of the World Social Forum', *Critical Sociology*, 33 (3), 2007, p. 506.

48 Ibid., pp. 529-30.

49 Stephanie Guilloud and William Cordery, 'Fundraising is Not a Dirty Word', p. 107.

50 Dylan Rodriguez, 'The Political Logic of the Non-Profit Industrial Complex', In: INCITE! Women of Color Against Violence (eds.) *The Revolution Will Not Be Funded: Beyond The Non-Profit Industrial Complex* (Boston: South End Press, 2007), p. 35-6.

51 Stephanie Guilloud and William Cordery, 'Fundraising is Not a Dirty Word', p. 110.

52 Madonna Thunder Hawk, 'Native Organizing Before the *Non-Profit Industrial Complex*', pp. 105-6.

53 Two of the most influential liberal foundations, the Ford Foundation and the Rockefeller Foundation, created and continue to provide substantial financial aid to elite planning groups like the Council on Foreign Relations and the Trilateral Commission. For example, the Ford Foundation's 2006 Annual Report (p. 62) notes that they gave the Council on Foreign Relations a

$200,000 grant "For research, seminars and publications on the role of women in conflict prevention, post-conflict reconstruction and state building." Furthermore, as Roelofs (2003, p. 98-9) notes: "During the North American Free Trade Agreement (NAFTA) debate, the EPI [Economic Policy Institute] (funded by Ford and others) made technical objections to the models supporting the trade agreement. At the same time, a much greater effect was produced by Ford funding to the other side, which included grants to the Institute for International Economics, a think tank that emphasizes the benefits of NAFTA. In addition, "the Ford Foundation also awarded grants to environmental groups and the Southwest Voters Research Institute to convene forums on NAFTA. These resulted in an alliance of 100 Latino organizations and elected officials, called the Latino Consensus on NAFTA, which provided conditional support for the agreement."

Also see Laurence H. Shoup, and William Minter, *Imperial Brain Trust: The Council on Foreign Relations and United States Foreign Policy* (New York: Monthly Review Press, 1977); Holly Sklar, *Trilateralism: The Trilateral Commission and Elite Planning For World Management* (Boston: South End Press, 1980).

54 James Petras and Henry Veltmeyer, 'Age of Reverse Aid: Neo-liberalism as Catalyst of Regression', In: Jan P. Pronk (ed.) *Catalysing Development* (Blackwell Publishers, 2004), pp. 70-1.

55 Andrea Smith, 'Introduction: The Revolution Will Not Be Funded', p. 10.

56 Amara H. Perez, and Sisters in Action for Power, 'Between Radical Theory and Community Praxis: Reflections on Organizing and the Non-Profit Industrial Complex', In: INCITE! Women of Color Against Violence (eds.) *The Revolution Will Not Be Funded: Beyond The Non-Profit Industrial Complex* (Boston: South End Press, 2007), p. 93.

57 Dylan Rodriguez, 'The Political Logic of the Non-Profit Industrial Complex', pp. 35-6.

58 Brian Tokar, *Earth for Sale: Reclaiming Ecology in the Age of Corporate Greenwash* (Boston: South End Press, 1997), p. 214.

59 Stephanie Guilloud and William Cordery, 'Fundraising is Not a Dirty Word', p. 111. Making this transition may be easier than expected, because Rodriguez (2007) suggest that "the ongoing work to maintain and prospect foundation money, combined with administrative obligations and developing infrastructure, was more taxing and exhausting than confronting any institution to fight for a policy change." Dylan Rodriguez, 'The Political Logic of the Non-Profit Industrial Complex', p. 27.

60 Bob Feldman, 'Report from the Field: Left Media and Left Think Tanks - Foundation-Managed Protest?', p. 428.

61 Bob Feldman, 'Report from the Field', p. 445.

12. Strange Contours:
Resistance and the Manipulation of People Power[*]

Edmund Berger

> Without substantial social reform and redistribution of
> economic assets, representative institutions - no matter how
> 'democratic' in form - will simply mirror the undemocratic
> power relations of society. Democracy requires a change in
> the balance of forces in society. Concentration of economic
> power in the hands of a small elite is a structural obstacle to
> democracy. It must be displaced if democracy is to emerge.
>
> > Barry Gills, Joen Rocamora and Richard Wilson[1]

> All reformers, no matter how radical they thought
> themselves to be, could be (and have been) caught up in
> reform structures whose underlying purpose is to reduce the
> inharmonics of the existing social system.
>
> > James Weinstein[2]

Even as attempts to curb protests through evictions and violence are
conducted across the country, the movement is spreading - every day,
more and more flock to their local parks and city centers, rallying under

---

[*]   This article was first published in *Dissident Voice,* 21 December 2011.
<http://dissidentvoice.org/2011/12/strange-contours-resistance-and-the-manipulation-of-people-power/>

the banner of "Occupy!" First it was Occupy Wall Street, a call put out by Adbusters, a quasi-Situationist organization that has been at the forefront of the 'culture jamming' ethos since 1989. From there, it was Occupy Chicago, Occupy Los Angeles, Occupy Boston, Occupy Omaha. The movement has gone global, with protestors catching the *Zeitgeist* in London and Rome. Regionalized discontent led to international solidarity in Greece, as further austerity measures loom on the horizon - imposed by none other than a government that dares to call itself socialist.

The central concept of the OWS movement is populist in nature, harking back to those that resisted capitalism's harsh realities in the earlier parts of the 1900s: there is a major disconnect between the 99% of the population and the 1% that acts as the center of wealth and power. At the core, this division is rooted in Marxist terminology, the proletariat versus the bourgeois and their exploitation. We demand democracy, the multitude is saying, from Lexington, Kentucky to Madrid, Spain. We demand freedom from economic exploitation, freedom from indentured servitude to the moneyed class, freedom to live our lives with a higher degree of autonomy than has been allowed by those who seek to manipulate and oppress for their own material gain. Be they students in the universities, underpaid workers who need government aid to live, or citizens horrified that a piece of every paycheck is going to bail-out reckless firms and to support foreign wars, the multitude is gradually realizing that *they* are the engine of this world, and that it is time for them to sit in the driver seat. But all is not right in the movement. It is in times of unrest and cries to social change that hegemony rears its ugly head. Since time immemorial, overt repression has been swapped for the far more subtle process of assimilation - the system acknowledges its defects, and then harnesses people power and guides it by hand into compromises that leave the primary mechanisms of domination intact. Radical change is exchanged for the more 'mature' approach of working *within* the system. This is a very real threat to the Occupy movement, one that needs to be acknowledged and resisted by any member who truly believes in striving for a better tomorrow.

Egypt: the Inspiration

OWS's genesis lies not just in Adbusters, but in the Spanish Indignants movement, a coalition advocating grassroots democracy in reaction to the impact of the international financial crisis on their nation. Leading the coalition is a group by the name of ¡Democracia Real YA! (Real Democracy NOW!), which called for international solidarity and protests on October 15th. Adbusters responded with a poster portraying a dancer atop the Wall Street bull, and request for people to join together to occupy the 'second capital' of wealth and power in the United States - Wall Street.

¡Democracia Real YA!'s initial inspiration for the international protest was the shocking success of 'Arab Spring',[3] the multi-country revolt that succeeded in toppling one of the world's worst dictators, the US-backed Egyptian president Hosni Mubarak. The opposing coalition, consisting mainly of tech-savy youth organizations such as the Coalition of the Youth of the Revolution and the 6 April Youth Movement, has been a consistent icon and inspiration for the Occupy movement, and rightfully so - it is one of the rare examples of people pushing for social change and *getting it*. So often we see revolt being crushed under the wheels of power, organization shattered, and violence suppressing hope. But even with Egypt, questions must be asked.

Ideological solidarity is giving way now to direct ties being formed between these desperate threads that are disrupting the international order. Egyptian activist Mohammed Ezzeldin gave a rousing speech to protestors in NYC's Washington Square Park, discussing the direct lineage between the two revolts. "I am coming from there - from the Arab Spring. From the Arab Spring to the fall of Wall Street," he said. "From Liberation Square to Washington Square, to the fall of Wall Street and market domination, and capitalist domination."[4]

Wired magazine has also reported that Ahmed Maher, one of the founding members of the 6 April Youth Movement, has traveled from Egypt to Washington D.C.'s McPherson Square to directly interact with the Occupiers there and advise them on courses of action. For sometime now Maher has been communicating with the protestors in the multitude's medium of choice - "We talk on the internet about what happened in Egypt, about our structure, about our organization, how to organize a flash mob, how to organize a sit-in, how to be non-violent with police"[5] - but this will mark the first time that he has come face to face with the people he refers to as his "brothers".

Behind and Below the Masses: the Revolution Factory

The Egyptian revolt, much like its counterparts in Tunisia and Libya, was a direct fall-out from the processes of globalization; namely, the domestic impact of US policies that were driving high the price of essential living commodities. As reported in the McClatchy Newspapers:

> The Fed [Federal Reserve Bank] has been engaged in what economists call 'quantitative easing,' buying U.S. Treasury bonds to attack the threat of deflation - the phenomenon of falling prices across an economy.
>
> Quantitative easing has the effect of raising asset prices, whether they're the prices of stocks or what traders are willing to pay for commodities such as wheat or corn. One of the side effects of this policy is that the dollar weakens against other currencies, and that's helped push up the global prices of commodities.[6]

As the article notes, the Fed's quantitative easing has led to wheat prices rising 70% over the past year, certainly bad news for the country of Egypt, which stands as the US's eight largest export market. With an economy pried open by the International Monetary Fund to a flood of international products under the banner of benevolent 'structural adjustments', the skyrocketing prices in the US means skyrocketing prices in Egypt. With an oppressive leader under the thumb of the United States military, the stage was ripe for revolution. In other words, Egypt, like the other countries involved in 'Arab Spring', was on the surface revolting against domestic policies; at its core; however, the revolt was against the structures of Late Capitalism, the mechanics of what Michael Hardt and Antonio Negri refer to as "Empire" - the international monetary system that is rapidly rendering the concept of the 'nation-state' obsolete.

So Mubarak is toppled and the Egyptian people seemingly liberate themselves. And what is the result? The country comes under the rule of the Supreme Council of the Armed Forces. Led by Mohamed Hussein Tantawi (a man described as "Mubarak's poodle" for his loyalty to the disposed leader[7]) the Council has declared to honor all existing political treaties and agreements, as well as maintaining the neoliberal stance of its predecessor. "We are not moving back to a socialist past," Egypt's temporary government has declared,[8] as the World Bank, the International Finance Corporation, and the European Investment Bank plan to descend upon the country with an "action plan" for foreign investment and "sustainable growth".[9]

Thus, Washington and the IMF's program will go unchanged as it moves from Mubarak's dictatorship to the new parliamentary democracy. How did it happen? How did we get from point A (the masses, infused with revolutionary potential) to point B (a cosmetic facelift of the prevailing economic system)? An analogous situation can be found in South Africa, where the spirit of the revolution was laid down in a document known as the Freedom Charter. In this document we can find declarations such as "the national wealth of our country, the heritage of South Africans, shall be restored to the people... the Banks and monopoly industry shall be transferred to the ownership of the people as a whole."[10] Yet when the dust settled after 1994, a radically different picture emerged: the apartheid-era finance minister, Derek Keyes, remained in his position as head of the South African bank; the ANC signed onto the international General Agreement on Tariffs and Trade; the World Bank was free to impose restrictions on socialized business models; and the IMF exerted authority over the approach to issues such as minimum wage. In the words of one activist, "they never freed us. They only took the chain from around our neck and put it around our ankles."[11]

The dominant system will always resist widespread structural change, and the most common method of doing this is through the power of non-governmental institutions. (See also Merz, Chapter 10, Barker, Chapter 11, Berger, Chapters 18 and 19 and Fisher, Chapter 20.) Foundations constitute a main apparatus of this process - "everything the Foundation did could be regarded as 'making the World safe for capitalism', reducing social tensions by helping to comfort the afflicted, provide safety valves for the angry, and improve the functioning of government," said McGeorge Bundy, the long-time president of the Ford Foundation.[12] There is also the National Endowment for Democracy (NED), a brainchild of the Reagan administration that seeks to provide a capitalist economic framework for developing nations, and ease former left-wing states into a financial and militaristic stance in line with Washington's key values. The NED receives its funding from the State Department through the US Agency for International Development (USAID), and in turn funnels the money into four subsidiary organizations: the National Democratic Institute (NDI), the International Republican Institute (IRI), the Center for International Private Enterprise (CIPE), and the American Center for International Labor Solidarity (Solidarity Center). The NDI and IRI are allied with their respective American political parties, while the CIPE is affiliated with the US Chamber of Commerce. The Solidarity Center, on the other hand, is a program of the AFL-CIO labor union consortium. Other NED funds flow into Freedom House, a US-based human rights organization that has been described as a "Who's Who of neoconservatives from government, business, academia, labor, and the press."[13] American libertarian politician Ron Paul has provided an excellent analysis and critique of the whole 'democracy promoting' apparatus:

> The misnamed National Endowment for Democracy is nothing more than a costly program that takes US taxpayer funds to promote favored politicians and political parties abroad. What the NED does in foreign countries, through its recipient organizations the National Democratic Institute and the International Republican Institute would be rightly illegal in the United States. The NED injects 'soft money' into the domestic elections of foreign countries in favor of one party or the other. Imagine what a couple of hundred thousand dollars will do to assist a politician or political party in a relatively poor country abroad. It is particularly Orwellian to call US manipulation of foreign elections 'promoting democracy.' How would Americans feel if the Chinese arrived with millions of dollars to support certain candidates deemed friendly to China? Would this be viewed as a democratic development?[14]

After playing a role in the 'color revolutions' of Georgia and the Ukraine, the NED's attention then turned to Egypt. (See also Berger, Chapter 19.) A recent *New York Times* article has revealed, citing WikiLeaks cables, that the disparate bands of dissident groups have been receiving "training and financing from groups like the International Republican Institute, the National Democratic Institute, and Freedom House."[15] Verification independent of the *New York Times* article can be found as well. Madeleine Albright, former Clinton-era Secretary of State and chairman of the NDI, appeared on MSNBC's Rachel Maddow Show to give her analysis of the events in Egypt. "You mentioned that I was chairman of the board of the National Democratic Institute," Albright says to Maddow in the interview, responding to the pundit's questions concerning the post-Mubarak government. "We have been working within Egypt for a very long time, in terms of developing various aspects of civil society, and dealing with various and talking to opposition groups who are prepared to participate in a fair and free election."

Freedom House also openly admits their role in fomenting the unrest. In a May 2009 report, the organization discusses their "New Generation Project" within Egypt, seeking to empower the nation's "Youtube generation" by "promoting exchange" between "democracy advocates" and "emerging democracies" to "share best practices," "providing advanced training on civil mobilization" and helping them understand the benefits of 'new media.'[16] In 2008, representatives from the organization attended the Alliance of Youth Movements, an activist summit funded by the State Department, Facebook, MTV, Google, and Youtube to provide a fertile meeting ground for 'digital activists' and the corporate leaders behind 'new media.' The summit has subsequently been the topic of a set of leaked WikiLeaks cables, describing an unnamed activist who presented there "his movement's goals for democratic change in Egypt." This same unnamed activist then met with a series of US Congressmen, discussing with them an "unwritten plan for democratic transition" of Egypt into a parliamentary democracy, a plan that had been accepted by "several opposition parties and movements."[17]

Disturbingly, this is the same milieu that Ahmed Maher, now an adviser to OWS, travelled in. As researcher Tony Cartalucci has reported:

> This of course isn't Maher's first trip to the United States. Years before the Egyptian revolution, the United States was quietly preparing a global army of youth cannon fodder to fuel region wide conflagrations throughout the world, both politically and literally. Maher's April 6 organization had been in New York City for the US State Department's first Alliance for Youth Movements Summit in 2008. His group then traveled to Serbia to train under the US-funded 'CANVAS' organization before returning to Egypt in 2010 with US International Crisis Group (ICG) operative Mohamed ElBaradei to spend the next year building up for the 'Arab Spring'.[18]

CANVAS (Centre for Applied Non Violent Action and Strategies) was founded in 2003 by the Serbian youth organization Otpor! (Resistance!), which utilized nonviolent methods of revolt to bring down Slobodan Milošević. Not surprisingly in the least, the organization had received millions of dollars in funding from both the NED and IRI[19] while CANVAS itself has worked closely with Freedom House.[20] Given the close ties between these youth-based activist organizations and US State Department's bureaucracy, perhaps it is distressing to note that former Otpor! Member and leader of CANVAS, Ivan Marovic, has given talks at the OWS rallies in NYC.[21]

The Right's Favorite Boogeyman – and a Useful Opportunity

Perhaps the centerpiece of the Egyptian Revolution was the individual Mohamed ElBaradei, a director general of the International Atomic Energy Agency and presidential hopeful for Egypt's parliamentary democracy. ElBaradei, however, has ties of his own to suspicious Western interests - he sits on the board of trustees of the International Crisis Group, which has been described by Madeleine Albright as a "full-service conflict prevention organization." Despite this astute observation, the membership rosters of the Crisis Group's various chairmen, trustees, and directors shows a significant overlap with affiliates of the National Endowment for Democracy: Zbigniew Brzezinski, Morton I. Abramowitz, and Stephen Solarz are just a handful of Crisis Group members who represent the interests of both. Here we can find the favorite whipping boy of the right-wing media, the billionaire philanthropist George Soros. Vilified as some sort of a socialist by the likes of Glenn Beck and Michael Savage, Soros, in truth, is far from that sort of ideology. A key figure in the transition of former Soviet states into the world of globalized capitalism, Soros helped engineer the economic 'shock therapy' that thrust Poland into a financial tail spin as extensive structural adjustments rattled the already crumbling economy.[22]

Soros, despite being a clear member of the 1%, has publicly stated his support of OWS:

> Billionaire financier George Soros says he sympathizes with protesters speaking out against corporate greed in ongoing protests on Wall Street... Soros says he understands the frustrations of small business owners, for instance those who have seen credit card charges soar during the current crisis.[23]

There are ties, albeit indirect ones, that can tie Soros to the fledgling Occupy movement. MoveOn.org, a regular recipient of Soros funding, has thrown its weight behind the protestors in an apparent sign of solidarity. As *TruthOut*'s Steve Horn writes:

> On October 5, Day 19 of Occupy Wall Street, MoveOn.org sent out an email calling on clicktivists (as opposed to activists) to 'Join the Virtual March on Wall Street.' "The 99% are both an inspiration and a call that needs to be answered.

So we're answering it today, in a nationwide Virtual March on Wall Street to support their demand for an economy that serves the many, not the few... Join in the virtual march by doing what hundreds have done spontaneously across the web: Take your picture holding a sign that tells your story, along with the words 'I am the 99%,'" wrote Daniel Mintz of MoveOn.org.[24]

MoveOn.org has a long history of left-wing co-option; as people flooded the streets of American cities in protest of the Iraq War, the online institution dove right into the populist fervor and proceeded to utilize people's discontent with the Bush administration to garner support for John Kerry's presidential campaign. The same process was repeated just a handful of years later, with MoveOn.org acting the second largest lobbying organization for Barack Obama (aside from the President's own Organizing for America). Through a strategic ad campaign - one of MoveOn's personnel is John Hlinko, a "social media marketing expert" - the organization managed to create a literal army of voters for Obama, reinforcing that the same "hope and change" imagery that was being pumped out by the campaign itself. Both MoveOn and Organizing America's methodology was a foreshadow to the systems of new media utilized by the Arab Spring protestors; this tool is now being called "netroots," the transporting of traditional grassroots activities into the virtual sphere.

MoveOn.org is not the only group chiming in to support for OWS. Rebuild the Dream, a progressive-style organization founded by former Obama White House adviser Van Jones, has championed the protestors - "Let's all support Occupy Wall St." reads a blurb on their website homepage. During an MSNBC interview, Van Jones directly linked the OWS movement to the Arab Spring, stating "you are going to see an American Fall, an American Autumn, just like we saw the Arab Spring."

However, the institution changes that OWS is calling for contrast sharply with Jones' vision of how to take America back: "We're talking about U.S. senators who want to run as American Dream candidates - soon to be announced. We've reached out to the House Democratic Caucus; there are House members who want to run as American Dream candidates."[25] Simply put, Rebuild the Dream is an unofficial organ of the Democrat Party, much like how MoveOn.org utilized, mobilized anti-war protestors to generate a large sector of the Democrat's voting base. In actuality the ties run closer than that - Jones had worked hand in hand with MoveOn.org to initially launch Rebuild the Dream. Furthermore, he had been a senior fellow at Center for American Progress; the progressive institution has received funding from both George Soros[26] and the Democracy Alliance organization, where Soros sits on the board of directors.

Co-option of social activism has always been the *modus operandi* of the Democrat Party. They play "the role of shock absorber, trying to head off and co-opt restive [and potentially radical] segments of the electorate" by posing as "the party of the people".[27] President Obama, riding the crest of the MoveOn.orgs of the country - and not to mention a well orchestrated propaganda campaign - has fit this concept to a T, something that has even been noted by members of the liberal establishment:

> Two and a half weeks after Obama's victory in the 2008 presidential election, David Rothkopf, a former Clinton administration official, commented on the president-elect's corporatist and militarist transition team and cabinet appointments with a musical analogy. Obama, Rothkopf told the *New York Times*, was following 'the violin model: you hold power with the left hand and you play the music with the right'.[28]

Liberal commentator Thomas Frank has observed the process of "voting for one thing, getting another" at work in the Republican Party:

> The trick never ages; the illusion never wears off. Vote to stop abortion; receive a rollback in capital gains taxes. Vote to make our country strong again, receive deindustrialization... Vote to get governments off our backs; receive conglomeration and monopoly everywhere from media to meatpacking... Vote to strike a blow against elitism; receive a social order in which wealth is more concentrated than ever before in our lifetimes, in which workers have been stripped of power and CEOs are rewarded in a manner beyond imagining.[29]

Is it really any different for the Democrat Party? Vote to end wars, receive troop escalation and change only years after the fact. Vote to allow workers to retain their rights, receive trade agreements that export jobs overseas. Vote to reign in the power of Wall Street, receive taxpayer-funded bail-outs that create moral hazards and prop up corrupt financial regimes. From the left to the right, the story is the same - the great violin keeps playing cheerfully as the world burns. It's only the hands grasping it, not the system that change.

One of the clearest portraits of co-option in recent history would be the history of the conservative Tea Party Movement. In its infancy, the Tea Party was a movement launched by libertarian politician Ron Paul, a staunch opponent of the government's infringement on civil liberties, its use of military force on foreign soil, the monopolization of the financial market by entities such as the Federal Reserve Bank, and the crony capitalism that eventually erupted into the bail-outs. Aside from certain economics view, there is certainly a great deal in Ron Paul's - and the early Tea Party Movement's - agenda that is entirely compatible with the demands of the Occupy Movement; it is for this very reason that libertarians have begun to reach out and join in solidarity with the protestors. Furthermore, given the anti-foreign aid and anti-Federal Reserve stance of the early Tea Party Movement, there can perhaps be observed an unspoken lineage between the Tea Party and the uprisings in Egypt and surrounding countries, triggered by Western support of the people's oppressors and the monetary policies of the Federal Reserve.

Just as Soros controls the purse strings to disrupt and redirect leftist movements into positions aligned with the Democrat Party, the right can find his counterpart in the Koch brothers, the billionaire owners of the little-known Koch Industries. With their money bankrolling organizations such as Americans for Prosperity, David and Charles Koch were able to train torrents of so-called Tea Party activists whose espoused viewpoints far more in line with typical Republican dialogue than with Ron Paul's libertarian ethos. The focus was shifted from attacking the Fed and ending the wars and towards union-busting, securing borders, and more often than not, reinforcing unequivocal US support for Israel - a direct clash with stance that Paul has taken on the topic.

This 'astro-turfing' of grassroots movements, of course, requires multiple organizations and front groups to create the veneer of a unified public opinion, and operating alongside Americans for Prosperity is FreedomWorks. Perhaps it is worthy to take into consideration that when the organization was created from a 2004 merger between the Koch-funded Citizens for a Sound Economy and the neoconservative Empower America, several prominent NED officials sat on the board of directors of the former - including Vin Weber (an adviser to Mitt Romney's ill-fated 2008 presidential campaign), Jeane J. Kirkpatrick (one of the most prominent of Cold War-era hardliners), and Michael Novak (an expert at the neoconservative think-tank American Enterprise Institute).

The Tea Party's assimilation into the broader spectrum of the Republican political arena was marked by the establishment of the Tea

Party Caucus, a coalition of House of Representatives and Senate members that represents perhaps the most powerful political body sitting in the US government - this consortium of leaders are essentially calling the shots when it comes to the right-wing of the American political system. Its members show utter disregard for the original protests of the Tea Party: Louie Gohmert has been a strong and vocal supporter of the war in Iraq, Steve King has openly supported the lobbying industry for their "effective and useful job[s]"[30] and Dennis A. Ross was a member of the United States House Oversight Subcommittee on TARP, Financial Services and Bailouts of Public and Private Programs. Joe Barton eviscerated any ideological tie between himself and the early stages of the movement that he claims to rally behind (not to mention a disregard for any allegiance to the notion of really existing free markets) by arguing that the removal of subsidies to oil companies would act as a 'disincentive' and result in the corporations going out of business.[31]

Curiously, the place where this whole process of right-wing co-option began - the corporate-financed milieu of Americans for Prosperity and FreedomWorks - was intended to be a "powerful answer to the challenge presented by the Left and groups like America Coming Together (ACT), MoveOn.org, and the Media Fund."[32] All three of these organizations are Soros-financed, revealing the hidden irony that ultimately, these seemingly opposing institutions are simply moving potentially disruptive individuals into an entirely compatible paradigm of power that sits in the dual capitals of Washington D.C. and Wall Street. However, this odd dialectic can be entirely useful. Realizing this process will allow individuals who yearn for legitimate change on either side of the aisle to separate themselves from the system, and hopefully, discover the disparate strands that are ideologically compatible between them and their counterparts. It is a rare opportunity for the discontents of 'left' and the 'right' to shake off the labels applied to them and create an open dialogue and eventual solidarity with one another.

Conclusions and Other Thoughts

Though it may certainly seem like it, this essay was not written to belittle the OWS movement, or attack the actions of those who stood in opposition to Milosevic, apartheid, or Mubarak. However, it was my intention to acknowledge the shortcomings in the aftermath of these fights - Serbia and South Africa both jumped into bed with the IMF, imposing austerity measures in their nations that allowed persistent poverty to fester and even continue to grow. Egypt is certainly following suit now, so even though the brutal fist of the American-backed regime is gone, the slow-burning fires of neoliberalism continue to carry on the torch. For Serbia and Egypt, their revolts, though brilliant displays of the potential of people power, were in no small part shaped by the technicians in State Department, operating through the long arm of the NED. For South Africa, money from George Soros ended up in the coffers of activist groups who quickly changed their tune from the ANC's quasi-socialist demands to jump starting South African neoliberalism.[33] Not surprisingly, these same groups showed a willingness to work closely with the NED.[34]

The NED, much like Soros' civil society empowering programs, promotes a little known methodology called low-intensity democracy.

> Low-intensity democracies are limited democracies in that they achieve important political changes, such as the formal reduction of the military's former institutional power or greater individual freedoms, but stop short in addressing the extreme social inequalities within... societies. ... they provide a more transparent and secure environment for the investments of transnational capital... these regimes function as legitimizing institutions for capitalist states, effectively co-opting the social opposition that arises from the destructive consequences of neoliberal austerity, or as Cyrus Vance and Henry Kissinger have argued, the promotion of 'pre-emptive' reform in order to co-opt popular movements that may press for more radical, or even revolutionary, change.[35]

Thus, it can be considered to be worrisome that individuals who were trained under institutions that implement this system are turning up at OWS rallies. While the NED's agenda is to establish low-intensity democracies around the world, this is precisely the type of governance that we are dealing with in the United States, the very system that produced the antagonism found in both the Tea Party and OWS. To consent to it would be a rejection of the spirit of the protest and an embrace of what is opposes.

It is the Democrat Party that could possibly represent this system even more so than the Republicans. It is the party of Social Security, government-provided medical care, and other welfare programs. Does this function of the party not dim and obfuscate the fact that it is also the party of bail-outs and NAFTA? Realizing this simple fact is paramount to creating a movement of legitimate change in the world; we must seek to deconstruct low-intensity democracy and replace it with Really Existing Democracy. We have already seen this functioning in a micro-sense at OWS rallies, where leadership positions are voluntary and voted in by the whole of the people. Decisions are made in a similar matter, putting the course of action and the direction of the movement in its entirety in the hands of the protestors, not in bureaucrats and moneymen with agendas of their own. It is organic and autonomous, and on an international level holds to be what Gilles Deleuze and Félix Guattari referred to as a 'rhizome' - "a nonhierarchal and noncentered network structure".[36]

There are further reasons to be optimistic about the movement's direction. The official OWS website hosts a petition with a "formal demand that MoveOn.org leaves" - "this is OUR movement and it is NOT Obama's personal reelection campaign," it reads.[37] The leftist online newspaper *TruthOut* has called attention to MoveOn.Org and Rebuild the Dream's attempts to cozy up to the protestors, while Michel Chossudovsky, the professor emeritus of the economics department at the University of Ottowa, has published a piece for his Centre for Research on Globalization detailing the arrival of NED associates at OWS rallies.

There is an opportunity here. We live in a time marked by crisis, catastrophe, poverty, and war, but it is in times of disruption like these that rifts open in the landscapes of the global system, providing people with a chance to take the wheel, if they so choose. For America, this time arises from the great disappointments of our so-called democratic process - the hookwinking of the masses by the left-right one-two punch by the back to back presidencies of George W. Bush and Barack H. Obama has led more people to step back, reconsider their presumptions about the world's machinery, and begin to demand that their voices be heard. What happens from here, with the choices marked by the path to liberation or the well-worn roads of hegemony, is entirely contingent on the will of the people.

Notes

1   Barry Gills, Joen Rocamora, and Richard Wilson, *Low Intensity Democracy: Political Power in the New World Order* (London: Pluto Press, 1993), quoted in Michael Barker, '*Do Capitalists Fund Revolutions? (Part 1 of 2)*', Znet, 4 September, 2007, and reprinted in this volume.
<http://www.zcommunications.org/do-capitalists-fund-revolutions-part-1-of-2-by-michael-barker>

2   James Weinstein, *The Corporate Ideal in the Liberal State, 1900-1918* (Boston: Beacon Press, 1968), p. 254, quoted in Michael Barker, 'Liberal Elites and the Pacification of Workers', *State of Nature*, Summer, 2010.
<http://www.stateofnature.org/liberalElitesAnd.html>

3   Lauren Frayer, 'Inspired by Arab Protests, Spain's Unemployed Rally for Change', *Voice of America, 19 May, 2011*.
<http://www.voanews.com/english/news/Inspired-by-Arab-Protests-Spains-Unemployed-Rally-for-Change-122237154.html>

4   Matt Sledge, 'Occupy Wall Street Egyptian Activist Goes 'From Liberation Square To Washington Square', *Huffington Post*, 8 October, 2011.
<http://www.huffingtonpost.com/2011/10/08/occupy-wall-street-washington-square_n_1001775.html>

5   Spencer Ackerman, 'Egypt's Top "Facebook Revolutionary" Now Advising Occupy Wall Street', *Wired*, 18 October, 2011.
<http://www.wired.com/dangerroom/2011/10/egypt-occupy-wall-street/>

6   Kevin G. Hall, 'Egypt's unrest may have roots in food prices, U.S. Fed Policy', *McClatchy Newspapers*, 31 January, 2011.
<http://www.mcclatchydc.com/2011/01/31/107813/egypts-unrest-may-have-roots-in.html>

7   '"Mubarak's Poodle" at Head of Egypt's Transition', *CBS News*, 16 February, 2011.
<http://www.cbsnews.com/stories/2011/02/16/501364/main20032166.shtml>

8   Emad Mekay, 'Egypt takes a step back from IMF ways', *Inter Press Service*, 20 February, 2011. <http://ipsnews.net/news.asp?idnews=54544>

9   'Multilateral banks join forces to aid Arab nations', *Yahoo! News*, 14 April, 2011.
<http://news.yahoo.com/s/afp/20110414/bs_afp/imfworldbankeconomyfinancemideastafrica>

10 Naomi Klein, *The Shock Doctrine: The Rise of Disaster Capitalism* (New York: Picador, 2007), pp. 247-248.

11 Ibid., pp. 256-257.

12 Quoted in Michel Chossudovsky, 'Manufacturing Dissent', *Center for Research on Globalization*, 20 September, 2010.
<http://www.globalresearch.ca/index.php?context=va&aid=21110>

13 Diana Barahona, 'The Freedom House Files', *Monthly Review*, 3 January, 2007.

<http://mrzine.monthlyreview.org/2007/barahona030107.html>

14 Ron Paul, 'National Endowment for Democracy: Paying to Make Enemies of America', 11 October, 2003. <http://www.antiwar.com/paul/paul79.html>

15 Ron Nixon, 'U.S. Groups Helped Nurture Arab Uprisings', *New York Times*, 14 April, 2011. <http://www.nytimes.com/2011/04/15/world/15aid.html?_r=2>

16 Freedom House, 'New Generation of Advocates: Empower Civil Society in Egypt', <http://www.freedomhouse.org/template.cfm?page=66&program=84>

17 'Egypt protests: secret US document discloses support for protesters', *The Telegraph*, 23 April, 2011.
<http://www.telegraph.co.uk/news/worldnews/africaandindianocean/egypt/8 289698/Egypt-protests-secret-US-document-discloses-support-for-protesters.html>

18 Tony Cartalucci, 'US State Department Funded Agitator in DC Advising #OWS', *Land Destroyer Report*, 18 October, 2011.
<http://landdestroyer.blogspot.com/2011/10/us-state-department-funded-agitators-in.htm>

19 Roger Cohen, 'Who Really Brought Down Milosevic?', *New York Times*, 26 November, 2000.
<http://www.nytimes.com/library/magazine/home/20001126mag-serbia.html>

20 Peter Ackerman, 'Skills or Conditions: What Key Factors Shape the Success or Failure of Civil Resistance?', *Conference on Civil Resistance & Power Politics*, St Antony's College, University of Oxford, 15-18 March 2007.
<http://www.nonviolent-conflict.org/PDF/AckermanSkillsOrConditions.pdf>

21 Michel Chossudovsky, 'Occupy Wall Street and "The American Autumn": Is It a "Colored Revolution?", *Centre for Research on Globalization*, 13 October, 2011. <http://www.globalresearch.ca/index.php?context=va&aid=27053>

22 This topic is covered extensively in Klein, *The Shock Doctrine*, pp. 215-229 and pp. 241-243.

23 'George Soros Says He Sympathizes With Occupy Wall Street Protesters', *Huffington Post*, 23 October, 2011.
<http://www.huffingtonpost.com/2011/10/03/george-soros-occupy-wall-street_n_992468.html>

24 Steve Horn, 'MoveOn.Org and Friends Attempt to Co-Opt Occupy Wall Street Movement', *TruthOut, 11 October, 2011. <http://www.truth-out.org/moveonorg-and-friends-attempt-co-opt-occupy-wall-street-movement/1318259708>*

25 Ibid.

26 Laura Blumenfeld 'Soros's Deep Pockets vs. Bush', *Washington Post*, 11 November, 2003. <http://www.washingtonpost.com/ac2/wp-dyn/A24179-2003Nov10?language=printer>

27 Paul Street, 'Obama's Violin: Populist rage and the uncertain containment of change', *Zcommunications,* May 2009.
<http://www.zcommunications.org/obamas-violin-by-paul-street>

28 Ibid.
29 Thomas Frank, *What's the Matter With Kansas? How Conservatives Won the Heart of America (New York:* Henry Holt & Company, 2004), p. 7.
30 Bara Vaida, 'Rep. King: "Lobbyists Are Useful"', *The National Journal's Under the Influence, 1* March, 2010.
    <http://undertheinfluence.nationaljournal.com/2010/03/lobbyists-are-useful-says-rep.php>
31 Brian Beutler, 'Barton: Govt Subsidies Necessary To Keep Exxon From Going Out Of Business', *Talking Points Memo, 10* March, 2011.
    <http://tpmdc.talkingpointsmemo.com/2011/03/barton-free-market-oil-subsidies-necessary-to-keep-exxon-from-going-out-of-business.php>
32 Adam Brandon, 'Citizens for a Sound Economy (CSE) and Empower America Merge to Form FreedomWorks', Media release, 21 July 21, 2004.
    <http://www.freedomworks.org/press-releases/citizens-for-a-sound-economy-cse-and-empower-ameri>
33 This topic is covered in Michael Barker, 'George Soros And South Africa's Elite Transition', *Swans Commentary, 31* May, 2010.
    <http://www.swans.com/library/art16/barker51.html>
34 This is not the only case of NED/Soros collaboration; I have covered the role of both in fomenting unrest in Iran in, 'Soros and the State Department: Moving Iran towards the Open Society', *Foreign Policy Journal, 14* May, 2011.
    <http://www.foreignpolicyjournal.com/2011/05/14/soros-and-the-state-department-moving-iran-towards-the-open-society/>
35 William Avilés, *Global Capitalism, Democracy, and Civil-Military Relations in Columbia (New York:* State University of New York Press, 2006), pp. 18-19.
36 Michael Hardt and Antonio Negri, *Empire* (Cambridg, Massachusetts: Harvard University Press, 2000) p. 299.
37 'Formally demand that Moveon.org leave', 16 October, 2011.
    <http://occupywallst.org/forum/formally-demand-that-moveonorg-leave/>

13. On Shock and Organisation:
Riots, Resistance and the Need for Consistency

The Free Association

La hora sonó, la hora sonó. NO permitiremos mas, mas tu doctrina del shock.
[The hour has struck, the hour has struck. We will allow NO MORE, no more your doctrine of shock.]

Lyrics to 'Shock' by Ana Tijoux
- the anthem of the 2011 Chilean student movement.

Shock can have debilitating effects on social movements. It can disorient us, it can be exploited as part of a concerted effort to discipline our thought and action, and it can prompt us to fall back on reactionary tropes. But, rather than seeking to avoid shock, **The Free Association** suggest that we need more resilient forms of political organisation that help mitigate these paralysing effects.

"Criminality, Pure and Simple", or The Death of a Princess

In September 1997 England was overtaken by mass hysteria. Following the death of the Princess of Wales ('Princess Di') on August 31 there was a 'massive public outpouring of grief' that would not have seemed amiss in North Korea. More than a million people lined the route of Diana's funeral cortege in London while the BBC reported that an estimated 2.5 billion people watched the funeral - an incredible number, implying that just about every human being on the planet with access to a television tuned in to the event. Elton John's tribute 'Candle in the Wind 1997' challenged Bing Crosby's 'White Christmas' for best-selling record of all time.

Fourteen years later, England was gripped by a more malign form of hysteria, this time in response to the riots that broke out in London and a dozen or so other cities and towns in August 2011. While many of those who took part in the riots reported familiar feelings of excitement, intensity and festival, the dominant response of large sections of Britain's population was a profound sense of shock, not just on an intellectual or moral level but also on an affective one.[1] This shock was underpinned by a sensation of fear, and even panic, as some old certainties threatened to collapse. Reinforced by the endless looping footage of shops set alight with apparently little regard for those living above, this affective reaction was leveraged by political and media elites into a hysterical right-wing backlash.

The aim of this campaign was simple: to prevent any association of the riots with their socio-economic context - that is, crisis and austerity. And it was frighteningly effective. The widespread sense of shock was quickly mobilised into a prohibition on thought, which was then ruthlessly policed. Anybody asking if the events could be understood as a response to the economic crisis, and the subsequent imposition of austerity, was vigorously condemned: 'to understand is to condone', went the mantra. London Mayor Boris Johnson tellingly responded to a question about the shooting that sparked the first riot by declaring: "It is time that people who are engaging in looting and violence stopped hearing economic and sociological justifications for what they are doing."[2] Prime Minister David Cameron insisted that there was nothing to understand about the riots, suggesting that it was "criminality, pure and simple".[3] (See also Pollard and Young, Chapter 14).

In the cold light of day this response looks rather ludicrous. Within a few months of Diana's funeral, the hysteria had given way to a mood of embarrassment as people recalled their absurd response to her death. The same process is under way now, as people attempt to excise from public memory the kneejerk reactions, the suspension of thought and the many untenable positions held over those few weeks.[4] Just as the inner-city riots of the 1980s went down in history as a response to the austerity of that period (administered by a Conservative government led by Cameron's heroine Margaret Thatcher), it was obvious that the August riots would also be recorded as one event in a varied series of responses to the 'great recession' of the early years of the 21st century.[5]

There is a lot that can still be said about the causes of the riots and the motivations of the participants, but we want to focus instead on the aftermath of the riots. More specifically we want to use these events to think through the political effect of *shock* upon social movements. While explosive events, like the riots or the 'Arab Spring', can cause the rapid unravelling of state power, they can be equally disruptive for social movements, exposing movements' limitations and isolation. In fact, shock can derail and destroy movements just as quickly as outright repression - and often far more effectively. Examining the nature of shock will draw out crucial lessons about how to respond to new social eruptions without falling back into positions that simply shore up the status quo. There are some differences between state-engineered shock and shock 'from below' (and also 'natural' shock, such as that visited on New Orleans by Katrina), and it's certainly the case that corporations and the state were not 'neutral' bystanders in the August 2011 events - it was corporate media that chose to endlessly loop the footage of the blazing shopfront, for example. However, we are more interested here in the way we can anticipate and counter shock, and thus evade the prohibition on thought.

From the Millbank Boot to the 'Broom Army': 2011's Syncopated Rhythm of Resistance

In a blog post of February 2011, later expanded into a book, *Why It's Kicking Off Everywhere*, Paul Mason identifies three key social actors in the upsurge of militancy that swept across the globe in 2010-11: organised labour, 'the graduate with no future' and the urban poor.[6] Situating these forces alongside an analysis of networked technologies, he asks, "What if - instead of waiting for the collapse of capitalism - the emancipated human being were beginning to emerge spontaneously from within this breakdown of the old order?"

Mason's argument is that these "three tribes of discontent" can be seen coming together at the most important points of social unrest during that period, from the 'Arab Spring' and the movement of the *Indignados* in Spain to the wave of Occupy actions right across the globe. In the UK, we can perhaps see this most clearly in the November 10 2010 demonstration against education cuts and the tripling of tuition fees, a demonstration which ended in the occupation of Conservative party headquarters at Millbank. The day's lasting image was that of a masked demonstrator kicking in the building's plate-glass windows, propelling a notion of antagonist street politics onto the front pages and, in so doing, creating the space for the emergence of a more militant politics in the run-up to the 'March for the Alternative' anti-austerity demonstration on March 26 2011. In other words, the circulation of this image served to unlock a latent militancy.

Instead of traditional organisational politics, Mason conceptualises this movement as networked protest, with actions and spaces organised along horizontal lines rather than from the top down. But this approach is still limited to a fairly conventional notion of politics as something that proceeds mechanically by means of formal and informal alliances and agreements. Such a view has trouble accounting for the enormous speed of events in 2010-11. The formal and informal links between Tahrir Square, for example, and anti-cuts actions in the UK were minimal, yet many of those taking part were in no doubt about the connections. It is probably more useful here to think of the way that social movements spread by *resonance*. People see or hear something that speaks to their lives; they then interpret it, apply it and pass it on; their actions add further density to the movement, increasing its chances of being picked up and played out elsewhere. Building mechanical linkages, then, is less important than the task of enhancing the resonance and avoiding the *dissonance* between different struggles. That's precisely how the 'Arab Spring' worked. And it's equally true of the August riots.

Seen in this light, we can think of a *rhythm* of resistance in the spring of 2011. Those who were part of that rhythm were bound by weak ties, with the result that the rhythm was mobile, highly responsive and able to grow very quickly as new people adopted, and adapted, the beat. But in the absence of more coherent forms of organisation, those weak ties made the rhythm vulnerable to disruption, and that is exactly what happened in the aftermath of the August riots. If the enduring image of winter 2010-11 was of a boot going through a window, then the aftermath of the summer was captured in those photographs of the 'Broom Army'. Co-ordinated by the Twitter hashtag #riotcleanup, these volunteers were promoted as law-abiding citizens reclaiming the streets, and heralded as the 'Big Society' in action.

Of course it could be argued that the 'Broom Army' was not entirely reactionary (and it almost certainly included a number of erstwhile rioters in its ranks). But what concerns us here is the speed with which it emerged and the way it bulldozed through any other way of thinking about events. How did the "three tribes of discontent" fall apart? How was a rhythm of resistance so quickly transformed into its opposite - hundreds of people banging the drum for law and order with brooms, bin bags and dustpans? And how did we allow it to happen? Or, to put it another way, if Millbank represented a moment of expansion, a point when it was possible to see the opening-up of possibility and a re-shaping of social relations, how did that moment get closed down? How did those shifting social relations contract into clearly defined, unmoving positions?

'Panic on the Streets of London, Panic on the Streets of Birmingham': Understanding Shock

Let's be clear: we are not concerned here with *avoiding* shock. Far from it. If shock is a break in the normal unfolding of life, then that disruption can be inflected in an anti-capitalist direction. After all, it is not inevitable that those suffering shock will fall back onto comforting old tropes, such as the innate criminality of the urban poor. Indeed it can often take a shock to provoke new thinking. The rupture offered by events like the August riots can knock us out of habitual patterns and make us question the usually unthought presuppositions of existing society. The problem is not how to avoid shock; it is how social movements can learn to respond to shock by opening up possibilities rather than allowing them to be closed down.

The question is all the more vital because of the problematic that has dominated and structured contemporary anti-capitalist movements. Neoliberalism's real strength is proving to be its domination of common sense, as this structures political possibility at a level that is difficult to reach in the normal course of politics. Put briefly, neoliberalism has colonised our sense of the possible. As Hardt and Negri put it: "Such transcendental powers compel obedience not through the commandment of a sovereign or even primarily through force but rather by structuring the conditions of possibility of social life."[7] (See also Fisher, Chapter 2).

To put it another way, our capacity to act, as human beings, is very closely tied to our capacity to first imagine our actions and their likely effects. In the capitalist mode of production, as in all social organisations, we are imprisoned by our near horizons. The neoliberal mantra that 'there is no alternative' has become more than just dogma: it has been repeatedly applied and extended through every aspect of our lives, so much so that it has become part of our operating system. This has profound implications for emergent forms of dissent: when the market form, for example, is widely taken for granted as the best way of organising society, it is hard to develop alternative models that challenge this notion. Anti-capitalist movements which do promote such a vision are quickly condemned as 'unrealistic', a problem compounded by the fact that it is a Tory-led government which is imposing austerity. It is too easy for activists to imagine that a Labour administration might be any different. A similar process happened in the aftermath of the riots where the terms of the debate were narrowly framed to exclude anything other than criminality: the only question on the table was the length of the sentences.

The problem then is how to challenge, exceed and change the sense of the possible without producing the type of shock that will disorientate a population to such an extent that it falls back on familiar but reactionary tropes. But first we need to clarify what we mean when we talk about 'shock' in a socio-political context.

In *The Shock Doctrine* Naomi Klein argues that neoliberal policies have consistently taken advantage of the disorientation that follows shock in order to implement policies that a more coherent 'civil society' might resist. More than this, Klein suggests that these shocks are often engineered, at least partly, for that very purpose and indeed are often caused by the speed and scale of the neoliberal reforms themselves. Her approach is structured around Milton Friedman's famous quotation:

> Only a crisis - actual or perceived - produces real change. When that crisis occurs, the actions that are taken depend on the ideas that are lying around. That, I believe, is our basic function: to develop alternatives to existing policies, to keep them alive and available until the politically impossible becomes politically inevitable.[8]

Such a model certainly fits the implementation of austerity in the UK. The sheer scale and diversity of the cuts in public services, for instance, has so far tended to produce political entropy. While the closure of a single library might serve as a focal point for opposition, when a whole range of services are being closed or constrained all at once, it becomes much harder for a coherent and collective response to emerge. In any case, the 'need' to reduce the deficit has been repeatedly hammered home by all politicians, with the result that it's become part of everyday common-sense thinking. In this restricted space, closures, cuts and lay-offs come to appear as 'politically inevitable' even though they are nothing of the sort.[9]

Klein's concept of shock is drawn from CIA torture manuals, which discuss how to rupture a prisoner's "ability to make sense of the world around them".[10] One recommended technique is the literal application of electric shocks; another is the use of sensory deprivation followed by overstimulation through recordings of barking dogs or endless heavy metal. This understanding of shock can be traced right back to the First World War: as thousands of shell-shocked soldiers returned from the trenches, the question of how an organism can protect itself against over-stimulation was taken up by Sigmund Freud and others.

We can think of shock as having two major consequences. The first is exhaustion - the body simply cannot cope with new stimuli and starts to shut down. In order to counter this, it is possible to embark on a training regime to get a body used to shock, and to help anticipate its arrival. We can think of the disciplining undertaken by soldiers or boxers, where they acclimatise their bodies to repeated shock by programming in autonomic sub-routines which are triggered at critical moments: soldiers often talk of 'the training taking over' as a reaction that prevents immobilisation and debilitation. But this sort of military training is, of course, designed for a particular command structure and depends on fixed notions of 'the body', 'the enemy' and so on. It is not a very useful model for emancipatory social movements (and in any case, acclimatisation is, by definition, a limited strategy for dealing with events that are wholly contingent or unexpected).

The effect of shock is the same whether those bodies are individual organisms (you, me, everyone else) or collective bodies of people (parties, unions, workplaces, local communities, etc.). But traditional hierarchical organisations are ill-equipped to cope with shock. They operate with a pre-conceived framework and strategy, and will try to squeeze new events into their pre-existing outlook. In this respect, they are more likely to seek to close down movements rather than allow themselves to be opened up to new stimuli. Of course, the rigid structure of such organisations also makes them brittle: like skyscrapers in an earthquake, they may simply shatter when pushed to the point of exhaustion.

Networked forms of organisation, by contrast, have proved far more effective at adapting to new information. Naomi Klein points to the example of Latin America where movements are learning to "build shock absorbers into their organising models" by adopting forms which are "less centralized than the sixties, making it harder to demobilize whole movements by eliminating a few leaders."[11] More importantly, the weak ties of these more diffuse forms of power have made these movements very elastic, able to flow around potential blockages and recombine forces with greater power. Closer to home, we can see an example of such viral adoption and adaptation in the case of UK Uncut. A small group of Camp for Climate Action veterans imported the direct action techniques developed there into the anti-austerity movement by blockading and occupying shops and businesses that had avoided large tax bills. The tactic had an immediate impact on the public debate by revealing austerity as a political decision and not the result of a 'law of nature'. The model quickly spread across the country, self-generating groups who identified with the tactic. This viral method worked because the story of the action was instantly understandable, because the actions were easily replicable and because participation carried a low entry level of risk.

However, shock does not simply produce exhaustion. It can also create disorientation and panic. The Italian writer Bifo talks about "an epidemic of panic" amid the hyper-productivity of modern capitalism:

> The mental environment is saturated by signs that create a sort of continuous excitation, a permanent electrocution, which leads the individuals, as well as the collective mind, to a state of collapse.[12]

We can think of shock as a massive intensification of this 'chatter' of everyday twenty-first century life. Politicians, experts, church leaders, talking heads... everyone had their answer for the riots yet very little thought was involved. Faced with such a sensory overload, the most effective counter-strategy is to slow things down, to allow time and space for sudden and unexpected bursts of stimulation or information to be absorbed and processed. For social movements, this reflection has to happen on a *collective* level, at the level of *organising*.

But here we come up against the weakness of the network model. The weak ties it generates have only seemed capable of generating a weak coherence, one that is very vulnerable to disruption. In the aftermath of the riots, social bodies across the UK were literally disoriented, losing their bearings along with any sense of direction. In many cases it seemed as if social media were acting to *reinforce* the affect of shock and thus police the prohibition on thought. Computer-mediated social networks proved a poor medium for dealing with shocked metrosexuals who had suddenly discovered their inner fascists, realising their sympathies lay with the state's draconian clampdown. One tweet we received summed it up. It suggested the day after the riots be henceforth known as "The Great Day of De-Friending and De-Following".

'Live Fast Die Young': On Speed and Consistency

If social movements are to become shock-resistant, the weak ties of network forms and social media need to be supplemented by the stronger ties that are formed through sustained engagement with a political project. We have to develop forms of organisations that are open enough to allow resonance but also coherent enough to collectively receive, analyse and process new stimuli. We need to develop repertoires, techniques and technologies which can help set the conditions for collective analysis. This may well involve techniques and organisational forms that slow down the pace of events and lower the level of intensity so reflection and analysis can take place. Finally, we need to find some sort of consistency or coherence, one that enables bodies to come together and stay together, so that we can sustain political organisation across the ebb and flow of distinct waves of protest.

There are two reasons why this is especially important now. First, we have to take a long-term view of the economic crisis that engulfed the world in 2007-8. Even in simple fiscal terms, we are going to be living through its consequences for at least the next decade. And politically its impact may be even greater, as austerity becomes the new normal. In 50 years' time, people might look back and see Keynesianism and social democracy as temporary blips in the normal, brutal functioning of capitalism. Over the next few years, then, there are bound to be waves of resistance followed by periods of quietism and troughs of defeat.

And when we take this long-term view, we need to think again about how social movements *move*. Events like Millbank, the 'Arab Spring' and the August riots highlight the incredible speed of politics organised on a virtual plane, via Facebook, Twitter and internet memes. But as longterm anti-capitalist scholar, George Caffentzis, has pointed out, the experiences of the last year have also shown that speed is not enough for political effect.[13] We need momentum as well. In physics, momentum is mass multiplied by velocity, so it can mean a small group travelling very fast. But if we're serious about change, it must also mean a much larger number of people moving at a slower pace. In the 'Arab Spring', for example, what was decisive in the end was massive numbers of physical bodies in physical spaces. So we can think of consistency as a way of bridging that gap between huge numbers of people and small groups moving fast.

This brings us on to the second reason why finding consistency is crucial. As austerity begins to bite, social conflict will intensify. Without developing some sort of coherence, our social movements will remain fragile, tentative and prone to collapse. We do not wish to lose the flexibility, speed and responsiveness offered by the network form. But, if we are to avoid the creation of dissonance, we must move beyond these and learn how to handle shock.

Notes

1   We're using the term 'affect' here in an attempt to move beyond the binary thinking that underpins much political theory, separating 'consciousness' from 'action' in much the same way that 'the mind' is often split from 'the body'. Affect here signifies something more than an emotional, psychological or sensory state. Indeed it would be a mistake to see it as a personal feeling at all. Instead, it might be more accurate to think of affect as *potential*, as an increase (or decrease) in a body's capacity to act. This seems a more productive way of dealing with the problems of agency and change than a traditional 'class consciousness' approach which often assumes that awareness of class exploitation plus the 'correct' class analysis adds up to a revolutionary subject.

2   Caroline Davies, 'Boris Johnson heckled in Clapham Junction over London riots', *The Guardian*, 9 August, 2011.
<http://www.guardian.co.uk/politics/2011/aug/09/boris-johnson-clapham-junction-london-riots>

3   Seumas Milne, 'These riots reflect a society run on greed and looting', *The Guardian*, 10 August, 2011.
<http://www.guardian.co.uk/commentisfree/2011/aug/10/riots-reflect-society-run-greed-looting>

4   The post-riots hysteria has persisted, however, in the incredibly draconian sentencing for those passing through the courts in relation to the events. One 21-year-old was infamously jailed for 39 months simply for sending a BBM from his BlackBerry telling his friends to "kick off" during disorder in Nottingham. (See also Anderson, Chapter 16.)

5   Indeed *Reading the Riots: Investigating England's Summer of Disorder*, a joint study by the LSE and the *Guardian* newspaper drawing on interviews with 270 participants in the riots, showed that austerity provided more than just a general context. Alongside other issues such as hostility to the police, it formed a central part of the self-understanding of the riots by participants. As the report summarised: "Rioters identified a range of political grievances, but at the heart of their complaints was a pervasive sense of injustice. For some this was economic: the lack of money, jobs or opportunity. For others it was more broadly social: how they felt they were treated compared with others. Many mentioned the increase in student tuition fees and the scrapping of the education maintenance allowance."

    <http://www.guardian.co.uk/uk/series/reading-the-riots>
6   Paul Mason, 'Twenty reasons why it's kicking off everywhere', 5 February,
    2011.
    <http://www.bbc.co.uk/blogs/newsnight/paulmason/2011/02/twenty_reasons_
    why_its_kicking.html>; Paul Mason, *Why It's Kicking Off Everywhere: The New
    Global Revolutions,* (London: Verso, 2012).
7   Michael Hardt and Antonio Negri, *Commonwealth* (Cambridge, MA: Harvard
    University Press, 2009), p. 6.
8   Milton Friedman, *Capitalism and Freedom* (Chicago: University of Chicago
    Press, 2002), p. xiv, cited in Naomi Klein, *The Shock Doctrine* (London:
    Penguin, 2007), p. 6.
9   Austerity is always a political choice, not a neutral fix, and the form it takes
    will depend on the strength of those attempting to impose it and those able
    to resist it. The most well-known period of austerity in the UK, at the end of
    World War II, had a very different flavour. Then, the UK's public debt was
    more than double the size of GDP, and sovereign debt three times what it is
    today (relative to output). But this was the era of the welfare state, with the
    creation of a national health service, free education, social security and huge
    state investment.
10 Klein, *The Shock Doctrine,* p. 16.
11 Ibid. p. 453.
12 Franco Berardi, *After the Future* (Oakland/Edinburgh: AK Press, 2011), p.94.
13 George Caffentzis, 'In the desert of cities: notes on the Occupy movement in
    the US', 27 January 2012. <http://www.reclamationsjournal.org/blog/?p=505>

14. "Criminality Pure and Simple": Comparing the Response to the Student Protests and the August Riots

Katie Pollard and Maria Young

Two struggles happened within the space of a year in the UK, both dominated by young people and both rejecting left parties and organisations: the student struggle which reached its height in a series of demonstrations in November and December 2010; and four days of riots in August 2011. Although the form and participants of the events overlapped, they were responded to very differently by both the state and the media. The student movement was recognised as a legitimate struggle that at times overstepped its boundaries, while the August riots were seen as nothing but a problem that needed solving. We argue that, whereas the riots on the student demonstrations could be recuperated as actions that made demands of the state - breaking the law to improve the law - the August riots broke the law to break the law, and so were harder to recuperate. As David Cameron said, they were "criminality pure and simple."

As soon as they formed a government with the Conservatives, the Liberal Democrats reneged upon their pre-election pledges not to raise tuition fees. In autumn 2010, a bill was drafted to triple fees to £9,000 a year, restructure higher education towards a market model and scrap the Education Maintenance Allowance (EMA), a £30 a week benefit for 16-18 year olds in full-time education with parents on low wages.

In early November, the National Union of Students (NUS) called a demo to ask Liberal Democrat MPs - many of whom had enjoyed considerable student support in the last election - if they would 'please' change their minds and vote against the bill. Middle class and working class university students and college students left the demonstrations to smash the Tory party headquarters at Millbank. By condemning this action as 'despicable', the NUS leadership lost any remaining support it had amongst the students. But the vacuum they left was filled by the various university occupations: they made websites, put out press releases and set up their own Twitter, Facebook and flickr accounts. Like the NUS, they directed their demands at politicians, particularly the Liberal Democrats. The choice these politicians were faced with - to support their leader and the tuition fees raise or to keep their promises to decrease tuition fees - was presented as a moral one: "Nick Clegg shame on you! Shame on you for turning blue!"

But although the university occupations and older Trotskyist student groups addressed the media and called the subsequent demos, they were not in control of the movement's nature or representation. The sight of a megaphone wielding student screaming at people that they were going in the wrong direction or hitting the wrong targets - "Stop doing that, we're not against the police, we're against the government!", "Go the other way, I'm in control!" - was not uncommon. They were not in control. The people they were trying to lead weren't listening. They were angry. And they knew that marching along pre-arranged routes to a boring rally didn't stop the war.

For two months there were weekly local demonstrations in which school students joined college and university students, walking out of lessons and rampaging through the streets. Most demonstrations ended with people being contained in one place by police until late at night. On the final national demonstration, when the vote was due to take place, police contained thousands at Parliament Square. Inside the kettle, people danced together to sound systems, smashed the windows of the Treasury, destroyed bus-stops, fought the police, and burnt park benches and school books. Some people broke away from the kettle, and, after a failed attempt to light the Trafalgar Square Christmas tree, ran down Oxford Street, smashing shops and attacking Prince Charles's cavalcade on the way.

The form of these protests in many ways anticipated the riots the following August: they refused to follow planned routes or to stay as one mass; property was destroyed; people fought off the police; and there was a feeling of criminality and of taking the streets. At moments the violence superseded demand making. But, unlike the riots, all this took place in central London, and so the protests' targets of destruction were largely symbols of power and state authority - the Conservative party headquarters, the Treasury, the Cenotaph and Prince Charles.

Right-wing journalists recognised the students' right to protest, but argued that violence was not consistent with that right. "The irony of attacking and defacing monuments to the freedom which allowed this demonstration to take place clearly escaped the mob".[1] Students were criticised for not having a serious enough relationship to their demands, and for having little understanding of the reality of the cuts - they were either too poor or too posh: the working class students were 'thugs', 'yobs' and 'troublemakers', and the middle-class students were a privileged elite who were being subsidised for three years so that, "between agitprop they can drift into the odd sociology lecture".[2]

The Left took the students seriously. It was understood that the demands of the demonstration extended beyond those made explicit: commentators declared that the protest "shouldn't be understood simply in economic terms as a complaint against fees" but also as opposition to "the ideological devastation of the education system" and "the increasingly utilitarian approach to human life that sees degrees as nothing but 'investments' by individuals".[3] There was a willingness on the Left to attribute even the violent actions to a shared political consciousness. It was commonly argued that, as the violence was targeted at property, it was not really violence at all, and that, if it was violence, it was nothing compared to the violence that the government was doing to the education system. One journalist said cheerfully, "Protesters have broken windows and made their way onto the roof. Twitter reports indicate that some have taken a sofa from inside Millbank and put it outside, with the quite *reasonable* argument that 'if we're going to be kettled we may as well be comfy'".[4] Understood as a movement making self-conscious defensive and reformist demands of the state, the Left enjoyed the property destruction as the 'reasonable' effervescence of a movement which was on their side.

Shaken by these protests, the government brought the vote forward so that it coincided with the beginning of the Christmas holidays. The vote was lost and tuition fees were tripled. Despite the intensity and size of the student demonstrations, the government hadn't listened. A proposed walk-out in early 2011, on the day that EMA was due to be scrapped, was attended by less than 200 people. The initial optimism had vanished, and with harsh penalties imposed on school students who skipped school, all subsequent demos were smaller, capable of less, and eventually fizzled out completely.

An interview at the time with two gang members who went to the student demonstrations to steal wallets and mobile phones gave some idea of what was to come:

> I'm not there to 'Tory scum this and that'...I'm there for a reason [to make money], just like they [the students] claim to be there for a reason, and they've got music pumping and that. I know that if I was going to somewhere to protest, and I had two, three thousand people behind me and they was all saying right we're listening to you, there wouldn't be no music, there would be nothing, it would be pure silence and you'd hear man, that's exactly what you would hear, it would be like two, three thousand titans walking down the road, that's exactly what it would be like, mate.
>
> We do know that these Tories that are in now, obviously they seem to be messing a lot of things up, and everybody's angry, everybody seems to have come to a point where they've just had enough, and that's where it's going to spill over see, at the moment it's all up [central] London, and some sort of control, but it's going to break free from that soon, and it's going to be in your high street, in your normal high street, in your Greenwiches, your Woolwiches, those sorts of places.
>
> When it gets to the actual streets, and it stops coming off these main tourist attraction sorts of spots and that yeah, and when it starts coming to the actual place where you live and sleep. Wow.[5]

By not meeting their demands, the government removed a rhetoric within which to frame the young people's dissent. But on the demonstration in which the vote was lost, students vowed to come back. "This is just the beginning," one blogged defiantly. Another shouted to the media, "We'll be back!". Did what was left escalate into the action that happened the following August?

The following summer, riots spread across the country. Gangs held a four day truce. Many of the same teenagers who had taken part in the student protests now took to rioting without music or slogans. The riots spread from Tottenham in North London, to South, West and East London. For three days, people in the capital looted and burnt out shops, set up burning barricades and battled with the cops. Whereas the students had been largely contained in police kettles, the police were running far behind the riots, afraid of advancing too close, until, on the fourth day, police forces from across Britain came to London to patrol the streets in armoured cars. That night was quiet in London, but the riots had spread to other major cities - Birmingham, Manchester, Liverpool, Nottingham... These were finished the following day, and the #riotcleanup began. Courts were in session throughout the night, and thousands of people were imprisoned for years at a time.

Unlike the student demonstrations, the riots had no media reps. Cameras were smashed, and journalists took cover on the cop side of the barricades. The media on the Left and the Right refused to see any continuity between the actions of the students and the actions of the rioters. After all, the riots couldn't be seen as legitimate, whichever way you looked at them.

The right-wing press described the rioters as feral children, running wild because they lacked fathers and family values. Although the same journalists had heavily criticised the violent actions of the students, it was only for the August rioters that they pulled out racism and eugenics. On prime time TV, a popular historian quoted a fascist speech by sixties politician Enoch Powell, and told viewers that the reason this riot included both white and black people was that "the whites have become black".[6] In one mainstream right-wing newspaper, a picture of Hackney teenagers in masks was accompanied by the caption, "Do rioters... have lower levels of a brain chemical that helps keep behaviour under control? Scientists think so."[7] One of their journalist wrote: "Their behaviour on the streets resembled that of the polar bear which attacked a Norwegian tourist camp last week. They were doing what came naturally and, unlike the bear, no one even shot them for it".[8]

Despite implying that they were sub-human or comparing them to wild animals, the Right still considered the rioters human enough to be held responsible for the riots. David Cameron even suggested that children (and perhaps their parents too) should be considered fully responsible for their actions. He insisted the unrest was nothing to do with the socio-economic situation, but was "criminality pure and simple and it has to be confronted and defeated... You will feel the full force of the law, and if you are old enough to commit these crimes, you are old enough to face the punishments".[9]

Most of the Left argued that responsibility lay not with the rioters, but with the rich and powerful. From the mainstream Left to Trotskyist and anarchist groups, it was commonly argued that 'we can neither condone nor condemn' the rioters. Just like we cannot condone or condemn the polar bear that attacked the Norwegian tourist camp. We can only condone or condemn responsible human beings. While content during the student protests to argue for the reasonableness of a responsible human being stealing a sofa when they are being contained by police, the Left was uninterested in exploring the reasonableness of stealing a new pair of trainers when you might need to run from the police (or might want to sell them). And they certainly didn't consider the reasonableness of acting criminally for criminality's sake. Rather than condone or condemn the rioters, it was easier to suggest that responsibility for the riots lay elsewhere.

The Left made an effort to identify the riots' external 'causes' - the closing down of youth centres, the end of EMA, the aggression of the police, incessant advertising, and unemployment. They suggested that these causes could be ended if bankers were less greedy and politicians changed their policies. The only people who were responsible for the riots, then, were the politicians and the bankers who should put the system back in order. Not only is the Left wrong that the politicians and the bankers have the power and ability to do this, but they are wrong that the rioters have no agency or power.

Fearful of this battle without slogans, music or demands, all the Left could do was hope that the politicians would bring it back onto the terrain of policies and solutions, putting a stop to it kindly. Placing the responsibility for the rioters' actions with the politicians, the Left exaggerated how much agency the politicians have and downplayed the agency of the rioters. By doing so, they attempted to embrace the rioters again in the system that their criminality, for four days, threatened to escape.

The riots were not simply the result of the action or inaction of politicians, but were the reasonable actions of people with nothing to lose consciously refusing their situation, taking revenge on that situation. Of course the rioters didn't choose to have nothing to lose, but they did choose to respond in the way they did. The Right understood the riots better than the Left in this respect: the rioters were responsible for their own criminality. In one of the few media interviews conducted during the riots, a journalist asks a mask-wearing rioter:

> If you're law-abiding and you've got no reason to fear the police, you wouldn't need to hide your identity would you?

The rioter answers:

> I'm not law-abiding, mate.[10]

The riots were not crime as a means to a message, being violent to get heard, but were criminality for criminality's sake - criminality pure and simple. Not breaking the law to make demands of the state, but breaking the law to break the law.

Recognising the agency of the rioters does not mean we have to argue that they had hidden demands, as some on the Left did. For the word 'demand' - even when implicit or unanswerable - suggests that a third party is involved: a demand involves mediation, you have to demand something *of* someone or something. Although the loss of EMA, the aggression of the police, the closing of youth centres, were all part of the situation that contributed to people rioting, and, indeed, were cited by many rioters as reasons for rioting, this does not make the bringing back of EMA, the re-opening of youth centres, or a less aggressive police force implicit demands of the riots. You might say you wouldn't have shoplifted food if you hadn't lost your job, but that doesn't mean that by shoplifting you demand your job back, even implicitly. Neither is shoplifting a demand for food. You are not demanding food. You are taking it. When you throw something at a cop you don't demand they feel pain, you make them feel pain. You don't demand revenge, you take it. You don't demand the streets, you take them. The rioters were not demanding to be treated better, they were saying 'fuck off'. They were not demanding what we want, they were getting what we want. As people said at the time, "That's what it's all about, it's showing the police we can do what we want, and now we have".[11] They were the days when "we could have run of the streets".[12] The riots were about taking, not demanding. Significantly, the only slogan that survived from the student demos was answered by itself: "Whose streets? Our streets!".

And they were our streets for four days. Those days were joyous. Many of the rioters said they were the best days of their lives and, given the opportunity, they would do it again. The riots were victorious as long as they lasted. But they didn't last long. Repression against the student movement was nothing in comparison to the repression against the rioters. Whereas the government ended the student protests by not listening, there was no option of refusing to listen to the riots, for the rioters didn't want to be listened to. They were going to continue as long as they could, not as long as it seemed that they might be heard. All the state could do was frighten off or physically remove them from the streets. "You will feel the full force of the law," was the only response that could be made to a struggle that refused to recognise or address itself to politicians; that refused to be recognised or addressed.

Notes

1   Paul Harris, 'Defacing the Cenotaph, urinating on Churchill... how young thugs at student protest broke every taboo', *The Daily Mail*, 10 December 2010. <http://www.dailymail.co.uk/news/article-1337315/TUITION-FEES-VOTE-PROTEST-Thugs-deface-Cenotaph-urinate-Churchill.html>

2   Harry Phibb, *The Mail Online*, 'Self indulgent student agitprop shows the case for tuition fees', 9 November 2011. <http://phibbsblog.dailymail.co.uk/2011/11/self-indulgent-student-agitprop-shows-the-case-for-tuition-fees.html>

3   Nina Power,'Student protest: We are all in this together', *The Guardian*, 10 November, 2010. <http://www.guardian.co.uk/commentisfree/2010/nov/10/student-protests-conservative-party-hq-occupation#start-of-comments>

4   Ibid.

5   Vice Media Inc, 'Rule Britannia: Teenage Riot – Part 5', 2011. <http://www.vice.com/rule-britannia/rule-britannia-teenage-riot-episode-5>

6   David Starkey, *Newsnight*, BBC, 12 August 2011.

7   Daily Mail Reporter, 'Rioters may have 'lower levels' of a brain chemical that keeps impulsive behaviour under control', *The Daily Mail*, 9 August, 2011. <http://www.dailymail.co.uk/sciencetech/article-2024173/Rioters-lower-levels-brain-chemical-keeps-impulsive-behaviour-control.html>

8   Max Hastings, *Mail Online*, 'Years of liberal dogma have spawned a generation of amoral, uneducated, welfare dependent, brutalised youngsters', 12 August 2011. <*http://www.dailymail.co.uk/debate/article-2024284/UK-riots-2011-Liberal-dogma-spawned-generation-brutalised-youths.html*>

9   David Cameron, Downing Street Statement on the riots in London and other cities, 9 August, 2011. <http://www.telegraph.co.uk/news/uknews/crime/8691034/London-riots-Prime-Ministers-statement-in-full.html>

10   Sky News, 9 August, 2011.

11   BBC News, 'London rioters: "Showing the rich we do what we want"', 9 August, 2011. <http://www.bbc.co.uk/news/uk-14458424>

12   *The Guardian*, 'Reading the Riots: Investigating England's summer of disorder'. <http://www.guardian.co.uk/uk/series/reading-the-riots>

Part 4

Legitimating the Repression of Dissent

15. Repression in the Neoliberal University

Charles Thorpe

On November 9, 2011, when students attempted to set up an Occupy encampment in the main plaza of the University of California (UC) Berkeley campus, in order to protest rising tuition fees and the *de facto* privatization of the University, they were met with heavily-armed police in riot-gear. The police jabbed protesting students and staff with batons and pulled protesters by the hair. A little over a week later, on November 18, police officer Lieutenant John Pike pepper-sprayed seated student demonstrators at UC Davis campus, causing outcry across the US.

The University administration responded to the uproar by quickly disowning and distancing itself from the violence. UC Davis Chancellor Linda Katehi expressed her "sadness." Chair of the University's Board of Regents Sherry Lansing said she was "shocked and appalled" by footage of the police actions.[1] President Yudof declared himself "appalled by [the] images" and said, "We cannot let this happen again."[2]

Despite these disavowals and statements of regret, it has become clear that the University administration played a key role in the move toward a violent crackdown on protest. The repression stemmed directly from the University's determination not to have Occupy-style protests on campus. Two days before the Berkeley occupation, Chancellor Robert Birgenau sent a letter to the campus community stating that "destructive" or "disrupt[ive]" activities, including "occupying buildings [or] setting up encampments... will not be tolerated." He would not allow any activities that might "disrupt with anyone's ability to conduct regular activities - go to class, study, carry out their research, etc."[3] Even in the face of widespread outrage following the violence against protesters, Birgenau defended his "no encampments" policy on the grounds of the "hygiene, safety, space, and conflict issues that emerge when an encampment takes hold and the more intransigent individuals gain control."[4] Such concerns about "intransigence," he suggested, had proven well-founded: "It is unfortunate that some protesters chose to obstruct the police by linking arms and forming a human chain to prevent the police from gaining access to the tents. This is not non-violent civil disobedience."[5]

Katehi was similarly concerned to prevent the Occupy movement taking hold on the Davis campus. For her, Occupy conjured images of chaos and debauchery:

> We were worried at the time about... [non-affiliates] because the issues from Oakland were in the news and the use of drugs and sex and other things, and you know here we have very young students... we were worried especially about having very young girls and other students with older people who come from the outside without any knowledge of their record... if anything happens to any student while we're in violation of policy, it's a very tough thing to overcome.[6]

Davis's Vice-Chancellor John Meyer said,

> our context at the time was seeing what's happening... in other municipalities across the country, and not being able to see a scenario where [a UC Davis Occupation] ends well... Do we lose control and have non-affiliates become part of an encampment? So my fear is a long-term occupation with a number of tents where we have an undergraduate student and a non-affiliate and there's an incident. And then I'm reporting to a parent that a non-affiliate has done this unthinkable act with your daughter, and how could we let that happen?[7]

The Davis administration seem to have been working with a view of their role in relation to students as *in loco parentis*, a view combined with a conception of the campus as an environment insulated from the outside world, and sexually charged anxieties about the supposedly chaotic character of the Occupy movement.

A detailed report into the Davis pepper-spray incident by former California Supreme Court Associate Justice Cruz Reynoso finds that the administrators' concerns about safety "were not supported by any evidence."[8] It finds the same about the police officers' claim that they feared violence from the student protesters who had gathered around them while officers awaited transport for people they had arrested. Pike felt that he was justified in using pepper-spray because the seated protesters were, from his point of view, preventing officers from leaving with their prisoners. The investigation by Kroll Inc. (which informed the Reynoso Task Force), however, found no basis for the idea that students would forcibly prevent officers from leaving. Kroll note that the very fact that Pike was able to step over protesters in order to target pepper-spray into their faces shows, to the contrary, the lack of physical resistance that police faced.[9]

The idea that the crowd were hostile and potentially violent was the officers' "*subjective* belief."[10] This pattern of stereotyping protesters as chaotic and violent, and this characterization justifying the use of force against them was evident also when, a few months after the Berkeley and Davis incidents, the UC Regents met on the UC Riverside campus. The UC Board of Regents is an exclusive politically appointed body, composed largely of members of California's politically-connected business elite, which oversees and makes policy for the entire University of California system. Again, when students and staff gathered to protest increases in tuition fees, they were met with extremely repressive and violent policing. In addition to campus police, hundreds of Riverside County Sheriffs were brought onto campus, raising tensions in what had been an entirely peaceful protest. Police then proceeded to strike and jab students and staff with batons and to fire paint-balls into the crowd at close range. In contrast with the incidents at Berkeley and Davis, the administration responded defensively to complaints about the police action. UC President Mark Yudof responded to complaints made by faculty by asserting that the demonstrators were an "angry mob" who "provoked the response from the police."[11] The fact that demonstrators blocked exits, preventing Regents and staff from leaving the building, constituted, in his view, "mob" behavior. And the fact that nine officers were injured was further evidence marshaled in the depiction of protesters as unreasonable. Some perspective on this latter fact is provided by the University newsletter, which notes, "Nine UC police officers sustained injuries, including bruises, cuts, and scratches. None required major medical attention."[12] Apparently, cuts and scrapes incurred by police officers in the course of repressing peaceful protest provide unquestionable justification for that repression. Photographs and testimony from protesters involved in the events at Riverside suggest a non-violent festive atmosphere, until the arrival of large numbers of police with drawn batons changed the atmosphere to one of fear and outrage.[13]

In his letter, Yudof insists that "The right to peaceful protest on all our campuses must be protected" and that "free speech is part of the DNA of the University of California." But, the overall tenor of Yudof's letter is that disruption caused to senior administrators fully warranted the police response. Police repression seems to be the default response when administrators feel what Birgenau called a loss of "control," or disruption of the "regular activities" of the organization.

At Davis, Katehi described her immediate concern as being for the protection of supposedly vulnerable female undergraduates from supposedly dangerous 'non-affiliates'. But her antipathy toward protest on campus would also seem to derive from a view that political activity threatens the mission of the university. Athens-born Katehi played a significant role in the abolition of asylum for Greek universities. This meant lifting restrictions on police access to campus that had underpinned the freedom of Greek students and scholars since the downfall of the military junta in 1974. In 2010-2011, she served on an "International Committee On Higher Education In Greece," and co-authored its report that provided the rationale for ending university asylum.[14] The report states: "Greek university campuses are not secure. While the Constitution allows University leaders to protect campuses against elements that seek political instability, Rectors have been reluctant to exercise their rights and responsibilities, and to make decisions needed in order to keep faculty, staff and students safe. As a result, University leaders and faculty have not been able to be good stewards of the facilities they have been entrusted with by the public." A key justification for the end of the asylum law was that, according to Greek officials, "criminals had repeatedly taken advantage of this law during the protests against the Greek austerity measures," in addition to reports of campuses as havens for drug-trafficking.[15] There are striking parallels with Katehi's anxiety about Occupy at UC: an idea of the campus being made unsafe by criminals or 'non-affiliates' and the paramount responsibility of administrators to maintain order on campus. But the report also suggests a deeper motivation to the shutting down of the encampment at Davis: a view of political activity as antithetical to, and potentially undermining, the proper activities of university campuses. Greek universities had suffered from "The politicization of the campuses - and specifically the politicization of students - [which] represents a beyond-reasonable involvement in the political process. This is contributing to an accelerated degradation of higher education."[16] Instead of fostering oppositional politics, the report's authors urge Greek universities to become "engines of innovation and economic development," encouraging "entrepreneurship" so that graduates "innovate" and "start their own businesses"[17] Katehi and her co-authors' desire to end the 'politicization' of the Greek university was part of proposals to implement a neoliberal model of the university in which academics are disciplined through "measur[ed] performance" and the goal of education is primarily constructed in service of business.[18] As sociologist Panagiotis Sotiris notes, this neoliberal model is also an authoritarian one "without democratic procedure and participation and without strong and politicized student and faculty movements."[19] It is a corporate model of top-down management, at odds with the conception of the university as a public sphere. It aims to construct a university appropriate to what Slavoj Zizek calls "a depoliticised technocracy in which bankers and other experts are allowed to demolish democracy."[20]

UC administration trumpets California's higher education and research institutions as modeling the 'entrepreneurial' university through university-industry links with science and technology "spin-off" firms that make the university an "economic engine that is driving the future" for the state of California.[21] But this neoliberal model is overlaid on a public university, with a historic notion of education and research as a public good, as codified in the Master Plan created in 1960 by University President Clark Kerr. This far-reaching plan established tuition-free higher education, and a framework through which California's youth could access higher education en masse. As *The Economist* points out, this framework has, to a large extent, been undone and the public university is now, in effect, being privatized. Since 2010, the state has contributed less than half the cost of an undergraduate education, and state funding continues to fall. *The Economist* notes that "In some ways, California has now inverted" the priorities embodied in the Master Plan, so that "Spending on prisons passed spending on universities in around 2004."[22]

The attacks on UC students by militarized police are indicative of this inversion of priorities in California, which has left its education system trailing and has massively expanded its prison-industrial complex.[23] As Dylan Rodriguez, a Professor of Ethnic Studies at UC Riverside, points out, the actions of Lieutenant Pike were entirely continuous with the routine violence of the American police against the poor and communities of color, those who are "least likely to send their young people to places like UC Davis."[24] Students resisting neoliberalism found themselves facing the same kind of violence routinely used by the American state apparatus against the poor. The violent repression of protest is part of the structural violence of the imposition of neoliberal 'shock doctrine' in California, as the effective privatization of the public university steals the future of California's youth. UC Davis English professor Nathan Brown, who has been a trenchant critic of the administration's role in the Davis pepper-spray incident, argues that "Police brutality is an administrative tool to enforce tuition increases."[25] The manifest brutality of the police, however, became a source of embarrassment for the University administration. The administration must navigate the deep divide between their neoliberal agenda and surviving (albeit weakened) notions of education as a public good and of the university as a public sphere that has a key democratic function as a site of unfettered rational public discourse.

Although this conception of the University as a public sphere and public good is continually being undermined by the administration's neoliberal agenda, these ideas cannot be entirely jettisoned without a significant weakening of the University's institutional legitimacy. (See also Whyte, Chapter 3 and Robinson, Chapter 4.) This continuing legitimizing function of public values for the University is made evident in the draft report on the policing of campus protest prepared for Yudof in the wake of the Berkeley and Davis incidents by UC Berkeley Dean Christopher Edley, Jr. and the University's General Counsel Charles F. Robinson, and recently made available for public comment. The report represents much more nuanced thinking about protest and policing than hitherto displayed by the University administration. It focuses on civil disobedience and recognizes the legitimacy of non-violent civil disobedience as a form of protest that has a deep history at the University of California and as a legitimate form of political expression. They call for policies on free expression "to recognize explicitly the important and historic role of civil disobedience as a protest tactic."[26] They write of the "importance to university life of expressive protest activity."[27] Civil disobedience, they state, "is not generally something to be feared and will not necessarily require force in response."[28] The report's recognition of the historic legitimacy of civil disobedience is framed within an understanding of the public university as an institution that has a special significance in relation to broader democratic free expression of ideas.[29] Edley and Robinson call on the administration to shift their "mindset" away from one "focused... on the maintenance of order and adherence to rules and regulations" toward an understanding of civil disobedience as expression in the context of the University as a "community" based on "peaceful discourse."[30]

The report implicitly rejects Birgenau's view of the demonstration at Berkeley by urging that new guidelines "should specify that administrators will not authorize any physical police response against protesters non-aggressively linking arms unless the protesters were significantly interfering with the academic mission of the campus."[31]

And Edley and Robinson reject the exclusionary stance of the Davis administration toward 'non-affiliates.' They write that "as a public institution, barring non-affiliates from campus is usually inappropriate, as well as physically all-but-impossible for most of those portions of our campuses designated as public forums for free speech activity."[32] Edley and Robinson's conception of the University as a public sphere not only underpins the legitimacy of civil disobedience on campus; it is also important for the legitimacy of the university as an institution. The report can be seen to be motivated by the administration's recognition that violent police attacks on demonstrators on campus seriously undermine relationships within the University between administration, staff and students and between the University and the broader public on which the institution still depends and which it is still supposed to serve. Edley and Robinson repeatedly emphasize dialogue and communication as the key to avoiding conflict and the use of force against protesters, and perhaps to avoiding civil disobedience altogether.[33] Recognizing that the University cannot resort to force against protesting students and staff and members of the public without generating massive outcry and weakening the institution's public legitimacy, Edley and Robinson appeal to values of dialogue and community as the key to avoiding a rerun of the chaotic scenes at Berkeley and Davis last year.

However, standing in tension with this kind of appeal to public-sphere values in the report is a competing technocratic-bureaucratic language of "the *management* of... protests."[34] While recognizing the legitimacy of civil disobedience to the extent of calling for "recognition" of its "important" role in the University, the report also emphasizes that civil disobedience entails breaking rules and is disruptive to the institution, and therefore must involve "consequences" for those engaging in it, including "legal consequences."[35] (See also Anderson, Chapter 16.) This is ultimately a report written for the University administration, embodying an institutional interest in maintaining the current social and authority relations of the University, handling dissent with minimum friction, and maintaining administrative control. The report's recognition of the legitimacy of civil disobedience is tied to an interest in rendering civil disobedience compatible with the bureaucratic structures of the University as an organization. Civil disobedience is recognized so as to be routinized and made subject to bureaucratic procedure. The report recommends establishing an "event response team on each campus to plan and oversee the campus response to demonstrations."[36] It is desirable that this team should "Identify and contact members of the demonstration group - preferably one or more group leaders - in advance of the demonstration to establish lines of communication." The aim should be to "understand the protesters' concerns and objectives" but also to "explain the ground rules" such as regulations about where and when protest gatherings are allowed to take place.[37] The University should "Establish a mediation function at the campus or regional level to assist in resolving issues likely to trigger protests or civil disobedience." It should also "Consider deploying this mediation function as an alternative to force, before and during a protest event."[38] The mediators should be trained in "communication techniques" that will "de-escalate tensions."[39] Here, dialogue appears as a set of techniques for integrating protest in such a way as to render it manageable by the campus bureaucracy.

Despite the emphasis on dialogue, there remains the recourse to force by those in power, in this case the University administration acting through the University's Police Department.[40] The report calls for "limit[ing] the use of force against protesters" but qualifies this with "wherever possible."[41] "Force," or in other words violence by the authorities, is still available when protest goes beyond the limits of what the institution is willing to tolerate.[42] While not ruling out the use of police violence, the Edley-Robinson report seeks to rationalize it by subjecting it to rationalistic procedures. Instead of the kind of overt police brutality seen at Berkeley and Davis, the report recommends "that campus police utilize hands-on pain compliance techniques before pepper spray or batons whenever feasible."[43] For example in a situation such as at Berkeley when protesters "are non-aggressively linking arms and when the event response team has determined that a physical response is required, principles should specify that administrators should authorize the police to use hands-on pain compliance techniques rather than higher levels of force... unless the situation renders pain compliance unsafe or unreasonable."[44] The report advocates the development of a "response continuum" whereby there are consistent protocols across the UC campuses for what level of force is employed in relation to different kinds of protest action or resistance.[45] There should be consistent system-wide guidelines for which "less lethal" weapons such as pepper-spray can be used by campus police forces.[46] It advocates "targeted" arrests aimed at particular individuals rather than "mass arrests [which] can substantially escalate tensions."[47] And the report recommends documenting what takes place, using "neutral observers" and videotaping protests, something that could be a check on police action, but also clearly has the potential to be used against demonstrators.[48]

Where chaotic acts of violence by police create a crisis of legitimacy for the institution, the bureaucratic response is to seek to rationalize the use of violence, subjecting it to procedure, "accountability" and "audit," and rendering it consistent.[49] In this way, the institution retains the ability to clamp down on protest, but in a way that is defensible as measured, consistent with procedure, and as having followed attempts to engage protesters in dialogue. The management of protest uses dialogue or mediation, but always with the option of a resort to, and escalation of, violence by the authorities. But now this escalation is a rational application not of chaotic 'violence' but of 'force' measured to achieve a desired outcome. This is the rationalized violence of 'pain compliance'.

For protesters, this rationalization of institutional response is double-edged. It does imply a check on the actions of police to the extent that it means a set of rules to which protesters and their allies can appeal in disputing excessive police actions. The Edley-Robinson report's recognition of civil disobedience as political expression and the report's language of 'dialogue', 'communication' and 'mediation' could signal a greater institutional openness and willingness to engage with protesters. However, it holds the danger of protest becoming a routinized and managed affair, stripping civil disobedience of the very disruptive and spontaneous qualities that make it powerful.[50] This is the power that Judith Butler refers to when she writes: "Their bodies are their last resource and their most important resource-and it is the power they have... So bodies in the street can stop traffic or bring attention that [there are] very basic needs to be satisfied, including shelter, food, employment, and freedom of mobility and freedom of expression."[51] Managed protest is in the interests of the bureaucracy, but is this kind of protest likely to change anything? A key part of what participants have found uplifting about the Occupy movement, and what has provoked the violent repression by authorities from federal and state governments to city and campus police, has been the way in which it has taken place outside the established institutions. Arguably, the movement's promise and its threat have derived precisely from its being *unmanageable*. Being managed entails being controlled and subordinated. The managers reserve the right to determine what they consider "tolerable," when dissent has gone too far, and when the time has come for "pain compliance" and an escalation of the "force continuum."

The contradiction in the Edley-Robinson report is the social contradiction between its image of the University as a dialogic community - "literally and figuratively a community of students, faculty, and staff" - and the reality of the transformation of the University of California on a neoliberal model.[52] This model points toward exclusion and inequality, rather than community. Drastic fee increases exacerbate class inequality in access to higher education. Many potential students are put off or priced out of higher education, forced into debt, or are trying to study while holding down full-time or near-full time jobs in order to make ends meet.[53] While fees are increased, a growing managerial class of senior administrators see their pay boosted.[54] Rather than serving the California public, the University is increasingly oriented to the needs of private business, whether pharmaceutical, biotech and agro-business companies, computer and electronics firms, or weapons manufacturers. Most fundamentally, UC is presided over by a body - the Regents - that is composed primarily of members of the 1% whose ability to represent the public interest in a public university is highly questionable.[55] It is a hierarchical and unequal structure antithetical to genuine dialogue. A report calling for reform of the Regents notes: "When Regents speak, they demonstrate a patronizing tone... [This] condescension is built into the Regental structure. Because they are unaccountable, Regents and their appointees face no recourse for their condescension."[56]

The Edley-Robinson report epitomizes the tension between the impulse toward recognizing the legitimacy of protest within the University as an aspect of the University's place within the democratic public sphere and the competing impetus to manage dissent within the context of a depoliticized and unequal neoliberal university. The way in which the University is more and more an adjunct of private business and an instrument of class exclusion rather than mobility and opportunity should lead us to expect the coercive management of protest to take precedence over dialogue, shaping the form and context of communication and setting its parameters. The purest expression of neoliberal management is pain compliance.

Notes

1   'Chancellor calls for task force to review Friday arrests', 19 November, 2011. <http://news.ucdavis.edu/search/news_detail.lasso?id=10083>; 'Regents chair Lansing with a message to UC community', 21 November, 2011. <http://www.universityofcalifornia.edu/news/article/26709>

2   'President Yudof Responds to Campus Protest Issues', 20 November, 2011. <http://www.universityofcalifornia.edu/news/article/26702>; 'Yudof meets with chancellors, outlines action on protests', 21 November, 2011. <http://www.universityofcalifornia.edu/news/article/26708>

3   Quoted in http://en.wikipedia.org/wiki/Robert_J._Birgeneau [accessed July 5,

2012].

4   'Message to Campus Community about "Occupy Cal"', 10 November, 2011.
     <http://newscenter.berkeley.edu/2011/11/10/message-to-the-campus-
     community-about-occupy-cal/>

5   Ibid.

6   Quoted in *UC Davis November 18, 2011 "Pepper Spray Incident" Task Force
     Report – "The Reynoso Task Force Report"*, p. 8.
     <http://reynosoreport.ucdavis.edu/reynoso-report.pdf>

7   Quoted in *Reynoso Report*, p. 8. See also David Greenwald, 'Vanguard
     Analysis: Vice Chancellor Meyer's Critical and Fateful Decisions on Clearing
     the Tent Pave Way For Incident', *Davis Vanguard*, 12 April, 2012.
     <http://davisvanguard.org/index.php?option=com_content&view=article&id=
     5262:vanguard-analysis-vice-chancellor-meyers-critical-and-fateful-
     decisions-on-clearing-the-tent-pave-way-for-incident&Itemid=114>

8   *Reynoso Report*, p. 9. See also 'The Reynoso Report: A Portrait of
     Administrative Malice, Stupidity, Incompetence, and Immaturity', *Reclaim
     UC*, 11 April, 2012.<http://reclaimuc.blogspot.com/2012/04/reynoso-report-
     portrait-of.html>

9   Kroll, *Report Concerning the Events at UC Davis on November 18, 2011*, pp. 119-
     120. <http://reynosoreport.ucdavis.edu/reynoso-report.pdf>

10   *Kroll Report,* p. 119 [emphasis in original].

11   Mark G. Yudof to Charles Thorpe, 2 February, 2012. <http://ucsdfa.org/wp-
     content/uploads/2012/01/let.pdf>; 'Open Letter to the UC Regents: Police
     Violence at UC Riverside', 26 January, 2012. <http://ucsdfa.org/open-letter-
     to-the-uc-regents-police-violence-at-uc-riverside/546>

12   'UC Regents Able to Meet at UC Riverside Despite Protests', *UCR Today*, 20
     January 20, 2012. <http://ucrtoday.ucr.edu/2177>

13   Diana Delgado, 'Occupy Riverside Student Injured by Police', *The Nation*
     Blog, 19 January, 2012. <http://www.thenation.com/blog/165800/occupy-
     riverside-student-injured-police>

14   Mark Ames, 'How UC Davis Chancellor Linda Katehi Brought Oppression
     Back to Greece's Universities', *Naked Capitalism*, 23 November, 2011.
     <http://www.nakedcapitalism.com/2011/11/mark-ames-how-uc-davis-
     chancellor-linda-katehi-brought-oppression-back-to-greece's-
     universities.html>; Panagiotis Sotiris, 'Linda Katehi and the neoliberal
     reform of Greek Higher Education', *Greek Left Review*, 24 November, 2011.
     <http://greekleftreview.wordpress.com/2011/11/24/linda-katehi-and-the-
     neoliberal-reform-of-greek-higher-education>

15   *Report of the International Committee on Higher Education in Greece*, February
     2011, p.
     8.<http://www.tsoukalas.org/attachments/313/INTERNATIONAL%20COMMI
     TTEE%20ON%20HIGHER%20EDUCATION%20IN%20GREECE_EN.pdf>;
     'Greek University Asylum Abolished', *ScienceGuide*, 25 August, 2011.
     <http://www.scienceguide.nl/201108/greek-university-asylum-

abolished.aspx> See also "Styx and Stones," *Times Higher Education Supplement*, 24 May, 2012.
<http://www.timeshighereducation.co.uk/story.asp?storycode=420077>

16 *Report of the International Committee*, p. 8.

17 *Report of the International Committee*, pp. 4, 5.

18 *Report of the International Committee*, pp. 10-11 (under the title "Enforce Accountability: *Measuring Performance*").

19 Sotiris, "Linda Katehi".

20 Slavoj Zizek, 'Save Us From the Saviors', *London Review of Books*, Vol. 34, No. 11, 7 June, 2012. <http://www.lrb.co.uk/v34/n11/slavoj-zizek/save-us-from-the-saviours>

21 UC San Diego Annual Report, 2012. <http://www.annualreport.ucsd.edu/2012/economicImpact.html> (Accessed June 18, 2012).

22 'Excellence for Fewer', *The Economist*, 10 September, 2011. http://www.economist.com/node/21528635>

23 Ruth Wilson Gilmore, *Golden Gulag: Prisons, Surplus, Crisis, and Opposition in Globalizing California* (Berkeley: University of California Press, 2007). The California Legislative Analyst's Office notes that "[O]ver the past two decades, prison costs have increased... [with, among other factors,] increases in the inmate and parolee populations. Meanwhile, the state cost of educating university students has declined as the universities have enacted student fee increases that shift a portion of costs onto students": 'Prisons vs. Universities Proposal Would Unwisely Lock Up Budget Flexibility', 26 January, 2010. <http://www.lao.ca.gov/reports/2010/edu/educ_prisons/educ_prisons_012610.aspx> On militarized policing at UC, see Max Blumenthal, 'From Occupation to "Occupy": The Israelification of American Domestic Security', *Al-Akhbar*, 2 December, 2011. <http://english.al-akhbar.com/content/occupation-"occupy"-israelification-american-domestic-security>

24 Dylan Rodríguez, 'De-Provincializing Police Violence: On the Recent Events at UC Davis', *Race and Class*, Vol. 54 (2012), pp. 99-109, p. 104.

25 Nathan Brown, 'Five Theses on Privatization and the UC Struggle', *Keep California's Promise*, 15 November, 2011. <http://keepcaliforniaspromise.org/2186/five-theses-on-privatization-and-the-uc-struggle> See also Jennifer Doyle, 'Silent Majority: California's War on its Students', *Nation Blog*, 28 November, 2011. <http://www.thenation.com/blog/164819/silent-majority-californias-war-its-students#>

26 Christopher F. Edley Jr. and Charles F. Robinson, *Response to Protests on UC Campuses: A Report to President Mark G. Yudof*, 4 May, 2012, p. 12. <http://campusprotestreport.universityofcalifornia.edu/documents/Robinson-Edley-Report-043012.pdf>

27 Edley and Robinson, *Response to Protests*, p. 17.

28 Edley and Robinson, *Response to Protests*, p. 12.

29 Edley and Robinson, *Response to Protests*, p. 8-9, 19.

30 Edley and Robinson, *Response to Protests*, p. 5.

31 Edley and Robinson, *Response to Protests*, p. 37.

32 Edley and Robinson, *Response to Protests*, p. 6.

33 Edley and Robinson, *Response to Protests*, pp. 5, 13, 20, 21, 22, 37, 55, 62.

34 Edley and Robinson, *Response to Protests*, p. 9 [emphasis added].

35 Edley and Robinson, *Response to Protests*, p. 12, 16.

36 Edley and Robinson, *Response to Protests*, p. 39.

37 Edley and Robinson, *Response to Protests*, p. 55.

38 Edley and Robinson, *Response to Protests*, p. 61.

39 Edley and Robinson, *Response to Protests*, p. 62.

40 'The University of California Police Department (UCPD) is the police agency charged with providing law enforcement to the campuses of the University of California system.' <http://en.wikipedia.org/wiki/UCPD>

41 Edley and Robinson, *Response to Protests*, p. 2.

42 Edley and Robinson, *Response to Protests*, p. 77.

43 Edley and Robinson, *Response to Protests*, p. 38. 'Hands-on pain compliance' refers to techniques such as applying pressure to sensitive points on the body and applying twist-locks and wristlocks. On the use of pain compliance by police at UC Santa Cruz, see University of California Santa Cruz, *Senate Executive Committee Tent University Report*, 1 February, 2006, p. 2. <http://senate.ucsc.edu/archives/campus-demonstration-response/TUSCreptSCP1479.pdf> See also Richard Nance, 'Pain Compliance vs. Body Mechanics', *Officer.com*, 15 March, 2007. <http://www.officer.com/article/10250067/pain-compliance-vs-body-mechanics> For controversy regarding the use of pain compliance in policing anti-abortion demonstrations in the US, see '"Pain Compliance" -- New Sector Lodges Brutality Complaints Against Police', *The Seattle Times*, 14 January, 1990. <http://community.seattletimes.nwsource.com/archive/?date=19900114&slug=1050745>

44 Edley and Robinson, *Response to Protests*, p. 39.

45 Edley and Robinson, *Response to Protests*, p. 78.

46 Edley and Robinson, *Response to Protests*, p. 82.

47 Edley and Robinson, *Response to Protests*, p. 63.

48 Robinson and Edley, *Response to Protests*, pp. 13, 89. The report does state that videotaping "should be conducted in a manner that avoids chilling speech" (p. 89).

49 Quoting Edley and Robinson, *Response to Protests*, p. 96.

50 Edley and Robinson acknowledge that "some believe an approach that asks protesters to work with the Administration is the antithesis of what civil disobedience is." They also insist that "This Report emphatically is not

concerned with stopping protests, curbing criticism of the University, or discouraging debate about larger social issues": *Response to Protests*, p. 9.

51 Judith Butler, quoted in Charlie Smith, 'Feminist scholar Judith Butler foresees rising repression against protests in the western world', *Straight.com*, 23 May 23, 2012. <http://www.straight.com/article-692066/vancouver/prof-foresees-rising-brutalit>

52 Edley and Robinson, *Response to Protests*, p. 6.

53 'I'm Borrowing My Way Through College', *Left Business Observer,* No. 125 (February 2010). <http://www.leftbusinessobserver.com/College.html>

54 'Despite Angry Protests, UC Regents Raise Administrators' Salaries', *The Bay Citizen*, 28 November, 2011. <http://www.baycitizen.org/education/story/protesters-demand-uc-regents-raises/> 'Behind Closed Doors, UC Regents Again Vote to Raise Admin Salaries', *Reclaim UC*, 28 November, 2011. <http://reclaimuc.blogspot.com/2011/11/behind-closed-doors-uc-regents-again.html>; 'UC's Administrators Crossed the Line', *Keep California's Promise,* 19 September, 2001. <http://keepcaliforniaspromise.org/2001/ucs-administrators-crossed-the-line> [accessed July 5, 2012].

55 Will Parrish and Darwin Bond-Graham, 'Who Rules the University? To What Ends Do They Rule?', *Reclamations,* Vol. 2 (April 2010). <http://reclamationsjournal.org/issue02_parrish_bondgraham.html>; Bob Samuels, 'Will the Regents Protect the Middle Class?', *Changing Universities*, 17 May, 2011. <http://changinguniversities.blogspot.com/2011/05/will-regents-protect-middle-class.html>; 'The 21st Century Strong Public University: A Proposal for the Reform of the Structure of the Board of Regents of the University of California', 7 December, 2009. <http://ucdemocracy.org/RegentsReformProposal_Main.pdf>; 'Accountable UC', <http://www.ucwatch.org/accountableUC.html> [accessed July 3, 2012]; Bob Meister, 'They Pledged Your Tuition to Wall Street', *Keep California's Promise*, 11 October, 2009. *<http://keepcaliforniaspromise.org/383/they-pledged-your-tuition>* [accessed July 5, 2012]; Peter Byrne, 'Investors' Club: How the University of California Regents Spin Public Money into Private Profit', 21 September, 2010. <http://www.berkeleydailyplanet.com/issue/2010-09-21/article/36292?headline=The-Investors-Club-How-the-University-of-California-Regents-Spin-Public-Money-into-Private-Profit>; Michael Hiltzik, 'Is UC Regent's Vision for Higher Education Clouded by his Investments?', *Los Angeles Times*, 14 July, 2010. <http://articles.latimes.com/2010/jul/14/business/la-fi-hiltzik-column-20100714>; Peter Byrne, 'University of California Invests $53 million in Two Diploma Mills Owned by a Regent', *SF Public Press*, 14 July, 2010. <http://sfpublicpress.org/news/2010-07/university-of-california-invests-53-million-in-two-diploma-mills-owned-by-a-regent>

56 'The 21st Century Strong Public University', p. 25. See also Concerned Students, Faculty, Staff and Community Members at UC Riverside, 'Open

Letter Re: January 19th Regents Meeting' <http://ucaft.org/content/open-letter-re-january-19th-regents-meeting-ucr>

16. When Co-option Fails

Tom Anderson

> *I rejoice that I live in a country where peaceful protest is a natural part of our democratic heritage.*
>
> Tony Blair[1]

> *The right to protest is an important aspect of a democratic society but when people cross the line into criminal activity they should be aware they may well find themselves facing prosecution.*
>
> Rob Turnbull, Chief Crown Prosecutor for North Yorkshire (Speaking before the guilty verdict was passed against twenty-two environmental activists who interfered with the transporting of coal, 2009).[2]

The British government, like all liberal 'democracies', frequently proclaims itself a defender of freedom of expression and assembly. However, this is usually accompanied by the words 'rule of law'. As this article will show, this provides a get-out clause, enabling governments to justify the repression of the same political freedoms they claim to defend. Since this 'rule of law' is created and developed by governments and the judicial system, it ensures governments can devise new ways with which to repress those who threaten state and corporate interests in response to changing circumstances and changing patterns of dissent. In this way the 'rule of law' serves to protect capitalist interests, in the name of public order, security and democracy. By using labels such as 'terrorist' and 'domestic extremist', particular forms of activity can be cast as beyond the pale, as having crossed the line from legitimate dissent into criminal activity. Meanwhile, activity which does not fundamentally challenge or disrupt the structures of capitalism can be promoted as proof of societies' 'democratic' nature. This power to set these lines of right and wrong, lawful and criminal in parliament and in the courts, and often by extension in the mainstream media and dominant discourses, are reserved for the state and justify its deployment of coercive strategies - including judicial punishments, repression and the use of violence - against those who threaten the interests of capitalist 'democracy'. In this way, the 'rule of law' serves a vital function in the organisation of consent and the protection of capitalism from the dissent that inevitably arises out of the structural inequalities that the capitalist system is predicated upon.

This article will look at UK governments' recent strategies to repress individuals, social movements and communities who try to remain unco-opted and uncontrolled, and at the ways in which this repression is legitimated via the ideological and material application of the 'rule of law' as a central, defining tenet of 'democracy'. It will explore how the ability to define 'legal' and 'illegal' provides a crucial means by which political dissent is channelled into 'legitimate' forms which do not fundamentally threaten capitalist interests, while dissent which cannot be channelled or co-opted is criminalised and rendered illegitimate, pernicious and therefore deserving of repression.

In contemporary liberal 'democracies' it is claimed that the right to political dissent is protected and that dissent will only be punished if it is expressed through criminal means, and even then that punishment will be lawful and just. However, the rule of law does not always adequately serve the purpose of repressing forms of dissent which cannot be controlled and co-opted. As a result the state adopts strategies aimed at controlling and repressing even those who have *not* broken any law. Authorities justify these strategies by invoking the need to protect the public and prevent crime. These strategies include: the systematic undermining of dissent; smear campaigns against activist groups; the use of fear, threats and intimidation; and use of judicial and extra-judicial means of repression against political groups which can even contravene the rule of law.

This article looks at the state in the UK's strategies towards those who engage in acts of dissent over, roughly, the last 30 years. The terms 'dissent' and 'act of dissent' are used here to describe all actions aimed at altering the current status quo. The term 'status-quo' is defined as the current state of affairs, thus 'dissent', defined in this way, encompasses both acts aimed at challenging the system itself and those at achieving limited change to one aspect of how society and/or culture are currently manifested. Thus, this article focuses on the actions of individuals and groups who have taken, or planned to take, some form of collective action or an action, whether taken independently or with others, expressly intended to achieve the collective purpose of criticising, obstructing or altering the way society currently operates. Of course, this does not encompass all possible forms of dissent, for example shoplifting could be seen as an act of dissent against capitalism or the concept of private property but is not typically overtly seeking to effect change for a collective or serve a collective purpose. Such individual acts are, of course, criminalised and repressed, but with less recourse to the ideology of democracy and freedom of expression as, however disruptive they are to the operations of capitalism, they are not commonly treated as an expression of political dissent.

Legislating to Manage Dissent

It is possible to see the political nature of the rule of law in the legislative responses to conditions in which dissent cannot be co-opted and disrupts or challenges the operations of capitalism. In the UK there has been a marked acceleration over the past thirty years in the creation of new police powers and new criminal law, much of which has had the effect of realigning the parameters of lawful and unlawful dissent, criminalising forms of collective action which threaten capitalist interests, and promoting forms of dissent which do not. This is not to suggest that legislation is always made with the express purpose of curtailing dissent. The systems which protect the principles of private property and the primacy of private profit (such as the legal system or the media) are the aggregate results of tacit agreements and shared values that evolve over time, rather than the result of pre-planned, coordinated and coherent construction. The end product, nevertheless, is a legal system which overwhelmingly reflects corporate and elite interests, and serves to demonise and repress those who challenge them.

One major new piece of legislation which has had a dramatic impact upon the management of dissent in the UK was Thatcher's Conservative government's Criminal Justice and Public Order Act (CJA), introduced in 1986 and refined and amended by the Major Government's 1994 Public Order Act.[3] The Conservative governments justified the introduction of what the then Home Secretary Michael

Howard dubbed "the most comprehensive programme of action against crime that has ever been announced by any Home Secretary",[4] by invoking the need to "make sure that it is criminals who are frightened not law abiding members of the public."[5] The protection of 'democracy' from terrorism was used as justification to restrict the right to silence[6] while convenient scapegoats such as Travelling communities, hunt saboteurs and organisers of raves[7] were deployed to justify new repressive legislation, such as the new offence of aggravated trespass, which serves to protect private property.[8] However, despite these justifications, the provisions of the act were drawn up in response to the needs of various elite groups: from the British Field Sports Society (BFSS) which lobbied for legislation against hunt saboteurs,[9] scientific lobby groups seeking to protect pharmaceutical companies from animal rights activists,[10] landlords seeking to remove squatters, politicians seeking to enact unpopular legislation, police pushing for greater powers and corporations seeking to exploit workers and the environment free from restraint.

The 1986 CJA, enacted by the Thatcher government, gave the police the power to restrict public gatherings and marches[11] and allowed the police to make arrests for a variety of offences relating to speech, for example, language or behaviour likely to cause harassment, intimidation, alarm or distress under section 5 of the act.[12] Section 5, in practice, has been used to restrict the shouting of political slogans at demonstrations,[13] prevent animal rights activists from displaying placards depicting vivisection[14] and for stepping on the flag of the USA outside an American air base.[15]

The Conservative Major government increased police powers further with the 1994 CJA, which created the new crime of aggravated trespass (trespass on land with the intent to disrupt lawful business)[16] and expanded police powers to conduct searches.[17] The introduction of the crime of aggravated trespass was particularly significant in consolidating the power of land owners as it allowed police, for the first time, to order trespassers to leave land, and potentially to charge them, if they were deemed to be disrupting 'lawful business'. Previously, the removal of trespassers had been a civil matter between the landlord and the occupier. The legislation originally only applied to trespass on land 'in the open air',[18] as it was originally packaged as a measure to deal with hunt saboteurs. However, it was soon amended to apply inside buildings too, apparently in response to indoor anti-arms fair demonstrations[19] and also to lobbying from groups close to the pharmaceutical industry, which had been targeted by the animal rights movement.[20]

Tony Blair's Labour government further amended the CJA by

granting police powers to restrict marches and assemblies, reducing the number of people that can lawfully constitute an illegal assembly from 20 to 2,[21] and specifically authorising senior police officers to order the removal of masks for the first time.[22]

The CJA allows police and prosecutors a degree of latitude in using these powers to arrest and prosecute. Authorities are able to choose whether or not to invoke their special powers. For instance, they can choose to request the removal of masks or impose conditions on the route or behaviour of a demonstration, based upon available intelligence on who will be taking part in the demonstration, the focus of the demonstration and the perceived likelihood of any crime taking place. When utilised, these special powers send a message to the public that demonstrators must be behaving illegally in some way to be subject to such restrictions. This demonisation then becomes self-perpetuating: the repression often defines the image of the protest in people's understanding, rather than the content of the demonstration or the action itself. Such a negative portrayal is no doubt also intended to dissuade people from taking similar action.

The CJA also allows, under Section 11,[23] police to request that demonstrators notify them when organising a march or static protest. In practice, when notification takes place the police request meetings with organisers and enter into a negotiation process over, for example, the route of marches and stewarding.[24] The purpose of this provision is to allow the police to pursue a divide and rule strategy, as those demonstrations whose organisers have come forward are held up as examples of 'good' protesters who are protesting within the law. However, negotiating with the police serves to limit the potential effectiveness of protest as those who negotiate are subjected to bureaucratic controls and the possibility of being held responsible for the actions of other protesters. For example an organiser of a demonstration in Brighton in 2006 whose participants marched on the road when the police had stipulated prior to the event that they must walk on the pavement was warned under Section 11 of the Act.[25] On the other hand, those who refuse to negotiate are often held to be intent on criminality and as a result deserving of police repression such as surveillance, violence, arrests and the application of special measures such as kettling.[26]

Extensive legislation has also been developed in order to control organised workers' movements, which can pose a threat to private profit and act as a restraint on, and potentially even a threat to the operations of capitalism. The potential for workers to organise effectively on issues like wages, conditions, hours or the business practices of their employers has long been legislated against. However, the Thatcher and Major governments did more than any other governments since the Second World War to hamstring effective collective action in the workplace by erecting bureaucratic hurdles to and criminalising forms of collective action, while legislating to protect state approved, less effective trade union action. Between 1980 and 1993 six pieces of legislation had a dramatic effect on workers' struggles. These were the introduction of compulsory ballots before industrial action from 1984;[27] the stipulation that these ballots must be postal from 1992,[28] the introduction of cumbersome ballot procedures;[29] the placing of restrictions on the use of union funds for political aims;[30] restrictions on picketing[31] and the criminalisation of secondary action (sympathy picketing).[32] The legislation has meant in practice that trade unions are only able to organise around specific issues of pay and conditions in specific workplaces rather than striking in sympathy with their fellow workers in other workplaces or challenging an employer's general business practices. For example it would be very difficult, due to the cumbersome procedures, for employees working for the same employer in different workplaces, facing job losses and a deterioration of working conditions resulting from their employers' strategy of privatisation to organise action against privatisation itself. The legislation also made trade unions that had taken 'unlawful' action under the new balloting procedures subject to large fines and ultimately to the sequestration of funds, as happened to the National Union of Mineworkers in 1984.[33] In this way this legislation limited the potential of trade unions in the UK to act effectively for their members in securing better pay and conditions from employers and provided further protection for the interests of private business. The measures were sold to the population by claiming that trade unions required proper oversight and scrutiny in order to ensure that society could operate effectively, safe from the potential for trades unions to abuse their power. This was part of the rhetoric propagated by Margaret Thatcher and others in the Conservative Party that the unions were a threat to democracy and had to be reined in. In 1984 Thatcher famously compared the war against the "enemy without" in the Falklands to the "enemy within", i.e. the trade union movement, which is "much more difficult to fight and more dangerous to liberty".[34] The effect of this legislation has been to channel trade union activism into state sanctioned actions which do not present a systemic threat. Paid trade union officials could put their positions at risk if they took radical political action, so they have a vested interest in avoiding full-scale confrontation with employers and the authorities, where they could be portrayed as breaking the law and thus risk both the union's assets and their own positions. As a result, the trade union movement has increasingly focused on organising in the public sector,[35] where there is comparatively less risk of falling foul of secondary picketing legislation as large numbers of workers are employed by the same employer, and on pursuing legalistic strategies such as workplace tribunals, rather than more visible and collective forms of action.[36]

Far from guaranteeing civil liberties as they claimed, the Labour government further extended police powers to repress the freedom to protest, supposedly a defining element of British democracy. On top of extending the provisions of the CJA, legislation was introduced to make it unlawful to withhold your name from a police officer if that officer has reason to believe you have been involved in anti-social behaviour,[37] and restricting the right to protest outside parliament[38] or in the vicinity of nuclear sites[39] and some other military bases.[40]

Labour also introduced new legislation specifically targeted at animal rights activists. The animal rights movement's adoption of anti-corporate campaigning, focusing on targeting the shareholders in and service providers to companies involved in vivisection, threatened their profits and had the potential to affect the viability of those companies. The Labour government under Tony Blair introduced legislation which made some acts illegal but only in relation to organisations involved in animal testing. In 2005, an amendment to the Serious Organised Crime and Police Act (SOCPA) made it illegal to "interfere with the contractual relations of an animal research organisation" or to "intimidate employees of an animal research organisation".[41] The intent of this was to demonise the actions of the entire animal rights movement as having crossed the line into criminality. The consequent state repression served to discourage others from getting involved out of fear of judicial punishments and to channel public sympathy away from the cause. Harsh sentences for those who breached the new law (which included a four and a half year prison sentence for Sean Kirtley simply for updating a website with animal rights related information[42] and even harsher sentences of up to sixteen years in prison handed down to activists involved in the Stop Huntingdon Animal Cruelty (SHAC) campaign for conspiracy to blackmail[43]) served to label animal rights campaigners as dangerous criminals and justify the removal of their right to exercise dissent and even express their views.[44] This is a typical use of legislation and harsh sentencing to discourage and demonise effective anti-corporate political activities.

The current Conservative/Liberal Democrat Coalition has attempted to reshape some of the legislation that the Labour governments were unable to implement. For instance, in 2011, after a long campaign against them,[45] the Coalition government repealed the restrictions on protest in parliament square, and replaced them with a new list of restrictions on the use of loudhailers and the erection of tents.[46] In addition, it has taken steps to restrict protest outside Kensington Palace.[47] The Coalition also sought to consolidate the protections given to private landlords by the CJA by, in September 2012, making it illegal to squat in a residential building, something which the Conservative Party had long been advocating.[48] However, the Coalition's legislative programme has so far been largely focused on the implementation of the privatisation of public services and cuts to the welfare state, which have been accompanied by statements mandating the police to use violence against those attempting to resist them. The Coalition's next steps may be to bring in a new swathe of repressive legislation to control public anger at these policies.

These legislative changes have served to limit the possibilities for dissent in the UK and to shift the legislative goalposts, in order justify the demonisation, criminalisation and imprisonment of particular target individuals and communities. People who breach any of these new provisions are defined as having crossed a line into unlawfulness, whether that line be protesting without permission outside parliament, picketing in solidarity with your fellow workers, wearing a mask to protect yourself from police surveillance, demonstrating outside a laboratory or US air base or living as a Traveller or a squatter. The impact of making these acts unlawful is to render them illegitimate, pernicious and in opposition to the dominant ideology of British democracy.

Setting Up Specialised Political Police Forces

In order to control dissent effectively and away from the public eye a number of specialised police units have been set up to target particular forms of dissent. These units act with the bare minimum of visibility, allowing the majority of the public to remain unaware of their existence. They are effective tools, not only to enforce government legislation, but to enable the use of a greater variety of tactics and methods to undermine and repress dissent. These tactics have included arrest and prosecution, the use of undercover officers, overt and covert surveillance, harassment and intimidation, and the promotion of a negative image of particular groups in the media and in public opinion. The creation of such police units often ensures both that the law is applied with its full weight to certain groups involved in certain forms of dissent when they break the law, and that some people involved in acts of dissent who *have not* broken any law are nonetheless criminalised and delegitimised. This illustrates that the function of these police units is less about protecting the population than protecting the powerful from challenges.

The direct political use of specialised police units is evident in the creation in 1968 of the Special Demonstration Squad (SDS), following the militant protests against UK government support for the US' war in Vietnam, with the aim of "preventing serious crimes associated with protest".[49] Until 2008, this operated as part of the Metropolitan Police Service.[50] Bob Lambert, an undercover police officer who infiltrated animal rights, environmental and anti-racist groups in the 1980s and 1990s was working, at least partly, for the SDS. (See also Anderson, Chapter 17.) Other units were established in the 1980s and 1990s, including the Animal Rights National Index (ARNI), set up as part of Scotland Yard[51] in 1986[52] in response to the success of the animal rights movement in targeting businesses involved in vivisection. ARNI's original role was "advising regional forces"[53] on how to deal with animal rights activists but its remit was extended in 1991, and consequently Anti-Terrorist Branch Officers were deployed against the animal rights movement.[54]

Since 1999 several new political units of the police force have been created,[55] many of which operate under the aegis of the Association of Chief Police Officers (ACPO) which was registered in 1997 as a private limited company[56] funded partly by the Home Office and through fees paid by local police forces.[57] This private company status means that the police departments operating under ACPO are freer from public scrutiny than traditional police units.[58] ACPO's status as a private company made it exempt from Freedom of Information legislation until this was reviewed in 2011.[59] Its incorporation as a private company also ensures it can retain a surplus from its income from membership fees and state funding and therefore has a degree of flexibility and independence in allocating its budgets.[60] Political units of the police force which have been under the command of ACPO include the National Domestic Extremism Unit, the National Extremism Tactical Coordination Unit (NETCU), the National Domestic Extremism Team (NDET) and the National Public Order Intelligence Unit (NPOIU). The fact that these units are arms of a private limited company rather than public bodies ensures their activities are conducted in relative secrecy. This is helpful in hiding the fact that the political repression meted out by these units to some groups of activists and protesters contradicts the dominant discourse which claims that the state guards our democratic rights to protest.

The creation of the NPOIU can be traced to concerns about the how to respond to changing patterns of dissent. It was set up by ACPO in 1999[61] following the publication of a HM Inspectorate of Constabularies (HMIC) report which claimed that some protest groups "have adopted a strategic, long-term approach to their protests employing new and innovative tactics to frustrate authorities and achieve their objectives" and noted in alarmed tones the existence of "evidence that some elements operate in cell like structures in a quasi-terrorist mode to keep secret their movements and intentions."[62] The NPOIU was located within the Metropolitan Police Service (MPS) and funded by the Home Office to gather and coordinate "intelligence".[63] The NPOIU has been responsible for deploying undercover officers within several UK direct action campaigns as well as carrying out overt surveillance of direct action groups.[64] (See also Anderson, Chapter 17.) Similarly, the NETCU was created in 2004 as a response to the animal rights movement. ACPO described the NETCU's role as to "promote a joined up, consistent and effective response to local police forces dealing with single-issue extremism of any character - including animal rights extremism"[65] and to provide "a central support and liaison service to animal research and related industries".[66] It was based in Huntingdon, Cambridgeshire, close to one of the UK animal rights movement's major corporate targets, Huntingdon Life Sciences (HLS). NETCU began referring to 'domestic extremism', a term which for a long time had no formal definition but which was defined in a HMIC report published in 2011 as: "activity, individuals or campaign groups that carry out criminal acts of direct action in furtherance of what is typically a single issue campaign. They usually seek to prevent something from happening or to change legislation or domestic policy, but attempt to do so outside of the normal democratic process".[67] The label 'domestic extremist' is, in practice, applied to those groups who do not compromise on their principles or tactics, particularly with regards to negotiating with the police, or over their use of direct action tactics. This could, until recently, be seen by glancing at NETCU's news-feed of information on domestic extremism which has included information on a broad range of people and groups from anti-G8 activists to campaigners against climate change and animal rights activists.[68]

The current statement on 'domestic extremism', from the ACPO website, claims that there is no hard and fast definition of a 'domestic extremist' but that "the term only applies to individuals or groups whose activities go outside the normal democratic process and engage in crime and disorder in order to further their campaign." The website notes that "[e]xtremists may operate independently, but will sometimes try to mask their activities by associating closely with legitimate campaigners. The police work hard to ensure that the majority of protesters can campaign peacefully while stopping the few individuals who break the law."[69] It is clear from this explanation that if and when dissent breaks the law then it will be considered to be 'domestic extremism' and thus, labelling activists as 'domestic extremists', whether or not they have committed criminal offences, implies that they have committed acts which are outside the law and are therefore no longer to be deemed 'peaceful' or 'legitimate' campaigners.

One of NETCU's key tasks was to undermine activist groups defined as 'domestic extremist' groups by feeding negative stories to the media. For instance, the NETCU worked closely with Timothy Lawson-Cruttenden, a lawyer working on behalf of a number of corporations (see below). Cruttenden's litigation against anti-corporate campaign groups like anti-arms industry group Smash EDO, climate change activists Plane Stupid and animal rights activists SHAC was accompanied by ideological justifications in the media which sought to delegitimise campaigners through demonisation. One story, published in *The Times* in 2004, archived on the 'media' section of the Lawson Cruttenden & Co website,[70] portrayed anti-arms trade campaigners as dangerous extremists seeking to "intimidate" employees and operate outside the just parameters of democracy, despite its generous, legal provision for dissent.[71] The article quotes Lawson-Cruttenden: "Two years ago I was vocally against the Iraq war, but this is not about war and peace, it is about the right not to be harassed in a liberal democracy."[72] Such stories could even amount to blatant slander. In 2008 NETCU released a 'green-scare' story to *The Observer* which aimed to tarnish ecological activists as dangerously Malthusian,[73] claiming that activists had expressed the need to cull the human population for the good of the planet. The story, which had been sourced solely from the NETCU, was found to have no basis in fact and was retracted by its author.[74] There are also suspicions that hundreds of disruptive postings, from a government IP address to the activist open-posting news website, Indymedia, website originated from the NETCU.[75]

Another police unit with the explicitly political purpose of controlling political, usually left wing, activist groups is NDET, which was formed in 2005, and initially focused on the animal rights movement but fanned out to counter 'crimes' "linked to single issue-type causes" such as anti-militarist campaigns. [76] Similarly, the Public Order Operational Command Unit or Central Operations II (COII) is part of the Metropolitan Police Force in London and coordinates ground policing of protests in London, as well as running many of the Forward

Intelligence Teams (see below).[77]

In 2010 it emerged that NETCU, NPOIU and NDET would be merged and that a review of the role of ACPO would occur.[78] The SDS, the NPOIU and "other units under the National Domestic Extremism Unit (NDEU) were subsumed"[79] in January 2011 within the MPS.[80] The effects of this are yet to be seen but it is extremely unlikely that the reorganisation will drastically alter police practices, nor impact upon their abilities to manage dissent with minimal levels of transparency and accountability.

Blurring of Civil and Criminal Law

Between the late 1990s and early 2000s the Labour government introduced legislation which has resulted in blurring the distinctions between criminal and civil law, and has allowed the imposition of criminal penalties in cases where only a civil offence, and in some cases no offence known to law, has been committed. This has provided the police and prosecutors with a wider range of possible legal measures with which to repress dissent. The 1997 Protection from Harassment Act (PHA) and Anti-Social Behaviour Orders, introduced in 1998, allow the imposition of orders preventing activity which is not necessarily a criminal offence and make breaching such orders punishable with imprisonment. This represents a massive inflation in the possible penalty for certain types of behaviour, and allows for selective applications of the law, for such offences often have no statutory definition and are open to subjective interpretation by the courts. As a result, a more selective application of the rule of law has evolved allowing the criminalisation of behaviour that is simply considered unacceptable, and is therefore dependent upon the actions and subjective judgements of politicians, the judiciary and specialised police organisations.

Anti-Social Behaviour Orders (ASBOs), introduced in 1998,[81] allow magistrates to impose orders on people who have engaged in behaviour deemed to be anti-social. Criminal penalties can be imposed on people who break the orders,[82] despite the facts that ASB cases are heard by magistrates sitting in a civil, rather than criminal, capacity and that ASBOs often proscribe behaviour which is not normally considered criminal, and may not even be tortious (i.e. cause someone to suffer a loss of some kind). Closed court hearings and hearsay evidence (i.e. evidence heard from a third party who is not present at court) are also allowed in ASB cases which can ensure that defendants have less opportunity to challenge prosecution evidence than in criminal cases.[83] ASBOs may be imposed for an open-ended period of time and there is no clear definition of behaviour which may be deemed to be antisocial. The success rate of ASBO applications is high, with only 3% being turned down.[84] Over 20,000 ASBOs were approved between 1999 and 2010.[85] ASBOs have frequently been used as a tool to undermine and criminalise dissent. For example, four of the defendants in a criminal trial relating to the SHAC campaign received indefinite Criminally Sought Anti Social Behaviour Orders (CRASBOs) which restricted them from protesting against animal experimentation.[86]

The introduction of ASBOs and CRASBOs allow crown prosecutors and judges to define for themselves which acts are inside or outside the law, without reference to everyday or legislative definitions of what is criminal. A cursory glance at the geographical and social breakdown of ASBOs issued suggests that ASBOS have been used disproportionately against working-class communities, a fact which is illustrated by the disproportionately high numbers of ASBOs being issued in Greater Manchester, West Yorkshire and the West Midlands,[87] areas which correspond to the some of the highest levels of poverty in the UK.[88] ASB legislation allows state judicial institutions which at root, operate to protect the principle of private property and are overwhelmingly dominated by those with the most class privilege. (See also Fisher, Chapter 2.) It could be argued that the state has a particular interest in criminalising the behaviour of those lacking economic privilege as, put bluntly, they have more reasons to rebel against the capitalist system. The ASB legislation is aided in this purpose by the mainstream media's eagerness to ridicule, patronise and demonise working class recipients of ASBOs, who are routinely branded 'ASBO yobs' and such-like.[89]

Theresa May, Conservative Home Secretary, has announced that ASBOs will be replaced by new measures but, at the time of writing, this change is yet to take place.[90] The proposed changes to ASB legislation comes in response to criticism over the efficacy of the measure in 'preventing anti-social behaviour'. However, the new proposals, including community triggered, i.e. complaint driven, 'Community Prevention Injunctions' and 'Criminal Behaviour Orders'[91] are a populist attempt to rebrand the orders as community driven. In fact the proposed changes will almost certainly continue in the same trajectory of attaching criminal penalties to civil offences.

The 1997 Protection from Harassment Act (PHA)[92] enabled state authorities to prosecute individuals for acts of harassment,[93] which may not have been in themselves criminal or even tortious, and enabled private individuals to apply to the courts for the imposition of orders against people they deemed to be harassing them. The act was developed, through precedents set in cases brought by solicitor-advocate, Timothy Lawson Cruttenden,[94] to ensure that groups of people could have injunctions passed against them and that corporations could seek injunctions against individuals or civil society groups which they alleged were harassing them.[95] The idea that a corporation can be 'harassed' was yet another step in the long-running transformation of corporations into entities that enjoy the same legal rights as human beings but which cannot be punished by measures like imprisonment as they are not human.[96]

These PHA injunctions were used to impose conditions on individuals for behaviour that would not otherwise be considered criminal: examples include using a camera, a megaphone or playing musical instruments.[97] The penalty for breaching PHA injunctions is a sentence of up to five years in prison and several people, including anti-militarist activists Paul Robinson[98] and Jaya Sacca,[99] spent time in prison on remand for alleged breaches.

The first use of the PHA to protect corporations from dissent was a case brought by Timothy Lawson-Cruttenden on behalf of Huntingdon Life Sciences. In the HLS case, Lawson-Cruttenden argued in the High Court that HLS was not only a corporation being harassed, but that it did not need to name its harassers. HLS claimed it was not one person, or even several named people, who were 'potential harassers'; it was anyone who protested against them. An interim injunction was thus granted against *all* protesters, i.e. anyone who sought to demonstrate against HLS. The injunction restricted the time and duration of protests and the noise levels at protests, meaning that anyone who did not observe these stipulations was in breach and risked fines or even imprisonment.[100]

Following the HLS success, Lawson-Cruttenden went on to apply for injunctions on behalf of Bayer, DHL, Harrods, Oxford University, TNT and others that had been targeted by the SHAC.[101] A close relationship developed between Lawson-Cruttenden and NETCU which supplied Lawson-Cruttenden with intelligence about the campaigns against which he was seeking injunctions.[102] Thus, corporate-friendly lawyers and specialist police departments have developed the PHA in such a way that it enables corporations such as HLS[103] or arms company EDO MBM[104] to claim blanket protection from anyone, including unnamed individuals, they choose to label a 'protester'. This allows corporations and other powerful groups, often with enthusiastic backing from specialised police units, to shape what is lawful and unlawful for those opposing them. The use of the PHA against groups of protesters has been effectively challenged in court by participants in the Smash EDO campaign,[105] SHAC[106] and the 2007 Heathrow Climate Camp[107] and as a result, its use has tailed off, except against animal rights activists, The PHA therefore remains a powerful potential tool for corporations seeking to repress dissent.

Surveillance

Overt surveillance is another method employed by the state to manage and suppress dissent, both as a means of information gathering and of intimidation. Pre-eminent among the justifications for surveillance is the claim that it will protect people's private property and personal security. For example, an article written for the website of the 2012 EUROSATORY defence and security fair[108] argued that surveillance tactics and technology, used to monitor social movements, could help prevent "destruction of property, injuries to innocent people and in some cases, death".[109] One aim of overt surveillance *is* the protection of private property but it also serves to deter, and protect the powerful from dissent. The proliferation of Closed Circuit Television (CCTV) cameras and increased use of overt police surveillance add to an atmosphere where disruptive action can seem risky or even unthinkable. Since the 1990s Britain has, it has been claimed, deployed more CCTV cameras per capita than any other country.[110] One 2005 study estimated that, at the time, 4.8 million cameras had been installed UK-wide. In addition, private businesses often employ advanced CCTV systems, with which to track, monitor and record activity surrounding their premises.

People involved in acts of dissent in the UK over the past decade have increasingly been subjected to overt police surveillance. The increased police attention given to those under surveillance implies that they are 'criminals' whether or not they actually have committed any criminal offence and irrespective of what they have actually done, which undermines their popular support. Overt police surveillance is also used to push potential supporters away from radical social movements by sending the message that associating with those under surveillance will be rewarded with the same treatment. The psychological impacts of being under surveillance can also severely impair individuals' ability to take political action.

Over the past fifteen years the police have also developed the use of overt surveillance against political activists. Forward Intelligence Teams (FITs) and Evidence Gathering Teams (EGTs) became a common fixture at protests, other large events, and even political meetings from the late 1990s.[111] FITs are groups of police officers equipped with cameras and video cameras, who aim to document the attendees at an event, photograph them and in doing so, broadcast to their targets the fact that they are being monitored.[112] FITs also carry with them 'capture cards' with photographs of people who are of interest to the police[113] whether or not they have previous convictions,[114] which mark the subject out for increased attention from police spotter teams.

Often FITs have been deployed more for their chilling effect on political movements than the prevention of 'disorder'. For instance, in 2009, during the trial of nine defendants prosecuted for conspiring to cause hundreds of thousands of pounds worth of damage to the EDO MBM factory in Brighton, FITs were regularly deployed at small demonstrations, of under fifteen people, outside the EDO factory.[115] This increased use of overt surveillance gave the impression that activists who attended the demonstrations would be criminalised, in the same way as the defendants in court and, as a result, put many people off being involved in the campaign.[116]

To an extent, the FITs have been effectively countered in the UK by activists, who began monitoring FIT teams and impeding their work by encouraging all demonstrators to wear masks, while organising groups of 'FIT Watchers' to block police cameras at demonstrations. At one anti-arms trade demonstration in 2008, the FIT teams were effectively forced to leave the protest by the counter-tactics of these 'FIT Watchers'.[117]

Another overt surveillance tactic is the deployment of officers from national police units during the trials of protesters. For instance, officers from the NPOIU were deployed at court cases of activists associated with the Smash EDO campaign during 2009-10 and SHAC during 2009. Officers provided an overt, oppressive presence in the court wearing lanyards to identify themselves and taking notes of snippets of overheard conversations in the public gallery.[118] This gave the impression, to the judiciary, jury and press, that the defendants, although not convicted, were seen as a threat to the rule of law, as well as presumably providing a practical intelligence-gathering purpose.

Following the death of Ian Tomlinson after being struck with a baton and pushed to the ground by Simon Harwood, a police officer at the G20 protests in 2009, police tactics have come under increased scrutiny. The resultant 2009 HMIC review[119] attempted to give the impression of an honest investigation and review of police tactics in an attempt to subdue public anger. The use of FITs has decreased somewhat since in favour of a more graded approach. For instance, at more recent demonstrations during the early stages of the student movement in

2010,[120] FITs used only notebooks rather than the more intrusive long-lensed cameras.

Of course, the police also practise covert surveillance, which, out of the public limelight, requires far less ideological justification. When exposed however, such as following the revelations in 2011 that undercover police officers had infiltrated various environmental and political movements in the 1990s and 2000s, the same claims to be protecting law and order were utilised. However, in this case, such arguments gained little traction, especially given that the groups infiltrated were not easily portrayed as 'dangerous' or 'a threat to society', which, as we have seen, has been a crucial ideological strategy to justify repression. Of course, infiltration is partly motivated by information gathering but it also shows the need for today's 'democracy' to control and influence people's political activities, undermine their autonomy and independence, and destroy their collective morale. (The strategy one undercover officer used to achieve this goal is explored in Anderson, Chapter 17.)

In 2012, following the HMIC enquiry into undercover policing, several police forces introduced Police Liaison Officers (PLOs),[121] officers who are deployed to engage in dialogue with protesters and to diffuse confrontation in public order situations as well as, in some instances, gather intelligence.[122] They are also deployed as a tactic to divide 'legitimate' protesters who engage with the authorities (in this case the police) from the 'illegitimate' ones who do not. Those protesters who do not engage with the police can then be portrayed as a potential threat, whose motives are suspicious since they must have something to hide, and whose actions can then be treated as having crossed the line into criminality. The role of PLOs was explained candidly by one PLO at an anti-fascist demonstration in Brighton, stating that he was there to "engage" with those present and "find out what your intentions are". When asked what happened if people refused to "engage" he replied that he would call in his colleagues with the "truncheons and pepper spray".[123]

Politicised Sentencing

After periods of social unrest the state and judiciary often work to ensure that sentences for those arrested are disproportionately heavy, with the view to create deterrents for future unrest. They clearly exercise a measure of discretion as to when and to what degree to exercise their power to impose harsh sentences. This discretion can be seen to correspond to role of the legal system in protecting the social order from political challenge, in particular from those with less power and less investment in and integration into the capitalist system. It very often results in political dimensions in sentencing, for instance in the differential treatment of less privileged, minority and marginalised communities. This can be seen in the disparity between the judicial treatment of the 2010-11 student movement and the 2009 Gaza solidarity movement.

The 2010-11 student movement involved rioting which exceeded any of the events during the 2009 Gaza solidarity movement yet those arrested were treated comparatively leniently. Meanwhile, the mass demonstrations outside the Israeli embassy at the time of the Israeli massacre in Gaza in 2009 known as 'Operation Cast Lead' ended in the arrest of 119 people[124] and the prosecution of 78.[125] The vast majority of these demonstrators were young Muslims and it was clear that the police wanted to punish them severely in order to avert a repeat of the demonstrations, and due to the inflated sense of threat that accompanies Muslim identity in a still deeply racially biased society. On giving sentence Judge Denniss, who presided over most of the hearings, made clear that the harsh sentences were intended, in part, to act as a "deterrent for those who may commit such of offences in the future"[126] and that those who took part in such protests "do so at their peril".[127] While such intentions have been voiced during other occurrences of unrest, including the 2010-11 student protests, harsh sentences to deter repeat offending are usually given to a small number of individuals, whereas in the case of the Gaza defendants the harsh treatment was almost across the board. Judge Denniss used the the 2001 Bradford riots cases as a benchmark. This prompted the Islamic Human Rights Commission (IHRC) to ask the rhetorical question in a commentary piece about the trials: "Could the presence of young Muslim males in both London and Bradford have been the deciding factor?"[128]

What seemed to have been most troubling to the authorities about the resistance to the Gaza massacre was the new unity between young, disenchanted Muslims and the more established Palestine solidarity movement, as well as their move towards more militant action. Sentences were harsh: those pleading guilty received between twelve months to two and a half years imprisonment. One man was sentenced to a one year prison sentence for throwing a plastic bottle in the direction of the police.[129] In court almost all of the defendants were required to surrender their passports and, despite the fact that the vast majority of those charged were British citizens, many were served with immigration notices which stated that they could be deported depending on the outcome of criminal proceedings.[130]

The 2001 Bradford riots, which Judge Denniss had used as a benchmark, were also the subject of much controversy as many commentators claim that the treatment of the 115 people who were convicted and who received, on average, sentences of four and a half years in prison,[131] was far harsher than sentences given for other riots around the UK which did not involve marginalised, minority communities.[132]

On the other hand, although there was some involvement from working class communities, the 2010/11 student movement against the rise in tuition fees and the scrapping of the Education Maintenance Allowance was at its core an issue which affected predominantly white middle class young people. The movement began with a group breaking away from a National Union of Students (NUS) demonstration on 11 November, 2010, breaking into and trashing the Conservative Party HQ at Millbank.[133] Later demonstrations that year saw the trashing of police vehicles,[134] damage to the Treasury building,[135] riots in Oxford Street[136] and an attack on a royal convoy carrying the Prince of Wales.[137] Altogether, 325 people were arrested and many of their cases are still ongoing at the time of writing. Sentences were harsh - up to two years and eight months custodial sentence for one demonstrator who threw a fire extinguisher off the roof of Millbank into a crowd of police below. However many have been dealt with by way of community service orders, suspended sentences and electronic tags.[138] According to the Legal Defence Monitoring Group, of the 180 cases where defendants were alleged to have been involved in serious 'disorder' which had been dealt with by March 2012 eighteen were handed a custodial sentence; twenty-one were given community service; twelve were given suspended prison sentences; seven were dealt with by way of electronic tagging; nine with curfews; one with a bind over to keep the peace; one with a fine; four were thrown out before they were brought to court; ten were found not guilty by juries and in one case the judge instructed the jury to reach a not guilty verdict.[139] Thus, while some of defendants from the student demonstrations were given harsh, exemplary sentences as deterrents to others, these were the worst examples, in stark comparison to the Gaza defendants, where non-custodial sentences were the exception.

The riots which took place in several English cities in August 2011 resulted in the imprisonment of 1,292 people and can be seen as another example of political sentencing.[140] Those convicted were predominantly from working class backgrounds and sentences were invariably harsh. Some of the most shocking examples include two men who were sentenced to four and a half years in prison for posting messages on Facebook which the court found had been intended to incite rioting;[141] a woman who was given a five month prison sentence for receiving a pair of shorts looted from a store during the riots; and a man who was sentenced to six months in prison for stealing £3.50 worth of bottled water.[142] A senior justice-clerk had issued advice to judges nationwide to disregard normal sentencing guidelines[143] when considering riot cases, mirroring David Cameron's statement before the Commons that anyone convicted of riot offences should go to jail.[144]

The current dominant political discourse in the UK places equality, and particularly equality before the law, as a fundamental and inviolable principle at the foundation of British democracy. However, when confronted with disorder the state and its judicial system use their latitude in choosing and recommending sentences to treat people in ways that are far from equal. As we have seen, when marginalised groups, whose integration within, and thus consent to, the capitalist system is less reliable, are involved in acts of rebellion, they are treated in a disproportionately harsh manner. This is because these communities gain comparatively little from capitalism and their consent requires shoring up with coercion and intimidation. (See also Pollard and Young, Chapter 14).

Democracy and the 'War on Terror'

George Bush stated the supposedly democratic purpose behind his policies of militaristic aggression and domestic repression in a speech to Congress on 20 September, 2001 when he launched the 'War on Terror': "Americans are asking, why do they hate us? They hate what we see right here in this Chamber, a democratically elected government. Their leaders are self-appointed. They hate our freedoms - our freedom of religion, our freedom of speech, our freedom to vote and assemble and disagree with each other".[145] He called for a global war which would, he said, be "civilization's fight",[146] adding without irony, "This is the fight of all who believe in progress and pluralism, tolerance and freedom".[147]

The language of the 'War on Terror' shows how integral the concept of 'the rule of law' is to the rhetoric of democracy, yet in practice it has facilitated the use of extra-judicial measures such as illegal invasion, 'extraordinary rendition', assassinations, torture, detention without trial and collective punishments. These measures show that the rule of law is not enough to ensure a sufficient degree of compliance for the imperialist foreign policies of capitalist 'democracies'. Governments invoke the 'terrorist' threat to 'democracy' in order to go beyond their legal powers both nationally and globally. The 'War on Terror' ironically utilises a rhetoric of democracy and the rule of law to justify and extend state repressive and extra-legal powers which in practice contravene both 'democracy' and the 'rule of law'.

The 'War on Terror' has served as a smokescreen for imperialist capitalist expansion and the maintenance of US global military and economic dominance. The 'War on Terror' has thus engendered a very unstable process of ideological and military warfare, in which support for US 'liberation' is sorely lacking, and wars in Iraq and Afghanistan that were conceived as quick, military ventures turned into prolonged military occupations.

In the UK, in the context of the 'War on Terror', Muslim people have been singled out by the state for special treatment. 'Islamic terrorism' and 'Islamic extremism' have become categories of dissent which are dealt with using strategies of repression which are often entirely different from those used against other groups. The government's PREVENT strategy for counter-terrorism defines extremism as: "the vocal or active opposition to fundamental British values, including democracy, the rule of law, individual liberty and mutual respect and tolerance of different faiths and beliefs" and includes "calls for the death of members of our armed forces, whether in this country or overseas".[148] The definition of 'domestic extremism' deployed by the police is quite different: a "single-issue campaign" which goes "outside the normal democratic process".[149] The two definitions of 'extremism' differ because they are intended to provide a justification for the repression of two separate forms of dissent: 'domestic extremists', dealt with by public order law, police infiltration and surveillance and specialist police departments, and 'terrorism', dealt with by anti-terror legislation.

Although the rhetorical justification for the 'War on Terror' and for anti-terrorist measures in the UK are primarily aimed at the Muslim community, the repressive strategies themselves have a potentially universal application, which has so far been applied selectively by the state. The 'War on Terror' has been used successfully to enact a huge raft of measures which provide the state with a plethora of judicial and police powers with which to repress dissent. The use of terror legislation often has little to do with anything that could be described as terrorism.

Schedule 7 of the Terrorism Act 2000 for example, allows immigration officers, customs officers or police officers to detain a suspect at an airport or port of entry into the UK for up to nine hours and question them.[150] Unlike elsewhere in English criminal law, suspects do not have the right to remain silent and if you fail to answer questions you can be fined or imprisoned.[151] According to the Institute of Race Relations, in 2010-11 the power to question under Schedule 7 was used over 65,000 times, 84% of those questioned for over one hour were from Black/Minority/Ethnic backgrounds.[152] Schedule 7 has also been used to question anti-globalisation activists,[153] anti-militarist activists,[154] Palestine solidarity campaigners,[155] anarchists,[156] climate change activists,[157] and alternative media activists.[158]

In 2000, even before the events of 11 September, 2001, the Blair government legislated a number of counter-terrorist powers including: arrest without a warrant;[159] new powers of stop and search;[160] expanded the list of proscribed organisations that it is illegal to be a member of[161] and allowed police to detain terrorist suspects for questioning for up to seven days without charge.[162] Later acts created the offence of 'glorifying terrorism'[163] and allowed the retention of communications data.[164]

Section 44 of the Terrorism Act 2000 allowed police to search in a designated area if a senior officer has authorised it.[165] Stop and search under Section 44, like Schedule 7, has disproportionately affected Black/Minority/Ethnic (BME) communities.[166] Section 44 was also used against protesters at, for example, the protests against the 2003 DSEi arms fair in Docklands[167] and the 2005 Labour Party conference.[168] Following a successful appeal to the European Court over use of Section 44 at the DSEi arms fair the power has been suspended. However, a revamped raft of stop and search powers has been enacted by the 2012 Protection of Freedoms Bill.[169] Thus legislation introduced under the guise of protecting society from 'terrorism' has been applied to domestic, political contexts where the threat is not terrorism, but other forms of political dissent.

In 2003 the period of detention for terrorist suspects was increased to fourteen days[170] and in 2006 it was increased, temporarily, to twenty-eight days.[171] The Labour government sought to increase the maximum period of detention without charge to up to ninety days but was outvoted. A 2011 parliamentary review[172] found that the maximum period of detention should be fourteen days. This fourteen day limit has been reaffirmed by the 2012 Protection of Freedoms Bill.[173]

The 2001 Anti-Terrorism Crime and Security Act, which allowed the indefinite detention of foreigners,[174] paved the way for the detention without trial of foreign nationals at Belmarsh prison.[175] After eight of these detainees won their appeal in the House of Lords in 2004 they were released but subjected to a new measure, control orders.[176] Control orders could be made in the interest of "protecting members of the public from a risk of terrorism"[177] and could be imposed against individuals in the absence of any charge. The orders could be used to restrict movement, employment, association, to restrict access to bank accounts and to confiscate passports.[178] There was no limit on the duration of a control order. This act was, however, repealed[179] in 2011 after persistent legal challenges made it untenable.[180]

The checks that parliament and the judiciary placed on the government during the Blair and Brown governments (for example the European Court's restriction on the use of Section 44, the British courts restriction on the use of Control orders and Parliament's curtailing of the period of detention without charge that is legally permissible) demonstrate how governments are not always able to mould the law to their satisfaction. As a result successive governments have resorted to extra-judicial measures.

When the 'Rule of Law' is Not Enough

It is apparent from the above that obstacles posed by the court system and parliament have prevented recent governments from implementing all of the measures they sought to use to control the general populace. However, illegality is not always a restraint on state power and over the course of the 'War on Terror' the UK government, both Labour and the Coalition have, in conjunction with other governments, resorted to extra-judicial measures which can be best described as the outsourcing of repression. These measures include the involvement of British security officials in interrogations at the US's Guantanamo Bay facility,[181] - where detainees are held for unlimited periods without trial - the rendition for interrogation and torture to countries such as Egypt, Libya and Pakistan,[182] and the complicity of the British military in the CIA's programme of targeted assassinations in Pakistan.[183]

The fact that these measures are outsourced reflects the need for the state to maintain the façade of the centrality of the rule of law and the primacy of parliament in today's 'democracy'. While public awareness of these extra-judicial measures can threaten the state's legitimacy, those measures also reaffirm the state's preparedness to be ruthlessly coercive in the protection of its interests. This has a chilling effect on dissent by illustrating the dangers of challenging power. With regard to the 'War on Terror' this has the most impact on Muslim people as they are the community most affected by extra-judicial repression.

However, even these extra-judicial measures are still, to some extent, masked by the rhetoric of the rule of law. Within state discourses, they are carried out in the interests of protection of democracy. Their subjects are portrayed as the enemies of democracy who should be controlled and punished. Mainstream media coverage largely abides by this discourse, and when the gory details do emerge criticism rarely extends beyond portraying extra-judicial measures as occasional abuses of power or mistakes, rather than an inherent part of how the capitalist system operates. Crucially those who experience the extra-judicial state repression of the 'War on Terror' are invariably Muslims, foreigners or migrants to the UK, who do not come from the dominant racial and economic groups in British society and have already been demonised by politicians and the mainstream media. Extra-legal measures have been taken against other demonised communities, for example the 1970s Labour policy of internment in Northern Ireland enabled detention without trial.[184] Similarly, the contemporary Home Office measures against immigration detainees enable practices such as child detention which would be unlawful if used against other groups within society.

Circuses Without The Bread

The state often uses fear and spectacle to suppress potential resistance and to consolidate social control. This typically occurs when governments need to maintain order in order better to implement controversial and/or unpopular measures. One way to achieve this stability is through the strategy of 'bread and circuses': that is, the creation of public approval through diversion, distraction and shallow populism. The phrase 'bread and circuses' was coined in the 1st Century AD by the Roman satirist Juvenal to describe the way that people were kept satisfied by the provision of public holidays and events such as chariot races, public games and executions coupled with the creation of jobs and the distribution of grain to all citizens of Rome.

In keeping with this long-standing method of subduing public dissent through distraction and spectacle the Conservative-led Coalition government has sought to capitalise upon three large public events, and use them to divert public attention from its unpopular 'austerity' policies, which have included cuts to welfare benefits and widescale privatisation. The government promotion of the April 2011 Royal Wedding, the Royal Diamond Jubilee in June 2012 and the Olympic Games in Summer 2012 amidst a brutal regime of 'austerity' seems to offer only circuses with very little bread. These events were also accompanied by the promotion of nationalism, repressive measures, militarisation and widespread publicity for increased security measures which had the effect of projecting the unassailable power of the state and the impossibility of resisting the status quo.

The wedding of Prince William on the 29 April 2011 was accompanied by a highly publicised £20 million security operation,[185] talk of snipers on London's rooftops and[186] military personnel lining the route of the procession.[187] There was wide speculation about threats to the event and the media reported a "severe"[188] threat of terrorism, a "muslim" threat,[189] an "anarchist"[190] threat and, recalling Thatcher, a "trade union threat".[191] Although the evidence of these supposed threats was flimsy at best the Metropolitan Police commissioner Bob Broadhurst announced that "the threat to the wedding is a threat to principles, it is a threat to democracy".[192] Before the 2011 royal wedding this opaque threat was used to justify real and tangible repression of demonstrators. Several people were pre-emptively arrested ahead of the ceremony[193] and police took the opportunity to raid several squats, including a protest site and a radical social centre.[194] Similarly, the Diamond Jubilee in 2012 was accompanied by massive security,[195] military spectacle[196] and talk of threats from "Al Quaeda and dissident Irish Republicans".[197] House visits were carried out by police forces on known political activists.[198] The Olympic Games later that Summer were accompanied by the militarisation of central London, missiles installed on rooftops in East London[199] and announcements that soldiers had been trained in snatch squad tactics to deal with public order situations ahead of the games.[200] London's Critical Mass bike ride's focus on the Games resulted in the pre-emptive arrest of 182 people.[201]

The repression related to these national events had very little to do with any real, or even perceived threat. Arguably, one aim was to create a feeling of awe at the spectacles the state is able to organise and to discourage potential opposition, through widespread publicity for massive security measures by the police and military, and thereby creating the impression that state control is absolute and that resistance is foolhardy. More importantly, the show of force, and the fabrication of the threat of social disorder projects the need for the state to maintain such a repressive arsenal. The generation of a perception of threat also creates opportunities for increased repression against opposing groups as can be seen, for example, from the raids prior to the Royal Wedding and the mass arrest of Critical Mass participants in the context of the London Olympics. Most of all these spectacles set out the things that 'we' were for: nationalism; patriotism; the monarchy; the state; 'democracy' and the 'rule of law'. Those opposed to these vague notions were set aside as enemies of democracy and thus their repression was presented as legitimate.

Conclusions

This article has explored how 'democracy' is used as an ideological weapon to justify the repression of political dissent through the promotion of the rule of law in its ever-changing and government defined forms, implemented with variable force depending on the target and circumstances, and even via extra-judicial measures which contravene the 'rule of law' upon which the ideology of democracy rests.

Contemporary dominant discourse insists that repression of 'illegitimate' dissent is necessary and right. However the state is constantly redrawing the lines of lawfulness and unlawfulness, setting and resetting the parameters of 'legitimate' dissent, in order to meet its need for continued social control. And while equality before the law is a central tenet of the ideology of democracy, the law is not applied equally: the authorities are able to strategically deploy special legal powers as well as the political interventions of specialised police departments against those who they believe may pose a systemic threat, particularly working class and minority communities. We have also seen that the repression of dissent is not entirely circumscribed by the rule of law, and that the UK government is prepared to flout laws and use extra legal measures in order to achieve social control. However these tactics are presented by the state and the media as necessary exceptions to protect democracy and, ironically, the rule of law.

Such justification of political repression within a supposedly free and tolerant 'democracy' is enabled by the creation of lines of acceptable, reasonable, and lawful dissent. Thus dissent which can be depended upon not to trespass across these mutable lines of acceptability, demonstrators who engage with the police before and during protest and who can be relied upon to limit themselves to unchallenging forms of political activity such as such as lobbying and state controlled forms of protest and organisation are promoted, providing democratic cover and adding weight to the lie that we live in a tolerant and free society, governed by the rule of law. Unauthorised, uncontrolled and unpredictable dissent does not come with these assurances. Dissent which refuses to engage with the police and their regulations, or which targets, disrupts or challenges capitalist interests, most importantly private property and the inalienable freedoms of corporations to maximise their profits, is portrayed as unreasonable, undemocratic, pernicious, and a threat to public security, in order to legitimate its repression. These words by former Labour Prime Minister Tony Blair exemplify this discourse: "I rejoice that I live in a country where *peaceful* protest is a natural part of our democratic heritage".[202] *Peaceful* protest, within dominant discourses, means dissent which is controlled, compliant and ultimately ineffective.

Thus the ideology of democracy and the rule of law enables the repression of groups which remain unco-opted and uncontrolled by the state. When internalised, this ideology can channel dissent along permitted routes, thereby protecting state and corporate interests. Our challenge is to question continually the legitimacy of government-defined laws and assert our own legitimacy and our need for true freedom of political expression. We must fight back against the legal and extra legal repression of dissent, and most importantly, keep resisting.

Notes

1   Tony Blair, Speech given in Glasgow, 15 February, 2003, quoted in Chris Atkins, dir. *Taking Liberties*, (2007).
    <http://www.youtube.com/watch?v=xV2LlcmAOpw&feature=relmfu>
2   'Drax protesters guilty over train ambush', *The Yorkshire Post*, 3 July, 2009.
    <http://www.yorkshirepost.co.uk/news/around-yorkshire/local-stories/drax-protesters-guilty-over-train-ambush-1-2358123>
3   *Public Order Act 1986, c. 64, Table of Contents.*
    <http://www.legislation.gov.uk/ukpga/1986/64/contents>
4   Stuart Trotter, 'Crime crackdown cheers the party', *The Herald*, 7 October, 1993. <http://www.heraldscotland.com/sport/spl/aberdeen/crime-crackdown-cheers-the-party-1.738905>
5   Ibid.
6   Ibid.
7   Ibid.
8   *Criminal Justice and Public Order Act 1994, c. 33, Part V, Disruptive trespassers, Section 68.* <http://www.legislation.gov.uk/ukpga/1994/33/section/68>
9   See Hunt Saboteurs Association, 'Briefing on introduction of CJA', originally written in April 1994, last updated 27 August, 2012.
    <http://hsa.enviroweb.org/index.php/component/content/article/52-legal-articles/219-briefing-on-introduction-of-cja>
10 Understanding Animal Research, 'Outlawing animal rights extremism'.
    <http://www.understandinganimalresearch.org.uk/policy/animal-rights-

extremism/outlawing-animal-rights-extremism>

11 *Public Order Act, 1986, c. 64, Part II.*
    <http://www.legislation.gov.uk/ukpga/1986/64/part/II>

12 *Public Order Act, 1986, c. 64, Part I, Section 5.*
    <http://www.legislation.gov.uk/ukpga/1986/64/section/5>

13 As was the case at a demonstration against an arms factory where an activist
    was convicted under Section 5 for allegedly shouting the words 'murdering
    scum' and 'you are complicit in murder' at the managing director of an arms
    company; Regina V. Osmond, Brighton Magistrates Court, 2007.

14 FreeB.E.A.G.L.E.S, 'Leafleting – A Guide to your Rights', last updated
    September, 2004. <http://www.freebeagles.org/articles/leafleting.html#41>

15 Rob Jerrard, 'Percy Again Conviction for defacing flag is incompatible with
    Article 10 of the European Convention on Human Rights', *Internet Law Book
    Reviews.*
    <http://www.rjerrard.co.uk/law/cases/percyvdppQBD2001times21janCHTML.
    html>

16 *Criminal Justice and Public Order Act, 1994, c. 33, Part V, Disruptive trespassers,
    Section 68.* <http://www.legislation.gov.uk/ukpga/1994/33/section/68>

17 *Criminal Justice and Public Order Act, 1994, c. 33, Part IV, Powers of police to stop
    and search, Section 60.*
    <http://www.legislation.gov.uk/ukpga/1994/33/section/60 >

18 *Criminal Justice and Public Order Act, 1994, c. 33, Part V, Disruptive trespassers,
    Section 68.* <http://www.legislation.gov.uk/ukpga/1994/33/section/68>

19 Thanks to Lydia Dagostino of Kelly's Solicitors for giving some context on
    the introduction of these provisions.

20 Understanding Animal Research, 'Outlawing animal rights extremism'.
    <http://www.understandinganimalresearch.org.uk/policy/animal-rights-
    extremism/outlawing-animal-rights-extremism>

21 See *Public Order Act, 1986, c. 64, Part II, Section 16.*
    <http://www.legislation.gov.uk/ukpga/1986/64/section/16> and *Anti Social
    Behaviour Act, 2003, c. 38, Part 7, Section 57.*
    <http://www.legislation.gov.uk/ukpga/2003/38/section/57/prospective>

22 *Criminal Justice and Public Order Act, 1994, c. 33, Part IV, Powers of police to stop
    and search, Section 60AA.*
    <http://www.legislation.gov.uk/ukpga/1994/33/section/60AA>

23 *Public Order Act, 1986, c. 64, Part II, Section 11.*
    <http://www.legislation.gov.uk/ukpga/1986/64/section/11>

24 Author's experience of policing of demonstrations in Brighton, 2000-2012.

25 Ibid.

26 For example, see, 'Smash Edo plan Brighton protest during Jubilee weekend',
    The Argus, 1 March 2012.
    <http://www.theargus.co.uk/news/9564953.Smash_EDO_plan_Brighton_prot
    est_during_jubilee_weekend/r/?ref=rss>

27 Dave Lyddon/The Union Makes Us Strong: TUC History Online, 'Anti-Union

Legislation: 1980-2000'.
<http://www.unionhistory.info/timeline/1960_2000_Narr_Display.php?Wher
e=NarTitle+contains+%27Anti-Union+Legislation%3A+1980-2000%27>

28 *Trade Union and Labour Relations (Consolidation) Act, 1992, c. 52, Table of
Contents.* <http://www.legislation.gov.uk/ukpga/1992/52/contents>

29 *Trade Union Reform and Employment Rights Act, 1993, c. 19, Part I, Industrial
Action.*
<http://www.legislation.gov.uk/ukpga/1993/19/part/I/crossheading/industrial

30 *Trade Union and Labour relations (Consolidation) Act, 1992, c. 52, Part I,
Restriction on use of funds for certain political objects.*
<http://www.legislation.gov.uk/ukpga/1992/52/part/I/chapter/VI/crossheadin
g/restriction-on-use-of-funds-for-certain-political-objects>

31 *Trade Union and Labour relations (Consolidation) Act, 1992, c. 52, Part V,
Criminal offences, Section 241.*
<http://www.legislation.gov.uk/ukpga/1992/52/section/241> ; Gov.uk, 'Guide,
Taking part in industrial strikes and actions. Going on strike and picketing',
last updated 22 October, 2012. <https://www.gov.uk/industrial-action-
strikes/going-on-strike-and-picketing>

32 *Trade Union and Labour relations (Consolidation) Act, 1992, c. 52, Part V, Action
excluded from protection, Section 224.*
<http://www.legislation.gov.uk/ukpga/1992/52/section/224>; Gov.uk, 'Guide,
Taking part in industrial strikes and actions. Going on strike and picketing',
last updated 22 October, 2012. <https://www.gov.uk/industrial-action-
strikes/going-on-strike-and-picketing>

33 James G. Moher, 'Trade unions and the law – history and a way forward?',
History and Policy. Connecting historians, policymakers and the media,
September, 2007. <http://www.historyandpolicy.org/papers/policy-paper-
63.html>

34 Paul Wilenius, 'Enemies within: Thatcher and the unions', *BBC News*, 5
March, 2004. <http://news.bbc.co.uk/1/hi/3067563.stm>

35 Beth Lawrence, 'Partnership or Struggle', *Corporate Watch Magazine: The Rules
of Engagement*, Summer, 2011, No. 49.
<http://www.corporatewatch.org.uk/?lid=4049>

36 Martin Schneider, 'Employment Litigation on the Rise? Comparing British
Employment Tribunals and German Labor Courts', in *Comparative Labor and
Law & Policy Journal*, Vol. 22, No. 2/3.

37 *Police Reform Act, 2002, c. 30, Part 4, Chapter 2, Power to require name and
address, Section 50.* <http://www.legislation.gov.uk/ukpga/2002/30/section/50>

38 *The Serious Organised Crime and Police Act 2005 (Designated Area) Order 2005,
2005 No. 1537, Table of Contents.*
<http://www.legislation.gov.uk/uksi/2005/1537/contents/made>

39 *Terrorism Act 2006, c. 11, Part 1, Offences involving radioactive devices and*

materials and nuclear facilities and sites, Section 12.
<http://www.legislation.gov.uk/ukpga/2006/11/section/12>

40 For example, see this map of the 'controlled area' surrounding RAF Menwith
Hill, North Yorkshire, 'RAF Menwith Hill SOCPA (Serious Organised Crime
and Police Act) 2005'. <http://www.mod.uk/NR/rdonlyres/0042D0BE-030A-
4375-83AF-E487E14D4EBB/0/menwith_hill_socap.pdf>

41 The Serious Organised Crime and Police Act 2005, c. 15, Part 5, Protection of
activities of certain organisations, Section 145.
<http://www.legislation.gov.uk/ukpga/2005/15/section/145>

42 Kirtley was later released on appeal. See Corporate Watch, 'Sean Kirtley freed
after sixteen months in prison', Corporate Watch Latest News, 16 October,
2009. <http://www.corporatewatch.org/?lid=3434>

43 Corporate Watch, 'Political Sentences handed down in second SHAC trial',
Corporate Watch Latest News, 10 November, 2010.
<http://www.corporatewatch.org/?lid=3830>

44 Several animal rights campaigners have been restricted from making contact
with other animal rights activists and ASBOs handed down to SHAC
campaigners could be interpreted to restrict them from speaking publicly
against vivisection.

45 See Repeal-SOCPA.info. <http://www.repeal-socpa.info/index.html>

46 Police Reform and Social Responsibility Act 2011, 2011, c. 13, Part 3.
<http://www.legislation.gov.uk/ukpga/2011/13/part/3/enacted>

47 The Serious Organised Crime and Police Act 2005 (Designated Sites under Section
128) (Amendment) Order 2012, No 1769, Article 2.
<http://www.legislation.gov.uk/uksi/2012/1769/article/2/made>

48 Legal Aid, Sentencing and Punishment of Offenders Act 2012, c. 10, Part 3,
CHAPTER 9, Offence of squatting in a residential building, Section 144.
<http://www.legislation.gov.uk/ukpga/2012/10/section/144/enacted>

49 HM Inspectorate of Constabulary (HMIC), A review of national police units
which provide intelligence on criminality associated with protest, (2012), p. 14.
<http://www.hmic.gov.uk/media/review-of-national-police-units-which-
provide-intelligence-on-criminality-associated-with-protest-20120202.pdf>

50 Ibid.

51 Corporate Watch, 'Farewell to NETCU: a brief history of how protest
movements have been targeted by political policing', Corporate Watch Latest
News, 19 January, 2011. <http://www.corporatewatch.org/?lid=3868>

52 Understanding Animal Research, 'Outlawing animal rights extremism'.
<http://www.understandinganimalresearch.org.uk/policy/animal-rights-
extremism/outlawing-animal-rights-extremism/>

53 Ibid.

54 Ibid.

55 HM Inspectorate of Constabulary (HMIC), A review of national police units
which provide intelligence on criminality associated with protest, (2012), p. 5.
<http://www.hmic.gov.uk/media/review-of-national-police-units-which-

provide-intelligence-on-criminality-associated-with-protest-20120202.pdf>

56 See Companies House, 'WebCheck – Select and Access Company
    Information'.
    <http://wck2.companieshouse.gov.uk/510fdd06d9f82e9e272725a6e6c130a4/c
    ompdetails>. The Association of Chief Police Officer's company number is
    03344583.

57 ACPO, *Full Accounts Made up to 31/03/11 for the Association of Chief Police
    Officers of England, Wales and Northern Ireland (Company No. 03344583)*,
    accessed via Companies House, November 2012.

58 What Do They Know.com, 'Freedom of Information Requests to National
    Extremism Tactical Coordination Unit'.
    <http://www.whatdotheyknow.com/body/netcu>

59 Association of Chief Police Officers, 'Freedom of Information (FOI)
    Requests'.
    <http://www.acpo.police.uk/FreedomofInformation/ACPOpublicationsFoI.as
    px>

60 What Do They Know.com, 'Freedom of Information Requests to National
    Extremism Tactical Coordination Unit'.
    <http://www.whatdotheyknow.com/body/netcu>

61 Tom Griffin, 'Mission Creep: How the ACPO empire hyped eco-terrorism',
    OurKingdom, power and liberty in Britain, 16 January 2011.
    <http://www.opendemocracy.net/ourkingdom/tom-griffin/mission-creep-
    how-acpo-empire-hyped-eco-terrorism>

62 HM Inspectorate of Constabulary (HMIC), 'Chapter 1. Assessing the Risk of
    Disorder', *Keeping the Peace: Policing Disorder*, (1999) p. 3.
    <http://www.nationalarchives.gov.uk/ERORecords/HO/421/2/P2/HMIC/disor
    d1.pdf>

63 HM Inspectorate of Constabulary (HMIC), *A review of national police units
    which provide intelligence on criminality associated with protest*, (2012) p. 5.
    <http://www.hmic.gov.uk/media/review-of-national-police-units-which-
    provide-intelligence-on-criminality-associated-with-protest-20120202.pdf>

64 Authors experience of the policing of the Smash EDO campaign 2004-12.

65 Powerbase, a project of Spinwatch, 'National Extremism Tactical
    Coordination Unit', *The Counter-Terrorism Portal*.
    <http://www.powerbase.info/index.php/National_Extremism_Tactical_Coord
    ination_Unit>

66 Ibid.

67 HM Inspectorate of Constabulary (HMIC), *A review of national police units
    which provide intelligence on criminality associated with protest*, (2012), p. 11.
    <http://www.hmic.gov.uk/media/review-of-national-police-units-which-
    provide-intelligence-on-criminality-associated-with-protest-20120202.pdf>

68 This is a summary of information viewed by the author on www.netcu.org.uk
    from 2004-2009; the website is currently unavailable and is not accessible via
    archive.org.

69 Association of Chief Police Officers, 'National Domestic Extremism Unit'.
    <http://www.acpo.police.uk/NationalPolicing/NationalDomesticExtremismU
    nit/Default.aspx

70 The original *Times* article is no longer available online. However it was
    reposted by Anonymous, 'Anti-war activists adopt guerilla tactics of animal
    rights campaign', *Infoshop News*, 12 April,
    2005.<http://news.infoshop.org/article.php?story=20050412195003515>

71 Ibid.

72 Ibid.

73 Malthusianism refers primarily to ideas derived from the writings of
    Reverend Thomas Robert Malthus, as laid out initially in his *An Essay on the
    Principle of Population*, 1798. Advocates of population control schemes are
    often referred to as neo-Malthusian.

74 Corporate Watch, 'Whose agenda do reports of 'eco-terrorism' serve?',
    Corporate Watch Latest News, 30 November, 2008.
    <http://www.corporatewatch.org/?lid=3179>

75 'INTER-NETCU: As Government Agency Caught Infiltrating Activist Media
    Outlet', *Schnews 755*, 21 January, 2011.
    <http://www.schnews.org.uk/archive/news755.php>

76 The NDET were involved in house visits and raids of activists houses after
    the 2009 decommissioning of the EDO MBM arms factory; authors
    experience of the policing of the Smash EDO campaign 2004-12.

77 Corporate Watch, 'Farewell to NETCU: a brief history of how protest
    movements have been targeted by political policing', *Corporate Watch Latest
    News*, 19 January, 2011. <http://www.corporatewatch.org/?lid=3868>

78 Ibid.

79 HM Inspectorate of Constabulary (HMIC), *A review of national police units
    which provide intelligence on criminality associated with protest*, (2012), p. 6.
    <http://www.hmic.gov.uk/media/review-of-national-police-units-which-
    provide-intelligence-on-criminality-associated-with-protest-20120202.pdf>

80 Ibid.

81 *Crime and Disorder Act 1998, c. 37, Part I, Chapter I, Crime and disorder: general,
    Section 1.* <http://www.legislation.gov.uk/ukpga/1998/37/section/1>

82 Ibid.

83 'About ASBOs', *Anti-Social Behavioural Orders*.
    <http://www.asbos.co.uk/AboutASBOs.aspx>

84 Matt Foot, 'A Triumph of hearsay and hysteria', *The Guardian*, 5 April, 2005.
    <http://www.guardian.co.uk/politics/2005/apr/05/ukcrime.prisonsandprobati
    on>

85 Ministry of Justice, *Statistical Notice: Anti-Social Behaviour Order (ASBO)
    Statistics England and Wales 2010*, 30 October, 2011.
    <http://www.homeoffice.gov.uk/publications/science-research-
    statistics/research-statistics/crime-research/asbo-stats-england-wales-
    2010/asbo10snr?view=Binary>

86 Corporate Watch, 'How the state protects corporations from dissent: jailed SHAC activists receive indefinite ASBOs', *Corporate Watch Latest News*, 29 January, 2009. <http://www.corporatewatch.org/?lid=3194>

87 Justice Statistics Analytical Services within the Ministry of Justice, 'Anti-Social Behaviour Order Statistics – England and Wales 2008', p. 15. <http://webarchive.nationalarchives.gov.uk/20110218135832/http://rds.home office.gov.uk/rds/pdfs10/asbo2008.pdf>

88 Simon Rogers, 'The Poverty Maps of England', *The Guardian*, 6 March, 2012. <http://www.guardian.co.uk/news/datablog/interactive/2012/mar/06/poverty-map-england-experian>

89 Metrowebukmetro, 'Asbos "badge of honour" for yobs', *The Metro*, 2 November, 2006. <http://www.metro.co.uk/news/23530-asbos-badge-of-honour-for-yobs>

90 'Asbos to be abolished under new Government plans', *Channel 4 News*, 7 February, 2011. <http://www.channel4.com/news/asbos-to-be-abolished-under-new-government-plans>

91 John Hall, 'Theresa May reveals "community trigger" to replace ASBOs and target anti-social behaviour', *The Independent*, 22 May, 2012. <http://www.independent.co.uk/news/uk/crime/theresa-may-reveals-community-trigger-to-replace-asbos-and-target-antisocial-behaviour-7777600.html>

92 *Protection from Harassment Act, 1997, c. 40, Table of Contents.* <http://www.legislation.gov.uk/ukpga/1997/40/contents>

93 *Protection from Harassment Act, 1997, c. 40, England and Wales, Section 2.* <http://www.legislation.gov.uk/ukpga/1997/40/section/2>

94 Lawson-Cruttenden & Co., 'Harassment & Stalking'. <http://www.lawson-cruttenden.co.uk/practice-areas/harassment-stalking>

95 This precedent was partly set by this ruling: House of Lords, *Opinions of the Lords of Appeal For Judgment in the Cause – Majrowski (Respondent) v. Guy's and St. Thomas' NHS Trust (Appellants)*, [2006] UKHL 34, 12 July, 2006. <http://www.publications.parliament.uk/pa/ld200506/ldjudgmt/jd060712/majro-1.htm#1>

96 For more on this see Corporate Watch, 'Corporate Law and Structures: Exposing the roots of the problem', 2004. <http://www.corporatewatch.org.uk/?lid=2592>

97 All of these were imposed in the interim injunction granted to EDO MBM. See *EDO MBM Technology v Campaign to Smash EDO & Others*, [2005] EWHC 837 (QB) 2005 WL 3661971. <http://www.smashedo.org.uk/resources/gross%27s%20judgement.pdf>

98 Smash EDO, 'Bomb Builders Drop Injunction', 10 February, 2006. <http://www.smashedo.org.uk/pressreleases/06-02-10.htm>

99 Ibid.

100 'Legal injunction granted to Huntingdon Life Sciences', Case No. HOO3X01149. <http://www.legalinjunction.com/hls/hls.html>

101 For a list of cases brought by Timothy Lawson-Cruttenden see, 'Lawson-Cruttenden & Co., 'Key Cases'. <http://www.lawson-cruttenden.co.uk/index.php/key-cases/>

102 Paul Lewis and Rob Evans, 'High court injunction – the weapon of choice to slap down protests', *The Guardian*, 27 October, 2009. <http://www.guardian.co.uk/uk/2009/oct/27/high-court-injunctions-protests>

103 'Legal injunction granted to Huntingdon Life Sciences', Case No. HO03X01149. <http://www.legalinjunction.com/hls/hls.html>

104 *EDO MBM Technology v Campaign to Smash EDO & Others*, [2005] EWHC 837 (QB) 2005 WL 3661971. <http://www.smashedo.org.uk/resources/gross%27s%20judgement.pdf>

105 See the Smash EDO Campaign film, *On the Verge*, Schmovies, 2008. <http://www.schnews.org.uk/schmovies/index-on-the-verge.htm>

106 'Putting on the writs', *Schnews 581*, 23 March, 2007. <http://www.schnews.org.uk/archive/news581.htm>

107 'Climate activists fight injunction', *The Guardian*, 27 July, 2007. <http://www.guardian.co.uk/environment/2007/jul/27/activists.travelandtransport>

108 *Eurosatory: Land and Airland Defence and Security*, <http://www.eurosatory.com/#/home>

109 Alex Chitty and Kylie Bull, 'Predicting a riot', *'Eurosatory 2012 News*, 12 June, 2012.<http://www.ihs.com/events/exhibitions/eurosatory-2012/news/jun-12/english/Predicting-a-riot.aspx>

110 Paul Lewis, 'Every step you take: UK underground centre that is spy capital of the world', *The Guardian*, 2 March, 2009. <http://www.guardian.co.uk/uk/2009/mar/02/westminster-cctv-system-privacy>

111 'Brief account of Resisting FIT at DSEi public meeting', *Fitwatch*. <http://www.fitwatch.org.uk/2007/07/01/brief-account-of-resisting-fit-at-dsei/>

112 See www.fitwatch.org.uk for general information about FITs.

113 'Who are the police spying on? A spotter card revealed, *The Guardian*, 27 October, 2009. <http://www.guardian.co.uk/uk/interactive/2009/oct/27/police-spotter-cards-revealed?INTCMP=ILCNETTXT3487>

114 'Spotter cards: What they look like and how they work', *The Guardian*, 25 October, 2009. <http://www.guardian.co.uk/uk/2009/oct/25/spotter-cards>

115 Police disclosure to C Osmond in Regina V. Saibene and others.

116 Authors experience of the policing if the Smash EDO campaign, 2004-12.

117 'Fitwatch at Carnival Against the Arms Trade', *Fitwatch*. <http://www.fitwatch.org.uk/2008/05/27/fitwatch-at-carnival-against-arms-trade/>

118 Data disclosed to the defendants in Regina V. Saibene and others.

119 HMIC, 'Policing protests reviews: Adapting to Protest', published 7 July, 2009. <http://www.hmic.gov.uk/inspections/policing-protest-review/>

120 Author's direct observation.

121 Accessed in September 2012 but is no longer available online.

122 Ibid.

123 Tom Anderson and Val Swain in conversation with PLOs in Brighton, 3 June, 2012.

124 Palestine Solidarity Campaign, 'Emergency Meeting: Harsh Sentencing of Gaza Protestors is clearly "Political"', *PSC News*.
<http://www.palestinecampaign.org/index7b.asp?m_id=1&l1_id=4&l2_id=24&Content_ID=1176>

125 Simon Hattenstone and Matthew Taylor, 'Sent to jail for throwing a single bottle', *The Guardian,* 13 March 2010.
<http://www.guardian.co.uk/theguardian/2010/mar/13/gaza-protesters-sent-prison>

126 Harmit Athwal, 'Gaza Protesters Defence Campaign launched', *Institute of Race Relations - Comment*, 12 March, 2010. <http://www.irr.org.uk/news/gaza-protesters-defence-campaign-launched/>

127 Dr. Hanan Chehata, 'Harsh sentences seem more likely to deter lawful protest rather than violent disorder', *Middle East Monitor*, 16 February, 2010. <http://www.middleeastmonitor.com/articles/62-europe/677-harsh-sentences-seem-more-likely-to-deter-lawful-protest-rather-than-violent-disorder>

128 Dr. Hanan Chahata, 'Gaza protesters to be sentenced despite allegations of police brutality', *Islamic Human Rights Commission*, 10 February, 2010. <http://www.ihrc.org.uk/news/articles/9228-gaza-protesters-to-be-sentenced-despite-allegations-of-police-brutality>

129 Palestine Solidarity Campaign, 'Emergency Meeting: Harsh Sentencing of Gaza Protestors is clearly "Political"', *PSC News*.
<http://www.palestinecampaign.org/index7b.asp?m_id=1&l1_id=4&l2_id=24&Content_ID=1176>

130 Harmit Athwal, 'Gaza Protesters Defence Campaing launched', *Institute of Race Relations - Comment*, 12 March, 2010. <http://www.irr.org.uk/news/gaza-protesters-defence-campaign-launched/>

131 Arun Kundnani, 'IRR expresses concern over excessive sentencing of Bradford rioters', *Institute of Race Relations - Press Release*, 5 July, 2002. <http://www.irr.org.uk/news/irr-expresses-concern-over-excessive-sentencing-of-bradford-rioters/>

132 Ibid.

133 Sean Coughlan, 'How the student fees protest turned violent', *BBC News*, 10 November, 2010. <http://www.bbc.co.uk/news/education-11729912>

134 John Domokos, Matthew Taylor and Richard Sprenger, 'Student protesters turn on abandoned police van', *The Guardian*, 24 November, 2010. <http://www.guardian.co.uk/education/video/2010/nov/24/student-protests-turn-ugly>

135 Michael White, 'Student protests: this time, police came prepared as anger

boils over', *The Guardian,* 10 December, 2010.
<http://www.guardian.co.uk/education/2010/dec/10/student-protests-police-come-prepared>

136 P. Nutt, 'Oxford Street Topshop Attacked by Students After Tuition Fees Vote', *Demotix.com*, 9 November, 2010.
<http://www.demotix.com/news/533015/oxford-street-topshop-attacked-students-after-tuition-fees-vote>

137 Kevin Schofield and James Clench, 'Charles and Camilla's car is attacked in London as students protest', *The Sun*, 4 November, 2010.
<http://www.thesun.co.uk/sol/homepage/news/3268159/Charles-Camillas-car-is-attacked-in-London-as-students-protest.html>

138 Legal Defence and Monitoring Group, 'Sentencing Summary from recent Student and Anti-Cuts Protests', http:ldmg.org.uk/, 2 March, 2012.
<http://ldmg.org.uk/files/sentencing_summary.pdf>

139 Ibid.

140 'One in five jailed rioters let out of prison early', *The Guardian*, 18 August, 2012. <http://www.guardian.co.uk/uk/2012/aug/18/one-in-five-rioters-prison-early>

141 Owen Bowcott, Haroon Siddique and Andrew Sparrow, 'Facebook cases trigger criticism of "disproportionate" riot sentences', *The Guardian*, 17 August, 2011. <http://www.guardian.co.uk/uk/2011/aug/17/facebook-cases-criticism-riot-sentences?intcmp=239>

142 Owen Bowcott and Stephen Bates, 'Riots: magistrates advised to disregard normal sentencing', *The Guardian*, 15 August, 2011.
<http://www.guardian.co.uk/uk/2011/aug/15/riots-magistrates-sentencing>

143 Ibid.; Owen Bowcott, Haroon Siddique and Andrew Sparrow, 'Facebook cases trigger criticism of "disproportionate" riot sentences', *The Guardian*, 17 August, 2011. <http://www.guardian.co.uk/uk/2011/aug/17/facebook-cases-criticism-riot-sentences?intcmp=239>

144 Owen Bowcott and Stephen Bates, 'Riots: magistrates advised to disregard normal sentencing', *The Guardian*, 15 August, 2011.
<http://www.guardian.co.uk/uk/2011/aug/15/riots-magistrates-sentencing>

145 Quoted in Pierre Tristram, 'Full Text: President Bush's Declares "War on Terror"', *About.com: Middle East Issues*, 20 September, 2001.
<http://middleeast.about.com/od/usmideastpolicy/a/bush-war-on-terror-speech.htm>

146 Ibid.

147 Ibid.

148 HM Inspectorate of Constabulary (HMIC), *A review of national police units which provide intelligence on criminality associated with protest*, (2012), p. 11.
<http://www.hmic.gov.uk/media/review-of-national-police-units-which-provide-intelligence-on-criminality-associated-with-protest-20120202.pdf>

149 Ibid.

150 *Terrorism Act 2000, c. 11, Schedule 7.*

<http://www.legislation.gov.uk/ukpga/2000/11/schedule/7>

151 Rizwaan Sabir, 'Schedule 7: A law unto itself', *Cage Prisoners*, 14 July, 2010.
<http://www.cageprisoners.com/our-work/opinion-editorial/item/310-schedule-7-a-law-unto-itself>

152 'Anti-Terrorism statistics', *Institute of Race Relations*.
<http://www.irr.org.uk/research/statistics/anti-terror/>

153 IMCista, 'You don't have the right to silence', *Indymedia UK*, 17 April, 2008.
<http://www.indymedia.org.uk/en/2008/04/396863.html>

154 Author's personal experience.

155 Author's interviews with International Solidarity Movement activists, March 2010.

156 Anarchist Federation, 'Anarchists Detained by Counter-Terrorism Police', *Indymedia UK*, 16 August, 2008.
<http://www.indymedia.org.uk/en/2012/08/499056.html?c=on>

157 Author's interview with Chris Kitchen, November 2012.

158 Author's personal experience.

159 *Terrorism Act 2000, c. 11, Part V, Suspected Terrorists, Section 41.*
<http://www.legislation.gov.uk/ukpga/2000/11/section/41>

160 *Terrorism Act 2000, c. 11, Part V, Power to stop and search, Section 44.*
<http://www.legislation.gov.uk/ukpga/2000/11/section/44>

161 *Terrorism Act 2000, c. 11, Part II, Offences, Section 11.*
<http://www.legislation.gov.uk/ukpga/2000/11/section/11>

162 *Terrorism Act 2000, c. 11, Schedule 8.*
<http://www.legislation.gov.uk/ukpga/2000/11/schedule/8>

163 *Terrorism Act 2006, c. 11, Part 1, Encouragement etc. of terrorism.*
<http://www.legislation.gov.uk/ukpga/2006/11/part/1/crossheading/encouragement-etc-of-terrorism>

164 *Anti-terrorism, Crime and Security Act 2001, c. 24, Part 11.*
<http://www.legislation.gov.uk/ukpga/2001/24/part/11>

165 *Terrorism Act 2000, c. 11, Part V, Power to stop and search.*
<http://www.legislation.gov.uk/ukpga/2000/11/part/V/crossheading/power-to-stop-and-search>

166 'Section 44 Terrorism Act', *Liberty*. <http://www.liberty-human-rights.org.uk/human-rights/justice/stop-and-search/section-44/index.php>; and 'Anti-Terrorism statistics', *Institute of Race Relations*.
<http://www.irr.org.uk/research/statistics/anti-terror/>

167 Alan Travis, 'Stop and search powers illegal, European court rules', *The Guardian,* 12 January, 2010.
<http://www.guardian.co.uk/world/2010/jan/12/stop-and-search-ruled-illegal>

168 Philip Johnston, 'The police must end their abuse of anti-terror legislation', *The Telegraph*, 3 October 2005.
<http://www.telegraph.co.uk/comment/personal-view/3620110/The-police-must-end-their-abuse-of-anti-terror-legislation.html>

169 'Section 44 Terrorism Act', *Liberty*. <http://www.liberty-human-rights.org.uk/human-rights/justice/stop-and-search/section-44/index.php>

170 *Criminal Justice Act 2003, c. 44, Part 13, Detention of suspected terrorists, Section 306.* <http://www.legislation.gov.uk/ukpga/2003/44/section/306>

171 *Terrorism Act 2006, c. 11, Part 2, Detention of terrorist suspects, Section 23.* <http://www.legislation.gov.uk/ukpga/2006/11/section/23>

172 *Protection of Freedoms Act 2010-12 – Progress of the Bill.* <http://services.parliament.uk/bills/2010-12/protectionoffreedoms.html>

173 Gavin Berman and Alexander Horne, 'Pre-Charge Detention in Terrorism Cases – Commons Library Standard Note, *UK Parliament Standard notes*, 16 March, 2012. <http://www.parliament.uk/briefing-papers/SN05634>

174 *Anti-terrorism, Crime and Security Act, 2001, c. 24, Table of Contents.* <http://www.legislation.gov.uk/ukpga/2001/24/contents>

175 Denise Winterman, 'Belmarsh – Britain's Guantanamo Bay?', *BBC News* , 6 October, 2004. <http://news.bbc.co.uk/1/hi/magazine/3714864.stm>

176 'Eight terror detainees released', *BBC News*, 11 March, 2005. <http://news.bbc.co.uk/1/hi/uk/4338849.stm>

177 *Prevention of Terrorism Act 2005, c. 2, Control Orders.* <http://www.legislation.gov.uk/ukpga/2005/2/crossheading/control-orders>

178 Ibid.

179 *Terrorism Prevention and Investigation Measures Act 2011, c. 23, New regime to protect the public from terrorism, Section 1.* <http://www.legislation.gov.uk/ukpga/2011/23/section/1>

180 Andy Worthington, 'Ruling sends message on control orders', *The Guardian*, 28 July, 2010. <http://www.guardian.co.uk/commentisfree/libertycentral/2010/jul/28/court-ruling-sends-message-control-orders>

181 For example, see Rajeev Syal and Owen Bowcott, 'Guantánamo Bay detainee says interrogation record was blanked', *The Guardian*, 18 July, 2010. <http://www.guardian.co.uk/world/2010/jul/18/guantanamo-bay-interrogation-detainee>

182 'UK government "approved Abdel Hakim Belhaj's rendition"', *BBC News*, 9 April, 2012. <http://www.bbc.co.uk/news/uk-17651797>

183 Mark Townsend, 'GCHQ civilian staff face war crimes charge over drone strikes in Pakistan', *The Guardian*, 11 March, 2012. <http://www.guardian.co.uk/world/2012/mar/11/gchq-staff-war-crimes-drones>

184 Martin Melaugh, 'Internment – Summary of Main Events', *CAIN Web Service*. <http://cain.ulst.ac.uk/events/intern/sum.htm>

185 Richard Hartley-Parkinson, 'No stone unturned: The massive operation to protect Prince William and Kate along the royal wedding route', *The Daily Mail*, 19 April, 2011. <http://www.dailymail.co.uk/news/article-1378387/Royal-Wedding-route-Security-operation-protect-Prince-William-Kate-Middleton.html>

186 Ibid.

187 Ministry of Defence, 'Military path-liners for Royal Wedding named', *People in Defence*, 28 April, 2011.
<http://www.mod.uk/DefenceInternet/DefenceNews/PeopleInDefence/MilitaryPathlinersForRoyalWeddingNamed.htm>

188 Traci Watson, 'Despite "severe" terrorist threat, London police vow safe royal wedding', *USA Today*, 27 April, 2011.
<http://www.usatoday.com/life/people/2011-04-27-london-threat_N.htm>

189 Mike Sullivan, 'Poppy burning Muslim fanatics vow to hijack the Royal Wedding', *The Sun*, 29 March, 2011.
<http://www.thesun.co.uk/sol/homepage/news/3496166/Poppy-burning-Muslim-fanatics-vow-to-hijack-the-Royal-Wedding.html>

190 Max Pemberton and Neil Tweedie, 'The secret threat to the royal wedding', *The Telegraph*, 23 April, 2011.
<http://www.telegraph.co.uk/news/uknews/royal-wedding/8468814/The-secret-threat-to-the-royal-wedding.html>

191 'Tube strike threat on royal wedding day', *BBC News London*, 10 January, 2011.
<http://www.bbc.co.uk/news/uk-england-london-12153653>

192 Metrowebukmetro, 'Stop-and-search at royal wedding to stop anti-cuts protest anarchists', *The Metro*, 28 March, 2011.
<http://www.metro.co.uk/news/859275-stop-and-search-at-royal-wedding-to-stop-anti-cuts-protest-anarchists#ixzz25XlDSvrV>

193 'Man arrested in Cambridge for royal wedding protest plan', *BBC News*, 29 April, 2011. <http://www.bbc.co.uk/news/uk-england-cambridgeshire-13237702>

194 Sandra Laville, 'Police raid five squats before royal wedding', *The Guardian*, 28 April, 2011. <http://www.guardian.co.uk/uk/2011/apr/28/police-raid-squats-royal-wedding>

195 Ibid.

196 Daniela Relph, 'Diamond Jubilee: Military parade tribute to Queen', *BBC News*, 19 May, 2012. <http://www.bbc.co.uk/news/uk-18132607>

197 Daily Mail Reporter, '6,000 police put on terror watch to protect Royals',*The Daily Mail*, 2 June, 2012. <http://www.dailymail.co.uk/news/article-2153890/Diamond-Jubilee-Thames-Pageant-6-000-police-terror-watch-protect-Royals.html>

198 Jason N. Parkinson and Rob Evans, 'Sussex police criticised for harassment during protester liaison', *The Guardian*, 4 September, 2012.
<http://www.guardian.co.uk/uk/2012/sep/04/sussex-police-criticised-harassment-protester-liaison>

199 Corporate Watch, 'Security Games: Surveillance, repression and activism around the London 2012 Olympics', *Corporate Games: The Corporate Olympic Games in 2010*, 27 July, 2012. <http://www.corporatewatch.org.uk/?lid=4467>

200 Corporate Watch, 'Soldiers trained in snatch squad tactics for the Olympics', *Corporate Watch Latest News,* 6 July, 2012.

<http://www.corporatewatch.org/?lid=4389>
201 Shiv Malik, 'Critical Mass arrests: police charge three', *The Guardian*, 29 July, 2012. <http://www.guardian.co.uk/uk/2012/jul/29/critical-mass-police-arrest-three>
202 Tony Blair, Speech given in Glasgow, 15 February, 2003, quoted in Chris Atkins, dir. *Taking Liberties*, (2007). <http://www.youtube.com/watch?v=xV2LlcmAOpw&feature=relmfu>

17. Infiltrated, Intimidated and Undermined: How Police Infiltration Can Mute Political Dissent

An Interview with Verity Smith, from Cardiff Anarchist Network
By Tom Anderson

In 2010 a long-term environmental activist using the alias 'Mark Stone' was confronted and revealed to be an undercover police officer called Mark Kennedy. Since then, the tactic of police infiltration has received increased public and media attention. However, much of the debate has focused on the rights and wrongs of this tactic in terms of what 'intelligence' was gleaned, whether it forms a cost-effective way of safeguarding law and order, and of whether these groups 'deserved' infiltration. What has been absent from the mainstream debate is an analysis of how police infiltration serves as a tool to undermine and even destroy activist networks, and to channel their actions away from forms of political activity which threaten capitalist interests. This article will examine the use of police infiltration to contain political dissent, and explore, through an interview with Verity Smith, an activist from Cardiff Anarchist Network (CAN), which was infiltrated by an undercover officer calling himself 'Marco Jacobs', how undercover police officers achieve these aims in practice.

Before we look at the particular tactics used by 'Marco Jacobs' it is useful to set the context by exploring what has come to be known about the role of police officers in infiltrating activist groups. Although for obvious reasons exact figures are not available, it is fair to say that police infiltration of activist groups in the UK is more common than has previously been presumed and is certainly not limited to groups which engage in illegal activity. Indeed, when Mark Kennedy was outed he claimed that he knew of fifteen other undercover operatives, four of whom were still in service.[1] A 2012 report by the HM Inspectorate of Constabularies (HMIC), produced following the public outrage surrounding the 2010 revelations about undercover policing, indicates that undercover officers have been deployed by both the Special Demonstration Squad (SDS), and the National Public Order Intelligence Unit (NPOIU). The SDS was set up in 1968, in the wake of the militant protests against the Vietnam war with the aim of "preventing serious crimes associated with protest"[2] while the NPOIU was set up by the Association of Chief Police Officers (ACPO) in 1999[3] to gather and coordinate intelligence about the animal rights and ecological direct action movements.[4] The SDS and NPOIU operated independently of each other although some staff worked for both organisations.[5] HMIC claims that the NPOIU deploys officers to "develop general intelligence for the purpose of preventing crime and disorder or directing subsequent criminal investigations, rather than gathering material for the purpose of criminal prosecutions"[6] and that it "gathered both intelligence on serious criminality, and intelligence that enabled forces to police protests effectively."[7] These stated aims granted it considerable powers to police political movements.

The groups that were infiltrated were many and varied. Mark Kennedy was reportedly originally approached by the Animal Rights National Index (ARNI) and then recruited by the NPOIU in 2002.[8] (See Anderson, Chapter, 16.) He infiltrated a wide variety of groups, including Earth First,[9] Saving Iceland[10] Climate Camp[11] and Dissent.[12] He played a pivotal role in providing intelligence concerning the anti-G8 mobilisation in Scotland.[13] Meanwhile, 'Mark "Marco" Jacobs', the subject of this interview, infiltrated Smash EDO,[14] Dissent[15] CAN (see below) and Rising Tide,[16] had attended several anti-G8 mobilisations,[17] the Heathrow Camp for Climate Action (see below) and the Crawley No Borders Camp.[18] He had also been involved in environmental and anti-militarist campaigns in Wales (see below). 'Lyn Watson', who was also exposed in the wake of the 'Mark Kennedy' outcry, had been posing as an activist in the campaign against Aldermaston Atomic Weapons Establishment, the Save Titnore Woods campaign,[19] the Common Place social centre in Leeds, the Action Medics collective and the Heathrow Camp for Climate Action.[20] Jim Boyling ('Jim Sutton') was discovered to have had infiltrated 'environmental movements' and Reclaim the Streets from 1995-2000.[21]

The role of Bob Lambert ('Bob Robinson'), 'Simon Welling' and 'Peter Black' as undercover officers was also explored in the media after the revelations about Mark Kennedy. Lambert, who is now an academic at Exeter and St Andrews Universities,[22] worked as a Special Branch detective between 1980 and 2006 and was involved in the SDS. Lambert reportedly infiltrated London Greenpeace,[23] the Animal Liberation Front (ALF)[24] and anti-racist groups.[25] Black had infiltrated the No M11 campaign in the 1990s.[26] Welling had infiltrated Globalise Resistance from 2001-5 and traveled to many international anti-capitalist mobilisations including those in New York and Seville.[27] Two undercover officers who apparently used the pseudonyms 'John Barker' and 'Mark Cassidy' have also been mentioned in the press.[28]

Most of these undercover police officers are accused of forming sexual relationships with activists while in their undercover personae. The activists concerned were under the impression that the men were committed activists and had no idea they were, in fact, paid police officers. The police have justified this behaviour in response to the public outcry over these relationships with reference to their utility in terms of gaining intelligence: one undercover officer explains that officers used sex as a "tool" to maintain cover and "glean information".[29] The 2012 HMIC report called these relationships "collateral intrusion"[30] and suggested that officers should weigh up whether the "intrusion" is proportionate to the intelligence uncovered.[31] A case is being considered by lawyers for eight women who claim they suffered emotional and psychological trauma after having intimate relationships with undercover officers.[32] Scotland Yard have attempted to argue that the case should be moved to the Investigatory Powers Tribunal (IPT), a body set up in 2000 by the Regulation of Investigatory Powers Act (RIPA) to handle complaints over surveillance[33] which, according to its website, "operates within a necessary ring of secrecy".[34] Cases held at the tribunal cannot be appealed in the UK and the tribunal is under no obligation to hold oral hearings.[35]

One major public controversy concerns the withholding of intelligence obtained by undercover officers during court cases, including information that may benefit the defence case or undermine the prosecution case. Mark Kennedy was one of over a hundred people arrested at the Iona School in Nottingham in 2009.[36] He had been involved in the plan to shut down a coal-fired power station at Ratcliffe-on-Soar from an early stage. The arrests resulted in two trials for conspiracy to commit aggravated trespass, one where defendants argued that there was a 'necessity' to take action (in order to prevent deaths from the effects of climate change) and one where defendants claimed they had not agreed to any conspiracy.

The first trial of the defendants who attempted to give a legal justification for their actions ended with their conviction.[37] However, prior to the second trial, after the revelations that Mark Kennedy was an undercover officer, it came to light that evidence gathered by Kennedy had been withheld from the defence in both cases. The evidence, a recording of the meetings held prior to the mass arrest,[38] had not been disclosed to the defence by the CPS.[39] This resulted in the collapse of the second trial and the Director of Public Prosecutions (DPP) inviting the first set of defendants to appeal. In July 2011 their convictions were quashed on the basis that evidence had been withheld from the CPS which could have benefited the defence case. The DPP has also invited twenty-nine people who were convicted of disrupting the transport of coal to the Drax power station to appeal on the basis that vital evidence gathered by Kennedy may have been withheld.[40]

A crucial factor to consider in relation to undercover police officers is to the extent to which they are cleared by their superiors in the police force to break the law while undercover. This lawbreaking may be used as a strategy in discrediting movements and/or securing the arrest and possible convictions of activists, as well as a way to gain the trust of those groups they are infiltrating. Bob Lambert, during his time as an undercover officer infiltrating the ALF, is alleged to have successfully planted an incendiary device as part of a coordinated arson attack which caused fires at two Debenhams stores in July 1987, as part of a campaign against the sale of fur.[41] Kennedy claims that he was cleared by his handlers to commit crimes such as trespass and criminal damage.[42] There have been many claims that Mark Kennedy acted as an agent provocateur, pushing for more and more extreme actions.[43] In their judgment in the appeal of the Ratcliffe defendants the Lord Chief Justice of England and Wales, Mr Justice Treacy and Mr Justice Calvert-Smith commented that Kennedy arguably acted as an "agent provocateur"[44] in regard to of the action at Ratcliffe-on-Soar.

There is evidence that undercover officers have made false claims about the activities of radical groups. Such claims may be motivated by a desire to heighten the perception of a threat to society posed by them in order to discredit them or to influence court proceedings For example, Mark Kennedy is accused of fabricating allegations that French activists practiced constructing Improvised Explosive Devices (IEDs). Some of these activists were later arrested in the village of Tarnac and put under formal investigation for allegedly sabotaging high speed rail lines in 2008.[45]

The role of undercover officers in both undermining resistance and channeling the routes that it takes has been little explored in independent as well as mainstream media. However, it can be clearly seen as one of the ways in which the state attempts to avoid situations where resistance grows to levels it cannot easily control, at least not without resorting to coercive means. The presence of undercover police officers can help the police to shape and mould the activities of the groups that they have infiltrated. Undercover officers can also, as Jacobs did while infiltrating Cardiff Anarchist Network, undermine and disrupt political activity which challenges the system, and thus encourage other activists to refrain from doing the same.

This interview explores the various uses of infiltrating protest groups. Clearly, one of the prime reasons is to gain intelligence to inform their overall strategy with regard to day-to-day events like protest campaigns. This information can be used to target particular activists for arrest and or harassment by, for example, Forward Intelligence Teams. (See Anderson, Chapter 16.) Undercover officers are also invaluable assets in gaining insider access to and intelligence about new activist networks. Infiltration thus allows the police to pinpoint those activists who pose a potential threat and to undermine them. The amount of police attention that these activists receive serves as a warning sign to potential supporters.

'Jacobs' appears to have been primarily engaged in an additional strategy to undermine the effectiveness of activist networks. This behaviour shows that sometimes, where groups pose a perceived threat, undercover officers will act to neutralise that threat, and actively destabilise and undermine the group to the point of making it unable to operate.

Tom Anderson: Can you tell me about Marco and what kind of involvement you had with him and when and what you think he was aiming to do in the various engagements you had with him?

Verity Smith: I became aware of him just after we returned from the G8 in Scotland in 2005, apparently he had been to Cardiff before that but I only remember him starting to appear at meetings of what was then the Cardiff Anarchist Network (CAN) after the G8. I believe he was at the G8 but I don't remember meeting him there, but my memory's not the best.

He moved to Cardiff claiming that he'd come from Brighton but that (activists in) Brighton had been hostile to him, had not accepted him and that he'd felt excluded. He said he'd come to Cardiff because we were more open and more tolerant of new people becoming involved and that there was a lot going on in Cardiff in terms of activism and that he wanted to be where things were happening.

Largely that was true, it may have been naïve but we were committed to being open and welcoming to people, we wanted to be a group that was accessible and in a place like Cardiff where there isn't a huge tradition of activism there was a need to be as welcoming as possible. We took people at face-value.

We were also very active. We were, as a group, very much involved in mobilising for the G8 within the Dissent network, we had been active against the Iraq war and we had taken a number of direct actions in relation to that. After the G8 in 2005 the group became active in environmental activism through Climate Camp and other actions that took place. We were, I think a fairly active group.

TA: And how did Marco introduce himself to you?

VS: The first time I remember meeting him was him turning up at a meeting of CAN which was held in a pub in the centre of town and saying "Hi I'm Marco I wanna be involved". He'd already, by then, become friendly with a couple of people in the group. He'd made contacts and got to know a few people so that when he came to the first meeting he wasn't walking in out of the blue, he'd got some contacts established so from that point on it was very easy for him.

TA: And what did he say about his backstory?

VS: There was a large absence in backstory, which looking back we should have questioned further. He claimed to hail from Northampton and to be a Northampton Town supporter. He had a story which I can't remember the details of because I wasn't particularly interested at the time about his personal relationships and his family. He claimed that he was in the process of a messy break-up with a woman in Northampton and that was the reason he'd wanted to leave Northampton to create some distance between him and her.

TA: And after that, over the years, what kind of thing was he involved in that you know of?

VS: He was very involved in organising around the G8 in Heiligendamm in 2007. He had shown interest in going to the G8 in St Petersburg in Russia in 2006 and said that he'd go but, at the last minute, he pulled out. He also pulled out of attending planning meetings in Ukraine. I now think this was because the police tried but failed to get the Russians and Ukrainians to agree to undercover police working in their territory. But he did go to planning meetings prior to the German G8 in 2007 and travelled to a planning meeting in Poland with other members of the group. He traveled with us to the G8 protests in Germany. He was very keen on being involved in that level of international organising.

After that he became very enthusiastic about Climate Camp and environmental actions. But after a while, I think partly due to his interventions and influences, the level of action in Cardiff significantly tailed off and at that point he got involved in all sorts of things such as actions against an MOD establishment in South Wales and with the No Borders group. He simply got involved with whatever was going on. The anti-militarist group he got involved with, for instance, involved people who were non-violent and largely law abiding, so was hardly the sort of thing that would justify undercover cops. But he still got involved, still went to meetings.

TA: You mentioned that the level of activism in Cardiff dropped because of his interventions. Can you expand on that.

VS: What I think, looking back, that he did was to almost immediately create divisions and to isolate people who were particularly active within the group. His first actions seemed to be to launch into a getting to know you phase. He would be down the pub all the time, he would always have money for drinks, he would be very keen to encourage people to go out drinking with him and used that time to really probe people on what they thought and what their attitudes were and what their opinions were, what their vulnerabilities were. I also think he wanted to instil a drinking culture that automatically excluded those people who were not part of that party scene - because they were working or because they had children or because they were not of that age group or whatever. So immediately after he turned up there was a level of division there that hadn't been there before.

I believe he also used the information that he got from this phase to develop strategies to isolate particular individuals by bad-mouthing them, by disparaging them, or making lots of little humorous comments about them which put them down. He would play on and exacerbate any arguments or differences, the things that are said in any group. And he would say some downright unpleasant things about people. In the end a number of people were simply pushed out by feelings within the group, including myself. A group in a small city like Cardiff is inevitably made up of people who have various different outlooks on life. Some of us were working, some professionals, some students, some on the dole. Some of us were anarchists, some not. We were vulnerable to someone winding up political differences.

Up until he arrived we had been very business-like. We weren't just there because all our mates were there, we were there because we wanted to do something. There was a business approach to what we did: we met, we talked about what we were going to do and then we went and did it. Marco created a much greater role for people's personalities and exacerbated people's personal differences as well. He'd say all sorts of things; I know he'd say about me that I just was 'not a nice person', that I was disposed to confrontation and violence and that I was likely to get other people in trouble. He would use all sorts of things, whatever ammunition came his way he would ratchet it up and fire it out and try to stop the group functioning as a cohesive whole.

A number of people began feeling very isolated, feeling that instead of being involved in an active and important group they were under attack, that they were not wanted. It became an unpleasant environment so people left and walked away. I think that was one of the key ways in which he disrupted the workings of the group but it wasn't the only way.

He was very good at keeping hold of useful information. He would say "I'll go, I'll feed back to you". I believe now that the information that was fed back was filtered and not all of the information that we should have received we actually did receive. He frequently put himself in positions where he was able to disrupt communications between groups, particularly in national and international networks.

Of course, he did foster very personal relationships with people which I believe he used as another way to cause separation and to disrupt the workings. Nothing seemed out of bounds, he could lie, he could sleep with women, he could abuse the trust that he was given. He would exploit vulnerabilities. Nothing seemed out of bounds in attempting to undermine the group.

TA: And do you think that his main aim was to destroy the group or did he have other objectives too?

VS: Well CAN was useful to Marco as a means of tapping in to national and international activist networks. He was introduced to activists around the world on the back of his involvement with us. We were a reasonably respected group and that gave him access to other networks, which certainly was an advantage to him.

At the time we were one of the more radical local networks and had played a very strong part in the Gleneagles G8 mobilisation and that, I believe, made us a key target. The police made huge resources available to undermine the organization of protests at international summits. That extended to local, national and international groups and I think, initially at least, we were targeted as part of that agenda.

But after the G8 he shifted his focus to environmental activities and tried to tap into the local animal rights networks. Clearly his role was to undermine us as a group, not just use us to tap into international networks, although that would have clearly been useful.

He stayed in Cardiff even long after there was any real activity in terms of direct action. When he left there was no group left really, it was in tatters. He'd undermined a fairly decent group.

TA: Do you think he was trying to channel the group one way or another, was there a particular direction that he wanted the group to take?

VS: It was most noticeable when people suggested making any stand of resistance against the state or being involved in civil disobedience or direct action. He would say thing like "oh god look at them, they're not going to do that are they." It made people feel uncomfortable about suggesting things of that nature because they would put themselves in a position where they could be put down and ridiculed. It was very subtle, it wasn't particularly overt. It was a general laughing at people who were active or who took part in direct action or civil disobedience or stood up to the state or didn't comply with police directions. Those were the sort of people who he'd say "aren't they being ridiculous" and having formed strong relationships with other people in the group he had some support. It could make you take a little step back and question what you were doing because he undermined the sort of strength it took to be active. That's the best way I can put it I think.

TA: Do you think that was his purpose, to discourage direct action?

VS: Definitely, there was a very clear disruptive element to what he was doing. Clearly there was an information and evidence gathering element to what he was doing as well. He clearly did liaise with the police and we believe he was instrumental in the police making arrests at at least one environmental action. But the information gathering was definitely not the only aspect of what he did, there was a very clear agenda to disrupt.

TA: And were there any actions that he promoted?

VS: Well yes, he promoted everything in theory. He was prepared to drive the car, he was prepared to be supportive of various actions. Thinking back, I can't actually remember a time when he proposed anything or clearly supported anything. He hid behind this sort of amiable clown thing, he made a joke of everything, deflected everything and was part of everything without promoting anything. That's how I remember it, others may have different opinions.

TA: Are there any other tactics that Marco used that you want to flag up?

VS: I don't have evidence but I believe he liaised with the Public Order Unit in order to target people. I believe I was targeted for arrest as a result of information that he would have passed on. Marco also took every possible oppurtunity to make life as difficult as possible without us knowing that it all came back to him, it was all very subtle and all very carefully done.

TA: And when did Marco leave the group?

VS: Marco had been in a relationship with somebody but he had, I believe, broken that off. He invited us all for a goodbye meal, about fourteen of us turned up and I don't know if he was expecting that, perhaps he was expecting a smaller number. By that time a number of us had quite deep suspicions about him but there were such divisions within the group that we hadn't told each other about them. I didn't know, for instance, that a number of others in the group shared my suspicions.

I turned up at the goodbye dinner out of a sense of curiosity really. He said he was going off to Cyprus, that he'd got a job, that he was going off there and of course we could all come to stay and it would be lovely to see us all and here was his number in Cyprus.

And then he went, a couple of people who were close to him got texts saying bland things like "the weather's nice" and then - nothing. His MySpace sites stopped being updated, he didn't answer his phone or email, he just dropped off the edge of the universe and at that point people's suspicions consolidated and people started to talk to each other and ask whether he was a cop. The group got together and talked about it, there was broad agreement that we thought he probably was but we didn't know what to do about it. People outside the group were quite dismissive and often we weren't believed and it was only after the Guardian ran the story, after the Mark Kennedy disclosure, that it was confirmed and people finally believed us.

Notes

1   Caroline Graham, 'Mark Kennedy: Undercover policeman tells story of 8 years with eco-warriors', *The Daily Mail*, 17 January, 2011. <http://www.dailymail.co.uk/news/article-1347478/Mark-Kennedy-Undercover-policeman-tells-story-8-years-eco-warriors.html>

2   HM Inspectorate of Constabulary (HMIC), *A review of national police units which provide intelligence on criminality associated with protest*, (2012), p. 14. <http://www.hmic.gov.uk/media/review-of-national-police-units-which-provide-intelligence-on-criminality-associated-with-protest-20120202.pdf>

3   Tom Griffin, 'Mission Creep: How the ACPO empire hyped eco-terrorism', *OurKingdom, power and liberty in Britain*, 16 January 2011. <http://www.opendemocracy.net/ourkingdom/tom-griffin/mission-creep-how-acpo-empire-hyped-eco-terrorism>

4   HM Inspectorate of Constabulary (HMIC), *A review of national police units which provide intelligence on criminality associated with protest*, (2012), p. 5. <http://www.hmic.gov.uk/media/review-of-national-police-units-which-provide-intelligence-on-criminality-associated-with-protest-20120202.pdf>

5   Ibid. p. 14.

6   Ibid. p. 7.

7   Ibid. p. 8.

8   Caroline Graham, '"I'm the victim of smears": Undercover policeman denies bedding a string of women during his eight years with eco-warriors', *The Daily Mail*, 17 January, 2011. <http://www.dailymail.co.uk/news/article-1347478/Mark-Kennedy-Undercover-policeman-tells-story-8-years-eco-warriors.html>

9   Tom Anderson, direct observation.

10 Saving Iceland Collective, 'The Real Facts Regarding Mark Kennedy's Infiltration of Saving Iceland', *Sheffield Indymedia*, 11 February, 2011. <http://sheffield.indymedia.org.uk/2011/02/473878.html>

11 Paul Lewis and Rob Evans, 'Mark Kennedy: A journey from undercover cop to "bona fide" activist', *The Guardian*, 10 January, 2011. <http://www.guardian.co.uk/environment/2011/jan/10/mark-kennedy-undercover-cop-activist>

12 Author's interviews with activists who had been involved in the Dissent Network, 2011-12.

13 Paul Lewis and Rob Evans, 'Mark Kennedy: A journey from undercover cop to "bona fide" activist', *The Guardian*, 10 January, 2011. <http://www.guardian.co.uk/environment/2011/jan/10/mark-kennedy-undercover-cop-activist>

14 'Dick Tracy', 'An account of Marco Jacobs' time in Brighton', *Sheffield Indymedia*, 19 January, 2011. <http://sheffield.indymedia.org.uk/2011/01/472391.html>

15 Ibid.

16 Rajeev Syal, 'Undercover police: Officer B identified as Mark Jacobs', *The Guardian*, 19 January, 2011. <http://www.guardian.co.uk/uk/2011/jan/19/undercover-police-officer-mark-jacobs>

17 Tom Anderson, direct observation.

18 Tom Anderson, direct observation.

19 Porkbolter, 'Exposed: police spy in Worthing', *Sheffield Indymedia*, 7 February, 2011. <http://sheffield.indymedia.org.uk/2011/02/473551.html>

20 Rajeev Syal and Martin Wainwright, 'Undercover police: Officer A named as Lynn Watson', *The Guardian*, 19 January, 2011. <http://www.guardian.co.uk/uk/2011/jan/19/undercover-police-officer-lynn-watson>; Porkbolter, 'Exposed: police spy in Worthing', *Sheffield Indymedia*, 7 February, 2011. <http://sheffield.indymedia.org.uk/2011/02/473551.html>

21 Paul Lewis, Rob Evans and Rowenna Davis, 'Undercover policeman married activist he was sent to spy on', *The Guardian*, 19 January, 2011. <http://www.guardian.co.uk/uk/2011/jan/19/undercover-policeman-married-activist-spy>

22 Rob Evans and Paul Lewis, 'Progressive academic Bob Lambert is former police spy', *The Guardian*, 16 October, 2011. <http://www.guardian.co.uk/uk/2011/oct/16/academic-bob-lambert-former-police-spy>

23 Graham Smith, 'Lecturer exposed as police spy-master who infiltrated Greenpeace and other groups "posing threat to public order"', *The Daily Mail*, 17 October, 2011. <http://www.dailymail.co.uk/news/article-2050051/Lecturer-exposed-police-spy-master-infiltrated-Greenpeace-groups-posing-threat-public-order.html>

24 Paul Lewis and Rob Evans, 'Police spy tricked lover with activist "cover story"', *The Guardian*, 23 October, 2011. <http://www.guardian.co.uk/uk/2011/oct/23/police-spy-tricked-lover-activist?newsfeed=true>

25 Paul Lewis, Rob Evans and Rowenna Davis, 'Undercover policeman married activist he was sent to spy on', *The Guardian*, 19 January, 2011. <http://www.guardian.co.uk/uk/2011/jan/19/undercover-policeman-married-activist-spy>

26 Rob Evans, Tony Thompson and Paul Lewis, 'Undercover police officer warns against giving Met control of spy unit', *The Guardian*, 24 January, 2011. <http://www.guardian.co.uk/uk/2011/jan/24/undercover-police-met-spy-unit>

27 Meirion Jones and Anna Adams, 'Undercover police work revealed by phone blunder', *BBC Newsnight*, 25 March, 2011. <http://www.bbc.co.uk/news/uk-12867187>

28 anon@indymedia.org (Nottingham Indymedia), 'Women sue Met over undercover cops', *Indymedia UK*, 26 December, 2011.

<http://www.indymedia.org.uk/en/2011/12/490541.html>; Rob Evans, 'Women start legal action against police chiefs over emotional trauma -their statement', *The Guardian*, 16 December, 2011. <http://www.guardian.co.uk/uk/undercover-with-paul-lewis-and-rob-evans/2011/dec/16/legal-action-over-police-spies>; Mark, 'Mark Cassidy undercover 1995-2000', *Sheffield Indymedia*, 4 February, 2011. <http://sheffield.indymedia.org.uk/2011/02/473378.html>

29 Mark Townsend and Tony Thompson, 'Undercover cop cleared "to have sex with activists"', *The Guardian*, 22 January, 2011. <http://www.guardian.co.uk/uk/2011/jan/22/undercover-police-cleared-sex-activists>

30 HM Inspectorate of Constabulary (HMIC), *A review of national police units which provide intelligence on criminality associated with protest*, (2012), p. 21. <http://www.hmic.gov.uk/media/review-of-national-police-units-which-provide-intelligence-on-criminality-associated-with-protest-20120202.pdf>

31 Ibid.

32 Rob Evans and Paul Lewis, 'Former lovers of undercover officers sue police over deceit', *The Guardian*, 16 December, 2011. <www.guardian.co.uk/uk/2011/dec/16/lovers-undercover-officers-sue-police>

33 See the Investigatory Powers Tribunal. <http://www.ipt-uk.com/>

34 Rob Evans and Paul Lewis, 'Metropolitan police want secret court to hear police spy cases', *The Guardian*, 2 October, 2012. <http://www.guardian.co.uk/uk/2012/oct/02/metropolitan-police-spy-cases-tribunal>

35 Ibid.

36 Juliette Jowit and Matthew Taylor, 'Police arrest 114 people in pre-emptive strike against environmental protesters', *The Guardian*, 13 April, 2009. <http://www.guardian.co.uk/environment/2009/apr/13/nottingham-police-raid-environmental-campaigners>;[2011] EWCA Crim 1885 [2012] Crim LR453, p.8. <http://www.judiciary.gov.uk/Resources/JCO/Documents/Judgments/barkshire-others-v-r.pdf>

37 James Meikle and Tim Webb, 'Ratcliffe activists found guilty of coal station plot', *The Guardian*, 14 December, 2010. <http://www.guardian.co.uk/environment/2010/dec/14/ratcliffe-coal-station-activists>

38 [2011] EWCA Crim 1885 [2012] Crim LR453, p.9. <http://www.judiciary.gov.uk/Resources/JCO/Documents/Judgments/barkshire-others-v-r.pdf>

39 Ibid.

40 Rob Evans and Paul Lewis, 'Mark Kennedy controversy: activists invited to challenge convictions', *The Guardian*, 3 July, 2012. <http://www.guardian.co.uk/environment/2012/jul/03/mark-kennedy-

activists-challenge-convictions>

41 Rob Evans and Paul Lewis, 'Call for police links to animal rights firebombing to be investigated', *The Guardian*, 13 June, 2012. <http://www.guardian.co.uk/uk/2012/jun/13/police>

42 Caroline Graham, '"I'm the victim of smears": Undercover policeman denies bedding a string of women during his eight years with eco-warriors', *The Daily Mail*, 17 January, 2011. <http://www.dailymail.co.uk/news/article-1347478/Mark-Kennedy-Undercover-policeman-tells-story-8-years-eco-warriors.html>

43 For example, Saving Iceland Collective, 'The Real Facts Regarding Mark Kennedy's Infiltration of Saving Iceland', *Sheffield Indymedia*, 11 February, 2011. <http://sheffield.indymedia.org.uk/2011/02/473878.html>

44 [2011] EWCA Crim 1885 [2012] Crim LR453, p.9. <http://www.judiciary.gov.uk/Resources/JCO/Documents/Judgments/barkshire-others-v-r.pdf>

45 Angelique Chrisafis, 'Police spy Mark Kennedy accused of fake claims in French case', *The Guardian*, 8 November 2012. <http://www.guardian.co.uk/uk/2012/nov/08/mark-kennedy-accused-fantasist-french>

Part 5

'Democracy Promotion'
in Pursuit of Global Hegemony

18. Grassroots Globalization: Underneath the Rhetoric of "Democracy Promotion"

Edmund Berger

It was a December morning in Cairo when the soldiers came. Armed for combat, they descended upon the offices of foreign NGOs, sequestering staffers inside their offices and shutting off communication to the outside. "We're literally locked in. I really have no idea why they are holding us inside and confiscating our personal laptops," tweeted one worker who was shocked to suddenly find herself a prisoner.[1]

The security forces had been ordered to raid the NGOs - ten in all[2] - by the Supreme Council of the Armed Forces (SCAF), the highest governing body of the Egyptian military. Since the resignation of President Hosni Mubarak in the face of the 'Arab Spring' protests, it was also the highest governing body in the nation. Upon the transfer of power between the dictator and his military confidants, the SCAF had closed Parliament, suspended the Constitution, dangled the promise of elections in front of the people - and now the assault on the NGOs had, in the eyes of the West, revealed that even though Mubarak was gone, his autocratic style of governance still lurked in post-revolutionary Egypt. American politicians quickly moved to reach a diplomatic solution as a handful of NGOs staffers were put on trial. Secretary of State Hillary Clinton warned Egypt's foreign minister that "failure to resolve the dispute may lead to the loss of American aid."[3] The warning sent a clear message about just how much had changed between the two countries: Egypt, like Israel, had long been the US's key strategic ally in the Middle East and North Africa region. During Mubarak's rule over the nation, a time when raids and suspensions of civil liberties were common place, Egypt was receiving $1.3 billion in US military aid.[4]

However, many of the NGOs in question are also recipients of US funding, and were even created through legislation passed in Washington. These included the National Democratic Institute (NDI) and the International Republican Institute (IRI), two organizations that operate under the mantle of the National Endowment for Democracy (NED). Freedom House, another target of the raid, began as a private NGO in the 1940s, yet over time its budget has received ample government money through the NED. Outfits like the NDI, the IRI, and Freedom House work in tandem in places of social unrest. They view themselves as an institutional manifestation of civil society, and thus the attacks on them are an attack on the people as a whole. Yet the SCAF is certainly not the first to crack down on them. In the aftermath of Iran's 2009 Green Revolt, the regime in Tehran barred some sixty NGOs, including the NED, IRI, the NDI, Freedom House, the Open Society Institute, and Human Rights Watch, from operating in the country on grounds that they were fomenting 'seditious' activity.

This particular network of NGOs is no stranger to crackdowns. In 1997, the government of Alexander Lukashenko in Belarus charged the Open Society Institute with tax fraud and seized the philanthropy's bank accounts, and in 2003 Eduard Shevardnadze in Georgia threatened to shut down its Tbilisi offices.[5] Figureheads from states worldwide outside the US's sphere of influence, from Venezuela to Russia, have attacked the NED in speech and in print, characterizing it as a tool of the Americans to intervene in the affairs of other countries. These are precisely the same accusations leveled at the NGOs by Egypt's SCAF.

Quasi-governmental NGOs like the NED and private NGOs such as the Open Society Institute profess that their work is not one of intervention, but an act of 'promoting democracy' in countries where governments enforce iron-fisted governance on its citizenry. But there are problems with this narrative. 'Democracy promotion' is implemented on an extremely selective basis, and a cursory glance inevitably leads one to conclude that ulterior motives lurk behind the veneer of democratic enlargement. (See also Fisher, Chapter 2.) For example, it is tough to see why the US was keen on promoting governmental change in Georgia when it supported authoritarian rule in nearby Azerbaijan, or why the NED worked so hard in Chile in the 1980s to undermine Augusto Pinochet when many of its principals openly supported the Contra rebels in Nicaragua.[6] By the admission of the NDI program director in Georgia, his organization's work had less to do with electoral democracy than it did with geopolitical primacy: "There was an overarching understanding that Russia having a lock on the movement of hydrocarbons to Europe is a problem," he reported, speaking of the Baku-Tbilisi-Ceyhan pipeline route.[7] And sometimes it had to do with economic incentive: George Soros, the founder and head of the Open Society Institute, made 'democratization' in post-Soviet Eastern Europe his raison d'etre in the 1990s. When the process was complete, however, he turned around and profited handsomely from his philanthropy's work. "... I have no rhyme or reason or right to deny my funds, or my shareholders, the possibility of investing there, or to deny those countries the chance to get hold of some of these funds," he explained.[8]

Critics of 'democracy promotion' NGOs frequently characterize these intervention platforms as the driving forces behind social unrest. While it could certainly appear that way (and the countries whose governments are targeted for 'democracy promotion' usually tout this line when justifying raids on offices and other crackdowns), this viewpoint ignores the dynamics of this system. The social unrest is not the creation of the State Department; instead, 'democracy promotion' generally piggy-backs preexisting grassroots movements. This is born from a very real dependent relationship that movements have with NGOs: as Clifford Bob, a political science professor at Duequesne University has observed, "outside aid is literally a matter of life of death. NGOs can raise awareness about little-known conflicts, mobilize resources for beleaguered movements, and pressure repressive governments."[9]

One of the more intriguing factors in 'democracy promotion' activities is the fact that Western backers, characteristically opposed to anything with even shades of socialism, frequently interact with left-wing movements. An excellent case in point was the Solidarity trade union movement in Poland, which successfully liberated the country from the Soviet sphere of control. While national independence was the primary goal of Solidarity, it envisioned sweeping reforms for the country more in line with early socialist philosophers than America's neoliberal market economy. "We demand a self-governing democratic reform at every management level and a new socioeconomic system combining the plan, self-government, and the market."[10] Even though the plan called for democratically operated worker co-operatives instead of corporate behemoths, participatory government structures and a regulated economy, aid came from the NED and Soros for the fledgling movement.

In the end, however, Poland was nothing like what Solidarity had planned. Structural adjustment plans drafted by the IMF forced the privatization of the former state-owned enterprises, so that before they could be transformed into the co-operative model they were picked up by foreign investors. Regulation was barred, and economics were formally separated from any form of political interference. A nationalist, left-leaning movement had been successfully utilized to break open a country into the purest form of neoliberalism possible. However, abandoning earlier goals or changing rhetoric isn't something uncommon for grassroots movements. Clifford Bob pointed out that the NGOs' "concerns, tactics, and organizational requirements create a loose but real structure to which needy local insurgents must conform to maximize their chances of gaining supporters."[11]

The Dialectic of Liberation

Despite its utilization of liberation movements as a medium for promoting strategic interests and capitalist integration, 'democracy promotion' paradoxically has a progenitor in the practice of colonialism. Colonialism, although dressed in a cloak of nationalism, has always been an affair of international economics. Cecil Rhodes sold imperialism to Great Britain by proclaiming that "in order to save the 40,000,000 inhabitants of the United Kingdom from a bloody civil war, we colonial statesmen must acquire new lands to settle the surplus population, to provide new markets for the goods produced by them in the factories and mines... If you want to avoid civil war, you must become imperialists."[12] Rosa Luxemburg's analysis of the internationalization of capitalism followed this argument closely: "All conquerors pursue the aim of dominating and exploiting the country, but none was interested in destroying their social organization."[13]

National liberation struggle built itself upon this pattern, and for a while it seemed as if Luxemburg's theories were being confirmed. From Algeria to Palestine to Vietnam, left-wing economic forms blended with the nationalist zeitgeist to produce revolutionary uprisings against the oppressors. Their post-revolutionary politics, however, paint a very different picture from these earlier ambitions. Just as Russia had to turn to the IMF and open up its market in order to keep itself afloat (the rapid economic 'shock therapy' implemented by the post-Soviet leadership under Yeltsin proved to be the catalyst for a major economic downturn),[14] liberated nations frequently find themselves in economic chaos and in need of a helping hand - a hand that international interests are willing to lend. Or as in the case of post-Apartheid South Africa, the exploiting elite remain a cog in the machinery of the nation. (See also Berger,

Chapter 12.) Franz Fanon, a psychologist and veteran of the Algerian struggle, wrote in *The Wretched of the Earth* that the post-revolutionary domestic elite's "vocation is to not transform the nation but prosaically to serve as a conveyor belt for capitalism, forced to camouflage itself behind the mask of neocolonialism. The national bourgeoisie, with no misgivings and great pride, revels in the role of the agent in its dealings with the Western bourgeoisie."[15] Michael Hardt and Antonio Negri have also written about this odd paradigm, describing the national liberation struggle as one of the key factors in the development of the globalized market economy:

> ... the equation nationalism equals political and economic modernization, which has been heralded by leaders of numerous anticolonial [sic] and anti-imperialist struggles from Gandhi and Ho Chi Minh to Nelson Mandela, really ends up being a perverse trick. This equation serves to mobilize popular forces and galvanize a social movement, but where does the movement lead and what interests does it serve? In most cases it involves a delegated struggle, in which the modernization project also establishes in power the new ruling group that is in charge of carrying it out... the revolutionaries get bogged down in 'realism', and modernization gets lost in the hierarchies of the world market... The nationalism of anticolonial and anti-imperialist struggles effectively functions in reverse, and the liberated countries find themselves subordinated in the international economic order.[16]

The relationship between the grassroots liberation struggle and world capitalism is further revealed by taking into consideration the changing nature of the capitalist system. During the heyday of colonialism, capitalism was certainly international but existed in a state-centric form, but with the collapse of much of the old colonialist world - which had accelerated with the breakdown of the statist forms of capitalism advocated by the adherents of Keynesianism - markets were unhinged from the state. It effectively transitioned into what Felix Guattari and other early theorists dubbed "Integrated World Capitalism,"[17] and what is commonly identified today as globalization. One of the by-products of this transnationalization of economics has been a shift in Fanon's 'domestic elites', who became what William Robinson calls the "transnational capitalist class (TCC)": the "the owners and managers of the TNCs [transnational corporations]" and the "transnational managerial elite" of the integrated world capitalist system.[18] In Robinson's analysis, the TCC reject the Fordist-Keynesian class compromise, instead charging that they are characterized by "'flexible' regime of accumulation" built on neoliberal programs such as deregulation, informationalization (the rise of computerized data systems and other digital networks), and a new fluctuating nature of labor. They are inherently technocratic, relying on transnational regulatory agencies such as the World Trade Organization (WTO), the World Bank, and the International Monetary Fund (IMF) to manage the stateless economic system. (See also Robinson, Chapter 4 and Carroll and Greeno, Chapter 9).

Individuals such as George Soros would fit into the TCC schema, as would many former activists involved in pro-democracy uprisings. We could use Vaclav Havel as an example here: he went from leading Czechoslovakia's Velvet Revolution against Soviet control (with NED support) to working with global capitalist institutions such as the New Atlantic Initiative, the Trilateral Commission, and the Orange Circle, an organization that assists transnational corporations invest in Ukraine. Global elite figures such as Soros and Havel operate within informal transnational networks; just as sociologist G. William Domhoff has argued that domestic elite networks constitute an inordinate degree of influence over electoral politics, scholars such as Anne-Marie Slaughter (who was a member of Secretary of State Condoleezza Rice's Advisory Committee on 'democracy promotion') have identified transnational networks as forming a sort of global governance.[19]

This 'global governance' is not to be viewed through the lenses of conspiratorial thinking; it is an inherent byproduct of the current epoch's transnational tendencies and not a creation of concentrated design. The problem does arise, however, when one considers that the power and influence of these elite networks creates a governance system where the underclasses have less and less say in matters that affect their daily lives. Under the regime of neoliberalism, the market is well insulated from the powers of politics. As such, the so-called democracy practiced in 'developed' nations - and the kind being promoted to 'developing' nations - is more akin to a form of management than an expression of autonomy and empowerment. (See also Fisher, Chapter 2 and Barker, Chapter 11.) It is best described, following William I. Robinson, as a "low intensity democracy". As William Avilés writes:

> Low-intensity democracies are limited democracies in that they achieve important political changes, such as the formal reduction of the military's former institutional power or

greater individual freedoms, but stop short in addressing the
extreme social inequalities within... societies. ...they provide
a more transparent and secure environment for the
investments of transnational capital... these regimes
function as legitimizing institutions for capitalist states,
effectively co-opting the social opposition that arises from
the destructive consequences of neoliberal austerity, or as
Cyrus Vance and Henry Kissinger have argued, the
promotion of 'pre-emptive' reform in order to co-opt
popular movements that may press for more radical, or even
revolutionary, change.[20]

Already practiced in the leading countries around the world, this is
precisely the form that 'democracy-promoting' agencies hand down to
grassroots movements seeking help in their domestic fights.

The National Endowment for Democracy, From 1967 to Beyond

In April of 1967, a Democrat congressman from Florida by the name of
Dante Fascell took a bill before Congress that would create an "Institute
of International Affairs," an "initiative that would authorize overt
funding for programs to promote democratic values."[21] The catalyst for
the proposal had been the recent revelations in *Ramparts* magazine that
the CIA had been passing funding through non-profits, NGOs, and
philanthropic foundations in a bid to influence events being conducted
at the grassroots level. Ideas had been floating around Washington for
some time about the creation of a sort of private CIA, one that could
conduct these kinds of operations without the bad press that comes with
covert action. Regardless, Fascell's bill was a failure. Undaunted, he tried
again eleven years later. Partnering with Congressman Donald M. Fraser,
a bill was drafted proposing a "quasi-autonomous non-governmental
organization" to fund and aid NGOs around the world. This
organization was to be called the Institute for Human Rights, and would
function identically to the future National Endowment for Democracy by
providing technical and financial assistance to organizations around the
globe under the rubric of human rights. But once again the idea failed to
catch on. It did catch the eye, however, of a political scientist by the name
of George Agree.

Agree had been conducting a study of West Germany's *Stiftungen*
complex, a set of government-subsidized foundations that worked with

developing political parties and movements around the globe. In the scheme, there were multiple *Stiftungen*, each aligned with a different power bloc in Germany's government - and each worked in comity to cultivate pluralist, Westernized forms of liberal democracy in the transitioning country. The project was of immense interest to Agree, himself affiliated with an American NGO by the name of Freedom House, which had been founded by a consortium of progressive internationalists brought together by Eleanor Roosevelt at the start of the 1940s. By the 1970s, Freedom House was already closely aligned with the Cold War effort, measuring the levels of freedom of countries outside the US's sphere of influence. In 1967 it worked closely with the United States Information Agency (USIA), a propaganda outfit that worked in conjunction with the US president's National Security Council. Noam Chomsky and Edward Herman have charged that Freedom House "has long served as a virtual propaganda arm of the government and international right wing",[22] while later researchers have dubbed the organization a *"Who's Who* of neoconservatives from government, business, academia, labor, and the press," thanks to the presence of high-profile figures such as Donald Rumsfeld (longtime corporate executive and Secretary of Defense for President George W. Bush), Samuel Huntington (right-wing political scientist and author of *The Clash of Civilizations*), Zbigniew Brzezinski (President Jimmy Carter's National Security adviser and adviser to transnational corporations), and Lane Kirkland (the hawkish president of the AFL-CIO labor union) on its board of trustees.[23]

For Agree and his Freedom House milieu, the *Stiftungen* model provided an excellent platform for 'democracy promotion' in a manner different from the covert actions of the intelligence community, and in 1979 he was joined by Charles Manatt (the chairman of the Democratic National Committee) and William Brock (the chairman of the Republican National Committee) in establishing the American Political Foundation to study the logistics of creating such an organization. The Foundation received the bulk of its funding from the major liberal philanthropies and its leadership was packed with Cold War-era heavy-weights from the foreign policy establishment, business, and labor: national security advisers such as Henry Kissinger and Brzezinski, representatives from the USIA, and Kirkland were just a few of the thinkers at work on the task at hand.[24]

Two years later President Ronald Reagan gave a speech at the Palace of Westminster in London, emphasizing America's commitment to cultivating democracy abroad by concentrating efforts on building "the infrastructure of democracy - the system of a free press, unions, political parties, universities - which allows a people to choose their own way, to develop their own culture, to reconcile their own differences through peaceful means." After the speech the US Agency for International Development (USAID) provided $300,000 to the American Political Foundation, which in turn put the money to use by creating the Democracy Program. This initiative brought together the informal network of 'democracy promotion' advocates - Fascell, Agree, Kirkland and others from the AFL-CIO, numerous congressmen, representatives from policy think-tanks, and political scientists from many of America's elite universities. A study of the works of these democracy scholars will reveal a common mentality on the necessity of power structures for social management, making the framework of low-intensity democracy essential to any 'altruistic' foreign policy. An example worthy of quoting is William Douglas, whose 1972 book *Developing Democracy* provided the intellectual cornerstone of the American Political Foundation's initiative:

> That a firm hand is needed is undeniable. However, it is harder to accept the claim that only a dictatorship can provide the sufficient degree of firmness. First, in regard to keeping order, what is involved is basically effective policy work, and there is no reason why democratic regimes cannot have well-trained riot squads... democratic governments may be able to do the same things as dictatorships to overcome centripetal social forces: use police to stop riots, strike bargains with the various groups to keep them reasonably satisfied, and call out the army when peaceful means fail... There is no denying the need for organization structures by which the modernized elite can exercise tutelage. However... it is common experience that in obtaining the desired behavior from a balky mule, a balky child, or a balky peasant, the real key is to find just the right balance between carrot and stick... Democracy can provide a sufficient degree of regimentation, if it can build up the mass organizations needed to reach the bulk of the people on a daily basis. Dictatorship has no monopoly on the tutelage principle.[25]

In 1983 the Democracy Program titled "The Commitment to Democracy: A Bipartisan Approach," to the Reagan White House. Chock full of patriotic imagery, quoting Abraham Lincoln and the latest President's Westminster address, the report outlined a model directly adapted from the German *Stiftungen* that they referred to as the National

Endowment for Democracy (NED). The NED would act as a clearinghouse for government funds, transferring them to four subsidiary organizations that existed under its umbrella. These subsidiary organizations would consist of two agencies aligned with the major American political parties, the National Democratic Institute (NDI) and the International Republican Institute (IRI), one aligned with the Chamber of Commerce, the Center for International Private Enterprise (CIPE) and a network of interrelated international labor organizations operating under the auspices of the AFL-CIO. These included the American Institute for Free Labor Development (AIFLD), the Free Trade Union Institute (FTUI), the Asian-American Free Labor Institute (AAFLI), and the African-American Labor Center (AALC). Much later these four would be consolidated into a single organization, the American Center for International Labor Solidarity, known more commonly as the Solidarity Center. Money from the NED would also be slated for Freedom House.

The ideal behind this structure is that it would provide a developing or transitional government with a series of checks and balances inside government, business and civil society - opposing political parties, a balance between capital and labor, and dialogue between capital and labor with the multiple parties in the government. However, such idealised Westernized 'democracy' frequently serves as a mask for interests of the powerful over the majority: rarely is there any true deviation between the left and right wings of the spectrum when it comes to the supremacy of the market or foreign policy. This false dichotomy is also found in the so-called conflict between capital and the AFL-CIO's moderate form of unionism, which William Domhoff has observed "involved a narrowing of worker demands to a manageable level. It contained the potential for satisfying most workers at the expense of the socialists among them, meaning that it removed the possibility of a challenge to the capitalist system itself..."[26] The AFL-CIO would take this mentality to the extremes during the Cold War (and certainly after), moving beyond its partnership with capital to becoming a tool of US foreign policy and defense. Early AFL-CIO leaders such as Jay Lovestone were on the payroll of the CIA, and the AIFLD worked extensively in Latin America in the 1960s, using funds provided by the US government and major corporations to undercut radicalized and militant labor union movements. Sometimes this involved the explicit use of violence: in one incident, AIFLD trainees firebombed the headquarters of the Brazilian Communist Party in Rio just prior to a US-backed coup that toppled the nation's left wing president, João Goulart.[27]

This 'democracy promotion' structure became activated through legislation with the passing of House Resolution 2915. This was introduced in part by Dante Fascell who briefly served as chairman of the NED, but stepped aside to allow John Richardson to take the helm. Richardson, a longtime fixture in the State Department having held prominent roles in a slew of CIA-linked organizations, oversaw the election of Carl Gershman (himself a former socialist from the hawkish Social Democrats USA and a close associate of the AFL-CIO leadership) as president of the NED. Gershman continues to hold this position today. Under his presidency the NED has become a major fixture in the world of transnational activism: in 1990 it began to publish a quarterly called the *Journal of Democracy*, which has published works not only by political scientists and State Department apparatchiks, but also by international figures such as the Dalai Lama and Vaclav Havel. In 2000, it helped set up the Community of Democracies, a global forum for democratic nations devised by Madeleine Albright (the longtime chairwoman of the NDI). A year earlier the NED itself had launched a sort of transnational civil society precursor to the Community of Democracies, the World Movement for Democracy (WMD). Joining with other 'democracy' promoting agencies such as the UK-based Westminster Foundation for Democracy, (see also Fisher, Chapter 20) the WMD links together pro-democracy activists from around the world to foster solidarity and establish the networks critical to cultivating ties between domestic movements and international NGOs. The WMD's steering committee's membership roster veers from the unsurprising (international political figures such as Kim Campbell) to the unexpected (Xiao Qiang, a famed Chinese dissident and an advisor to Wikileaks).

'Democracy Promotion' in the Post-Soviet Age

The collapse of the Soviet Union and its subsequent transition into neoliberal capitalism (a change assisted by the NED, among other US agencies) was heralded as a global victory for westernized 'democracies'. Conservative and liberal pundits alike lauded the accomplishment and the dawn of a new order; these attitudes were personified in the now-infamous *The End of History and the Last Man*, a Hegel-inspired tome by Francis Fukuyama that proclaimed that corporatist low-intensity democracy was the apex in cultural and political evolution. It should come as no surprise that Fukuyama has been an adviser to the NED, the *Journal of Democracy*, and Freedom House.

Still, there were scores of countries with dissident movements toiling under oppressive state regimes. For the western democratic project to be completed, these hold-outs would still need to be brought into or brought up to date in the transnational economic system, and as early anti-colonial struggles and 'democracy promotion' had proved, domestic grassroots movements provided the perfect vehicle for this integration. The post-Soviet globe saw the rise of non-state actors working for transition; the most notable being the hedge fund billionaire George Soros, whose Open Society Foundations have worked directly with the NED in promoting capitalist economics across central Europe and in Russia. Another major player has been the Carnegie Endowment for International Peace, a well-known but little discussed nonprofit that "has throughout its history been closely connected with the State Department, successive presidents, numerous private foreign affairs groups and the leaders of the main political parties."[28]

'Democracy promotion' received a new urgency in foreign policy during the administration of President Bill Clinton, thanks to the efforts of Larry Diamond, one of the founders of the *Journal of Democracy*. Diamond had also been an affiliate for the Progressive Policy Institute (PPI), a think-tank dedicated to promoting the "Third Way," a sort of American re-articulation of Europe's social market democracies; the organization had functioned as the 'brain trust' of the Democratic Party and can take credit for many of President Clinton's policy initiatives. While at the PPI, Diamond had drafted a report titled "An American Foreign Policy for Democracy", which pushed for a foreign policy outlook based on Democratic Peace Theory (DPT) - the idea that liberal democratic nations don't go to war with one another - as an alternative to the "Peace through Strength" mentality of the Reagan years.[29] Diamond was quick to identify the economic benefits inherent in DPT, writing that democracies provide equitable "climates for investment," and as such, America must seek "to reshape the world."[30] The report also served as the impetus for the creation of the earlier-mentioned Community of Democracies by recommending that the US establish an "association of democratic nations" that can provide transnational "action on behalf of democracy."

The Clinton administration's 'democracy promotion' agenda was furthered by the National Security Adviser, Anthony Lake. Lake, whose earlier credentials included having moved from the Carnegie Endowment for International Peace into Carter's State Department alongside Zbigniew Brzezinski (not to mention a later tenure on the board of Freedom House), went about establishing a task force to properly articulate this new foreign policy program. Together with Jeremy

Rosner, a speechwriter at the NSC and Vice President for Domestic Affairs at the PPI, he drafted a four-point "blueprint" for enlarging "the world's free community of market democracies".[31]

> ... (1) "strengthen the community of market democracies"; (2) "foster and consolidate new democracies and market economies where possible;" (3) "counter the aggression and support the liberalization of states hostile to democracy"; and (4) "help democracy and market economies take root in regions of greatest humanitarian concerns".[32]

Even as Clinton told Congress that "We have put our economic competitiveness at the heart of our foreign policy",[33] a sort of counter-intellectual current began to form in opposition to President Clinton amongst the neoconservatives in Washington. This coalesced in 1996 as the Project for the New American Century (PNAC), a think-tank that argued for a militarized effort to bring democracy to regions under the control of authoritarian regimes - most specifically, Iraq and Iran. Much has been made about the close-knit relationship between PNAC, pro-Israeli lobbying organizations, such as the American Israel Public Affairs Committee (AIPAC), and the defense industry, and rightfully so: everything that the neoconservatives were urging for strategically benefited Israel's supremacy in the Middle East and involved financial booms for firms specializing in warfare. But what hasn't been addressed is the close interlocking relationship between PNAC and the 'democracy' promoting agencies. The following chart illustrates this quite clearly:

Project for the New American Century Member	'Democracy Promotion' Affiliation
Elliot Abrams, *Assistant Secretary of State for Inter-American affairs under President Reagan*	Former member of the Social Democrats USA with Carl Gershman and many other NED and AFL-CIO principles; heavily involved in 'democracy promotion' activities in Augusto Pinochet's Chile.
Paula Dobriansky, *senior Vice President of the Council on Foreign Relation's Washington offices*	Board member of the NED, board member of Freedom House

Project for the New American Century Member	'Democracy Promotion' Affiliation
Steve Forbes, Jr., *heir to the Forbes family fortune*	Trustee of Freedom House
Francis Fukuyama, *author of* The End of History and the Last Man	Adviser to the NED, Freedom House, and the *Journal of Democracy*
Donald Kagan, *professor at Yale University*	Senior Associate at the Carnegie Endowment for International Peace
Peter W. Rodman, *longtime assistant to Henry Kissinger*	Trustee of Freedom House
Randy Scheunemann, *political consultant and lobbyist*	Director at the International Republican Institute; more recently, his firm has lobbied on behalf of George Soros' Open Society Institute
Vin Weber, *former congressman*	Former chairman of the NED
George Weigel, *theologian and adviser to the USIA*	Member of the American Political Foundation's Democracy Program
R. James Woolsey, Jr., *former director of the CIA*	Former chairman of Freedom House
Paul Wolfowitz, *former Undersecretary for Defense Policy*	Former member of the Social Democrats USA, board member of the NED

The majority of the people listed above went on to assume positions in the administration of President George W. Bush. Paul Wolfowitz was appointed as president of the World Bank; Elliot Abrams became a member of the National Security Council; Paula Dobriansky was appointed as Undersecretary of State for Global Affairs; Peter Rodman went on to serve as Assistant Secretary of Defense for International

Security; and Francis Fukuyama became a member of the President's Council on Bioethics. It should also be noted that Vice President Dick Cheney and Secretary of Defense Donald Rumsfeld had been members of the PNAC, and Senator John McCain - chairman of the IRI - had lent his name to letters issued by the organization, while Randy Scheunemann served as an adviser to Rumsfeld on matters pertaining to Iraq. Scheunemann also founded the pro-intervention lobbying outfit Committee for the Liberation of Iraq, whose members included John McCain, Stephen Solarz (a director of the NED), and R. James Woolsey, Jr.

The influence of these 'democracy promotion' advocates resonated sharply within the administration of President Bush, especially after the events of September 11th 2001 and the declaration of the 'War on Terror'. In the face of the new, essentially territory-less global enemy, Bush envisaged himself as the Ronald Reagan of the millennial era: at a 2003 address to the NED (where he was introduced by PNAC's Vin Weber), the president declared Reagan's Westminster speech as a "turning point... in history." As he applauded the NED's bipartisan commitment to the "great cause of liberty," he couldn't resist harkening back to the Clintonite directions in 'democracy promotion' by stating that "the advance of markets and free enterprise helped to create a middle class that was confident enough to demand their own rights... Successful societies privatize their economies, and secure the rights of property."[34] Bush also greatly enlarged the NED's funding, increasing it from $40 million in 2003 to $100 million in 2007.[35]

Much of the NED's work in this time period would focus on Afghanistan and Iraq - the two primary targets of the 'War on Terror,' interventions that were being sold to the international community not only as strikes against terrorism, but as 'democracy promotion' and nation building. The disastrous economic consequences of this agenda were felt most strongly in Iraq under L. Paul Bremer, the administrator of the US's Coalition Provisional Authority (CPA). Bremer, an American diplomat who had just finished a twelve year stint as the managing director of Kissinger Associates (the international consulting firm founded by former national security advisers Henry Kissinger and Brent Scowcroft; the latter being a board member of the IRI), had replaced the recently-sacked Jay Garner. Garner's crime had been to reject the Bush administration's program of forced privatization of Iraqi state-owned assets prior to the election process,[36] but Bremer's commitment to neoliberal orthodoxy allowed him to carry out the task. "Getting inefficient state enterprises into private hands is essential for Iraq's economic recovery," he said, and *The Economist* agreed whole-heartedly by reporting that the US's reform program was the "wish-list that foreign investors and donor agencies dream of for developing markets."[37] NED interests, unsurprisingly, entered into the CPA's fray - Larry Diamond joined in as a senior adviser, while Bremer brought in J. Scott Carpenter, a veteran of the IRI, to serve as director of the authority's governance group. Bremer, incidentally, would join the IRI's board in 2006.

However, not all involved in 'democracy promotion' activities were pleased with the Bush administration's efforts in the Middle East. Francis Fukuyama cut his ties with the neoconservative circles he had been so active in,[38] and Zbigniew Brzezinski, who by this point had served on the boards of the NED and Freedom House, attacked the ideology in an interview with *Le Figaro,* declaring that "the neoconservative formula doesn't work."[39] Yet Fukuyama is still insistent that the US follow a foreign policy based upon "realistic Wilsonianism," and Brzezinski has been no stranger to urging interventionist politics in the post-Iraq War world. Soros himself, while launching a crusade on Bush and the neoconservatives, worked closely with the NED in training and subsidizing the activists involved in Georgia's 'Rose Revolution' (2003) and Ukraine's 'Orange Revolution' (2004); both of these revolts were squarely in line with US policy towards Russia and also served to spearhead foreign investment in the markets of the former Soviet Union.[40]

Bush himself didn't feel that militarized hard power was the only mechanism for 'democracy promotion' in the Middle East; soft power via economic incentives (something far more in line with the ideas of Fukuyama, Brzezinski and Soros) drove Bush's proposal for a Middle East Free Trade Area (MEFTA), a "plan of graduated steps for Middle Eastern nations to increase trade and investment with the United States and with others in the world economy, with the eventual goal of a regional free trade agreement."[41] To assist this, Colin Powell in 2002 announced the creation of the Middle Eastern Partnership Initiative (MEPI) at the neoconservative Heritage Foundation. Critics in the Arab world reacted skeptically to MEPI, while experts at the Geneva Centre for the Democratic Control of Armed Forces have written of it as a "Trojan horse for Western ideals and values."[42] These suspicions seemed to be confirmed with the announcement that Elizabeth Cheney, the daughter of Vice President Dick Cheney, would head up MEPI. Cheney laid out the MEPI agenda in full at the 2003 World Economic Forum, where she was joined by Paul Bremer. Together, they would act as the vanguard of the new Middle Eastern neoliberal revolution.

In 2004, Cheney turned the reigns of MEPI over to J. Scott Carpenter, previously of the IRI and the CPA. MEPI subsequently began to fund NED-related enterprises; the program has allotted money to all four of the key NED subsidiaries, as well as the International Research and Exchanges Board (IREX) to cultivate 'independent media' in Middle Eastern countries. Carpenter also continued to work outside MEPI on 'democracy promotion' and other interventionist platforms. In 2006 he participated in the creation of the Office of Iranian Affairs within the US State Department, a program overseen by Elizabeth Cheney with an agenda to "promote a democratic transition in the Islamic republic."[43] Another cog in the State Department machine, David Denehy, moved into the Office;[44] like Carpenter, he had made the transition from the IRI to the Coalition Provisional Authority under Bremer.

Carpenter would also play a role in the establishment of Fikra Forum, "an online community that aims to generate ideas to support Arab democrats in their struggle with authoritarians and extremists."[45] Fikra Forum contributors come from across the Arabic world and frequently have ties to NED programs in their home countries. For example, the Syrian activist Radwan Ziadeh, who founded and (at the time of writing) directs the NED-financed Damascus Center for Human Rights Studies, and Abdulwahab Alkebsi, who served as the executive director of the NED-funded Center for Islam and Democracy before serving as the NED's Director of MENA programs. What Fikra fails to advertise openly on their website is that they are, in fact, a program of the Washington Institute for Near East Policy (WINEP), itself a program of the American Israel Political Affairs Committee (AIPAC), the central organization of the Israeli lobby in the US. [46] The fact that AIPAC, where, incidentally, current NDI director Kenneth Pollack spent a long-time residency, exists in such close proximity to political change advocates, 'democracy' promoters, and Israeli interests suggests that the Fikra Forum is geared towards promoting Western economic and military hegemony throughout the MENA region. It's near impossible not to see President Bush's entire so-called 'Freedom Agenda' - of which both MEPI and massive NED budget increases are a part - as pursuing this goal. When the White House announced National Security Presidential Directive 58: Institutionalizing the Freedom Agenda (NSPD-58), it ignored the complicity of the US in the 'color revolutions' in Georgia and Ukraine even as it held these up as examples of a model of what the citizens in the MENA region should follow. (For more on the 'color revolutions' see Berger, Chapter 12.) Bush saw the invasion of Iraq - an action of crony capitalism that had led to tens of thousands of casualties, a tattered economy at home and a nation sold off for pennies in the transnational economic auction that is mass privatization - as a shining pillar of hope that would inspire a democratic revolution across the region.

Just as the backlash had formed against Clinton that propelled the neoconservative ascendency in Washington, near-universal condemnation of the wars led to a presidential campaign that, for a large part, focused primarily on the contentious issue. On the conservative side was John McCain, the hawkish senator from Arizona and the head of the IRI, and on the other was Barack Obama, a former community organizer and centrist senator from Illinois. Obama rallied the support of a massive grassroots advocacy base; in addition to Obama's own Organizing for America, the most prominent of these was a coalition called Americans Against Escalation in Iraq (AAEI). While the AAEI maintained the veneer of an organic activist movement, it was in actuality a consortium of different Democratic Party-aligned organizations, in particular, the Open Society Institute-financed Center for American Progress. It is clear, however, that Obama's vision of American foreign policy was, in reality, hardly different from Bush's in its intentions and neoliberal ambitions. Obama "followed the violin model," said a former Clinton administration official. "You hold the power with the left hand you play the music with the right."[47] Joseph Biden, Obama's pick for vice president, had foreshadowed the administration's commitment to intervention by writing in the *Washington Post* that "Promoting democracy is tough sledding. We must go beyond rhetorical support and the passion of a single speech. It's one thing to topple a tyrant; it's another to put something better in his place."[48] This was further confirmed when Obama pledged to significantly increase the NED's funding.

The similarities between the left and right-wings of the American political spectrum when it comes to foreign policy, which concerns itself less with multinational balances of power than with the exporting of capital-led governance structures, establishes a firm basis on which critiques of the prevailing socio-economic conditions can be built upon. This, of course, is not a new tactic; it has been one of the longest-running methodologies of analysis that dissent utilizes. But for far too long the simple image of 'corporate colonialism' has been used to analyze the usage of militarized hard power; and the formations of soft-power and the 'democracy promotion' process itself have been pushed to the margins of discourse. 'Democracy promotion', especially in relation to liberatory struggles and seemingly grassroots movements, needs to be rearticulated as a fundamental strategy of current US and European foreign policy. Only then can we clear a way through the uncomfortable questions and complexities that 'democracy promotion' provokes. This is not to say that we can only utilize critiques and analyses of 'democracy promotion' to examine the external actions of a country; it also allows us a chance to look inward at the dynamics driving our own internal political systems, and find a way to change the status quo in a time when democracy is only a game of the rich and powerful.

Notes

1   Peter Beaumont and Paul Harris, 'US "deeply concerned" after Egyptian forces raid NGO offices in Cairo', *The Guardian*, 29 December, 2011. <http://www.guardian.co.uk/world/2011/dec/29/us-egyptian-forces-raid-cairo>

2   Rebecca Collard and Dan Murphy, 'US "deeply concerned" after Egypt raids NGO offices', *Christian Science Monitor*, 29 December, 2011. <http://www.csmonitor.com/World/Middle-East/2011/1229/US-deeply-concerned-after-Egypt-raids-NGO-offices>

3   'Egypt to put foreign NGO workers on trial for "banned activity" claims', *The Guardian*, 5 February, 2012. <http://www.guardian.co.uk/world/2012/feb/05/egypt-foreign-ngo-workers-trial>

4   Marian Wang, 'F.A.Q. on U.S. Aid to Egypt: Where Does the Money Go – And Who Decides How It's Spent?', *ProPublica*, 31 January, 2011. <http://www.propublica.org/blog/item/f.a.q.-on-u.s.-aid-to-egypt-where-does-the-money-go-who-decides-how-spent>

5   Mark MacKinnon, *The New Cold War: Revolutions, Rigged Elections, and Pipeline Politics in the Former Soviet Union* (New York: Carroll & Graf Publishers, 2007), pp. 65, 120.

6   For those interested, this issue is tackled in William I. Robinson's seminal work on democracy promotion, *Promoting Polyarchy: Globalization, US Intervention and Hegemony* (Cambridge: Cambridge University Press, 1996).

7   MacKinnon, *The New Cold War*, p. 119.

8   Naomi Klein, *The Shock Doctrine: The Rise of Disaster Capitalism* (New York: Picador, 2007), pp. 297-298.

9   Clifford Bob, *The Marketing of Rebellion: Insurgents, Media, and International Activism* (New York: Cambridge University Press, 2005), p. 4.

10 Klein, *The Shock Doctrine*, p. 218.

11 Bob, *The Marketing of Rebellion*, p. 21

12 Cecil Rhodes, quoted in Michael Hardt and Antonio Negri, *Empire*, (Cambridge, Massachusetts: Harvard University Press, 2000), p. 231

13 Ibid., p. 226.

14 Klein, *The Shock Doctrine* p. 275 - 304.

15 Franz Fanon, *The Wretched of the Earth* (New York: Grove Press, 2005, reprinted), pp. 100-101.

16 Hardt, Negri, *Empire,* p. 133.

17 Felix Guattari, Ian Pindar and Paul Sutto, *The Three Ecologies* (New York: Athlone Press, 2000), p. 73.

18 William I. Robinson, 'Global Capitalism Theory and the Emergence of Transnational Elites', *Critical Sociology*, vol. 38, no.3, May 2012, pp.349-363. <http://www.soc.ucsb.edu/faculty/robinson/Assets/pdf/emergencetnelite.pdf>

19 Anne-Marie Slaughter, *A New World Order* (New Jersey: Princeton University Press, 2005). For information on domestic elite power, see G. William Domhoff, *Who Rules America? Challenges to Corporate and Class Dominance* (New York: McGraw Hill, 2009, 6th edition).

20 William Avilés, *Global Capitalism, Democracy, and Civil-Military Relations in Columbia* (New York: State University of New York Press, 2006), p. 18-19.

21 David Lowe, 'Idea to Reality: The NED at 25'. <http://www.ned.org/about/history>

22 Noam Chomsky and Edward Herman, *Manufacturing Consent: The Political Economy of the Mass Media* (New York: Pantheon Books, 1988), p. 27.

23 Diana Barahona, 'The Freedom House Files', *MRZine*, 1 March, 2007. <http://mrzine.monthlyreview.org/2007/barahona030107.html>

24 Robinson, *Promoting Polyarchy*, p. 90.

25 William Douglas, *Developing Democracy* (Washington: Heldref Publications, 1972), pp. 16-22; cited in Robinson, *Promoting Polyarchy*, p. 84.

26 G. William Domhoff, *The Power Elite and the State: How Policy is Made in America* (New York: Walter de Gruyter, 1990), p. 73.

27 Gerard Colby and Charlotte Dennett, *Thy Will Be Done: The Conquest of the Amazon: Nelson Rockefeller and Evangelism in the Age of Oil* (New York: HarperCollins, 1996), p. 444; citing Eugene H. Methvin 'Labor's New Weapon for Democracy' *Reader's Digest*, October 1966, pp. 21-28.

28 Inderjeet Parmar, 'Engineering consent: the Carnegie Endowment for International Peace and the mobilization of American public opinion 1939–1945', *Review of International Studies*, vol 26, Issue 1 (2000), pp. 35-48, p. 35.

29 Inderjeet Parmar, *Foundations of the American Century: The Ford, Carnegie and Rockefeller Foundations in the Rise of American Power* (New York: Columbia University Press, 2012) p. 232.

30 Ibid.

31 Stephen Ambrose, Douglas G. Brinkley, *Rise to Globalism: American Foreign Policy Since 1938* (New York: Penguin Books, 2011), p. 407.

32 Ibid., pp. 407-408.

33 Ibid., p. 408.

34 'Remarks by President George W. Bush at the 20th Anniversary of the National Endowment for Democracy', National Endowment for Democracy, 6 November, 2003. <http://www.ned.org/george-w-bush/remarks-by-president-george-w-bush-at-the-20th-anniversary>

35 Lowe, 'Idea to Reality: NED at 25'.
36 Paul Krugman, 'What Went Wrong?', *The New York Times*, 23 April, 2004.
    <http://www.nytimes.com/2004/04/23/opinion/what-went-wrong.html>
37 Klein, *The Shock Doctrine* p. 436
38 Francis Fukuyama, 'The Neoconservative Moment', *The National Interest*,
    Summer, 2004, pp. 57-68, p. 76. <http://nationalinterest.org/article/the-
    neoconservative-moment-811>
39 Marie-Laure Germon, 'Zbigniew Brzezinski: The Neo-Conservative
    Movement Doesn't Work', *Le Figaro*, 21 October, 2004.
    <http://bellaciao.org/en/article.php3?id_article=3851>
40 Though this is certainly beyond the scope of this article, this issue is covered
    at length in MacKinnon, *The New Cold War.*
41 'Middle East Free Trade Agreement (MIFTA)', Office of the United States
    Trade Representative. <http://www.ustr.gov/trade-agreements/other-
    initiatives/middle-east-free-trade-area-initiative-mefta>
42 Alan Bryden and Heiner Hänggi, *Reform and Reconstruction of the Security
    Sector* (Münster, Lit Verlag, 2004), p. 271.
43 Elise Labott, 'U.S. to sharpen focus on Iran', *CNN*, 2 March, 2006.
    <http://www.cnn.com/2006/POLITICS/03/02/us.iran.index.html?section=cnn
    _latest>
44 Justin Raimondo, 'Scary Reunion', *Anti-War*, 26 May, 2006.
    <http://antiwar.com/blog/2006/05/26/scary-reunion/>
45 Fikra Forum, 'About Us'. <http://fikraforum.org/?page_id=2>
46 Maidhc Ó Cathail, 'Fikra: Israeli Forum for Arab Democrats', *Palestine
    Chronicle*, 21 February 2012.
    <http://www.palestinechronicle.com/view_article_details.php?id=19115>
47 Berger 'Strange Contours', reprinted in this volume, Chapter 12.
48 Hossein Derakhshan, 'Obama shares Bush's goals', *Al-Jazeera*, 17 September,
    2008. <http://www.aljazeera.com/focus/2008/09/20089151314357484.html>

19. Egypt and International Capital: Is this what Democracy looks like?

Edmund Berger

It was during the heyday of the Italian autonomist movement, as the country's mainstream Leftist factions moved into a close relationship with parties representing the dual Western interests of capital and militarization, that the militant psychiatrist and philosopher Felix Guattari made the observation that "a semi-tolerated, semi-encouraged, and co-opted protest could well be an intrinsic part of the system."[1] Fast forward to Egypt and the 'Arab Spring', and we can find those that opposed the Mubarak government, a puppet regime of the United States, utilized many of the same tactics as the autonomists - direct action, alternative media networks, and the occupation of public space. However, despite the fact that the interests of capital were opposed to those of the protestors, neoliberal interests were looking to this revolution with a keen eye. 'Democracy promotion', the ideological weapon of choice for neoliberalism, has long been at work in Egypt; this was confirmed by former Secretary of State, Madeleine Albright, in an interview with Rachel Maddow, "You mentioned that I was chairman of the board of the National Democratic Institute. We have been working within Egypt for a very long time, in terms of developing various aspects of civil society, and dealing with various and talking to opposition groups who are prepared to participate in a fair and free election."[2] (See also Berger, Chapter 18.) Indeed, the earliest recorded 'democracy promotion' activities date back to 2005, when it looked like Mubarak's reign was without end. This article will attempt to unravel the manner in which the 'democracy promotion' agencies have attempted to embed their agendas within the protean grassroots networks in Egypt, in particular following the uprisings, with the aim of subverting real or potential challenges to the neoliberal order.

Giving the Revolution a Helping Hand
Early Rumblings

While Hosni Mubarak had long been a key strategic ally of the United States, his relationship with the country became strained in the midst of the Bush administration's Freedom Agenda. In 2000, the Egyptian regime had jailed the popular dissident Saad Eddin Ibrahim, the founder of the pro-market Ibn Khaldun Center for Development Studies at the American University of Cairo, a common recipient of funding from National Endowment for Democracy (NED). Ibrahim, a future contributor to Fikra Forum (a program of AIPAC, the right-wing Israeli lobbying organization in the US), advisor to the *Journal of Democracy* (the official digest of the NED), and World Bank consultant, was moderate and pro-Western, unlike many of those who opposed the US's meddling in Egyptian affairs. He "favored peace with Israel, good relations with the United States, a secular state and free market reforms," it was reported in the *Los Angeles Times*.[3] Freedom House conducted a display of solidarity by awarding Ibrahim the organization's Bette Bao Lord Award for Writing on Freedom, and in 2000 the Bush administration withheld an important aid package to Egypt. The plan worked - he was released in 2003 without charge. Bush's relationship with Mubarak, however, had drastically changed. "You're not the only dissident," Bush told Saad Eddin Ibrahim in a meeting in 2007, "I too am a dissident in Washington. Bureaucracy in the United States does not help change. It seems that Mubarak succeeded in brainwashing them."[4] Clearly Bush saw himself in contrast with those in the government - including his own vice president - who continued to support the regime.

Two years prior to this meeting, however, the US government had already began to take an active role in shaping the resistance to Mubarak within Egypt's civil society. Ayman Nour, a leader in the El-Ghad Party, told *Guardian* journalist Mark McKinnon that "some Americans... had offered to stage a Ukraine-style revolution for him around Egypt's 2005 presidential vote."[5] El-Ghad's platform is moderate, supporting Palestinian rights and advocating the development of an Arab common market that would cooperate closely with the EU. The problem for Nour was that he "couldn't afford the price they were asking." [6] This statement was made without elaboration, but before the year was out, he would face circumstances similar to Ibrahim's five years earlier - he was jailed by the regime until 2009.

Even if Nour couldn't afford the price offered by the American 'democracy' promoters, they went to work in Cairo nonetheless in order to promote the version of 'resistance' they required. A private organization, the International Center for Nonviolent Conflict (ICNC), had "slipped into Cairo to conduct a workshop" on how to practice nonviolent resistance methods in the face of authoritarian governments.[7] The workshop was of particular interest to the April 6 Movement, which had been founded by two El-Ghad volunteers, Ahmed Maher and Israa Abdel-Fattah, and incubated in the party's official headquarters.[8] One participant, Dalia Ziada, reported that the ICNC's "trainees were active in both the Tunisia and Egypt revolts." Indeed, April 6 would play an essential role in the 'Arab Spring'.

At the helm of the ICNC is Peter Ackerman, a multimillionaire, member of the Council on Foreign Relations, and a longtime chairman of Freedom House. His commitment to nonviolent resistance derives from the teachings of his mentor, Gene Sharp, the author of the famed *From Dictatorship to Democracy*. The work has become a manifesto for pacifist activists around the globe; when Serbia's Otpor! movement was struggling against Slobodan Milosevic, the IRI dispatched the retired Army colonel Robert Helvey to give the dissidents a crash-course in Sharp's work.[9] After the success of Otpor's revolt, the students became teachers and disseminated Sharp's philosophy to the activists in Georgia's Rose Revolution and Ukraine's Orange Revolution. (See also Berger, Chapter 12.) When Ackerman was in Cairo, he provided the Egyptian democrats with *From Dictatorship to Democracy*. "Some activists translated excerpts of Mr. Sharp's work into Arabic, and... his message of 'attacking weaknesses of dictators' stuck with them," Ziada told the *New York Times*.[10] Though the topic is beyond the reach of this article, it is certainly worth mentioning that Sharp's protest strategies rely on his conception of power, which he articulates rather simply as the toil of the subject/people under the ruler/government. Thus, his tactics are always geared towards oppression rooted in states. The exploitative system of capitalism is completely ejected from his analysis and as a consequence he provides no clear methodology for resistance.[11] Anti-capitalist, and even more radical anti-statist movements are pushed to the margins, theoretically cut off from much of mainstream nonviolent activism. Unsurprisingly, the place where Gene Sharp cultivated the early stages of his theories - Harvard's Center for International Affairs - was conceived as part of a Cold War-era program designed to "provide training for civilians who might later be involved in the formation of defense policy."[12]

Ackerman continues to work closely with former Otpor activists, most notably Ivan Marovic. Joined by the filmmaker Steve York, the two have designed *A Force More Powerful*, an educational video game that allows the player to "organize street demonstrations to topple a fictional dictator."[13] This isn't the only multimedia project revolving around resistance - Ackerman and York had previously worked together in filming a documentary about the Otpor movement titled *Bringing Down a Dictator*. With frequent NED funding, the film has been shown around the world in troubled hotspots ripe with democratic unrest.

It's prudent at this time to review some of Ackerman's other connections, as his long resumé reveals certain dynamics about the world of 'democracy promotion'. A committed capitalist, he's a financier of the neoliberal Free Africa Foundation, the owner of the Chicago-based marketing consulting firm Upshot Inc., and an advisor to the libertarian CATO Institute's Project on Social Security, which advocates the privatization of the American social security system. He's also a member of the Business Advisory Council of the United States Olympic Committee, so it's interesting to consider that the Committee's president, William J. Hybl, is a board member of the International Republican Institute (IRI, the conservative subsidiary of the NED) and the chairman of the International Foundation for Election Systems. Meanwhile, Ackerman's wife, Joanne Leedom-Ackerman, is a former reporter for the *Christian Science Monitor* and a board member of Human Rights Watch. She's also a board member of the International Crisis Group, a connection deserving of further scrutiny.

The International Crisis Group (ICG) is a pro-interventionist conflict awareness organization that came into being in the build-up to NATO's involvement in the Kosovo War in the 1990s. Financed by liberal philanthropists, such as the Ford and Rockefeller Foundations, as well as the Open Society Institute, it generally keeps a low profile in the media (while its recommendations carry much weight in policy circles) and it has gained significant coverage several times in recent news cycles. When the Kony 2012 video, a short lived marketing piece urging intervention against the African warlord Joseph Kony, went viral on the internet, the fact that the ICG had already been urging the Obama administration to dispatch military advisors to Uganda became a repeated talking point amongst those skeptical of the movement's true aims. It had also garnered attention when it became known that the organization's board counted Mohamed ElBaradei, an Egyptian lawyer and former director general for the International Atomic Energy Agency, as a member.

When the 'Arab Spring' rocked Egypt, it seemed for a while that ElBaradei was on track to become the country's first post-Mubarak president. The April 6 Movement was particularly enamored with him - when he returned to Egypt in February of 2010 he was greeted by a reception organized by the movement.[14] "It is the biggest threat to President Mubarak since he came to power... ElBaradei has come to be a symbol now, a symbol to challenge that dinosaur," Abdullah al-Ashaal, a diplomat and political science lecturer at the American University in Cairo, told *Al Jazeera*. Abdul Rahman Yusuf, who ran a pro-ElBaradei Facebook group, expressed similar sentiments: "Our aim is to bring together activists on the ground who can galvanize a popular base [for his election] through peaceful means."[15]

Despite this support, ElBaradei's presidential ambitions quickly turned sour. Mamdouh Hamza, an Egyptian businessman and associate of the April 6 Movement who had helped nurture the early days of the Tahir Square occupation, lambasted the lawyer, charging him with "having strong ties to Zionist institutions" and for his affiliation with the ICG.[16] The association is indeed problematic: the ICG's board is crammed full of individuals with connections to the world of interventionist foreign policy and 'democracy promotion' networks. It also features prominent Zionists such as Shimon Peres in its management, as well as individuals from the transnational capitalist class such as Stanley Fischer, the former head of Israel's central bank and managing director of the IMF (Fischer had become renowned for his role in 'democraticizing' the former Soviet Union). The following chart gives a cursory outline of some of the ICG's connections:

International Crisis Group	Affiliations
Morton Abramowitz, *US ambassador*	Former president of the Carnegie Endowment for International Peace; director at the NED; director at Freedom House
Joanne Leedom-Ackerman, *novelist, journalist, wife of Peter Ackerman*	Board member of the Albert Einstein Institution

International Crisis Group	Affiliations
Ken Adelman, *former US ambassador to the United Nations*	Secretary at Freedom House
Martti Ahtisaari, *former President of Finland*	Advisor to the Open Society Institute
Zainab Bangura, *former chairman of Sierra Leone's Movement for Progress Party*	Former fellow at the NED; recipient of the 2006 NED Democracy Award; Steering Committee of the World Movement for Democracy
Zbigniew Brzezinski, *former National Security Adviser*	Director at the NED; advisory board member of the *Journal of Democracy*; trustee at Freedom House; director at the Council on Foreign Relations
Kim Campbell, *former Canadian prime minister*	Steering committee of the World Movement for Democracy
Wesley Clark, *former Supreme Commander of NATO*	Director at the NED
Stanley Fischer, *president of CitiGroup International*	First Deputy Managing Director of the International Monetary Fund; Vice President of Development Economics and Chief Economist at the World Bank
Leslie H. Gelb, *chairman of the Council on Foreign Relations*	Trustee of the Carnegie Endowment for International Peace
Rita Hauser, *international lawyer*	Advisor to Freedom House
Asma Jahangir, *UN's Special Rapporteur on Freedom of Religion or Belief.*	Advisor the Democracy Coalition Project

International Crisis Group	Affiliations
Elliot F. Kulick, *international lawyer and corporate consultant*	Board member of the NDI
Matthew McHugh, *counselor to the president of the World Bank*	Secretary of the NED, recipient of the 2004 NED Democracy Award
Ayo Obe, *Nigeria-based lawyer and peace activist*	Steering committee of the World Movement for Democracy
Samantha Power, *President Obama's Senior Director for Multilateral Affairs*	Strategy Committee for the Project for Justice in Times of Transition (financed by the NED and the Open Society Institute); founder of the Carr Center for Human Rights Policy
Stephen Solarz, *former Congressman from New York*	Consultant to the Carnegie Endowment for International Peace; former director of the NED, election observer for the NDI; recipient of the 2001 NED Democracy Award
George Soros, *president and chairman of Soros Fund Management*	Founder and chairman of the Open Society Institute; advisor to the Democracy Coalition Project

Returning to Peter Ackerman, both he and his wife can be found alongside the aforementioned Robert Helvey as directors of the Albert Einstein Institution, a non-profit founded in 1983 by Gene Sharp himself to study and promote nonviolent conflict resolution. Over the years the Institution has garnered grants from the NED, the IRI, and the Open Society Institute, and this money has allowed individuals from the organization to travel around the globe, consulting with pro-democracy dissidents and providing them with lessons in activism. While it may be true that the Albert Einstein Institution's work is progressive in nature, its intimate connection with the world of 'democracy promotion' begs certain questions, particularly given how, as we have already seen, 'democracy promotion' utilizes progressive idealism as a vehicle.

As well as reviewing Ackerman's ties to Freedom House and his extended relationship with the ICG, it is also beneficial to look to his partner at the ICNC, Jack Duvall. Duvall, the director for Ackerman's film *Bringing Down a Dictator*, has been listed as a contributor to Gozaar, an initiative of Freedom House tasked with 'democracy promotion' activities directed towards Iran (other contributors include Peter Ackerman, the Carnegie Endowment's Thomas Carothers, the NED's Carl Gershman, and Larry Diamond). Duvall can also be found alongside Freedom House's R. James Woolsey on the board of directors of the Arlington Institute, a "nonprofit research organization" founded by John L. Peterson, a futurist[17] specializing in long-term strategic planning and leadership tactics. The organization maintains close ties to the corporate world and that of the government - "Clients include Boeing, Honda, all four branches of the U.S. military, and IBM Corp," brags one write-up.[18] The Institute is also partnered with the Global Business Network, where Peterson is listed as a network member.

Serving beneath Ackerman and Duvall at the ICNC in the capacity of vice president is Berel Rodal, a longtime consultant to the Canadian government on management issues. Notably, Rodal's extracurricular activities includes an advisory position at the Myrmidon Group, "a small New York based consultancy with a representation in Kyiv that works with investors and corporations seeking entry into the complex but lucrative emerging markets of Ukraine and Eastern Europe."[19] What is alarming here is that Myrmidon was founded by Adrian Karatnycky, a former affiliate of Social Democrats USA, alongside Carl Gershman and many other NED principles and early neoconservative figureheads, as well as the longtime president and CEO of Freedom House. Karatnycky thus holds close ties to the American interests that played a role in pushing the 'Orange Revolution' in Ukraine. This is something important to take note of - by managing a company that assists corporations entering into the Ukrainian market, there exists a potential conflict of interest. Indeed, Karatnycky has written about the 'Orange Revolution' in terms of its relevancy to economic interests:

> ... the growing influence of business on Ukraine's parties is a by-product of the intense political struggle. Since 2000 there have been two presidential and three parliamentary elections, as well as numerous local contests. The frequent elections generate a need to finance increasingly expensive campaigns. In turn, business leaders leverage financial support into a direct presence on party lists and influence over party programmes. As a result, the big parties all

espouse business-friendly, centrist economic policies when in office.[20]

Rodal is no stranger to apparent cronyism of this type. In 2003 he was an advisor to Trireme Partners LP, a "venture capital firm" established shortly after September 11th by Henry Kissinger and Richard Perle (an associate of the Social Democrats USA, Project for the New American Century (PNAC) member, and Rumsfeld's pick to chair the Defense Policy Board) to "invest in firms developing products and services relevant to homeland security and defense."[21] Trireme's first investor was Boeing, which provided Perle with some $20 million in start-up funds. Perle subsequently became a champion of Boeing, publishing op-eds lauding the corporation's multimillion dollar defense contracts with the Pentagon. Trireme's other board members also betray an explicit pro-corporate agenda, a case in point being the presence of the Canadian media mogul Conrad Black (the CEO of Hollinger International, the media giant that counts Perle and Kissinger on its director board). Black's name has been linked to the Fraser Institute, a hard-right think-tank that escalated fears of the Canadian debt crisis in a bid to privatize the nation's state-owned assets.[22] The gambit was successful, and was carried out behind closed doors and away from the public's eye.

These are strange bedfellows for pro-democracy advocates to have. From Ackerman to Duvall to Rodal, there has been a consistent pattern of corporate agenda-setting. When these conflicts of interests occur, the veneer of democracy quickly fades, and it begs the questions of just how altruistic the motives of 'democracy' promoters really are. At the same time, however, the last ICNC member to be examined here, Stephen Zunes, stands in sharp contrast to his predecessors. The chair of Middle Eastern Studies at the University of San Francisco, Zunes has been one of the most outspoken proponents of nonviolent resistance, drawing heavily on the writings of Gene Sharp in formulating his owns theories for effective means of social change. His opposition to American hegemony, the disastrous meanderings in Iraq and the treatment of the Palestinians at the hands of Israel's military has led him to being included in a list compiled by the neoconservative ideologue David Horowitz of the "101 most dangerous academics" in the educational system. Despite this, however, Zunes held a senior fellowship at the United States Institute for Peace, a taxpayer-funded institution that operates in a manner similar to the NED.[23]

Aside from the USIP, Zunes is listed as a staff member of the Centre for Applied Nonviolent Actions and Strategies (CANVAS), "an

International network of trainers and consultants" founded in 2003 by two former members of the NED-linked Otpor movement in Serbia.[24] One of these individuals, Slobodan Djinovic, has risen from activist to telecommunications mogul after he founded Serbia's first wireless internet provider; he uses his wealth to fund around half of CANVAS's budget.[25] Additional funding comes from the IRI and Freedom House, according to a piece in the *Los Angeles Times*,[26] and thus it's unsurprising that the organization has partnered with Freedom House for workshops and seminars for prospective activists. The operations of CANVAS are remarkably similar to that of the ICNC, and the two maintain a close-knit relationship. Just as Zunes plays a role in both organizations, there are additional interlocks between the ICNC and CANVAS - Kurt Schock, an academic in the field of sociology and global affairs, and John Gould, an associate professor of political science at Colorado College, split their time between each.

CANVAS's appearance in the midst of the 'Rose' and 'Orange Revolutions' in Georgia and Ukraine raises questions over its relationship with the ICNC and its extended network of capitalist interest in the region. Several years later CANVAS popped up in Venezuela, providing training to anti-Chavez dissidents. While CANVAS maintains that its work exists separately from the sphere of US foreign policy, the work it did in Venezuela certainly dovetailed that conducted by the NED and the AEI in the country over the past decade.[27] By 2011 CANVAS had gone to Egypt to provide the April 6 activists with knowledge and training, continuing the Gene Sharp-inspired work of the ICNC beguun six years prior.[28] But by this point major efforts had already been under way for some time, as the NED and Freedom House continued to assist the moderate networks needed to remove Mubarak from power.

Activating Civil Society: The Alliance for Youth Movements Summit

In 2008, the State Department, along with corporate interests representing the transnational technology sector (Facebook, Google, AT & T, Howcast, etc.) held the first annual Alliance of Youth Movements Summit in New York City to bring together grassroots pro-democracy activists from around the globe for seminars and networking sessions with trainers, benefactors, and advisors. The summit was the brainchild of James K. Glassman, a Bush cabinet member and a senior fellow at the neoconservative American Enterprise Institute; and Jared Cohen, who had joined Condoleezza Rice's State Department in an advisory capacity (particularly pertaining to Iran). His forte was counter-radicalization tactics involving the then-emergent phenomenon of social media. This interest is clearly illustrated in the choice of key-note speaker for the summit: Oscar A. Morales Guevara, a Columbian-born peace activist who pioneered social media as a medium for raising awareness through his One Million Voices Against FARC organization.

Other high-profile players brought together under the rubric of the summit included Larry Diamond, Joe Rospars, the New Media Director for the Obama campaign, and Adnan Kifayat, who at the time was handling counter-terrorism issues and helping to give form to the proposed Middle East Free Trade Area (MEFTA) at Bush's National Security Council. Yet another individual was Stuart W. Holliday, an assistant to President Bush, a lifetime member of the Council on Foreign Relations, and board member of the NED-linked International Foundation for Election Systems. In addition to these credentials, in 2006 Holliday was the president of the Meridian International Center, a Washington, D.C.-based non-profit established to promote "international understanding through the exchange of people, ideas and the arts"[29] - a task it aims to accomplish with the help of deep-pocketed funders such as ExxonMobil, Lockheed Martin, Boeing, Chevron, Bechtel, and none other than Peter and Joanne-Leedom Ackerman.

Perhaps most relevant to the current discussion is the presence of Sherif Mansour at the Youth Summit. At the time the program officer of Freedom House's Middle East division, Mansour had been a longtime participant in 'democracy promotion' networks. He held a year-long fellowship at the Center for Islam and Democracy, which boasts a president who has served as both a member of CIPE's Development Institute and the NED's former program director for the MENA (Middle East and North Africa) region. Another critical connection for the Center for Islam and Democracy is the NED and AIPAC sponsored Saad Eddin Ibrahim's membership of the board, which may explain Mansour's own personal trajectory: before entering into the fray of the Center and Freedom House, he had spent time at Ibrahim's pro-market Ibn Khaldun Center as the leader of an election monitoring coalition during the 2005 presidential race.

Given this direct tie between State Department planners and corporate interests with the grassroots unrest in Egypt (especially in light of Ackerman and the ICNC's 2005 trip to Cairo), the disclosure by WikiLeaks of confidential diplomatic cables discussing the Summit should not come as a shock. The cable in question, circulated in the State Department's Bureau of Near Eastern Affairs, revealed that one leader of the April 6 Movement, Ahmed Saleh, had been in contact with "unnamed members of Freedom House" and had planned to travel to the New York summit.[30] Furthermore, Saleh reportedly had meetings with an "unnamed Amcit [American citizen] who advised him on potential Washington meetings and is working to include him in an early December dinner in New York with Egyptian activist Saad Eddin Ibrahim." An additional cable contained references to Ahmed Saleh (although the name had been redacted upon publishing of the cables), describing his Washington meetings as "positive", and revealed for the first time that "the Wafd, Nasserite, Karama and Tagammu parties, and the Muslim Brotherhood, Kifaya, and Revolutionary Socialist movements... [had] agreed to support an unwritten plan for a transition to a parliamentary democracy."[31]

These efforts seemed to have begun to pay off within a year of the summit: a leaked cable from 2009 finds Saleh hard at work networking in America on behalf of April 6.[32] He told the State Department that his trips across the Atlantic were being financed by Saad Eddin Ibrahim, and that he was operating in conjunction with Sherif Mansour at Freedom House to provide Ayman Nour with earlier electoral support. These efforts were reportedly being assisted by Dina Guirgis, an Egyptian expatriate living in Washington. Guirgis, the executive director of an NGO called Voices for a Democratic Egypt, had worked previously at the Ibn Khaldun Center, and cultivated additional ties inside the neoconservative establishment by holding a fellowship at WINEP's Fikra Forum.

At this juncture it would be prudent to examine the actions of State Department advisor, Jared Cohen, in the years following the 2008 Alliance of Youth Movements Summit. Cohen was kept on in Obama's adminstration, advising Hilary Clinton in the State Department on Iranian affairs. When the 'Green Revolution' hit Iran in 2009, he sought out the help of Twitter founder Jack Dorsey to ensure that the flow of social media continued undeterred.[33] The top brass of the administration, which had maintained a 'hands-off Iran' policy during the unrest (aside from continued NED funding to sectors of the protest movement),[34] was incensed at this intervention. "If it had been up to the White House, they would have fired him," an insider said.[35]

But Cohen did leave the State Department in 2010, and took a position at Google. Making the move with him was another veteran of 'democracy promotion' networks, J. Scott Carpenter, and the two former Washington officials went to work setting up Google Ideas, a 'think/do tank' tasked with generating political change on the global stage outside the usual power corridors of governments. An embodiment of the transnational capital-driven civil society, Google Ideas often partners with elite institutions to conduct its work. For example, the corporate branch partnered with the Tribeca Film Festival (one of the organizations involved in the initial 2008 Alliance of Youth Movements Summit) and the Council on Foreign Relations to host an 'Idea Summit', a platform to analyze how technological advancements can provide "freedom from fear."[36]

Cohen's new corporate position also allowed him opportunities to travel around the world to hot-spots of pro-democracy uprisings. In January 2011 he found himself in Egypt, where he had dinner with Wael Ghonim, the head of Google's marketing department for the corporation's Middle East and North Africa division. Ghonim was then on leave from the company, utilizing his time instead to assist in the burgeoning revolutionary movement. Like his friend Cohen, his specialty is in social media: the previous year he had used Facebook to rally activists following the torturing to death of an Egyptian citizen at the hand of the authorities. Through the digital space he built networks with the other opposition movements, and began to call for an Egyptian equivalent of the Tunisia uprisings, a demand that resounded through the politically charged civil society. The response was the mass demonstrations that shook the country on January 25th. Cohen's dinner with Ghonim, incidentally, took place the night before the launch of the revolution.

Cohen's trajectory from the State Department to Google and his propensity for revolutionary jet-setting caught the eye of Stratfor Forecasting Inc., a Texas-based global intelligence company that provides data analysis to governments, the media, and corporations. Particularly keen on investigating Cohen was Stratfor's vice president of counterterrorism, Fred Burton, who cultivated a series of contacts deep into Google's executive hierarchy. Burton's email correspondences concerning Cohen were released to the public through WikiLeaks, and their contents are quite revealing: "Jared Cohen, the Google policy official who met w/ [Ghonim] the Google Gypo Exec, ONE HOUR before the poor chap was nabbed, is off to Gaza next week... per a very good Google source," Burton reported to one intelligence analyst:[37] "Google is not clear if Cohen is operating w/a State Dept/WH license, or a hippie activist." However, in another message, this time between Burton and Stratfor's CEO and founder, Burton's Google sources seemed to have been leaning towards the notion that Cohen is not as divested from Washington as previously believed: "the inference is relative to Cohen working for the State Dept and WH to support Arab regime changes." Friedman responded with the brief note that he is "thinking I may be on the right track about him despite his denials."[38]

Aligning Economics and Political Parties

In 2009 the NED's funding to Egyptian activist networks totaled $1,409,621; a year later it had been increased to $2,399,457. Over the recent years a great deal of money has flowed to CIPE for a myriad of programs: to "work with universities to incorporate CIPE's Development Institute into their curriculum; and conduct workshops at the governorate [a division of a county] level to promote corporate citizenship"; to "build consensus on the reform priorities of Egypt's business community through the National Business Agenda process and engage Egyptian policymakers to effect legislative and/or regulatory change based on the agenda's recommendations"; and to "engage civil society organizations to participate in the democratic process by strengthening their capacity to advocate for free market legislative reform, and to build consensus on needed changes to the Egyptian legal environment to remove impediments to competition in a free market. CIPE will work with the Federation of Economic Development Associations (FEDA) to organize policy reform roundtables, draft policy position papers and an economic analysis report, and conduct policy and advocacy planning sessions for SME [Small to Medium Enterprise] business associations."

Large sums went to similar projects, such as $19,520 to the Cairo Liberal Forum in order to "expand the use of social advertising among young activists for the promotion of democratic ideas and values and build the capacity of a youth-led NGO."[39] The Cairo Liberal Forum, incidentally, is "an Egyptian NGO that seeks to promote individual rights and free market principles".[40] The head of the forum, Amr Bakly, appeared at a conference in 2011 hosted by Canada's Fraser Institute to address the potential opportunities for free market reform in the restructured, post-'Arab Spring' Middle East. Levels of financing were also increasing for the Ibn Khaldun Center, amounting to $65,000 the year before the uprising.

The NED was also in the business of providing money to Western organizations that could provide support for a revolutionary movement. Amongst these was Project on Middle East Democracy (POMED), which received $190,000 to "to build and strengthen the capacity of Egyptian NGOs to lead parliamentary tracking efforts and produce high quality policy and budget analyses."[41] Headquartered in Washington D.C., the

POMED's leadership draws from the usual 'democracy promotion' networks. There is Stephen McInerney, a foreign policy analyst and contributor to Fikra Forum; Lorne Kramer of the IRI and Kenneth Wollack of the NDI; the Carnegie Endowment for International Peace's Nathan Brown, Daniel Brumberg and Thomas Carothers; Larry Diamond; Noah Feldman from the Coalition Provisional Authority; Mark Palmer of Freedom House and the NED; Haleh Esfandiari, a former fellow at the National Endowment for Democracy; and Saad Eddin Ibrahim. $21,900 also went to the American Islamic Congress (AIC), yet another place where Ibrahim can be found, serving on their board.

The AIC is certainly worth elaborating on. If POMED's orientation is more liberal in its outlook, the AIC leans towards neoconservativism. For example, the AIC's founder, Zainab Al-Suwaij, worked with the neoconservative Foundation for the Defense of Democracies to launch the pro-interventionist Women for a Free Iraq in 2003.[42] The AIC and the Foundation also sided with the notoriously anti-feminist Independent Women's Forum to form the Iraqi Women's Educational Institute, and the aforementioned Haleh Esfandiari from POMED serves as an advisor to the organization. The AIC's interlocks with other neoconservative organizations through other board members, such as Khaleel Mohammed, a member of the pro-Zionist Intelligence Summit; and Hillel Fradkin, whose name has been linked to PNAC.

Certain opposition parties in Egypt maintained direct ties to this American neoconservative nexus. The most prominent of these has been Masr El-Om (Mother Egypt), which had been founded by Cynthia Farahat, an intellectual steeped in the market fundamentalism of Ayn Rand and a program officer at the Cairo offices of the Friedrich Naumann Foundation for Liberty[43] - one of the German *Stiftungen* that initially inspired the structure of the NED. Farahat is a member of the Middle East Forum, a WINEP-aligned organization founded by the hard-line Zionist Daniel Pipes. In addition to the Forum, Farahat spends time at the Center for Security Policy, the brainchild of Frank Gaffney, one of the "key ideologues who are the nerve center of the Islamophobia network."[44] To gauge the attitudes of the Center, advisors and board members have included Elliot Abrams and Dick Cheney, as well as a host of corporate executives from defense contractor firms like Lockheed Martin and Boeing.

The viewpoint espoused by the Middle East Forum and the Center for Security Policy is clearly expressed in Farahat's own words. For her, Egypt's ideal future would be "small government, laissez-faire capitalism, individual liberty, and the ideals of the American Founding

Fathers."[45] Echoing the anti-Islam lines of Pipes and Gaffney, she decries the prominence of the Egyptian Brotherhood, painting the multinational organization as dangerous theocrats in the model of Iran. For her, the 'Arab Spring' proved that the Americans were backing the Islamic movement, a concept that is parroted frequently in the far-right radio circuit in America: "The current administration and State Department obviously want the Muslim Brotherhood in power," she told Joshua Lipana, a conservative internet blogger.[46] There is a degree of truth in what she says, but she fails to take into account the 'common sense' factor. Parties like hers do not gain the critical traction needed in a mass movement because they run on platforms that oppose many key aspects of Arab identity. As is made clear by RAND Corporation's policy recommendation papers, moderate Muslim networks are the only truly viable vessel for 'democracy promotion' in the MENA region. The Muslim Brotherhood would fit the bill for this; the economic line given by the religious organization is certainly compatible with the West's preferred transnational capitalism. "The core of the economic vision of Brotherhood," said one member, "is extreme capitalist." Meanwhile, two primary leaders of the Brotherhood in Egypt, Hassan Malek and Khairat el-Shater, are described as the "neoliberal faces" of the organization.[47] Both are members of Cairo's business elite and are business partners, and have both made names for themselves in the new, post-Mubarak Egypt: el-Shater has been nominated as the deputy supreme guide of the Brotherhood's political arm, the Freedom and Justice Party, while Malek launched the Egyptian Business Development Association (EBDA). John Sullivan, executive director of CIPE, has been a speaker at at least one EBDA function.

The Muslim Brotherhood has garnered endorsements from the Egyptian Center for Economic Studies, a neoliberal think-tank that, in the past, has received NED grants via CIPE. It is also firmly locked into Robinson's TCC: the current executive director has been a longtime senior economist at the IMF, while the previous director has worked as an industrial economist at the World Bank since 1984. Consequently, the Muslim Brotherhood has found themselves unopposed to the idea of IMF aid to Egypt: "We will accept the loan, we don't have a preconceived position against the IMF" says Malek.[48]

Even so, the US has, for quite a while, kept the Brotherhood at arm's length. It wasn't really until 2007 that the foreign policy establishment began to make overtures towards the organization as a bid to foster dissent in Syria - a gamble that, if successful, would further isolate America's chief *bête noire*, Iran.[49] Even so, the Muslim Brotherhood was kept on the back-burner as the 'democracy' promoters descended on the country. Instead, the NED's annual reports for Egypt indicate that it was the El-Ghad Party, the political faction of which Ayman Nour was the leader that was the preferred vehicle. There exists a close relationship between NED grantees and El-Ghad: the party's former vice-president, Hisham Kassem, is Egypt's representative to the World Movement for Democracy,[50] while Dalia Ziada, the executive director of the Ibn Khaldun Center, a Fikra Forum contributor and attendee of the ICNC's workshop on Gene Sharp, is the founding chairwoman of the El-Ghad Party's Freedom and Rights Committee. Another primary NED grantee with a strong relationship to El-Ghad is the Egyptian Democracy Academy, a youth organization designed to teach 'students' "everything from how to evaluate a political candidate to how to use new media."[51] The Academy's media coordinator is none other than April 6 founder Israa Abd Al Fatah Rashed (yet another Fikra Forum contributor), and its chairman is Hossam El Din Ali, a member of the El-Ghad high council. Meanwhile, the organization's program director, Ahmed Badawy, has attended a summit of the NED's World Movement for Democracy as representative of the El-Ghad Party.[52] He has since become a contributor to Fikra Forum.

El-Ghad quickly moved itself into alignment with the Muslim Brotherhood during the 'Arab Spring'. It joined the Brotherhood's Democratic Alliance for Egypt alongside the Freedom Egypt Party, founded by Carnegie Endowment for International Peace's Amr Hamzawy. Another member organization of the Alliance was Justice Party, which had been founded by members of the April 6 Movement, and the National Association for Change, a political pressure group aiming to oust Mubarak, founded and headed up by Mohamed ElBaradei. Serving beneath him is Ayman Nour, Shadi Taha from El-Ghad's high council, and the Muslim Brotherhood's primary neoliberal ideologue, Saad El-Katany. But the road wasn't easy for the Brotherhood. "In the earliest days of the revolution last year, the Muslim Brotherhood drew criticism from many groups, accused of being latecomers to the uprising, then ultimately attempting to take it over," *Al-Monitor* reported.[53] Regardless, Ahmed Maher eventually announced that the April 6 Movement finally threw its weight behind the Muslim Brotherhood's candidate, Mohamed Morsi.[54] By the end of June 2012, the Supreme Council of the Armed Forces, the interim governing body of the country after the removal of Mubarak, was gone, and Morsi had been elected president.

Of Democracy and Politics: Concluding Thoughts

This piece has not been an attempt to retell the story of the Egyptian uprisings, but to provide a cursory outline of the foreign interest involved. Furthermore, the actions laid out in the previous pages should not be taken as an anti-'Arab Spring' tract, or some other attempt to smear the name of what is one of the most important paradigm shifts of the modern age, a true victory for people power and a warning to autocratic dictatorships around the globe. There are many works out there examining the same issue of 'democracy promotion' in Egypt, and a great deal of them castigate the uprisings as a planned revolution, a conspiracy birthed in the halls of the State Department and executed by agent provocateurs and useful idiots. I believe this approach to be wrong; espousing such a viewpoint has a built-in power system skewed towards the West, and reflects the same mentality that drove colonialism in the first place; that is, the idea that the developing world could not possibly accomplish something of this scale of its own accord.

As mentioned earlier, 'democracy promotion' does not catalyze social unrest, it simply utilizes preexisting discontents, identifies dissenters, provides help and support before adjusting to any political changes that ensue. For example, as the NED gave the Egyptian protests legitimate tools on how to raise voter awareness, monitor elections, etc, IRI chairman John McCain travelled to Egypt with John Kerry and a delegation of American businessmen representing firms such as Boeing, Coca-Cola, Dow, ExxonMobil, General Electric and Marriot, among others. The *New York Time*'s write-up on the trip described it as "part of a broader trip to advance American economic ties in the region" and quoted McCain as saying that "the success and failure of the revolution in this part of the Arab world will be directly related to the ability of providing investments and jobs for the Egyptian people."[55]

There is also the question of just how dynamic the relationship between 'democracy' promoters and their beneficiaries is. When I posed the question to Otpor's Ivan Marovic, he responded that "strong movements can engage with foreigners and maintain their independence. It is important to build the movement on your own first, because early support will eventually weaken the movement. It is better to spend some time on the margins and build your way up slowly so when this interaction happens you have enough leverage to drive the process." [56] Professor Stephen Zunes, on the other hand, was a bit more wary of the NED specifically. "The NED is much more designed to promote the U.S. foreign policy agenda... Personally, I would have a hard time working with them or accepting any money from them."[57]

Regardless of the opinions of those, like Marovic and Zunes, who operate on the periphery of the 'democracy promotion' apparatuses, subsequent events and agreements paint a clear portrait of why the State Department so eagerly engages in anti-regime activities. In early September, as the US government ironed out its debt-relief plans for Egypt, a delegation of over one-hundred businessmen - representing many of the same corporate firms that were involved in the Kerry/McCain expedition - travelled to Cairo to meet with Hassan Malik's Egyptian Business Development Association. Two weeks earlier, the IMF's managing director was also in Cairo, meeting with the top brass of the new government (including President Morsi himself) to draw up plans for a loan totalling somewhere between $3.2 and $4.8 billion.[58] As the protestors across the Eurozone know, entanglements with American business delegations and the IMF spell out one thing: austerity, despite whatever rhetoric about democracy flows down from the top as they make the painful cuts. There is no evidence to suggest that Morsi's government will be any different; he already "announced plans to privatize publicly owned enterprises, reduce the deficit via elimination of basic subsidies to the poor, de-regulate the economy to increase the flow of foreign capital and end labor strikes."[59]

But even as 'democracy promotion' preaches a message of global peace, and despite being driven primarily by economic imperatives, there absolutely exists the potentiality for negative reactions. This had already played out in Iraq, as America's actions fostered a massive counter-insurgency. It also shattered America's credibility on the world stage. When Russia emerged from the totalitarianism of the Soviet Union, the helping hand offered by the 'democracy' promoters, the World Bank, and the IMF quickly transformed it into a free-falling economy, with runaway wealth concentrating in the upper classes, while statistics relating to suicide and violent crime dramatically worsened. It has led to a place where authoritarian leaders such as Putin can put musicians behind bars for speaking freely, once again attracting the attention of the 'democracy' promoters in the State Department.

It is absolutely vital that real democracy be promoted, and from below, without the constraints and restraints of elite NGOs and the moneyed interests that they represent. Band-aids only have a limited effect, for only so long, and if the perpetual cycles of violence, poverty, and unrest are to be quelled, then a real structural and systematic change must occur.

Notes

1   Felix Guattari, 'The Proliferation of the Margins' in Sylvere Lotringer (ed.)
    Autonomia: Post-Political Politics Semiotext(e), 2007, p. 108.
2   Rachel Maddow, 'interview with Madeleine Albright', *The Rachel Maddow
    Show*, 3 February, 2011.
    <http://www.msnbc.msn.com/id/26315908/#41418459>
3   David Lamb, 'Activist Cleared of Defaming Egypt', *Los Angeles Times*, 19
    March, 2003. <http://articles.latimes.com/2003/mar/19/world/fg-egypt19>
4   Peter Baker, 'As Democracy Push Falters, Bush Feels Like a Dissident', *The
    Washington Post*, 20 August, 2007. <http://www.washingtonpost.com/wp-
    dyn/content/article/2007/08/19/AR2007081901720.html>
5   Mark MacKinnon, *The New Cold War: Revolutions, Rigged Elections, and Pipeline
    Politics in the Former Soviet Union* (New York: Carroll & Graf Publishers, 2007),
    p. 292, note 1.
6   Ibid.
7   Sheryl Gay Stolberg, 'Shy U.S. Intellectual Created Playbook Used in
    Revolution', *The New York Times*, 16 February, 2011
8   David Wolman, 'Cairo Activists Use Facebook', *Wired Magazine*, Issue 16:11,
    20 October, 2008. <http://www.wired.com/techbiz/startups/magazine/16-
    11/ff_facebookegypt>
9   MacKinnon *The New Cold War*, pp. 50-51.
10 Stolberg, 'Shy U.S. Intellectual'.
11 This topic is discussed further in Brian Martin, 'Gene Sharp's Theory of
    Power', *Journal of Peace Research,* vol. 26, no. 2, 1989.
    <http://www.bmartin.cc/pubs/89jpr.html>
12 David Horowitz, 'Sinews of Empire', *Ramparts*, October, 1969. According to
    Horowitz, the Center for International Affairs was "unmatched in its tight
    interlacing of the knots of power. Among the key individuals who were
    involved in the creation of the Center were: Robert R. Bowie, its first director
    and head of the State Department Policy Planning Staff under John Foster
    Dulles; Henry A. Kissinger, who became associate director; Dean Rusk of the
    Rockefeller Foundation, who followed J.F. Dulles first at the Foundation and
    then in the State Department; James A. Perkins of the Carnegie Corporation,
    who went on to become president of Cornell and a director of the Chase
    Manhattan Bank; Don K. Price, vice president of the Ford Foundation,
    formerly of the staff of Harvard's School of Public Administration, who later
    returned to become dean after his stint at Ford."
13 MacKinnon, *The New Cold War*, pp. 264-265.
14 'Egyptians welcome ElBaradei home', 19 February, 2010.
    <http://www.aljazeera.com/news/middleeast/2010/02/201021955830950565.h
    tml>
15 Ibid.

16 'ElBaradei says smear campaign relaunched against him', *Egypt Independent*, 30 November, 2011. <http://www.egyptindependent.com/news/elbaradei-says-smear-campaign-relaunched-against-him>

17 A futurist is a scientist who attempts, utilizing current trends and tendencies, to predict or analyze the probability of changes or developments in the future. They are frequently employed as consultants to corporations, non-profits, think-tanks and politicians in order to formulate long-term strategic planning in the unpredictable and short-term driven currents of neoliberal capitalism.

18 Michael Hardy, 'Institute aims to discern the future from media analysis', *Mass High Tech MHT*, 4 February, 2002. <http://www.masshightech.com/stories/2002/02/04/story44-Institute-aims-to-discern-the-future-from-media-analysis.html>

19 Myrmidon Group LLC, 'About Myrmidon'. <http://myrmidongrpllc.com/>

20 Adrian Karatnycky, 'Overcome rivalries and draw clear lines of authority', *The Financial Times*, 14 May 14, 2008;, quoted in Michael Barker 'Capitalizing on Nonviolence', *Swans Commentary*, 20 June 20th, 2011. <http://www.swans.com/library/art17/barker81.html>

21 Naomi Klein, *The Shock Doctrine: The Rise of Disaster Capitalism* (New York: Picador, 2007), pp. 404-405.

22 Ibid., pp. 324-326.

23 Investigative journalists Sara Diamond and Richard Hatch have written an excellent critique of the United States Institute for Peace (USIP) entitled, 'Operation Peace Institute', *Z Magazine*, July/August, 1990. They write: "The USIP is a funding conduit and clearinghouse for research on problems inherent to U.S. strategies of 'low intensity conflict' ... a careful analysis of the USIP's annotated list of 238 grant projects through early 1990 reveals undeniable favoritism toward researchers committed to Cold War paradigms." Diamond and Hatch also note that the USIP provided some $90,000 to the Albert Einstein Institution. Aside from the information provided by Diamond and Hatch, it may be worthwhile to note that Peter Ackerman has served as the director of the USIP.

24 Michael Barker, 'CANVAS[ing] for the Nonviolent Propaganda Offensive: Propaganda in the Service of Imperial Projects', *Countercurrents*, 26 March , 2011. <http://www.countercurrents.org/barker260311.pdf>

25 Ibid

26 Borzou Daragahi, 'Georgian unrolls the "velvet" revolution', *Los Angeles Times*, 3 September, 2008. <http://articles.latimes.com/2008/sep/03/world/fg-velvet3>

27 Venezuela has long been an object of NED penetration. For more information see Benjamin Duncan, 'Venezuela: What is the National Endowment for Democracy up to?', *Venezuela Analysis*, 4 May, 2004. <http://venezuelanalysis.com/analysis/491>; George Ciccariello-Maher, 'Einstein Turn in His Grave', *Counterpunch*, 1 April, 2008.

<http://www.counterpunch.org/2008/04/16/einstein-turns-in-his-grave/>

28 Tina Rosenberg, 'Revolution U: What Egypt Learned from the Students Who Overthrew Milosevic', *Foreign Policy*, 16 February, 2011.

29 Meridian International Center, 'Arts Intern'. <http://www.meridian.org/meridian/careers-and-internships/internships/item/663-arts-internship>

30 Wikileaks cable 08CAIRO243, 'April 6 Activist Describes Goe Harassment, Requests Information on Youth Movements Summit', *Embassy Cairo*, 26 November, 2008. <http://www.cablegatesearch.net/cable.php?id=08CAIRO2431>

31 'Egypt protests: secret US document discloses support for protesters', *The Telegraph*, 28 January, 2011. <http://www.telegraph.co.uk/news/worldnews/africaandindianocean/egypt/8289698/Egypt-protests-secret-US-document-discloses-support-for-protesters.html>

32 Wikileaks cable 09CAIR0695, 'April 6" Leader Plans U.S. Travel; Describes Movement in Disarray', *Embassy Cairo*, 23 April, 2009. <http://wikileaks.org/cable/2009/04/09CAIRO695.html,>

33 Ryan Lizza, 'The Consequentialist: How the Arab Spring Remade Obama's Foreign Policy', *The New Yorker*, 2 May, 2011. <http://www.newyorker.com/reporting/2011/05/02/110502fa_fact_lizza?currentPage=all>

34 This is covered in my 'Soros and the State Department: Moving Iran Towards the Open Society', *Foreign Policy Journal*, 14 May, 2011. <http://www.foreignpolicyjournal.com/2011/05/14/soros-and-the-state-department-moving-iran-towards-the-open-society/>

35 Rizza 'The Consequentialist'.

36 Stewart M. Patrick, 'The Google Ideas Summit: Some Reflections', *Council on Foreign Relations, The Internationalist blog*, 19 July, 2012. <http://blogs.cfr.org/patrick/2012/07/19/the-google-ideas-summit-some-reflections/>

37 Allison Deger, 'WikiLeaks: Google caught in spy games on execs and 'regime change' *MondoWeiss*, 21 March, 2012. <http://mondoweiss.net/2012/03/wikileaks-mossad-and-google-caught-in-spy-games.html>

38 '398679_GOOGLE's Jared Cohen update', *Alakhbar*, 14 February, 2011. <http://english.al-akhbar.com/node/5205>

39 'Egypt grants', *National Endowment for Democracy* website. <http://www.ned.org/node/242>

40 'Amr Bakly', *Atlantic Council*. <http://www.acus.org/users/amr-bakly>

41 'Egypt grants', *National Endowment for Democracy*.

42 Michael Barker, 'The Violence of Nonviolence', *State of Nature*, Spring 2010. <http://www.stateofnature.org/violenceOfNonviolence.html>

43 Joshua Lipana, 'Interview with Cynthia Farahat on Growing Up in Egypt,

Discovering Ayn Rand, and Fighting Islamists', *The Objective Standard; TOS Blog*, 10 February 2012.
<http://www.theobjectivestandard.com/blog/index.php/2012/02/interview-with-cynthia-farahat/>

44 Wajahat Ali, Eli Clifton, Matthew Duss, Lee Fang, Scott Keyes, and Faiz Shakir, *Fears Inc.: The Roots of the Islamaphobic Network in America* Center for American Progress (August 2011).
<http://www.scribd.com/doc/63489887/Fear-Inc-The-Roots-of-the-Islamophobia-Network-in-America>

45 Joshua Lipana, 'Interview with Cynthia Faraht on Growing Up in Egypt, Discovering Ayn Rand, and Fighting Islamists', *The Objective Standard,* 10 February, 2011.
<http://www.theobjectivestandard.com/blog/index.php/2012/02/interview-with-cynthia-farahat/>

46 Ibid.

47 Suzy Hansen, "'The Economic Vision of Egypt's Muslim Brotherhood Millionaires', "*BloombergBusinessweek*, 19 April, 2012. < http://www.businessweek.com/articles/2012-04-19/the-economic-vision-of-egypts-muslim-brotherhood-millionaires>

48 Ibid.

49 Seymour Hersh, 'The Redirection', *The New Yorker*, 5 March, 2007.
<http://www.newyorker.com/reporting/2007/03/05/070305fa_fact_hersh?currentPage=all>

50 Michael Barker, 'People Power in Egypt', *Countercurrents.org,* 15 March 2011.
<http://www.countercurrents.org/barker150311.pdf>

51 Lauren E. Bohn, 'Egyptians learn tough lessons in democracy', *CNN*, 10 March, 2011.
<http://www.cnn.com/2011/WORLD/africa/03/09/egypt.democracy/index.html>

52 'Sixth Assembly Participants', World Movement for Democracy website.
<http://webcache.googleusercontent.com/search?q=cache:http://www.wmd.org/assemblies/sixth-assembly/participants>

53 Vivian Salama,'Class Divisions in Egypt Make a Comeback', *Al-Monitor*, 4 August, 2012. <http://www.al-monitor.com/pulse/originals/2012/al-monitor/class-divisions-in-egypt-makes-a.html>

54 'April 6 declares support for Brotherhood's Morsi in Egypt presidency runoff', *AhramOnline*, 12 January 2012.
<http://english.ahram.org.eg/NewsContent/36/122/44667/Presidential-elections-/Presidential-elections-news/April--declares-support-for-Brotherhoods-Mursi-in-.aspx>

55 Dina Salah Amer, 'Egyptian Leader Assures McCain and Kerry on Transition', *The New York Times*, 26 June, 2011.
<http://www.nytimes.com/2011/06/27/world/middleeast/27egypt.html?_r=3>

56 Personal correspondence, March, 2012

57 Ibid.
58 Hayfa Zaaitar, 'IMF's $3.2 Billion Loan Tests Egypt's Islamist Regime', *Al-Monitor*, 23 August, 2012. <http://www.al-monitor.com/pulse/business/2012/08/imf-loan-make-of-break-for-egypt-economists.html>
59 James Petras, 'The Summer of Muslim Discontent', *Dissident Voice*, 22 September, 2012. <http://dissidentvoice.org/2012/09/the-summer-of-muslim-discontent>

20. The Insidious Nature of 'Democracy Promotion': The Case of the Westminster Foundation for Democracy

Rebecca Fisher

> *The Arab Spring and other popular protests around the world have shown us that the desire for fairer and more democratic societies is a universal one. It is fundamental that organisations like the Westminster Foundation for Democracy continue to provide support to embed democratic standards and practices, in response to the needs and demands of people around the world.*[1]

> Ed Miliband MP, Leader of the Labour Party

> *We're standing with dissidents and exiles against oppressive regimes, because we know that the dissidents of today will be the democratic leaders of tomorrow.*

> George W. Bush,
> Remarks to the National Endowment for Democracy, October 6, 2005.[2]

At the height of the uprisings in North Africa and the Middle East the UK government was already instigating its political and "strategic response"[3] to the changing political landscape of the region, readying itself to intervene and mould the political structures that would arise from the turmoil. The Arab Partnership was launched on 8 February

2011; it is a multimillion pound venture claiming to support "those in the region that want to put the building blocks of a more open, free societies, underpinned by vibrant economies, in place",[4] and focusing on "political participation, rule of law, corruption, public voice, youth employability, [and] private sector development".[5] As this article will argue, it provides a prime example of the thinly-veiled neo-colonialist practices of so-called 'democracy promotion'. Faced with a protean and unpredictable social rebellion in oil-rich areas, the UK government, among others, is jumping upon the dismantling of the authoritarian power structures in these countries as an opportunity to shape their replacements, and to counter the threat of the formation of any political groups or blocs of power that might resist integration into the neoliberal economy and refuse corporate access to the area's land, labour and resources. Or as the FCO puts it, to establish "[p]olitically and economically open and inclusive societies"[6] in the region. This intervention consists of both economic and political elements, the Arab Partnership Participation Fund (APPF) and the Arab Partnership Economic Facility (APEF). The APPF is led by the Foreign and Commonwealth Office (FCO), and aims at "political reform" including "not just free and fair elections, but stronger parliaments, media and judiciaries".[7] Meanwhile the aim of the APEF, led by the Department for International Development (DfID), is to to bring "expert advice on economic reform", by which they mean International Financial Institutions (IFIs) such as the World Bank and the African Development Bank, experts in the imposition of macro-economic policies which will aid economic liberalisation and corporate access.[8] This new advice is provided in order to, "support economic reform and to build more inclusive, vibrant and internationally integrated economies".[9] This twin strategy to open up and dominate the economies of this region, and to ensure that the domestic political and social structures will provide internal stability for these economic reforms demonstrates the geostrategic need to mould evolving governments, misleadingly called 'democracy promotion' in order to sustain today's crisis-ridden neoliberal economy. Through a close examination of one 'democracy promotion' organisation, the Westminster Foundation for Democracy (WFD), (which is one of the organisations tasked with undertaking the FCO's Arab Partnership) this article will explore the relationship between economic and political co-option and the aim of control in countries seen as fertile for the economic and political rule of neoliberal capital. What will be revealed is the attempt to use 'democracy promotion' as a rhetorical device to facilitate the exertion of power and influence over putatively sovereign states.

'Democracy Promotion'

'Democracy promotion' comprises the complex series of initiatives by governmental, intra-governmental or semi-private or private organisations and non-governmental organisations (NGOs) to influence, mould and direct political, economic and social change in ostensibly independent countries, in order to insulate the penetration of international capital in countries of geostrategic interest. (See also Berger Chapters 18 and 19.) The 'democracy' promoted by these organisations, is best characterised, following Robinson, as *polyarchy*, or "low-intensity democracy", a system in which "a small group actually rules and mass participation in decision-making is confined to leadership choice in elections carefully managed by competing elites."[10] Such limited democracy has proved very successful in suppressing more organic, autonomous popular politics and containing resistance to the capitalist system in the West, and it is via these political foundations that the same model is now being exported. (Fisher, Chapter 2 and Barker, Chapter 11.) However, as market dominance intensifies, restructuring societies at the centre and periphery of capital accumulation, widening the gulf between rich and poor, both between and within countries, accelerating privatisations and enclosures of the few remaining commons, and causing environmental and agricultural catastrophes, political instability is sure to increase. Efforts to build consent for these policies, both in terms of the politicians, bureaucrats and technocrats implementing them, and civil society and the general public acquiescing to them, acquire increasing importance to the maintenance of the neoliberal capitalist order. (See also Whyte, Chapter 3 and Robinson, Chapter 4.)

Since the early 1980s, the militaristic, coercive foreign policy of states such as the United States and Great Britain has been reinforced and complemented by the promotion of this empty form of democracy. While, of course, force and co-option have always been used in tandem, and direct coercion is clearly still a vital weapon of foreign policy - with ideological justifications such as humanitarianism now often aiding their legitimation - the use of 'democracy promotion' as a rhetorical device to mould the political structures of targeted countries has emerged as the political counterpart to neoliberalism, with the two in tandem enabling material and ideological social control. Rather than directly and covertly manipulating the political leaders and elites from above via military interventions, assassinations and coups to produce a regime which will adhere to transnational and corporate interests, as the

CIA did in Chile, Iran, Nicaragua and elsewhere, the preferred strategy is now to mould political systems, civil society organisations and political parties from below, in the name of 'democracy promotion'. (See also Fisher, Chapter 2, and Berger, Chapter 18.) This aims to hardwire the same result into their political landscapes under the cover of democracy. The intensified focus on civil society - i.e. social and political formations outside of the direct purview of the state such as churches, political parties, trades unions, NGOs, social movements and so on - is hardly surprising given their ability to channel popular opinion and political activity. The results of such interventions can be seen most visibly in the so-called colour revolutions of former Soviet countries.[11]

Today, a vast array of 'democracy promotion' organisations have emerged, primarily from North America and Europe, and operate all over the world. The most famous are the US-based National Endowment for Democracy (NED) and Freedom House but others include government and intra-government institutions such as USAID, DfID and the United Nations Development Program. (See also Berger, Chapter 18.) This article will investigate one, the Westminster Foundation for Democracy (WFD), that has so far received very little critical scrutiny, but which is integral to the UK government's attempts to use 'democracy promotion' as a foreign policy weapon. It is hard to ascertain how its programmes are received, and how much it influences the political and cultural identities and practices in their target countries; what we can do is examine the programmes' intentions, and the ways in which they try to mask their political agendas.

There is not space here to examine precisely the motivations of the individuals involved in the agencies, or whether they understand their work as explicitly aiming to protect the capitalist system. Doubtless many do sincerely believe, for pragmatic and ideological reasons, in the merits of representative democracy, and in global capitalism. Here the focus in not on such complicated issues of agency, but on the outcomes of the work of 'democracy promotion' organisations, whether or not they reflect deliberate intentions or are the result of more structural forces in which they are embedded, and which they support. I would also stress that I do not wish to criticise those in intervened countries who engage with such 'democracy promotion' agencies, for whom the offers of funding even with such an unequal power dynamic are often difficult to resist, and who, in any case, may still be able to use this funding to their own ends, subverting those of the 'democracy promotion' organisations.

The Westminster Foundation for Democracy

Like most other European 'democracy promotion' organisations, the WFD was a governmental response to the break up of the Soviet Union, in order to establish influence over the newly opened economies of Eastern and Central Europe. (See also Berger, Chapter 18.) It was established in 1992 by the FCO, modelled upon the far larger NED, which was founded in 1983.[12] It has since broadened its focus from the former Soviet states to include East and West Africa, the Middle East and to a lesser but growing extent Asia (currently Bangladesh and Pakistan).[13] Its work is divided into two main areas: firstly, its own 'parliamentary strengthening' programmes, in which the WFD fund carefully selected and closely monitored national and international civil society organisations; and secondly, 'political party development programmes' which provides ideological and political support, including trainings and exchange visits, via British political parties, to political parties in the WFD's target countries. In addition, the WFD is the lead partner in The Westminster Consortium (TWC) through which "leading experts in the fields of parliamentary practice, financial oversight and communications"[14] build capacity in the parliamentary process and management. The democracy training provided derives from the participants' experience of the British political system, the cultural caché of which is very much part of the WFD's marketing strategy. In this way the WFD essentially aim to export some of the practices and processes of the British parliamentary system, the "Westminster model", as the epitome of a truly democratic system, across the world.[15]

The WFD's work is conducted within a paternalistic narrative of the 'transition to democracy' in which infantilised 'transition' countries require expert advice to learn about and adopt the undisputed benefits of Western democratic culture. For instance, in reference to countries in the Middle East and North Africa the WFD's 2011-12 Business Plan insist that "the role of political parties in parliament and their representation in the public sphere is weak... Political parties tend to lack internal democratic procedures and do not work on the basis of clear and developed party platforms... The wider public do not tend to understand the roles and responsibilities of political parties".[16] Meanwhile, the Business Plan asserts that "in Africa... There is rarely a strong ideological divide between the parties, instead power tends to be concentrated in individuals and in support of individual ethnicities".[17] Thus via direct support to civil society and parliamentary bodies, and through facilitating the support of UK political parties, the WFD interventions echo Britain's imperial 'civilising' mission and achieve inherently ideological influence over the kinds of politics that arise in the 'emerging democracies' of strategic interest to the British Government, militating against the unpredictable and uncontrollable outcomes of popular politics which genuine democracy - in which there would be universal political freedoms and access to decision-making processes - might bring. The colonial language may have been toned down, but the attempts to control the politics of other countries remain current.

Who's Pulling the WFD's Strings?

The dominance of the UK government's strategic interests in the WFD's operations is achieved through close ties between the WFD and the FCO. Although apparently "independent from government and operat[ing] at arms length from the FCO"[18] the WFD must account to Parliament for its expenditure and its priorities, and objectives must "contribute to the delivery of the Government's strategic international goals".[19] To that end the WFD must agree its corporate plan and strategy with the FCO, "to ensure that it complements [its] overall objectives and priorities".[20] This consultation also extends into the more day-to-day running of the WFD. For instance, a meeting of the board of governors held in late January 2010, at which FCO staff members were in attendance, praised the "newly established arrangements for consulting and collating comments from FCO and others". Such 'consultation' aids the political deployment of the WFD in areas of strategic concern for the UK government, as this meeting demonstrates in acknowledging the "close alignment of WFD programmes with FCO and DfID priority countries" and agreeing to an extension of the WFD's "geographical reach" on the proviso that it remained "within the framework of a clear strategy and agreed criteria".[21] This kind of strategic thinking was encouraged in the WFD, as the meeting noted that the "WFD needed a 'political horizon scanning' capability that would raise its awareness of political change and provide sound intelligence on which to act".[22] The FCO are also consulted over specific project proposals. For example, a meeting of the 'Programmes and Projects Committee' in January 2010 noted that the "revised project/programme templates... now incorporate FO [Foreign Office] comments in the bids" while Chief Executive Linda Duffield, whose previous work had included several ambassadorial positions at the FCO, was minuted to encourage "Parties and HOPs [Heads of Programmes] to consult with FCO and Embassies at draft stage".[23]

Duffield is far from the only WFD staff member with close links to the British government. In fact, according to its constitution, all fourteen members of its Board of Governors must be appointed by the Secretary of State for Foreign and Commonwealth Affairs, with eight of them nominated by the Westminster parties with which the WFD works. In addition, its nine patrons are the Speaker of the House of Commons and the leaders of the main political parties in Westminster, currently David Cameron (the Conservatives), Ed Miliband (Labour), Nick Clegg (the Liberal Democrats), Alasdair McDonnell (the Social and Democratic Labour Party), Alex Salmond (Scottish National Party), Peter Robinson (Democratic Unionist Party), Ieuan Wyn Jones (Plaid Cymru), Tom Elliot (Ulster Unionist Party) and Caroline Lucas (the Green Party).

Such close ties are not openly admitted to however, ensuring that the UK government can hide behind the ostensible independence of the WFD in the pursuit of its political objectives. As the FCO admit, the WFD was established "to allow the FCO to support democratic political party development overseas and parliamentary strengthening without direct involvement".[24] The WFD's Annual Report is more candid: "WFD offers the FCO and HMG... a focus on political work which the FCO or the Government could not or would not wish to undertake directly: developing political parties and democratic institutions... where engaging directly with new/emerging political and civic groups and free media is politically sensitive, and where direct British government support could be interpreted as foreign interference."[25]

An FCO commissioned 2010 WFD review, authored by Global Partners & Associates, another UK-based 'democracy promotion' organisation, highlights the highly partisan nature of the WFD's party support work: "the purpose of party support - strictly defined - is not to show demonstrable improvements in the functioning of democracy."[26] Instead they note that party support "was part of the original rationale around which WFD was build, in that it allows the parties to engage in activity that would be impossible for the FCO to undertake" and which they praise as "the strength of the model".[27] This work involves an "overtly political set of activities, designed to help their ideological counterparts in other countries"[28] and "facilitates access to, and influence over parties in developing democracies", supporting the "UK government's diplomatic objectives by providing insights and access to parties that may form the government in priority countries in the future."[29] Thus the WFD clearly provides an important service for the UK government in providing intelligence about emerging political forces and helping to shape them. "It's difficult to put a value on this sort of soft power" as one interviewee for the Review remarked. [30] Peter Burnell, an UK-based academic tasked with writing up a WFD-organised conference, candidly stated, "trying to promote democracy is necessarily a political act."[31]

Where and How the WFD Operates

When and where the WFD chooses to operate strongly attests to the political nature of its work. For instance, given the UK's "vested economic interests in Eastern Europe, [and] future partners in the European Union",[32] it is unsurprising to find that the WFD are still active in the former Soviet states in Central and Eastern Europe, where it first began to operate. Similarly, today the WFD has been quick to capitalise on the "new opportunities for engagement" provided by the "Arab Spring [which] has seen democracy taking root in many countries in the Middle East".[33] Predictably, the people of such a geostrategically important, oil-rich area will not be left to choose their own political directions without interference from state and corporate interests. Before the uprisings, the WFD's work in Egypt had operated with caution; in 2009 they noted an "Absent [sic] of change in the 'rules of the game' allowing foreign bodies to openly assist political parties" and recommending that the programme "should... abstain from any activities related to supporting candidates in local or national elections, directly or indirectly" and should instead focus on providing support within the parliamentary system.[34] And while Mubarak's regime remained obligingly faithful to neoliberalism such political inference was not seen as such a priority. All this changed following Mubarak's deposition however: initially wrong-footed, organisations like the WFD are now crucial in the imperial powers' attempts to recapture effective political influence, through the manipulation of governments and civil society. In 2012 the WFD opportunistically launched a new programme to "support the new Parliament" including "induction training for MPs" and regional projects on "enhancing public policy".[35] As Chief Executive, Linda Duffield, hopes, "The technical training that we can deliver, and the opportunity to share experiences with members of the UK Parliament, should help give the People's Assembly the tools it needs to fulfil its role in Egypt's democratic transition."[36]

The WFD's 'support' involves intervention in the policy-making process of ostensibly sovereign states, influencing and shaping their society, economy and culture. However, the WFD is far less explicit in its promotion of specific market reforms than the US equivalent organisations.[37] It is nonetheless possible to see the WFD's influence over economic matters, such as the fact that their 'democracy strengthening' work includes advice on budget writing. The WFD's *Corporate Plan 2011-15* describes its work on financial oversight as focusing on "strengthening parliament's authority and ability to agree national spending priorities" which clearly has a very prescriptive role to "ensure that specific policy areas are being funded adequately to meet policy objectives, and conduct budgetary and expenditure oversight".[38] This demonstrates the WFD's intention to influence key decision-making concerning government spending. The WFD also actively attempts to influence policy-making more generally. For instance, the 2011 programmes in the Middle East and North Africa involve training "Researchers, activists and experts from Tunisia and Egypt... to write policy analysis and recommendations"[39] and developing a "guidebook on best practice in policy making".[40]

Policy 'support' given, coordinated or funded by the WFD can concern extremely contentious questions. In Uganda, where an estimated 3.5 billion barrels of oil reserves are located,[41] the WFD and the Westminster Consortium have been engaged in providing "constructive input" regarding the writing of new legislation relating to the Ugandan oil industry. However, this input seems to be very focused on the notoriously corporate-friendly form of oil contract which facilitate the de-facto privatisation of national oil reserves, called Production Sharing Agreements (PSAs). For instance, the agenda of a workshop which was held on 10-12 January 2012 indicates that the session concerning "Legal frameworks for achieving parliamentary oversight" was to detail "Legislation Treaties, Contracts between host government and private enterprises with focus on PSAs".[42] In addition, each of the three 'notable' action points or recommendations arising from this workshop concerned the implementation of PSAs.[43] The role of the WFD here, amongst other agencies and NGOs, is evidently to normalise the inevitability of PSAs, in light of the shock expressed by many Ugandan civil society organisations as to the degree of corporate power and freedom the contracts offered. In doing so, they serve to "dampen any political aspirations to fundamentally change the deals or even, as many were calling for in 2009, altering them so, say Murchison Park [a national park and potential site of a new oil well] is not drilled."[44]

The inherent bias towards economic liberalisation can be seen in the WFD's support for the accession of Macedonia, Montenegro and Serbia to the EU. Their programme in Macedonia was initiated following the European Commission's statement that the country was insufficiently "compatible with EU norms and regulations" and so the goal of "[a]chieving successful multiparty dialogue, in the context of the EU Accession Partnership" became the "foundation of the Macedonia programme."[45] The WFD therefore seems engaged in facilitating Macedonia's fulfilment of the EU's Accession requirements which include such economic reforms as the "implementation of the Central European Free Trade Agreement" and "strengthening... the functioning of the market economy".[46] Thus here we have the WFD acting to facilitate market liberalisation policies in order to pave the way for Macedonia's political and economic decision-making to be placed in the undemocratic hands of the EU, rather in the 'democratic' parliament the WFD purports to support.

'Support' to encourage specific policy decisions is undertaken even when faced with local political resistance. The Westminster Consortium Annual Report cites "Lack of political will for reform" as an "External Risk" of "Medium" probability and impact to their project. As a "Mitigation Measure" the Consortium suggests that they "[b]uild a good relationship with parliamentary leadership and continue to encourage reform".[47] This potential for resistance is well acknowledged by the WFD, who have tricks up their sleeve in order to legitimate their hoped for reforms, and to insulate them from the wider public, which is only symbolically 'consulted' at election times.

The WFD and Civil Society

In keeping with the tradition of 'democracy promotion', a major part of the WFD's work involves the training and cultivation of civil society. Like many other such organisations the WFD devotes considerable attention to political parties. Moulding non-state actors, who both provide the appearance of public engagement and construct policy, is crucial to influencing a government's decision-making and maintaining the illusion of democracy, and thus political stability. As the WFD former Chief Executive, David French, writes, "Parties are the bridge between government and society, both in the ways they translate society's demands into political ideas and programmes, and in the way they hold government to account on society's behalf."[48]

The WFD's political party development programmes are undeniably partisan and ideologically motivated, based around such themes as "Message and policy development"; "Development of party campaigning and communications"; "campaigning and election strategies" and strengthening parties' "political and ideological identity" and "ability to communicate with the electorate",[49] all of which present ample opportunity directly to shape the identities, ideologies and activities of local political parties, as well as to impart ideologically motivated 'truths' about the nature, role and functioning of Westminster-style 'democracy'. Further, supporting only those parties built on Westminster models, helps to confer legitimacy upon liberal, capitalist parties, and suggests the illegitimacy of others who deviate from this norm. Operating within a neo-colonial power dynamic, organisations like the WFD, and the Westminster political parties they coordinate, operate with superior financial and political resources than can be deployed by ideologically different political groupings who might be aiming at political influence. The result is that the successful parties and the 'democratic' structures of target countries are likely to owe more to whatever interests, foreign or local, interests deploy the greatest resources than to the wishes of their own constituents.

In addition to the skills trainings and technical advice, the three main Westminster parties attempt to mould the ideological make-ups of the parties they work with, while conveying an image of their work as non-ideological or 'technical', which is the preferred term. The British Conservative Party runs programmes in the Balkans, Eastern Europe, Africa and South Asia, much of which seems to focus on developing parties' ideological identities. In addition to the more standard party building, campaign and communications and policy development programmes, "[t]here is also, however, now an emphasis on the internal ideological consolidation of the party"[50] which, in keeping with the narrative of target countries' ineluctable transition to Westminster-inspired 'democracy' "emphasise the importance of Conservative principles and values as an alternative to identification with a leadership figure or national tradition".[51] The wish to support particular policies in opposition to others less favourable to transnational corporate investment and deregulation is evident: for instance, the Conservatives aim to aid "the development of a viable opposition to the ruling Democratic Party of Socialists, which has a clear policy programme and can draw support from across Montenegro".[52] That these interventions' real aim is to engender a stable social order, in which few challenges to the neoliberal status quo are permitted is demonstrated by the claim that this ideological tutelage is "a necessary process if the political spectrum in these countries is to stabilise", a statement which is then given the thin veil of 'democratic' legitimacy: "and voters are to be given a real choice", albeit only between Westminster modelled parties.[53]

The British Labour Party also attempts to ideologically mould the political parties it trains. In Eastern Europe it was observed that "[s]ocial democracy is weak" and so a "week long academy for young people" which "focused heavily on the ideology, principles and values" of "social democrats" was organised.[54] The Liberal Democrats aim to do the same, for instance, their support to the political parties within the Africa Liberal Network directly influences their manifestos to ensure that they are "founded on liberal ideas", which they justify by claiming that it "provided the electorate with greater choice".[55] Although they provide greater legitimacy, by imparting political training indirectly via the Westminster model the WFD risk diluting their main objectives. However, in case the individual MPs deviate from the WFD-defined rubrics the WFD have recommended that they be "carefully selected and adequately briefed" and given a "guidance note to help frame discussions".[56] Such political party work has grand, strategic ambitions. The Liberal Democrats hope that the "strategic impact" of their work with the Africa Liberal Network will be "the development of liberal democracy in Africa",[57] while the Conservatives intend "that the strategic impact of these projects [in Ghana, Uganda, Côte D'Ivoire, Liberia, and Kenya] will be to establish ideologically well defined and structurally sustainable centre-right political parties".[58]

The WFD does not limit its engagement with civil society to political parties. Wider civil society, which has at least the potential to remain outside established parliamentary structures, constitutes a crucial battleground, in which 'democracy promoters' around the world are determined to gain a dominant position, in order to win vital legitimacy and authority. If successfully influenced, co-opted or controlled, civil society organisations can provide a veneer of democracy while in fact remaining more responsive to interests other than of the local population, and malleable to their foreign donors through their close relationships with and ideological allegiances to them. NGOs especially, are traditionally deployed within established political structures to effect and sanction policy changes, obviating the need to engage with the wider populace. Further, civil society groups that are incorporated into these 'democratic' structures are rendered largely unable to offer structural critiques of the system they are now a part of, and so can channel public debate away from such critiques, redirecting or neutering people's disaffection. Such groups can thus act more as a buffer to protect powerful interests from the threat of broader popular participation, than as the buffer protecting the public from the abuses of power that they are frequently portrayed as being by the media and the 'democracy promotion' industry.

There is consequently a strong emphasis in WFD materials on encouraging these civil society groups, often foreign sponsored and/or trained, to put their energies into engaging with parliamentary decision-making. In this way, decisions made by those in power can seem to be subject to or even the product of public engagement, when in reality the public are represented by a select number of groups which have usually been heavily influenced by corporate-NGO methodology and foreign interests. It also ensures that the issues focused on are limited to very specific policies and reformist proposals, and take place in the rarefied and carefully circumscribed world of parliament, which does not readily allow for wider questions on who has the right to resources in a particular place, or how such decisions get made collectively and fairly. The Westminster Consortium, for instance, seeks to address "how opportunities are can be [sic] created within parliament to enable better CSO [civil society organisation] access to committees and members" and "looks at building evidence and advocacy skills needed to lobby and communicate their policy positions professionally".[59] Similarly, the Annual Report boasts about the WFD's success in "[d]eveloping the capacity of civil society organisations to produce evidence-based research to influence policy making in Ukraine"[60] and in "establishing close relations with parliamentarians and civil organisations" in Kyrgyzstan.[61] Not all civil society organisations are encouraged to have their capacities enhanced however. While the Evaluation of the Egypt programme June 2006-March 2009 recommends publicising "Opportunities for organisations (primarily civil society ones) to participate in, and compete for, implementation of activities supporting the programme" it suggests making such opportunities available only for "a limited number, say 7-15, NGOs and other relevant entities" who "should be identified and shortlisted for solicitation".[62] Thus the support and training provided by the WFD is not available to all, but only to a chosen, presumably fairly receptive few.

A particular focus for the WFD, as with most 'democracy promotion' organisations, is on women and youth movements. William Robinson suggests an ulterior motive in such apparent progressiveness may lie in the fact that such groups, are likely to have more grievances against the established local political structures over which power and influence is being sought, and therefore be receptive to 'democracy promotion', as well as being necessary to co-opt. This is corroborated by one specialist who observed that: "The youth of a growing population may very well play a major role in pressing for change. They are among those who are actually disproportionately disadvantaged they have less at stake in the existing structure of authority, more idealism, more impatience".[63]

'Democracy promotion' organisations may thus find it easier to build trust with and co-opt such disaffected groups, from which to leverage influence over protean political movements and systems.

The WFD is also involved in the establishment and training of educational and advisory bodies, through which they can channel their supposedly neutral expertise at arm's length, and thereby extend this expertise to other groups, organisations and bodies. In May 2011 the WFD launched a parliamentary think-tank in Iraq, called the Iraqi House of Expertise, to "provide specialist advice in parliamentary affairs and public policies to Iraqi MPs"; advice has consisted of "Policy recommendations in four sectors (education, health, gender and transparency)... to better inform policy discussions".[64] The WFD have also engaged University institutions in their attempts to influence both the teaching of students and the advice given to governments. In 2008, in partnership with the Arab Forum of Alternatives, the WFD organised a six-month project to train a pool of Iraqi university lecturers, which encouraged them to become more engaged with the Iraqi Parliament. The final report of the programme indicates that participants were provided with "tools to play to role of consultancy" through workshops covering such matters as "[e]lectoral laws... [n]egotiation skills, lobbying" and "policy recommendation writing" and listed as an achievement in the enhancement of "professors' interaction with legislators" and enabling them "to influence the legislative policies in the Iraq Parliament".[65] The academics were also given trainings on topics such as "parliamentarian systems... electoral laws and it's [sic] international standards" both of which illustrate the standardised, Western version of 'democracy' promoted by the WFD as if a neutral training exercise.[66] The programme certainly addresses some very un-neutral topics, such as "[t]he Constitution; the Petroleum oil law; the project of the US military troops deal".[67]

Another concern of WFD programmes is training and developing links with local journalists, in an attempt to influence how events and issues are reported. Journalism is seen as crucial to "informing and manipulating public opinion, educating a mass public, influencing the culture of a general population"; it thus can make a "major contribution to the shifts in power and social relations in an intervened country, to the relationships between leaders and masses and between parties and social groups, and to the political behaviour in general of the population."[68] Emphasis on media training is typical in 'democracy promotion' organisations. The WFD organises several trainings for journalists in which they promote a kind of false objectivity of the UK media that disguises the fact that certain ideologies, favourable to elites, are honoured while other are suppressed. (See also Cromwell and Edwards, Chapter 5.) The TWC's "Guide to Reporting Parliament", written by Thomson Reuters Foundation, declares that journalists must "strive for total impartiality" and stay "strictly neutral" even if this means disregarding their own opinions: "Some journalists have strong political views, which they need to suppress if they are giving a balanced report".[69] The Guidebook also cautioned journalists: "Politicians, particularly in coalition governments, are frequently required to modify or even drop policies according to changing circumstances. By concentrating on such shifts, reporters risk losing sight of the real issues".[70] This clearly demonstrates the WFD's promotion of both the fallacy of objectivity and the bias towards those in power in journalistic practice. As the Guide states, "the media has a vital role... in telling the politicians what ordinary people want or do not want".[71] According to this, it is the role of the media to articulate the needs and wants of the public to the politicians, who claim to represent them. This explains why control and influence of the media is so important to the 'democracy' the WFD seeks to promote.

When successfully de-fanged and incorporated into the parliamentary system where fundamental challenges are not permitted, civil society can act as shock-absorbers - absorbing social pressures from below and ensuring they do not reach, in any substantive form, the power structures above. Meanwhile, other social formations ostensibly separate from the state, such as media and research institutions, are also cultivated by the WFD, in order to ensure their participation and endorsement, active or tacit of the market 'democracy' they promote.

The WFD's Role in Achieving Hegemonic Control

The WFD is also active in networking, both among other international 'democracy promotion' organisations, and between the government and state officials and civil society organisations and individuals it trains. Networking has both practical and normative impacts upon their work, establishing "regular opportunities for a wide range of officials in government and international organisations to interact with democracy activists"[72] and establishing momentum, respectability and legitimacy to the work of 'democracy promotion'. For instance, their endorsement and funding will often unlock funding from other similar organisations, which "leverage each other and other groups... in growing efforts to collaborate and make progress in the spread of democracy."[73] The WFD's

Evaluation of its Business Plan for 2010-11 recommends "exploring new partnerships and investing in new relationships to enable WFD to be a leader in the democracy assistance field".[74] How to network is also part of the WFD's training programmes: the programme to train Iraqi lecturers dedicated a day to "networking experiences, strategies and mechanisms" in order to better link "this group to Organisations who are running parliamentary strengthening programmes in Iraq".[75]

The coordination and networking of the 'democracy promotion' industry ensures that its impact is not limited to the particular target countries. More generally, it helps to create powerful norms and standards which can define democracy in ways which open the doors to transnational corporate power and neoliberal ideals and practice. The cumulative effect of the programmes is to normalise the limited democracy they promote, and their proliferation adds to the apparent legitimacy and neutrality of their ventures. They thus provide considerable weight to an ideological hegemony supporting a 'democracy' which limits popular participation to within the parameters set by carefully managed electoral politics and fosters neoliberal economic policies. Any challenge to this dogma is deemed irrational. It is symptomatic of neoliberal hegemony that such efforts must be undertaken to ensure that this is accepted as the right option among both the public and dominant elites, particularly given the rise of public disorder and opposition in the wake of the financial crisis and the intrinsic incapacity of neoliberal policies to do anything but exacerbate the ecological crisis.

In many respects it is hard to miss the neocolonial impetus of 'democracy promotion' interventions, such as those of the WFD detailed here. Economic, political, and social norms of the global north can be cultivated and disseminated through many routes, to be internalised and normalised by the target populations, devaluing and delegitimising all others, and ensuring they all become bound into the logic, ideals and practice of neoliberal capitalism. The WFD represents one route, to mould the political and business culture in its target countries, and to normalise procedures and practices of representative democracy - in particular among politicians, political parties, civil society and the media. In *Decolonizing the Mind,* Ngũgĩ Wa Thiong'o wrote of this process in relation to the role of culture in the subjugation of the colonised but his insights are useful here in relation to the promotion of a political culture as a form of subjugation: he writes that colonialism's "most important area of domination was the mental universe of the colonised, the control through culture, of how people perceived themselves and their relationship to the world. Economic and political control can never be complete or effective without mental control. To control people's culture is to control their tools of self-definition in relation to others." [76] By intervening with putatively neutral and beneficial training, capacity building, and technical assistance 'democracy promotion' organisations like the WFD aim to secure neocolonial influence over the political culture of target countries and over the ways their populations conceive of their political agency, their relationship within and without the global system, and of what kinds of political decision-making processes and decisions are conceivable. In this way 'democracy promotion' aims to engender a situation in which target populations internalise this Western-derived liberal definition and practice of representative, market 'democracy', and discipline *themselves* to make decisions, adopt policies and work within political systems that work in consonance with and are conditioned, if not determined, by global corporations, international financial institutions and ultimately the neoliberal hegemonic order. As we've seen, options such as nationalisation of natural assets such as oil, or refusal to join the EU, are likely to be off-limits, regardless of public opinion. This way, ideas and rules are internalised, reducing the need to resort to coercive means to secure obedience, and thus providing more effective, and legitimate, protection for the capitalist social order from political unrest.

However, of course the use of coercion remains very much a part of neoliberal disciplinary practices. Indeed soft and hard power are difficult to extricate, as the latter is used as a threat if the terms of the former are not met. Yet these connections are often missed when examining 'democracy promotion', which so often is taken at face value as unquestionably beneficial, and entirely separate from coercive mechanisms of social control. Overt 'democracy promotion' programmes, conducted openly, and often highlighting their supposedly neutral aims, hide their agendas in plain sight. This has enabled neo-colonial powers such as the US and the UK in many instances to rely upon less repressive mechanisms to engineer general consent via 'democracy promotion', rather than coercion. Soft power has not replaced hard power: the war on Iraq for example was a brutally coercive attempt to install a client regime, made up of Iraqi exiles, close to the US political establishment. Nor is it at all clear that 'democracy promotion' will retain the status it currently occupies as the current crisis of neoliberalism deepens and coercive mechanisms become increasingly utilised. (See also Whyte, Chapter 3 and Robinson, Chapter 4.) However, it is also true that in the wake of the failure swiftly to impose a client government on Iraq, 'democracy promotion' is now a predominant method to build in Iraq a pliant economic and political system whose markets and especially its oil will be open to transnational capital. Thus, while the attempts to spread and deepen neoliberal practices worldwide still rely heavily on coercion, a strategic deployment of a discourse and practice of 'democracy', as a supposedly neutral, beneficial intervention, has been developed to mask the same political, geo-strategic and economic objectives that motivated the covert and militaristic ventures.

The 'democracy' that is promoted does not receive the same degree of public scrutiny and condemnation as the military ventures, yet this serves to disguise a crucial part of the weaponry of North American and European governments and their fundamental support of neoliberal global capitalism. For organisations like the WFD directly intervene in policy-making and governmental structures, ideologically mould and train political parties, cultivate civil society organisations who will respect and engage with this limited democracy, and through networking among and between foundations and governmental and civil society actors normalise 'democratic' standards that facilitate the penetration of global capital across the world, the suppression of mass popular participation in the political decision-making process, and thus the foreclosing of the development of truly participatory democracies. 'Democracy promotion' organisations represent a subtle yet crucial means of accommodating other countries to the needs and ideals of global capitalism. It is only by examining them, including relatively small ones like the WFD, and seeing behind the language of neutrality to reveal their deeply ideological and undemocratic objectives, that we can fully discern the crucial mechanisms through which neoliberal capitalist norms and aims have been engineered, embraced, and embedded throughout the world.

Notes

1   Quoted in Westminster Foundation for Democracy, 'WFD Annual Review 2011', p.13.
    <http://www.wfd.org/upload/docs/Annual%20Review%202011%20MASTER%20COPY.pdf>
2   George W. Bush, 'Remarks to the National Endowment for Democracy', 6 October, 2005. <http://www.iefd.org/articles/bush_to_ned.php>
3   Foreign and Commonwealth Office, 'Arab Partnership: Leading the UK Government's strategic response to the Arab Spring'.

<http://www.fco.gov.uk/en/global-issues/mena/uk-arab-partnership/>

4   Ibid.

5   Department for International Development, 'Arab Partnership offers new opportunities for Middle East', 26 May, 2011.
    <http://www.dfid.gov.uk/news/latest-news/2011/uk-pledges-support-for-political-and-economic-reform-in-the-middle-east/>

6   Foreign and Commonwealth Office, 'The Arab Partnership Strategy'.
    <http://www.fco.gov.uk/en/global-issues/mena/uk-arab-partnership/the-arab-partnership-strategy/>

7   Foreign and Commonwealth Office, 'Arab Partnership Core Narrative', obtained via a Freedom of Information request and uploaded to www.whatdotheykonw.com, p. 2.
    <http://www.whatdotheyknow.com/request/79587/response/208972/attach/4/110823%20AP%20Core%20Narrative.pdf>

8   Foreign and Commonwealth Office, '10 Things to Know about the Arab Partnership'. <http://www.fco.gov.uk/en/global-issues/mena/uk-arab-partnership/010-ten-facts-arab-partnership/>

9   FCO, 'Arab Partnership: Core Narrative', p. 2.

10 *William I. Robinson, Promoting Polyarchy: Globalization, US Intervention, and Hegemony*, (Cambridge: Cambridge University Press, 1996) p. 49.

11 For more information, see Michael Barker, 'Taking the Risk out of Civil Society', Refereed Paper presented to the *Australasian Political Studies Association Conference, University of Newcastle, 25-27 September, 2006.*
    <http://www.google.co.uk/url?url=http://www.newcastle.edu.au/Resources/Schools/Newcastle%2520Business%2520School/APSA/INTLREL/Barker-Michael.pdf&rct=j&sa=U&ei=8onIUNzlBKLB0QX0hoDoDQ&ved=0CBUQFjAA&q=%22taking+the+risk+out+of+civil+society%22&usg=AFQjCNEfcjHMZVLhb_wcVUP9AbRFt-G7xQ>

12 The Westminster Foundation for Democracy is a Non-Departmental Public Body and a private company limited by guarantee with no share capital. It is funded each year by a FCO core grant-in-aid, which for both 2011-12 and 2012-13 was of £3.5 million, an increase of 3.1% on 2010-11. The FCO has indicated that it intends this figure to remain level for 2013-14 and 2014-15. In addition, the WFD receives further funding from FCO Embassies which in 2011-12 amounted to £602,033 (an increase of £420,142 on 2010-11); and in 2012-13 the WFD received a new Accountable Grant from the FCO of £2 million. The WFD also receives funding from the DfID to run a £1 million programme in Bangladesh and a five year contract worth £5 million to manage The Westminster Consortium as part of the DfID's Global Transparency Fund. In 2011 the WFD won its first grant from the European Union, £200,000 for a parliamentary strengthening programme in Lebanon. In 2012-13 this grant increased to £610,000. In 2011-12 the British Council granted the WFD £90,000. The WFD's overall funding has increased from £5.89m in 2011-12 to £8.07m in 2012-13. See Westminster Foundation for

Democracy, 'Annual Report and Accounts 2011/12', p. 31.
<http://www.wfd.org/upload/docs/HC%20478.pdf>; Westminster Foundation
for Democracy, 'Annual Report and Accounts 2010/11', p. 26.
<http://www.wfd.org/upload/docs/TSO%20WFD%20FY%202011%20Report%
20and%20Accounts%2018%20July%202011%20FINAL%20-
%20web%20accessible%20version.pdf>; Westminster Foundation for
Democracy, 'Business Plan 2012-13', p.19.
<http://www.wfd.org/upload/docs/Business%20Plan%202012-13_final.pdf>

13 During 2012-15 the WFD is planning to work in the following countries and
regions: Democratic Republic of Congo, East Africa Legislative Assembly,
Kenya, Mozambique, Nigeria, Uganda, Bangladesh, Indonesia, Pakistan,
Georgia, Kyrgyzstan, Ukraine, Western Balkans, Egypt, Iraq, Jordan, Lebanon,
Morocco, Tunisia, Middle East and North Africa in relation to women's
leadership and policy development. See Westminster Foundation for
Democracy, 'Annual Report and Accounts 2011/12',
p.10.<http://www.wfd.org/upload/docs/HC%20478.pdf>

14 The Westminster Consortium for Parliaments and Democracy, 'Foreword', in
Strengthening Parliaments and Democracies. Prospectus of Courses, (The
Westminster Foundation for Democracy, 2009).
<http://www.wfd.org/upload/docs/TWC%20Ukraine%20prospectus%20V8F%
20visual.pdf> The organisations that make up The Westminster Consortium
are: The Commonwealth Parliamentary Association UK Branch, House of
Commons Overseas Office, International Bar Association, National Audit
Office, Thomson Reuters Foundation, and the University of Essex Centre for
Democratic Governance.

15 Westminster Foundation for Democracy, 'Business Plan 2011-12', pp. 57, 59,
60.
<http://www.wfd.org/upload/docs/Publishable%20WFD%20Business%20Plan
%202011-12.pdf>

16 Ibid., p. 7-8.
<http://www.wfd.org/upload/docs/Publishable%20WFD%20Business%20Plan
%202011-12.pdf>

17 Ibid. p. 21.

18 Foreign and Commonwealth Office, 'Westminster Foundation for
Democracy. <http://www.fco.gov.uk/en/global-issues/human-
rights/democracy/westminster-foundation/>

19 WFD, 'Annual Report and Accounts 2011/12', p. 5.

20 FCO, 'Westminster Foundation for Democracy'.

21 The Westminster Foundation for Democracy Limited, 'Minutes of Meeting of
the Board of Governors held in Committee Room 17, Palace of Westminster,
on Wednesday, 27 January 2010', obtained by Corporate Watch via a Freedom
of Information request.

22 Ibid.

23 The Westminster Foundation for Democracy Limited, 'Minutes of the

Meeting of the Programme and Projects committee held in Committee Room 17, Palace of Westminster on Wednesday 13 January 2010 14:00', obtained by Corporate Watch via a Freedom of Information request.

24 FCO, 'Westminster Foundation for Democracy'.

25 WFD, 'Annual Report and Accounts 2011/12', p. 5.

26 Global Partners & Associates, 'Review of the Westminster Foundation for Democracy', February 2010, p. 12.
    <http://www.wfd.org/upload/docs/FCO%20Review%202009-10%20Final%20_2_.pdf>

27 Ibid. p. 12.

28 Ibid. p. 12.

29 Ibid. p. 11.

30 Ibid.

31 Peter Burnell, 'Building Better Democracies. Why political parties matter', (The Westminster Foundation for Democracy, 2004), p. 8.
    <http://www.wfd.org/upload/docs/WFDBBD5_noprice.pdf>

32 James M. Scott and Kelly J. Walters, 'Supporting the Wave: Western Political Foundations and the Promotion of a Global Democratic Society', *Global Society*, Vol. 14, No. 2 (2000), pp. 237-257, p. 246.

33 WFD, 'Annual Report and Accounts 2011/12', p. 7.

34 Westminster Foundation for Democracy, 'Evaluation of Egypt Programme: June 2006-March 2009', p. 2.
    <http://www.wfd.org/upload/docs/Egypt%20Programme%20Evaluation%20Summary%20Sheet.pdf>

35 WFD, 'Annual Report and Accounts 2011/12', p. 7.

36 Westminster Foundation for Democracy, 'Parliamentary training programme launched for Egyptian MPs', <http://www.wfd.org/wfd-news/latest/news.aspx?p=109546>

37 See Scott and Walters, "Supporting the Wave', p. 250.

38 Westminster Foundation for Democracy, 'Corporate Plan 2011-15', p. 7.
    <http://www.wfd.org/upload/docs/WFD%20Corporate%20Plan%202011-15.pdf>

39 WFD, 'Annual Report and Accounts 2011/12', p. 7.

40 See WFD, 'Business Plan 2011-12', p. 43.

41 See Elias Biryabarema, 'UPDATE 1 - Uganda ups oil reserves estimate 40 pct to 3.5 bln bbles', *Reuters*, 17 September, 2012.
    <http://www.reuters.com/article/2012/09/17/uganda-oil-idUSL5E8KH1MG20120917>

42 WFD, 'Revised Workshop Agenda, Legislative Oversight of Extractive Industries, 10-12th January 2012', obtained by Corporate Watch via a Freedom of Information request.

43 WFD, Legislative Oversight of Extractive Industries (Oil and Gas) for Members of Parliament Workshop Report', obtained by Corporate Watch via a Freedom of Information request.

44 Taimour Ley, personal correspondence.
45 Greg Power and Oliver Coleman of Global Partners & Associates, 'The WFD's work with the Macedonian Parliament', in *The Challenges of Political Programming: International Assistance to Parties and Parliaments. Discussion Paper for International IDEA* (International Institute for Democracy and Electoral Assistance, November 2011), p. 44. <http://global-partners.co.uk/wp-content/uploads/Challenges-of-political-programming1.pdf>
46 Europa, Summaries of EU legislation, 'Accession Partnership with the Former Yugoslav Republic of Macedonia', 27 May, 2009. <http://europa.eu/legislation_summaries/enlargement/ongoing_enlargement/former_yugoslav_republic_of_macedonia/r18013_en.htm>
47 The Westminster Consortium, 'GTF Annual Report 2011-12', p. 8. <http://www.wfd.org/upload/docs/GTF%20394%20Annual%20Report%202011-12%20Web.pdf>
48 David French, Foreword to Peter Burnell, *Building Better Democracies,* p. 1.
49 WFD, 'Business Plan 2011-12', p. 5.
50 The Westminster Foundation for Democracy, 'Evaluation of WFD's Business Plan 2010-11', p. 37.
51 Ibid. p. 16.
52 Ibid., p. 37.
53 Ibid., pp. 37, 6.
54 WFD, 'WFD Annual Review', p. 13.
55 WFD, 'Evaluation of WFD's Business Plan 2010-11', p. 14.
56 Ibid. p. 37.
57 WFD, 'Business Plan 2011-12', p. 22.
58 Ibid. p. 19.
59 The Westminster Consortium, 'GTF Annual Report 2011-12', p. 17. <http://www.wfd.org/upload/docs/GTF%20394%20Annual%20Report%202011-12%20Web.pdf>
60 WFD, 'Annual Report and Accounts 2011/12', p.9.
61 Ibid., p. 7.
62 WFD, 'Evaluation of Egypt Programme', p. 2.
63 Quoted in Robinson, *Promoting Polyarchy,* p. 103.
64 WFD, 'Evaluation of WFD's Business Plan 2010-11', p. 20.
65 Westminster Foundation for Democracy, 'Final Report, Submitted by: Arab Forum For Alternatives, Project Date 21 December 2008', obtained by Corporate Watch via a Freedom of Information Request.
66 Ibid.
67 Ibid.
68 Robinson, *Promoting Polyarchy,* p. 104.
69 Thomson Reuters Foundation/The Westminster Consortium,'A Guide to Reporting Parliament', 2011, obtained by Corporate Watch via a Freedom of Information request, pp. 42, 6.

70 Ibid., p. 8.

71 Ibid., p. 34.

72 Scott and Walters, 'Supporting the Wave', p. 241.

73 Scott Walters, 'Supporting the Wave', p. 254.

74 WFD, 'Evaluation of WFD's Business Plan 2010-11', p. 6.

75 WFD, 'Final Report, Submitted by: Arab Forum For Alternatives'.

76 Ngũgĩ Wa Thiong'o, 'The Language of African Literature', in Ngũgĩ Wa
    Thiong'o, *Decolonizing the Mind. The politics of language in African Literature*,
    (Nairobi: East African Educational Publishers, 1981), p. 16.

Index